Cinema 4D R14 Cookbook

Second Edition

Elevate your art to the fourth dimension with
Cinema 4D R14

Simon Russell

Michael Szabo

BIRMINGHAM - MUMBAI

D1716329

Cinema 4D R14 Cookbook
Second Edition

First published: February 2012

Second edition: August 2013

Production Reference: 1140813

Published by Packt Publishing Ltd.
Livery Place
35 Livery Street
Birmingham B3 2PB, UK

ISBN 978-1-84969-668-5

www.packtpub.com

Cover Image by Suresh Mogre (suresh.mogre.99@gmail.com)

Credits

Authors

Simon Russell

Michael Szabo

Reviewers

Pim Grooff

Marko Ilic

Vincent de Winter

Acquisition Editor

Kevin Colaco

Lead Technical Editor

Ankita Shashi

Technical Editors

Aparna Chand

Dylan Fernandes

Menza Mathew

Hardik B. Soni

Project Coordinator

Wendell Palmer

Proofreader

Linda Morris

Indexer

Rekha Nair

Production Coordinator

Conidon Miranda

Cover Work

Conidon Miranda

About the Authors

Simon Russell is a freelance animation director based in London. Originally from Bath in south-west England, he moved to London to study Moving Image Design at Ravensbourne college. He has worked for a number of companies before going it alone in 2010. Since then he has worked with commercial clients such as Nike, Land Rover, and EA as well as making his own shorts, plugins, and tutorials. When he's not doing that (which is pretty much most of the time) he likes running and making his cats chase lasers! You can find him online at simonrussell.blogspot.com or @simonfarussell.

Michael Szabo is a freelance motion graphics artist in Miami, FL who probably doesn't go a day without opening Cinema 4D and using it for both business and for fun. As a kid, he was always curious about moving images and his no-budget home movies inspired him to learn design applications, such as Final Cut Pro, Motion, Photoshop, After Effects, and Cinema 4D on his own, because they just weren't going to magically start teaching themselves to him. He has always been interested in learning new techniques and has always tried to design something better than he did the day before. You can find him at http://www.bigmikedesign.com and on Twitter at @bigmikedesign.

I'd like to thank my mom and dad for always giving me their full support and encouragement. Neither of you have any clue what the heck Cinema 4D is, but there's no way I could have written this book without the both of you.

About the Reviewers

Pim Grooff has worked with Cinema 4D since 2002, and he is still enjoying and learning it. His main focus is on animations, and over the past 4 years, he has concentrated on plugin development. He also creates Cinema 4D and Python tutorials and in that way, gives something back to the community. He lives in the Netherlands close to the beach, which gives him a lot of inspiration.

Marko Ilic has extensive experience with graphic and web design. He has mastered HTML, CSS, PHP, JavaScript, WordPress, Cinema 4D, After Effects, and Photoshop. He has learned by experimentation and gained practical knowledge. He started learning from an early age and has always tried to challenge himself. He is known for his extensive knowledge of computer systems and various technologies. He does freelancing and works for his school.

Vincent de Winter has worked in the broadcast industry for 15 years, wherein the last 9 years, he made animations for television. At first, he mainly concentrated on creating animations in After Effects, but that wasn't enough and so after a few years, he started to work with Cinema4D and the integration between the two programs. He worked for a crime reporting program, so most of his work was about explaining crime scenes to the viewers. After the program ended, he studied 3D Producer at the College of Multimedia in Amsterdam, where he got his degree and also became certified by Maxon. Now, he does more freelancing and all kinds of animations such as logo animations, medical animations, and architectural animations. Occasionally, he also makes short films, which combine real video footage and 3D animations.

www.PacktPub.com

Support files, eBooks, discount offers and more

You might want to visit www.PacktPub.com for support files and downloads related to your book.

Did you know that Packt offers eBook versions of every book published, with PDF and ePub files available? You can upgrade to the eBook version at www.PacktPub.com and as a print book customer, you are entitled to a discount on the eBook copy. Get in touch with us at service@packtpub.com for more details.

At www.PacktPub.com, you can also read a collection of free technical articles, sign up for a range of free newsletters and receive exclusive discounts and offers on Packt books and eBooks.

http://PacktLib.PacktPub.com

Do you need instant solutions to your IT questions? PacktLib is Packt's online digital book library. Here, you can access, read and search across Packt's entire library of books.

Why Subscribe?

- ▶ Fully searchable across every book published by Packt
- ▶ Copy and paste, print and bookmark content
- ▶ On demand and accessible via web browser

Free Access for Packt account holders

If you have an account with Packt at www.PacktPub.com, you can use this to access PacktLib today and view nine entirely free books. Simply use your login credentials for immediate access.

Table of Contents

Preface

Cinema 4D is becoming the most popular 3D design program in the world, and learning it now will only help you become a better and more valuable designer in the 3D design industry.

This book provides all the Cinema 4D knowledge you need to become well-versed with the software, in the form of short recipes, which get straight to the point about what you need to know to start designing great 3D projects.

Cinema 4D R14 Cookbook will guide you towards becoming an adept 3D designer, giving you all the tools to succeed in the field of 3D graphics. The book is set up to gradually introduce more sophisticated topics as you go deeper, and by the end of it, you'll have a great working knowledge of the program. Early on, you'll learn the basics of the program, and then jump right into how to start creating your own 3D objects to use in your designs. Along the way, you'll learn how to set up lights, cameras, and materials to turn your work into something that feels more like art and design. Towards the end of the book, you will be introduced to powerful tools such as XPresso, MoGraph, Thinking Particles, and Dynamics to take your work to the next level. You'll be impressed by how easy it is to design top-quality work once you lay the foundation for the entire program through this book. By the end of this book, you'll have opened new creative doors and given yourself the opportunity to be a more successful and versatile designer.

What this book covers

Chapter 1, The Fundamentals, gives you an essential introduction to the program.

Chapter 2, Super Modeling, uses many modeling tools available to create 3D objects.

Chapter 3, The Deformers, takes a look at the special tools used to modify and adjust your 3D creations.

Chapter 4, Cameras are Rolling, describes different methods to set up and use cameras within the program. You'll learn to create a realistic camera movement, as well match your 3D scene to photography to create special effects.

Chapter 5, Let there be Lights, gives you an overview of different lights and techniques for applying them to your 3D scene.

Chapter 6, A Material World, tells you how to apply textures and alter the look of the objects you create.

Chapter 7, Rendering Strategy, is a guide to quality and efficient rendering of your files.

Chapter 8, The Awesome Power of MoGraph, tells you how to use the MoGraph module to create complex designs.

Chapter 9, XPresso Shots, tells you how to use XPresso to create smarter projects.

Chapter 10, Configuring Dynamics, describes setting up dynamic scenes where your 3D objects interact with each other.

Chapter 11, Thinking About Particles, will show you how to create powerful and flexible particle simulations with both Standard and Thinking Particles.

What you need for this book

This book focuses on teaching the Cinema 4D software application, which at the time of this publication is set up to release 14. The files included with the book can be opened in the previous versions, but you may get error messages if the file utilizes aspects that are exclusive to the newer version. Parts of the book deal with certain advanced modules and tools within Cinema 4D, which may not be available in the bundle you have. If this is the case, Maxon offers a free download of Cinema 4D for trial use with all the necessary functionality you will need, located at the following link:

```
http://www.maxon.net/products/demo-version/download-form.html
```

You don't need to be familiar with Cinema 4D prior to using this book. *Chapter 1, The Fundamentals*, will get you started, and the book will explain and focus on the most widely used features of the program to make you an advanced user by the end. If you have used Cinema 4D a little bit before, you will certainly be able to build upon your knowledge of the program.

The screenshots and workflow are based on a PC, but Cinema 4D works equally great on a Mac. There aren't any differences in how the recipes are performed except for the notation of keyboard shortcuts.

Who this book is for

This book is for anyone who wants to quickly get up to speed with Cinema 4D to create 3D projects that run laps around simple 2D designs.

Conventions

In this book, you will find a number of styles of text that distinguish between different kinds of information. Here are some examples of these styles, and an explanation of their meaning.

Code words in text, database table names, folder names, filenames, file extensions, pathnames, dummy URLs, user input, and Twitter handles are shown as follows: "Use the Glass_Spiral.c4d file from the C4D Content Pack for this recipe."

New terms and **important words** are shown in bold. Words that you see on the screen, in menus or dialog boxes for example, appear in the text like this: "For our image, we want to render this in 1080 HD, so change the **Width** value to **1920** and the **Height** value to **1080**."

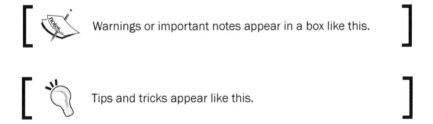

Warnings or important notes appear in a box like this.

Tips and tricks appear like this.

Reader feedback

Feedback from our readers is always welcome. Let us know what you think about this book—what you liked or may have disliked. Reader feedback is important for us to develop titles that you really get the most out of.

To send us general feedback, simply send an e-mail to feedback@packtpub.com, and mention the book title via the subject of your message.

If there is a topic that you have expertise in and you are interested in either writing or contributing to a book, see our author guide on www.packtpub.com/authors.

Customer support

Now that you are the proud owner of a Packt book, we have a number of things to help you to get the most from your purchase.

Downloading the C4D Content Pack for this book

You can download the C4D Content Pack for this book from your account at http://www.PacktPub.com. If you purchased this book elsewhere, you can visit http://www.PacktPub.com/support and register to have the files e-mailed directly to you.

Downloading the color images of this book

We also provide you a PDF file that has color images of the screenshots/diagrams used in this book. The color images will help you better understand the changes in the output. You can download this file from `http://www.packtpub.com/sites/default/files/downloads/6685OT_ColorGraphics.pdf`

Errata

Although we have taken every care to ensure the accuracy of our content, mistakes do happen. If you find a mistake in one of our books—maybe a mistake in the text or the code—we would be grateful if you would report this to us. By doing so, you can save other readers from frustration and help us improve subsequent versions of this book. If you find any errata, please report them by visiting `http://www.packtpub.com/submit-errata`, selecting your book, clicking on the **errata submission form** link, and entering the details of your errata. Once your errata are verified, your submission will be accepted and the errata will be uploaded on our website, or added to any list of existing errata, under the Errata section of that title. Any existing errata can be viewed by selecting your title from `http://www.packtpub.com/support`.

Piracy

Piracy of copyright material on the Internet is an ongoing problem across all media. At Packt, we take the protection of our copyright and licenses very seriously. If you come across any illegal copies of our works, in any form, on the Internet, please provide us with the location address or website name immediately so that we can pursue a remedy.

Please contact us at `copyright@packtpub.com` with a link to the suspected pirated material.

We appreciate your help in protecting our authors, and our ability to bring you valuable content.

Questions

You can contact us at `questions@packtpub.com` if you are having a problem with any aspect of the book, and we will do our best to address it.

1
The Fundamentals

In this chapter we will cover:

- ▶ Exploring the interface
- ▶ Moving around in Cinema 4D
- ▶ Meeting the managers
- ▶ Setting keyframes
- ▶ Utilizing the Content Browser
- ▶ Adjusting the scale of your objects

Introduction

Welcome to the warm-up chapter! Every textbook has one; some stretching and a little jogging before we get to the main exercises. This chapter will give you a brief introduction to Cinema 4D that many designers tend to agree as a very user-friendly program, especially compared to other longstanding 3D applications.

This chapter contains a few recipes to help you navigate through the program and get comfortable with Cinema 4D. It's important to get to know some good keyboard shortcuts and a few interface tips now, while you are still new and impressionable to the program. The objective of the chapter is to help you to look in the right direction and encourage you to explore some more features on your own. Let's not waste time and get started.

Exploring the interface

This first recipe is going to start by going over the interface inside Cinema 4D. The idea is to get used to where certain features are, to make it easier to understand recipes later throughout the book.

Getting ready

For most of the recipes in this chapter, we will be using the Obstacle_Course.c4d file. So load it up now and use it to get your feet wet inside Cinema 4D. Open the file by navigating to its location on your computer with the **C4D Content Pack** and double-clicking on it—it will automatically launch Cinema 4D. Likewise, you can open Cinema 4D first by double-clicking on its icon inside the folder where it is stored on your system, then going under the **File** menu and selecting **Open**, where you can navigate to the Obstacle_Course.c4d file on your system and load it from there.

Downloading the C4D Content Pack for this book

You can download the C4D Content Pack for this book from your account at http://www.PacktPub.com. If you purchased this book elsewhere, you can visit http://www.PacktPub.com/support and register to have the files e-mailed directly to you.

How to do it...

If this is your first time using Cinema 4D, you are probably unsure as to what all these fancy panels inside this project are for. If you have used Cinema 4D a little bit, you may have a general idea of what the different windows and menus do, but it's a good idea to go through this recipe once, just to make sure we are all on the same page. The following is an image of the Cinema 4D interface with each area of the layout numbered so that we can focus on each part individually:

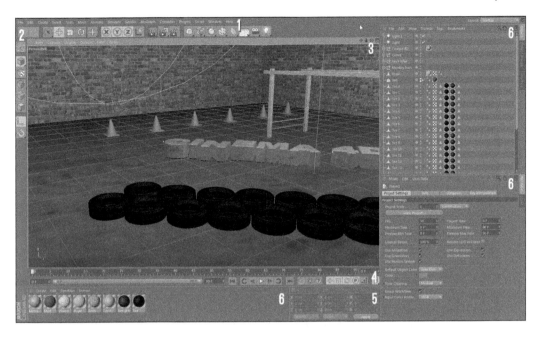

1. As with about every other software program, Cinema 4D has a menu bar along the top with many application-specific menus; it is labeled as #**1** in our image. There are some familiar ones, such as **File**, **Edit**, and **Help**, and there are plenty of other items in between. Many of the options within these menus can be activated in several ways apart from within the actual menus, and we will call upon plenty of them throughout the book.

2. In the **Edit** menu, you'll find Cinema 4D's **Preferences** setting all the way towards the bottom. Most of this stuff doesn't need to be tinkered with very often, or at all, but you may want to examine the first set of options for the **Interface**. You can set the program to have a dark or light color scheme and adjust font sizes, in case you want to make Cinema 4D look a little different or be more readable.

3. Take a look at the **OpenGL** tab, where you can control the quality and speed of your previews based on how sophisticated your computer graphics card is. The settings can be changed to get more detailed previews in the Viewer. If you have a very strong graphics card, you may want to increase these settings, or you may want to decrease or disable the settings if you are dealing with a very heavy and intensive 3D project. For detailed notes on your computer's **OpenGL** capabilities, click on the **Show OpenGL Capabilities** button.

4.   I'd also like to highlight the **Window** menu, the second to last tab on the right. Look inside and mouse over the **Layouts** submenu where you'll find all sorts of options for customizing the look of your Cinema 4D interface. As you work in the program and get the hang of it, I suggest you explore this menu to get a layout that you feel comfortable with. For now though, so that your interface looks the same as mine, select the **Standard** layout option in case your windows are out of place compared to mine. A new feature in Cinema 4D 13 is the **Layout** drop-down menu at the top right-hand corner of the application window, which allows you to quickly switch between the different layouts:

5.   The blue areas comprise item **#2**, the **Command Palettes**, located beneath the application menus and the column along the left-hand side. The buttons are either known as **Icons** or **Icon Palettes** if they contain multiple options within, noted by the small black triangle at the bottom right-hand corner of the icon. As indicated in the previous section, these icons are also found within the various menus up top, and they are the most frequently-used tools in the program made easily accessible with these icons. In the upcoming recipes, we will use these palettes to add objects, splines, lights, cameras, and more.

6. The **Viewer** is **#3**, the big green area; it's where you actually see your 3D scene. Whenever you add objects to your scene, like those from the icons in the Command Palette, they appear at the origin. The origin is located at (0,0,0) point inside your 3D space; the numbers correspond to your X, Y, and Z coordinates. The Viewer has a menu bar at its top with helpful tools that apply to only the Viewer. The menu options have a wide variety of features from managing your cameras to adjusting the look of your preview. The X axis moves across the length of your frame, the Y axis corresponds vertically over the height of your frame, and the Z axis is the key to 3D—it represents the depth in your scene from the front of the Viewer all the way to the back towards infinity.

7. Under the **Panel** menu, hover over the **Arrangement** option and you'll see different options for dividing up the Viewer into two, three, and four different windows to see your scene. You can set up different views and cameras in each window to see work from different perspectives and work a little faster at times. Try selecting the **4 Views** option and see how the viewer gets divided up. Change the option back to **Single View** to focus on just one window. Switching between different views can be very useful when modifying objects in your 3D environment; we'll explore this in *Chapter 2, Super Modeling*:

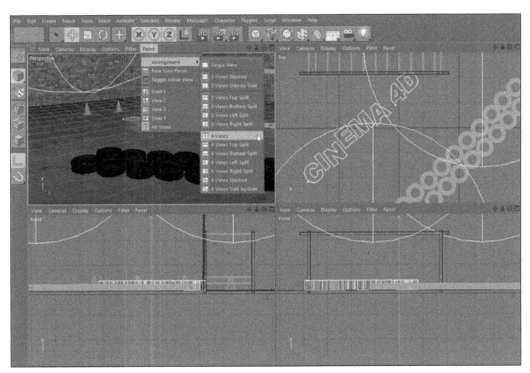

8. Towards the bottom of the screen you'll find **#4**, the purple Animation toolbar, which allows you to control the time of your 3D scene. The timeline bar has small tick marks representing each frame in your project, and you can pull the small green play head by clicking-and-dragging it back and forth. The small set of seven playback buttons give you control much like any video player you've ever used. The buttons have the following functions:

   ❏ *Shift + F*: Jumps to the start of the Animation toolbar

   ❏ *Ctrl* or *command + F*: Moves back to the previous key frame

   ❏ *F*: Moves back by one frame

   ❏ *F8*: Plays the animation

   ❏ *G*: Moves forward by one frame

   ❏ *Ctrl* or *command + G*: Moves forward to the next key frame

   ❏ *Shift + G*: Jumps to the end of the Animation toolbar

> You can adjust the length of your project by opening the **Project Settings** window inside the **Edit** menu. Change the number in the field for **Maximum Time** to shorten or lengthen your timeline. It's a good idea to keep your length as small as you need, so eliminate any extra frames via this setting. When you first open a new project, the **Project Settings** are available at the bottom right-hand side of the screen in the **Attribute Manager**.

9. The **Coordinate Manager** is **#5**; it's a panel that displays the position, size, and rotation of a selected object. You can enter adjustments to these parameters in the **Coordinate Manager** and the changes will appear to your object inside the Viewer.

10. The other windows that are labeled **#6**, the **Object Manager**, **Attribute Manager**, and **Material Manager**, are all more important managers, and they require their own recipe to go over all of their features.

The most useful tip in the book

"Help!" One extremely useful feature of Cinema 4D, which will really help you learn the program more thoroughly is the built-in help browser. You can right-click on any icon or menu option within the program and select **Show Help** from the menu. Try and use it whenever you come across a feature you are curious about or don't understand. You can also access it by going to the **Help** menu and selecting **Show Help**. The built-in help is extensive, helpful, and well written with numerous examples. This, probably more than any other tool in the book, will help you master Cinema 4D if you can get into the habit of using it.

Commander

The Commander is a very useful new feature that helps you to find what you're after, within Cinema 4D. You can press *Shift + C* and the Commander will appear. Then, begin typing and the Commander will search for the command or object you're looking for. It's kind of like Google for Cinema 4D and will help you find items without having to know where they are in the menus. You can also access the Commander by clicking in the magnifying glass at the very top right of the interface:

How it works...

This general preview of the interface hopefully gives you some bearings within Cinema 4D. Throughout this book, we will use all of these features so it's important to know where they are and generally what they do whenever they are referenced in the future.

There's more...

Check out the *Meeting the Managers* recipe in this chapter to learn more about **Object Manager**, **Attribute Manager**, and **Material Manager**.

Moving around in Cinema 4D

This recipe is designed to help you understand how to navigate the viewer in Cinema 4D, whether it be adjusting the angle of view or position objects in 3D space. A 3D application such as Cinema 4D has the added dimension of depth so we can view the object from any angle. There are several tools used for altering the perspective of our scene and positioning objects wherever we want in 3D space.

Getting ready

Continue using the `Obstacle_Course.c4d` file with this recipe.

How to do it...

If we were somehow able to teleport inside your project in Cinema 4D (Maxon will probably have this feature in Release 27 or 27.1), the Viewer would represent the perspective of looking at our 3D obstacle course with your own eyes. We could walk around and angle our head to look at this scene from any angle we want. This is what the default Viewer is like when you load a new project; you have a few mouse and keyboard controls, as well as some interface buttons at your disposal to change the view.

1. Let's focus on movements that go left and right as well as up and down. This would be the equivalent to us taking steps directly to either side, or let's say if we are climbing higher or lower on a ladder. Start by resetting the Viewer to the default view, by going to the **View** menu in the Viewer and selecting **Frame Default**. Now, take your mouse and hold down the *1* key while clicking-and-dragging throughout the scene. Your view is repositioned in any direction, but it remains on the same plane, only moving left, right, up, or down. You can also move through the Viewer in this manner by holding down the *Alt* or *option* key while clicking-and-dragging with the middle-mouse button if it's available. The same movement can be done with a button that is a circle surrounded by four arrows on the Viewer interface. Click on this button and drag the mouse in any direction and the view will shift accordingly. This movement is referred to as trucking or tracking with real cameras to represent a change in the X position of your view. Changing the Y position is called **dollying**, where you are moving vertically in your scene.

2. Now for that third dimension. Let's say we want to get closer or farther away from the objects in our scene. There are four main options for moving the camera in and out; reset your Viewer to the default view again before attempting the movements. If your mouse has a scroll wheel, try scrolling the wheel back and forth and you'll see the Viewer zooming in and out. Next, try holding down the *2* key while clicking-and-dragging with the mouse; it accomplishes the same result. You can also use the *Alt* or *option* key and then right-click and drag around to move deeper in the scene. The final method to move in and out is by clicking-and-dragging on the two-way arrow icon in the top right-hand corner of the Viewer. Moving closer or farther from the subject is a dolly zoom, and it helps utilize the depth available in your 3D environment.

3. Being in 3D means we can rotate in three dimensions as well, which would alter the view in the same way that turning your head around to any angle would. Try holding down the *3* key while clicking-and-dragging; you'll see this rotates the view along the X and Y axis, or you can hold the *Alt* or *option* key and drag the mouse while holding the left-click. The same effect can be done by clicking-and-dragging the icon at the top right-hand corner of the view with the circular arrows fixed around the dot. This movement corresponds to tilting the camera if you change the angle up and down, or panning if you move the angle side to side.

4. If you wanted to tilt the view, which is a technique called **Dutch Angle**, you have to hold down the *3* key and right-click while dragging the mouse. Likewise, you can right-click and drag the icon in the Viewer to get this tilted angle as well. Frame your scene to the default view for the next part of the exercise.

5. Changing the view is different from actually moving objects in space. All objects are created at the origin, when added to the scene so not every object can occupy the same coordinates; hence, we need to reposition them in 3D space. Click on the cube primitive icon and hold down the mouse, and select a new **Sphere** from the menu and load into the scene. It automatically snaps into place the origin, but we already have objects placed there. We need to have it occupy its own space somewhere else.

[

Whenever you click on one of the icons in the Command Palette just once, the object that appears on the icon will be automatically loaded into your scene. For example, our Primitives icon has the cube as the icon, and clicking on the icon automatically creates a cube in our scene.
]

6. When the **Sphere** object is selected, a red, green, and blue axis with arrows appears in the center, which can sometimes be referred to as a **gizmo** in Cinema 4D. This colored gizmo provides controls for the Move Tool, which allows us to change the position of our objects. The Move Tool, which can be activated by pressing the *E* key as well, is the yellow four-way arrow icon located in the Command Palette. It sits next to the Scale Tool (*T* key) and the Rotate Tool (*R* key), which alters the scale and rotation in the same way the Move Tool alters the position of an object. When any of these tools are selected within **Model mode**, which is represented by the icon with an orange outline around a gray cube on the left-hand side of the interface, you can make live adjustments by clicking-and-dragging in the Viewer. Click-and-drag the cube up higher in the scene so that it's above the other objects. If you click-and-drag the colored handles of the gizmo, you can move the cube in just the direction that the arrow on the gizmo is pointing. Zoom out with the Viewer if you want more room to operate.

7. Hit *Ctrl* or *command + Z* to undo the move you just did. A smart way to move objects is to grab-and-drag the red, green, or blue arrow on the gizmo and hold down the *Shift* key. This will move the object in intervals of 10. Grab-and-drag the green arrow on the axis and hold the *Shift* key and move your arrow up 50 units; you'll see how the counter in the center of the screen jumps up 10 units with every move, so you'll always get nice round numbers to work with. This makes calculations and adjustments a lot easier to work with and allows for more precision and organization in your projects.

How it works...

There are different ways to move our view and our objects in Cinema 4D. Our view can be adjusted with a variety of keyboard commands, mouse movements, and buttons on the interface. This makes it easy to adjust exactly how we want to look at our scene. Moving objects is easy with the combination of using our Move Tool and our Model Tool; we can drag the object anywhere in 3D space to make it fit within our project and prevent it from overlapping with other objects.

There's more...

Try using the Scale and Rotate tools, right next to the button for the Move Tool. You can click-and-drag to make those similar respective alterations to your cube, and holding the *Shift* key keeps those parameters nice and orderly too.

The View is your camera

Take this recipe a step further, and instead of thinking of the Viewer as your eyes, think of it as the image being captured by a camera. You have to position your camera wherever you want to capture your image, as well as place the objects into the field of view. We cover all sorts of techniques for moving and adjusting cameras in *Chapter 4, Cameras are Rolling*.

Change how you rotate

Your view will most often rotate around either the origin or a particular object if you have it selected. If you hold down the *Ctrl* key while you rotate, the view will rotate around from its own perspective, like if you were panning with a camera and looking through the viewfinder.

Highlighting and selections

You can see which object is selected in the viewer because it will have an orange outline surrounding it. If you move your mouse around the viewer a white outline will appear around any object the cursor is over. If you then left-click on the object, it will be selected.

Depending on the graphics card in your computer you may need to turn this function on manually by selecting **Options** from the viewport menus and then selecting **Enhanced OpenGL**

Also, if you put your cursor over almost any item or icons, an explanation will appear in the very bottom left of Cinema 4D. This can be very helpful in trying to understand what each element does and help you understand the program more deeply.

Meeting the Managers

If you think of Cinema 4D as the CEO of your design project, it employs several managers to focus on and control specific parts of your project. The three most important managers in Cinema 4D are the **Object Manager**, the **Attribute Manager**, and the **Material Manager**. This recipe will give you an overview of what kind of functionality these managers provide.

Getting ready

Keep using the `Obstacle_Course.c4d` project for this recipe. If you want to start your project fresh like it was before the previous recipes, click on **Revert to Saved** under the **File** menu.

How to do it...

1. **Object Manager** is the hub that lists all of the components of your project that comprise your scene. Whenever you add pieces like primitives, deformers, lights, cameras, and so on to your scene, they appear inside the **Object Manager** window. By default, it appears as the bigger panel on the right-hand side of Cinema 4D. As your scene grows in complexity, it's important to be able to keep your **Object Manager** window tidy and labeled so that objects remain organized, so you can clearly find the particular piece of the puzzle you need.

2. Look in the **Object Manager** window and find the **Tire** objects. They are all the same kind of objects but occur as separate instances, each with their own individual properties. However, it's smart to keep them grouped together for organizational purposes. Hold down the *Ctrl* key and select the items individually or select the first and last ones while holding the *Shift* key to select all of the objects, and then hit the *Alt* or *option + G* keys, and you'll see that the objects have now become a group. You could also right-click or context-click on the selected items and hit **Group Objects**. We can click on the **+** symbol at the top of the group name to unfold the group and view its contents, and click on the **−** symbol to close that group. The tires still retain their individual properties and can be modified, but they have now become part of a group with its own properties, so all of the tires can be moved, scaled, or rotated at once. Click on the name of **Group 1** and change it to **Tires** so that we know what it is, and fold it up by clicking on the - symbol:

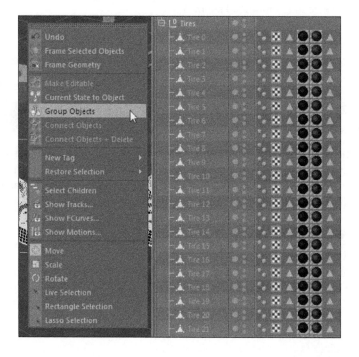

Objects in the **Object Manager** window do not follow any sort of vertical stacking rules like in programs such as **Photoshop** and **After Effects**. If you have object A listed first in the **Object Manager** window ahead of object B, it won't appear on top of, or in front of, the object like it would in other programs where the stacking order determines the visibility of the objects. Cinema 4D presents objects in terms of their position within 3D space, so you have to physically place objects in front, behind, on top, and so on, in order to get them to appear in the manner you choose. It makes no difference where they appear in the **Object Manager**.

3. Within our group of tires, you'll notice that each tire has small square icons to the left-hand side of their object names. Each tire contains different tags, which are specialized modifiers used to add different properties and functions to the objects we apply them to. The tags can be added from the **Tags** menu at the top of the **Object Manager** window, which actually contains several different groups of tags that are organized for you to browse. They are also accessed via right-clicking or context-clicking on an object that is selected in the **Object Manager** window. Select the **Tire 0** object in the group and go into the **Tags** menu, and then under **Cinema 4D Tags**, select the **Compositing** tag and notice how the image of a small slate has appeared at the end of our row of tags. Now, we can fiddle with extra parameters added by this tag to just the **Tire 0** object (the **Compositing** tag is one of the most useful; it has its own recipe within *Chapter 7, Rendering Strategy*):

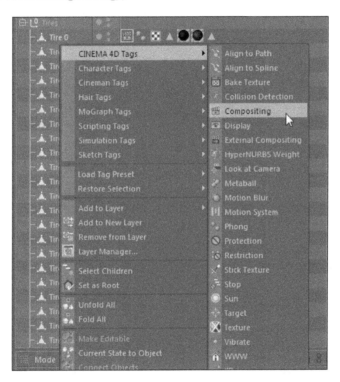

4. The next crucial feature of **Object Manager** is what is often referred to as the **Traffic Light** in Cinema 4D. It has two small dots very close to the right-hand side of the object's name. The dots default to a gray state, but these can be changed from red and to green by clicking directly on them. Find the **Monkey bars** object, click on the top dot to change it to green and then click on it again to change it to red. The monkey bars disappears from the scene as red, but reappears once you cycle back to gray or green. This traffic light toggles the visibility of objects in the editor, represented by the top dot, and the renderer, which is represented by the bottom dot.

Objects can be visible with both the default gray dot and the green dot. The difference is that when the green dot is active, it means that the visibility of the object is forced. For example, if you have several objects that are in a group and you force the group to have red dots, meaning that they are invisible in the editor and renderer, you could still have select objects within that group appear visible if you set their traffic lights to green. The objects that are left to the default gray dots will remain invisible:

5. Now, make sure the top dot is turned red, and the bottom dot is gray or green, and do a render preview by hitting the *Ctrl* or *command* + *R*. The scene renders the **Monkey bars** object even though you don't actually see it in the Viewer. By having control of both dots, you can show and hide different objects in a cluttered scene and still have them rendered as part of your previews and final output, which can be useful if you are working with scenes filled with high-polygon objects:

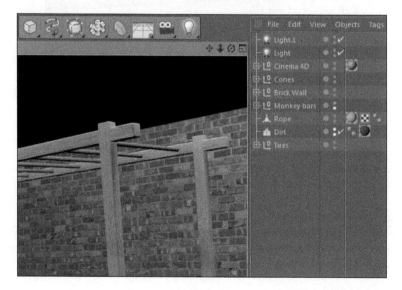

6. The green checkmark next to the traffic light controls if an object is active or not. It essentially eliminates an object from your scene without deleting it, and it's an easy way to turn an object completely off in both the editor and renderer with just one click. Click on any green checkmark you see in the **Object Manager** and watch it turn into a red X. The object no longer affects your scene and it will only become activated again if you change the setting back to the green checkmark.

7. The last main feature of **Object Manager** is the ability to place your objects in layers to keep your project organized. It takes ideas from the traffic light and the idea of grouping in Cinema 4D, but it can control as many objects as you wish at once, as long as they are all applied to the same layer. We already hit upon this a little bit by selecting all or certain objects in the **Object Manager** window and using the **+** and **−** symbols in groups to fold and unfold the contents. There are a few other options for these actions that help sort and organize our project. Highlight the **Cones** object in the scene and unfold the group by going under the **View** menu in the **Object Manager** window, followed by the **Folding** submenu, and then select **Unfold Selected**. With the **Cones** group selected, go under the **Edit** menu and click on **Select Children** to highlight all of the objects below. With everything highlighted, go under the **Edit** menu in the **Object Manager** window and select **Add to New Layer**. A small colored swatch pops up right next to the names of the objects. Click on any one of the color swatches and select the **Layer Browser...** option to open the panel that will list all the different layers we apply throughout our scene. It replaces the area where the **Attribute Manager** is found.

8. We can double-click on the name **Layer** and change it to something more descriptive, such as **Cones**. Click on the eyeball under the **V** column in the browser and you'll notice that in the Viewer our objects have disappeared. This row of options is a set of controls for all of the objects within our layer; toggling them affects all the objects equally. The dot in the **S** column acts as a solo switch, which isolates all the objects in that layer inside the Viewer.

9. In the **File** menu of the Layer Browser, select **New Layer**, and a new color swatch pops up in the browser. Take the color swatch for the new layer and drag it from the Layer Browser on top of the **Cones** group in the **Object Manager**. Then, click on the new swatch and drag your mouse down the column of swatches, where your cursor should change to a brush icon, and paint your swatches with the new color. An alternative is to select the **Cone** object and right-click or context-click on them and then select **Add to New Layer**, where you'll find both of your created layers, and select the layer that you want to add to them. Because our new layer has the eyeball option open, our cones become visible again. As a result, you can add multiple layers and freely switch the objects between them as you develop your project. Getting familiar with all the icons and buttons in the **Object Manager** is crucial for helping you navigate through your projects smoothly.

10. When an object is selected in **Object Manager**, the window directly below it (in the default layout) loads all the particular controls for that object into the **Attribute Manager**. This is where we can tweak the settings and parameters to make changes to our objects and set key frames to adjust parameters over time. The manager places these parameters inside different tabs to help organize all the information you have control of. The bottom window may still be set to the Layer tab on the right-hand side, so flip it over by clicking on the tab that says Attribute.

11. Almost every object has three main tabs to start: **Basic**, **Coordinates** (abbreviated as **Coord.**), and **Object**. Select the **Dirt** object in the **Object Manager** and click on the **Basic** tab in the **Attributes Manager**. The **Basic** tab contains some fundamental properties about the object selected. The **Name** field and **Layer** field are self-explanatory; they contain what the object is called and what layer grouping the object pertains to. The other most useful properties in the **Basic** tab are the **Visible in Editor**, **Visible in Renderer**, and **Enabled** options.

12. Switch the **Visible in Editor** field from the default setting to **Off**; you'll notice the **Attributes** object will disappear and the top dot in the traffic light is now red. These two fields are linked directly to the traffic light in **Object Manager**, so any changes made in one will affect the other. The same goes for the enabled checkbox; by un-checking the box, the green checkmark by the **Attributes** object name switches to a red **X**.

There are times you may want to switch **on** or **off** the visibility of an object, and that value can be controlled and key framed from inside the **Attribute Manager**, not the **Object Manager**. Simply set one key frame in the **On** state and the other in the **Off** state, and you'll get an action that is like someone hitting a switch to make your object disappear. We will discuss key framing in the next recipe.

13. The next tab over is the **Coord.** tab. This contains the properties that determine where and how your object occupies space in your 3D Scene. The three properties are broken down into **Position**, **Scale**, and **Rotation**, each with their own sub-properties that control the parameter in the X, Y, and Z dimensions.

14. Take the **Dirt** object and change its **X** position from **-250** to **0**, its **Y** position to **100**, and its **Z** position to **150**. Note how the object jumps to a new position every time you enter a new value and how our dirt is now in the entirely wrong position. These position coordinates are based on the **World Coordinates position**, where the center (0,0,0) is the origin and the position properties indicate how far away your object is from the origin. Change the dirt back to **-250** for **X** and **0** for both **Y** and **Z** dimensions.

15. The **Scale** parameters control the size of the object in the **X**, **Y**, and **Z** dimensions. Enter a value of **2** for all three scale values. Notice how the scale options are independent of each other and you can adjust the values to distort the object in any dimension; the values do not have to be uniform. Change the value back to **1** for each dimension, which represents the actual scale of the object.

Don't use scale to size up objects unless you absolutely have to. If you have a sphere object, change its radius to make it bigger instead of using the scale. Projects can get messy if you have different objects with varying scale values, and there are some instances where scale values will be ignored and overridden like when using cloners in **MoGraph**. Only change scale values when you want to perhaps keep a group of objects proportional in size because adjusting them individually will throw off their relation to one another. Or, you can use scale to change just one dimension to modify a shape, such as taking a sphere and increasing its scale in the X value to make it into more of an egg shape.

16. The last column is for the **Rotation** properties of your object. They are labeled as **R.H**, **R.P**, **R.B**, which correspond to the rotation in the **Heading**, **Pitch**, and **Bank** respectively. They will rotate the object around the origin of the Object Axis, which we can adjust to a different spot. Adjust the **R.H** value of the **Dirt** object to **45**, and you'll notice our object has turned 45 degrees. Reset the rotation value back to **0**.

17. Our dirt rotates around the exact center of itself, but there are times where we want to adjust to where the rotation point is and where our axis occurs.

18. This will be covered more in *Chapter 2*, *Super Modeling*, but we need to convert our dirt from its primitive state into a polygonal object. With the **Dirt** object highlighted in the **Object Manager**, press the *C* key on your keyboard and the object won't change the way it looks; it will just lose some of the editable properties that were in the **Attribute Manager**. We move from mathematically defined geometry to objects the user can define. All the magic lies in this transition. Now, we can freely reposition the axis within our **Dirt** object.

The **Make Object editable** button is found in the top left-hand side corner of the Command Palette. It has two spheres and a set of arrows showing that the object is turning into polygons. With your object selected, you can click on this button instead of hitting the *C* key to get the same result.

19. Look on the left-hand side of the Command Palette and click on the two orange arrows that form a right angle, which is the command for **Enable Axis Modification**. This tells Cinema 4D we want to reposition the actual axis by moving the gizmo around, rather than using the gizmo to move the entire object while the axis remains in place. Take the red, green, and blue colored axis in the center of the object and grab the red handle, and slide it to the left 500 units (directed towards the back of the scene). In order to keep your values nice and even, click-and-hold the *Shift* key down to get exact measurements in multiples of 10. With the axis now shifted, enter the **R.H** value of **45** again, and you'll notice the **Dirt** object has now rotated around the newer pivot point, and we have a different-looking rotation.

20. The **Object** tab is unique to every object; it contains the parameter specific to modifying that particular object. Unfold the groups and click on the different objects in our project file, and notice how their **Object** tab loads different controls each time you change objects. The **Attribute Manager** also contains tabs for any specific tags that are applied to your object. Click on your tags next to your tire objects and you'll see them instantly load into the **Attribute Manager**.

> Click on tabs while holding the *Ctrl/command* or *Shift* key and you will select multiple tabs at once to keep them all loaded in the **Attribute Manager**.

21. The final manager of the recipe is our **Material Manager**. This window loads at the bottom of the screen in the default layout, and it's reserved for viewing and sorting our materials, which are applied to objects in order to give them specific visual qualities such as color, texture, transparency, and reflection. Notice how there are materials already loaded in the manager, because they were applied to objects and saved into the project.

22. Double-click on the **Mud** thumbnail in the **Material Manager** and Cinema 4D will open up the **Material Editor**, which contains all of the channels we need to create the visual look we are going for. Each thumbnail in the **Material Manager** loads a different material, which can all have a unique combination of parameters for creating different materials like metal, wood, and glass.

23. Double-click on an empty space in the **Material Manager** to create a new material, and then double-click on the new thumbnail to open it in the **Material Editor**. Change the name of the material by entering the word New Material in the box under the thumbnail image of the gray sphere directly.

24. The column on the left lists the channels that are active and combine as properties of the material. The **Color** and **Specular** channels are on by default. Highlight the **Color** channel and note the color slider that appears inside the **Material Editor**. By default, it should be set to an RGB slider with values from 0-255; if it's not, you can change it to that mode by selecting those options inside the small-rounded rectangular button right below the color swatch. Adjust the sliders so that you have values of **204** for **red**, **87** for **green**, and **72** for **blue**, to create a reddish-pink color.

25. Now you can take this material and apply it to an object in your scene. Simply take the thumbnail from the **Material Manager** and drag it on top of any object in your scene or on the name of the object directly in the **Object Manager**. Apply it to the Cinema 4D group and note that a new texture tag appears in the **Object Manager**, represented by a small icon of the material. This can be loaded into the **Attribute Manager** to make adjustments to the way the material is applied to your object. This is how you get all three managers working together:

 You can drag a material from the **Material Editor** onto the **Texture** tag in the **Object Manager** in order to replace the texture. Simply adding the material to an object that already has a material on it will just add another texture on it, and you may want to replace it and not end up being confused by extra **Texture** tags on an object.

How it works...

The **Object Manager**, **Attribute Manager**, and **Material Manager** serve special purposes to help manage your projects in Cinema 4D. The **Object Manager** displays all our objects that are contained within your project, and we can use the *Alt* or *option + G* keys command to group them together, as well as assign layers to them, so our project stays organized. The **Attribute Manager** displays our editable parameters for whatever object we have selected, including any tags we add to provide extra functionality. The **Material Manager** is the key towards sorting and applying materials to our objects, and it can launch the **Material Editor** that we can use to design our materials to look a certain way.

Cinema 4D has a comprehensive list of all of the keyboard commands that come into Cinema 4D by default and it's where you can assign custom shortcuts. It's located inside the **Window** menu and under the **Customization** submenu, under Customize Commands. There are tons, and I mean tons, of shortcuts by default, and I will try to bring up many useful ones throughout the book, but if you are a keyboard shortcut fiend, you may need to sift through this manager and absorb all of them and maybe set your own once you get better acquainted with the program.

There's more...

Basically, you will be using these different managers in every recipe in this book, so it's important to get familiar with the different options and functionality they provide. As far as the **Material Manager** and **Material Editor** go, there's a whole chapter on materials that uses these features extensively.

Setting keyframes

Keyframes are the bookends of animation. They are specified values that we set at particular frames in a timeline and the differences between their values result in animation. Setting keyframes is the most basic method for generating movement and changing your scene from static to dynamic. If you can set keyframes, you can make the 3D objects you design jump, shake, dance, spin, slide, explode, and just about any other verb in the dictionary. This recipe will demonstrate how to set keyframes to get things moving in your scene.

Getting ready

Keep using the `Obstacle_Course.c4d` file from the C4D Content Pack.

How to do it...

1. Start by using the skills you learned to position our Viewer so we can see the rope on the back brick wall clearly. We are going to animate it swinging back and forth. Select the **Rope** object in the **Object Manager** and our rope will be highlighted inside the Viewer. Now, any transformations we apply with the Move Tool, Rotate Tool, or Scale Tool will occur on our rope.

2. The main focus of keyframing is done inside the **Attribute Manager**. Because the manager controls all the properties of our objects, it makes sense to be able to set keyframes inside it to animate the attributes of our object. Select the **Coordinates** tab for your rope inside the **Attribute Manager**, which contains the position, scale, and rotation properties of our rope. The property we are going to focus on is the **R.B** column or the bank of our **Rope** object, which is currently set to **0**.

3. Notice, that to the left of each property there is a small circle with a black outline; this is our indicator that tells us if the property is keyframed. To set a keyframe, make sure you are on frame 1 in your Animation toolbar, then hold down the *Ctrl* key or the *command* key and click on the circle, which should now become a red-filled dot. Congratulations on setting a keyframe. Let's move on to the next recipe then.

4. Just kidding! We need to do more than that to see how keyframes actually work; setting one keyframe will not animate anything. Make sure you switch back OFF the Enable Axis Modification icon on the left-hand side in the Command Palette if you just finished the last recipe. Now, select the Rotate Tool from the Command Palette and grab the blue ring around the rope that corresponds to the rotation of our **R.B** value. Drag the ring clockwise and hold down the *Shift* key so that we rotate in intervals of 10, and stop when you get to 45 degrees. Notice how your keyframe dot has changed from red to yellow, meaning that we have changed the value at which our keyframe was previously set. If we skip to another frame, then Cinema 4D will revert back to the previously-set keyframe value. Therefore, we need to do the same command to set a new keyframe with our value of 45. Hold *Ctrl* or *command* and click on the dot to change it from yellow to red, meaning our keyframe is set with our new value:

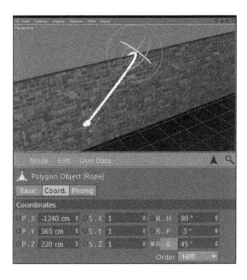

5. Movement by keyframes comes from the change in values between two or more keyframes, so let's set another one at another point in time. Move to frame 15 in your Animation toolbar, and instead of using the Rotate Tool, just enter a value of -45 directly in the **R.B** field in the **Attribute Manager**. The dot has turned into a yellow circle, meaning the value has been changed but not keyframed. Try setting a keyframe by right-clicking on the yellow circle and selecting **Add Keyframe** from the **Animation** menu. Go to the beginning frame of the timeline and click on the **Play** button in the Animation toolbar, and watch your rope swing from one side to the other.

It helps to think about the motion you want to achieve and try to translate that into numerical values occurring throughout the timeline. The rope's starting point is like you are holding it up high and waiting to let it go. Upon the release, it would swing and reach its farthest rotation on the initial swing then it would swing back and forth with a gradually decreasing rotation at similar intervals, which gives it the final look of slowing down and coming to rest.

6. Now's the time to go crazy and set the rest of our keyframes, one after another. Jump to frame **30** and set the keyframe for **R.B** to **25**, then go to frame **45** and set it to **-25**, then a value of **5** at frame **60**, **-5** at frame **75**, and finally back to **0** at frame **90**. Press the **Play** button in the Animation toolbar and watch your animation. Your rope should drop and swing back and forth and come to a complete rest.

7. If you would like to see the results of your keyframes visually, go into the **Window** menu at the top and select the **Timeline** option. This keeps track of all the keyframed values in your project and allows you to make adjustments to your keyframes as if they were points plotted on a graph. The default view shows your keyframes that you can slide into different moments in time, but we are more interested in the graphical view. Click on the small icon of a curve equation, next to the key in the top right-hand corner, and then select the **Rope** object on the far left-hand side, or press the spacebar to toggle between the two. You should see a curve that looks somewhat like a sine wave; this is the rotation value we plotted. These curves are called **F-Curves**, where the F stands for function, and you can use them to adjust the temporal (time) interpolation of the values between keyframes:

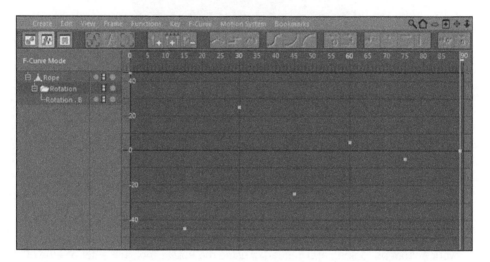

8. In this window, we can select individual points and slide them around the graph. The Y axis represents the actual rotation value, and the X axis corresponds to the frames in our composition. Click-and-drag your mouse to create a box around all the points on the graph, so that they are selected and highlighted in orange. Notice how the points have little levers called **Bezier** handles that can be stretched out or tilted in different angles to adjust the shape of the curve around the point representing the keyframe:

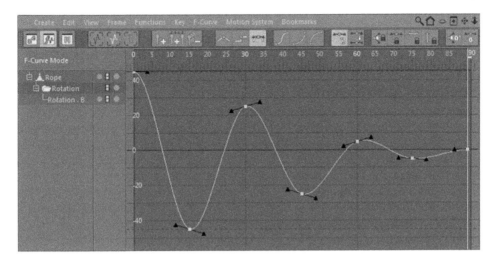

9. With the points selected, right-click and change the highlighted option from **Spline** to **Linear**. Your curve turns into straight lines, making a very sharp and jagged shape on your graph. Go play with your animation and observe what this has done to your rope, it now swings stiffly and sharply, changing direction just like the new shape of your graph would indicate. Hit *Ctrl* or *command + Z* to undo your change to the graph, so that we now have curves again, which represent a more appropriate motion for our rope.

How it works...

We use the properties inside the **Attribute Manager** to set keyframes to create animations inside Cinema 4D. The keyframes need to be set at different points in time and have different values in order to cause change and motion in our scene. We can also use the **Timeline** window to view a visual representation of our keyframes as points on a graph. This window allows us to adjust our points with Bezier handles and also change the way our keyframes ease from one to the next.

There's more...

You can keyframe any parameter with that small circle next to it. Technically, any object in Cinema 4D can be keyframed in some way. I promise we will make a better animation than this swinging rope if you keep reading my book.

Delete the track

If you end up keyframing a parameter and you hate the way it looks, you can delete all of your keyframes simply by right-clicking on the keyframed dot and selecting **Delete Track**.

Interpolation is the word

Interpolation is the method in which our animation changes between keyframes. Bezier curves represent the concept of easing into and out of different keyframe values. In the case of our rope, the rope doesn't change directions instantly and switch directions immediately; it slows down and gradually shifts back in the other direction. The linear method made our animation look awful, but in some cases it's the appropriate kind of interpolation for your keyframes. Let's say you have a fighter jet flying through your scene; if the position keyframes are set to Bezier, your plane will appear to gradually speed up in the beginning and slow down at the end of your keyframed animation. In actuality, the plane should be traveling at a constant rate through your scene, so you would want to have a linear interpolation between your keyframes. You have to picture how your object is supposed to move, and imagine how that looks plotted on a graph.

Don't fear the reeper

It's early in the book, but I like to include any extra tools I use just for reference. I easily created the rope used in this recipe using **Reeper X**, a free plugin for Cinema 4D that specializes in creating ropes (`http://www.codeworkers.de/garage-plugins-reeperx.html`).

Utilizing the Content Browser

Depending on which version you've purchased, Cinema 4D comes equipped with additional content and presets that you can easily import into your projects. These extra files are found in the **Content Browser**, which is an organized Viewer for you to browse through all the additional content that comes with Cinema 4D. The **Content Browser** has 3D models, materials, sample projects, and perhaps much more if you have Cinema 4D Prime, Visualize, Broadcast, or Studio. This recipe shows you where to find this additional content within Cinema 4D.

Getting ready

Start a new project for this recipe; you don't need to use the obstacle course any more.

How to do it...

1. Head up to the **Window** menu, look inside, and find the **Content Browser** option and click on it to open it. A new window pops up with a listing of folders and places on your computer located on the left-hand side. Untwirl the **Presets** folder to reveal even more folders inside; this is where the additional content is stored. It works very similar to your operating system's folder and file structure.

2. We are only going to explore the **Prime** folder because that is the most basic package available in Cinema 4D and all other versions should include those presets as well. Un-twirl the **Prime** folder, this reveals even more sub-folders. The folders should include **Example Scenes**, **Humans**, **Light Setups**, **Materials**, and **Misc**.

3. Double-click on the **Humans** folder and you'll find two models, **Fred** and **Lisa**, that you can double-click and they will import into your scene directly. Place **Fred** in the scene and notice how he resides at the origin of your new project:

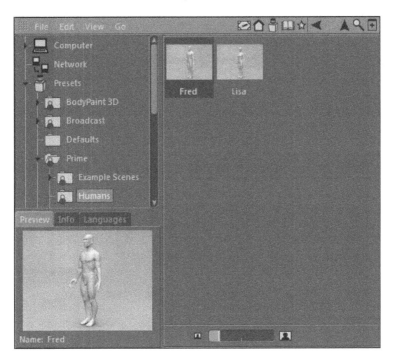

4. Reopen the **Content Browser** by pressing *Shift + F8* if you've closed it. Now, go under the **Light Setups** folder and double-click on the **3 Point Light Stage** option, and Cinema 4D will add a basic light setup to your scene with **Fred**:

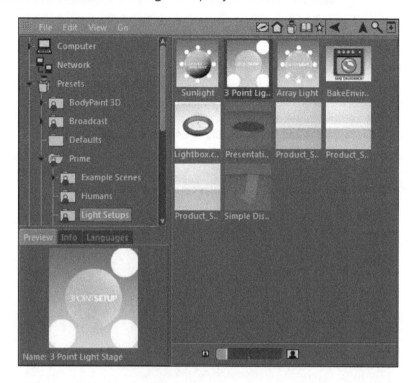

 At the top right-hand corner of the **Content Browser**, you'll find a set of arrows used for navigating through the different levels of folders. Use them to move back and forth through the content if you find yourself getting lost inside the browser's hierarchy.

5. Reopen the **Content Browser** once more, and now navigate to the folder labeled **Materials**. Once in this folder, go to the next level in the **Basic** folder and scroll down to find the material named **Metal 003**. Take this material and drag it directly onto **Fred**; on the release of your mouse, **Fred** will go from being made of flesh to being made of metal. The metal material is now also imported into your **Material Manager**:

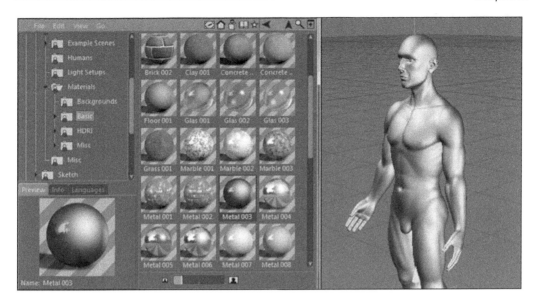

How it works...

The **Content Browser** is found inside the **Window** menu and is a great tool for using the extra presets and projects Maxon provides with their software. It's a great way to get quick results by using prebuilt items, and you can even add your own presets as well as purchase and install other content from third parties.

There's more...

Be sure to go through all of your folders inside the **Content Browser** to see what kinds of files are available to you. It can save tons of time by having professional quality presets ready to go at your fingertips. The **Content Browser** can import them into your scene instantly; use it to your advantage.

Reverse engineering

The beauty of the **Content Browser** and its presets are that you can easily import them into your project and open them up to learn how a particular effect is achieved. If you want to know some good techniques for creating metallic textures, examine the metal material we imported as well as the others available and determine what goes into creating a good metal texture. Once you examine all of the content available, open up any project or preset that piques your interest and examine how it's done.

Adjusting the scale of your objects

In case you haven't noticed yet, Cinema 4D uses actual units of measurement for their values for things, such as size and position. Mine is labeled in centimeters, and you can pick what kind of units you default to by going under the **Edit** menu, followed by **Preferences**, and then the options for Units, and selecting your Unit Display to be a bunch of different Metric or U.S. forms of measurement. The animators usually aren't concerned with what set of measurements they are using; your animation will look the same whether you are using miles or millimeters. But, let's say you are designing a model that needs to be accurate to scale, say for an architectural model, and you've designed a piece that is set in the wrong units. Whether it's too big or too small, there's a way in Cinema 4D to adjust the scale of your object so it's resized properly.

Getting ready

Open the `Trashcan.c4d` file from the **C4D Content Pack**. You'll be creating this object from scratch in the next chapter.

How to do it...

1. Add a **Cube** primitive to our scene, and in my case, it's the default 200 centimeters in every dimension, making it a bit taller than the size of my trash can. Use the Move tool to position the cube to the right of the Trash Can to compare the size. Let's say you want your Trash Can to appear much smaller but keep the cube at that size. You could click on the Trash Can group in the **Object Manager** and change the Scale X, Y, and Z values to a fraction of 1, so that the Trash Can shrinks in size:

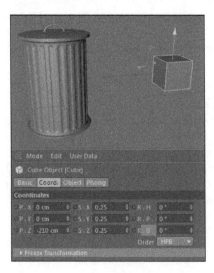

This method is good, but what if you want to keep your scale values proportioned at 1? The answer lies in the **Edit** menu under the **Scale Project** command. Delete the cube from the scene and then find the **Scale Project** option inside the **Edit** menu up top. A small pop-up window appears and asks you what your **Current Scale** is and what you want your **Target Scale** to be. If right now you have it set that 1 unit is equal to 1 centimeter, you'd have to decrease the **Target Scale** to have the Trash Can become smaller. Change the **Target Scale** from **Centimeters** to **Millimeters** and click on **OK**. The Trash Can just shrunk, but any new object we add will appear just as big as it would have before. Add a **Cube** object and you'll notice it is gigantic compared to our Trash Can, but it's the same size and measurement in centimeters as before.

2. If you want to undo the change you can't just hit your undo keyboard shortcut. You have to go back into the **Scale Project** setting and apply the opposite transformation. Change the **Target Scale** to have a value of **10** and watch how your Trash Can springs back to the size it was before. Create another **Cube** object and you'll see it is back to the proportion it was originally. You basically have to undo the math you did with new math by converting the units properly.

How it works...

This function is useful if you need to scale your scene to fit into an appropriate measurement. If your model appears absurdly large or small, then you can size it properly with the **Scale Document** function so it fits your scene better. We are able to quickly adjust the entire scale of what's in your .c4d file without messing up the scale settings in the **Coordinates** tab. This is just a more precise way to resize your models than applying fractions to your scale settings.

There's more...

This is a good tip in case you encounter a file that someone designed using a different unit of measurement in their version of the application, and it appears to be really large or small when you integrate it with your model. The same is true when you perhaps buy pre-made models; you'll be able to adjust the scale so they fit within your scene properly.

Use separate C4D files

The **Scale Project** function works on everything in your document, so you need to isolate only the objects you want to scale with the command. Copy and paste them into a new, empty C4D file and make the changes to the scale in there, then copy and paste the smaller version back into the C4D file you are working with.

2
Super Modeling

In this chapter we will cover:

- ▶ Working with primitives
- ▶ Subdividing, selecting, and editing polygons
- ▶ Creating from splines – extrude NURBS
- ▶ Using Lathe NURBS
- ▶ Using Sweep NURBS
- ▶ Modeling with Loft NURBS
- ▶ Punching holes with Boole
- ▶ Using the Atom array tool
- ▶ Best modeling advice – just go for it
- ▶ Getting to grips with sculpting
- ▶ Sculpting a head

Introduction

Don't let my very modest looks and gigantic appetite fool you, sometimes my job requires me to do a little bit of modeling. It's a tough job sometimes, but people like me are made for it. Nobody can pull off the T-shirt and jeans-look like I can when I'm modeling. OK enough with the homonyms; while it might be nice to make a career by being attractive and by getting pictures snapped by a professional photographer, we're going to have to focus on a different kind of modeling.

Be careful who you throw that word out to, because people tend to think of the headshot and swimsuit issues when you say you're doing some modeling. However, in Cinema 4D, modeling more closely resembles the craft store hobby of assembling small-scale recreations of things such as cars, planes, and boats. We can create anything we want in Cinema 4D, which allows you to design something as specific and detailed or delightfully abstract and creative as you desire.

By creating an object in 3D, we are able to position it, light it, and set up cameras to capture it, much like a photographer who takes pictures of models. The idea is the same: you work endlessly to get everything just right (in a photo studio or inside Cinema 4D), and the final result is the perfect image that you were looking for, and the model probably gets all the credit for being gorgeous. But you and I know who really made it happen and that it was all worth the effort:

There are so many different tools and techniques for creating models of what you need in 3D. This chapter will focus on the essential components of Cinema 4D used for generating something from nothing and creating a 3D object from scratch to use in your designs.

Working with primitives

Cinema 4D comes equipped with a series of 3D shapes to use as common starting points for your 3D models. They are called **Primitives** and they are what we call **Parametric objects**, meaning that they are generated by mathematical formulas with unique values to determine what they look like. These shapes can be adjusted and combined to form very simple models. In this recipe, we are going to create a stool out of two common primitives: the cube and the cylinder.

How to do it...

1. The **Primitives** are located inside the icon with the blue cube on it inside the Command Palette. If you click and hold down on the icon, you'll see all of the available shapes—everything from the common **Sphere** to the man-like **Figure** object. You'll probably use the **Cube**, **Cylinder**, and **Sphere** the most because those are some of the most common shapes, but it's important to take an inventory of all these menus to see what's available for creating future models:

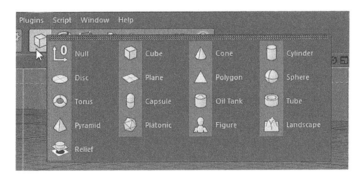

2. Inside the **Primitives** menu, select a **Cylinder** object and watch as one is instantly generated at the origin of your scene. It's automatically selected in the **Object Manager**, which loads its properties into the **Attribute Manager**.

3. Under the **Object** tab, you'll find all the parametric properties for the cylinder that you can control to change how it looks. The default cylinder is really tall, but we are looking to model the seat of our stool, which should be really short. Change the **Height** parameter from **200** to **15** and watch the cylinder shrink to a more suitable size.

4. Many primitives also come with the option to create a **Fillet**, which takes sharp edges and smoothes them out. Change from the **Object** tab to the **Caps** tab in the **Attribute Manager**, check the box to activate the **Fillet**, and change the **Radius** to **3.5**. Notice, how your cylinder now has a nice smooth edge around it. This is a much more pleasant-looking seat for our stool, as before you'd have to worry about cutting yourself on the edge when you sat down. Double-click on the name of the cylinder in the **Object Manager** and rename it to `Seat`, so you know what it is.

5. With the seat of our stool in place, we can now focus on the legs of our stool. Go back to the **Primitives** icon in the Command Palette and click once on it to create a cube, which is the default primitive. The default cube is huge; it's 200 units in every direction. If you take a peek into the **Attribute Manager**, you'll see that we have control over the size of our cube in the X, Y, and Z dimensions. This means we can create a rectangular prism of any size, instead of just a cube, which happens to be a very special version of one. Resize the **Size X** and **Size Z** from **200** to **10**, and now you'll have a tall and skinny leg for our stool. Check the box below for **Fillet** and reduce the **Fillet Radius** down to **1**, so that our edges are just a little smoother. Double-click on the name of the cube in the **Object Manager** and change it to `Leg`.

   Once you create a primitive, it can easily be duplicated in the **Object Manager** and repositioned with the **Attribute Manager** to keep the identical settings you gave it. With the **Leg** highlighted in the **Object Manager**, hold the *Ctrl* or *command* key and drag it away slightly. When the cursor features a **+** sign on it, you are making a copy of it, and when you release the mouse, you'll have a duplicate of your leg. Repeat this twice more, so you have four legs in total in the **Object Manager**.

   It still only appears that you have one leg because those copies of the leg all occupy the same coordinates, so they are overlapping each other. Select all four of your legs in the **Object Manager** and slide them down in the Y position with the Move Tool. Hold the **Shift** key and move the legs down by 100 units, so they appear to be coming from the bottom of the seat.

6. Now, switch the viewer from the **Perspective** view to the **Bottom** view so we can look at where exactly these legs are by clicking on the **Cameras** menu and selecting **Bottom**. All four of them are right in the middle, and we want to spread them out so that they balance out and create a stool suitable for sitting.

   Deselect all of the legs and then reselect only one in the **Object Manager**, and use the Move Tool while holding the *Shift* key to slide it over **-40** units using the red arrow handle for the X dimension. Select the next leg and do the opposite: move it over **40** units in the opposite direction on the x axis, so it's on the other side. Now, do the same with the other two legs; just move them up and down by **40** units in the Y position, so we have four legs evenly spread out underneath our stool for balance.

7. Switch back to the **Perspective** view and you'll see that our stool now has four legs, but we need to angle them a little bit so our stool doesn't seem so stiff and cheap. You'll need to rotate each leg in either the **R.B** or **R.P** setting either by **5** or **-5** degrees; it all depends on which leg sits on which spot around the stool. The first leg that you moved over **-40** in the X dimension should have a rotation of **5** in the **R.B**, so that it stands a little wider at the base than at the top. Now, the one that you moved in the opposite **40** units should be rotated by **-5** degrees in the **R.B**, since it needs to face the opposite direction on the other side. Repeat these steps for the other two with their values in the **R.P** setting, until you have all four legs tilted inwards:

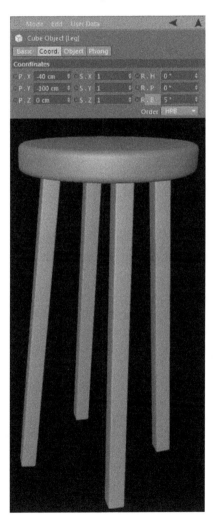

How it works...

This is about as easy as things will ever get in terms of modeling. The idea here is that there are set shapes in Cinema 4D called primitives, and we can change their parametric properties to fit what we are looking for. Our cylinder started out really tall, but we were able to shrink it down and make a seat for our stool. We made four thin legs from our original giant cube by reducing two of its size properties. Using the **Coordinates** tab in the **Attribute Manager** for each primitive allows us to position them individually and give them unique coordinates in the scene to add the final touches to our stool. Primitives are often the key starting points for your models, because they are based on common shapes and have flexible properties that you can use to control their look.

There's more...

Move on to the next recipe to learn how to convert simple primitives to editable objects when your models require more complex shapes.

Working with the Viewer

When modeling, you should get used to switching between all the available views in the Cameras menu inside the Viewer. It's much easier to see and change your model when you move around and check it out from different angles.

Subdividing, selecting, and editing polygons

Primitives are very useful and often the perfect base for starting to build a 3D model of just about anything. But, look at the world around you: objects may resemble certain primitives, but they most likely possess far more details than just the basic shapes. In this recipe, we will start with just a regular primitive and edit its structure so that it becomes a more realistic and detailed model.

How to do it...

1. We are going to construct a metal trash can by manipulating the polygons on a basic **Cylinder** object, which can be found under your **Primitives** icon in the Command Palette. Start by reducing its **Height** to **150**, so it's a little shorter. Pay attention to the fields below; they are crucial when modeling. At all times, you have the option of adjusting the number of segments, such as our **Height Segments** and **Rotation Segments** here. This aims to change your object's subdivision.

2. Subdivision is the number of polygonal that your model is divided into. Objects with less polygons tend to be more stiff and rigid-looking, but require less selecting and manipulating because they are simpler shapes. Objects that are dense with polygons take more time to adjust and work with, but they will give you more detail to model with because they are subdivided much more. You always need to roughly consider how many polygons you want your object to be made of; for our trash can, change the **Height Segments** to **32** and the **Rotation Segments** to **50**. You'll see the number of little rectangles, making up your cylinder, increase dramatically.

> Overall, the more polygons you have within the objects in your scene, the slower your system will respond and your rendering will probably take longer. Only use more polygons if you have to; if objects don't require a lot of detail, use fewer polygons.

3. Now, here's the key—primitives are parametric objects that are determined by math and have parameters we can edit in the **Attribute Manager**. What if we want to manipulate particular parts of the cylinder? In order to change the structure and target specific polygons on our cylinder, we have to make it editable, which removes the parametric properties. Double-click on the name of your cylinder in the **Object Manager** and rename it to **Trash Can**. With it still selected, hit the *C* key or click on the button towards the top left-hand side of the Command Palette with the orange sphere and with the arrows pointing to the subdivided sphere. This is the **Make Object Editable** command, and it turns our primitive into a polygon object. The icon in the **Object Manager** turns from a cylinder to a blue triangle, denoting that it's now made of polygons. We no longer have control over the radius and height in the **Attribute Manager**, and that's OK, because we need to be able to change the structure of our cylinder with specific polygons to make our trash can properly.

> Hold out for as long as you can before making your object editable. Once you convert an object into polygons and you start editing them, you can't change it back to a primitive. Your object won't look any different the instant you change it, and if you don't plan on editing its structure, then there's no reason to lose control over the convenient parametric properties you have when the object is a primitive.

4. Now what? Cinema 4D has a variety of tools to select and edit these little polygons, so we can create a shape that's more detailed than a plain old cylinder. Let's start by removing the top of our cylinder; a trash can needs to be hollow, so we can put trash in it. You have the ability to select three different parts of your polygonal object: points, edges, and polygons. **Points** are the intersections where the lines making up your shape cross each other. **Edges** are in fact those lines; they form the outlines of the subdivided pieces of your object. **Polygons** are the actual pieces of your subdivision, which we created during the initial stage where we determined our **Rotation** and **Height** segments. Cinema 4D has three modes for selecting each of these components, located on the left-hand side of the Command Palette. We want to edit our trash can's polygons for now, so click on the **Use Polygon** mode button to allow us to pick just the polygons.

5. Go up to the **Select** menu and click on the **Ring Selection** option. Simply hover over the top of your cylinder composed of all those wedges and notice how Cinema 4D is highlighting the entire top portion. The **Ring Selection** tool is great for selecting large groups of connected polygons. Click on the selected group so it turns orange, meaning it's officially selected, and then press the *Delete* key. And just like that, we now have an open container. Angle the viewer so you can see inside the object and notice how it's hollow on the inside:

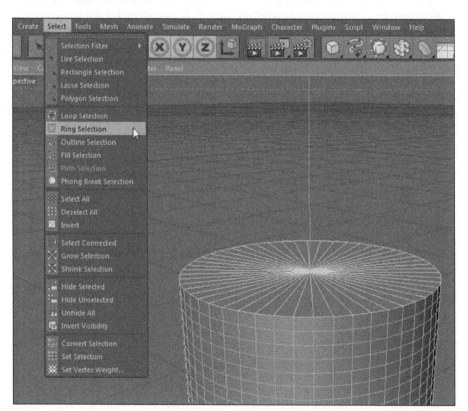

6. Now, take your **Ring Selection** tool and click on the top ring of polygons circling around your object. It should select the entire ring around your future trash can with just one click. Now, head to the bottom ring and hold the *Shift* key, and then click on it to add to the selection. Both the top and bottom ring of polygons should be selected. Now, go under the **Mesh** menu and select **Extrude** from the **Create Tools** submenu. This tool allows us to take our selection and extrude it either in or out from its current position and in relation to its fellow polygons. With the tool selected, click-and-drag to the right-hand side of your screen to make our two rings pop out slightly. Now, our cylinder has these two lips at the top and at the bottom. Go back to the **Create Tools** menu again and switch tools to the **Bevel** tool, which takes your current selection of polygons and lets you create beveled edges instead of the very angular kind of edge we have right now. With the same rings of polygons we just extruded still selected, click-and-drag to the right-hand side so that you have a sort of sloped edge that meets in the middle:

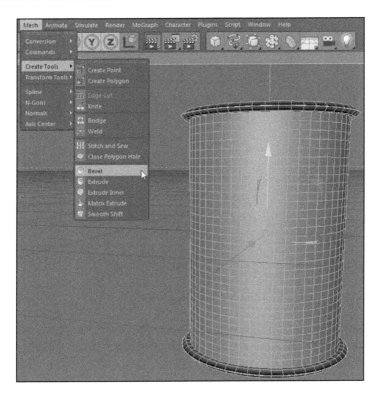

7. Now, we are going to create the metal dimples that wrap all the way around trash cans. Go back to the **Select** menu and pick your **Ring Selection** again. This step may be a little tedious, but you need to hover over each vertical column of every polygon and let the **Ring Selection** tool grab them. You need to skip one column and then select the next group, so that our cylinder alternates between orange and gray groups of selected and unselected rings of polygons. Hold the *Shift* key and click on the ring while hovering over it. The group of polygons turns white before you select it, so make sure you are selecting the vertical columns of polygons and not the rows. Work your way around the object entirely by rotating the angle of your viewer, so you can see your object in every perspective. Be patient and take your time, but if you click on the wrong row or column, just use the undo command, *Ctrl* or *command + Z*, to unselect that group:

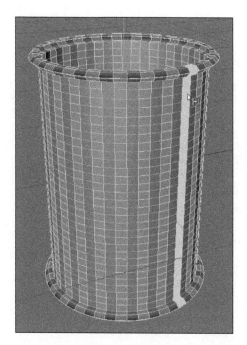

8. It's not always going to be as simple as just grabbing the **Ring Selection** tool and grabbing the exact amount of polygons you need. We need to actually remove some of these polygons, because we don't want the polygons at the top and bottom to be part of our dimples. Switch your Viewer to the **Front** view so we can see our trash can from head on, and zoom in on it so it fills your frame. Now, go in the **Select** menu and pick the **Rectangular Selection** tool, which will let us draw a rectangular box around a group of polygons to select or deselect it. Head to the **Attribute Manager** and uncheck the box that says **Only Select Visible Elements**. This means that our polygons at the back of our object will be selected if they fall within the rectangular box we draw, even though we can't see them.

With some selection tools, such as the rectangular selection, you need to completely incorporate the polygon within the box you draw in order for it to be selected. The border of the box needs to extend beyond it, so that it's included in its entirety. So, don't be scared to go a little further beyond the polygon you want with your selection; you'll be fine as long as it doesn't completely cover the next section of polygons you don't want to select.

9. As you saw earlier, holding the *Shift* key allows you to add polygons to your current selection; conversely, the *Ctrl* key will do the opposite and remove polygons from your selection. So, while holding down the *Ctrl* key, draw a box around the three highest rows of polygons: the two that are on our lip and the first one that's part of the middle of our trash can. Do the same for the corresponding group of polygons at the bottom of our trash can.

Use views such as the **Front** view, **Bottom** view, **Right** view, and **Left** view to move and manipulate points, edges, and polygons instead of the perspective view. These views are called Orthographic, where a 3D object is represented in just two dimensions. It's much easier to manage your selections and place objects correctly when you are looking in an orthographic view, so use and switch between these often.

10. With these polygons selected, we can use the **Extrude** tool again to create the dimples in our trash can. Click-and-drag with the **Extrude** tool to the left this time; this will extrude our polygons inward. Just a very small amount; the dimples on a trash can aren't that steep. So, now our polygons have moved inward, but the result is a very sharp and steep drop-off. The best tool for correcting this is the **HyperNURBS** object, which takes a polygonal object and applies an algorithm to further subdivide the object and smooth the object out, without actually affecting the subdivision. The most common use is to take sharp edges and round them off, or create smooth-looking models from an object with a lower number of polygons.

11. Click on the **HyperNURBS** object, which is the green blob inside the cube in the Command Palette, and it will be added to your scene automatically. It doesn't do anything until we make our trash can a child of it. So, in the **Object Manager**, take your **Trash Can** object and drag it below the **HyperNURBS** object to make it a child. Make sure the arrow faces down before you let go of the mouse, which signals that the object is going to be a child of the object over it, rather than simply being placed below it in the hierarchy. You should notice that our trash can is now smooth-looking, and it appears to have way more polygons—thanks to the **HyperNURBS** object we added. Do a render preview by holding *Ctrl* or *command* + *R*, and you'll see our trash can taking form with smooth dimples. Try deactivating the **HyperNURBS** object by clicking on its green checkmark in the **Object Manager** and doing the render preview; you'll see how different it looks with the **HyperNURBS** object turned off.

When you have any object selected, you can hold the *Alt* or *option* key and click on the **HyperNURBS** icon in the Command Palette, and it will make the selected object a child of the new **HyperNURBS** object automatically. This also works with other Command Palette items such as **Extruded NURBS**, the focus of our next recipe:

12. Now, our trash can needs a lid. Create a new **Cylinder** primitive and change its **Height** to **4**, its **Radius** to **56**, and its **Rotation Segments** to **60** inside the **Attribute Manager**. We then switch to the **Coordinates** tab, move the cylinder much higher in the Y position, and change it to **100**. Change the name of the cylinder to **Lid**, and press the **C** key to make it an editable polygon object.

13. Our lid is hovering above our trash can so we can see underneath it. Rotate your camera so you can see the underside of your lid. Go to the **Select** menu and pick the **Ring Selection** tool. Now, click on the bottom of your lid so that all of the polygon wedges are selected on the underside. Now, switch over to the **Extrude Inner** tool found inside the **Create Tools** submenu in the **Mesh** menu. Then, click-and-drag to the right-hand side so that we create a small gap, a new row of polygons, between the edge of the lid and our selected polygons. You can now hit the *Delete* key to delete the main middle portion here, leaving a lip around your edge.

14. Now, rotate your viewer up to see the top of your lid, and grab our **Ring Selection** tool once more. Grab the polygon wedges at the top by selecting them all and turning them orange. We'll use the **Extrude Inner** tool much like on the underside of the lid, but we'll drag it much closer to the center, until your selected polygons now go about halfway between the center and the edge. Now, we can simply use the Move Tool to take this ring of polygons and move it up very slightly in the Y position. So, grab the green handle on the object's axis and pull it up slightly. The objective here is to create a slight slope on our lid, so that it's not perfectly flat. It's now a little higher in the middle than around the edges. Now, select your lid in the **Object Manager** and then slide it further down in the Y position inside the **Coordinates** tab of the **Attribute Manager**. It looks good with a value of **74** in the **Y** position; it rests on top of the trash can.

15. Lastly, the lid needs a handle. Go up to your **Primitives** icon in the Command Palette and select a **Torus** object inside. The default **Torus** is gigantic, so head to the **Attribute Manager** and change its **Ring Radius** to **15**, the **Pipe Radius** to **2**, and its **Orientation** to **-X.** Then, switch over to the **Slice** tab and check the box for **Slice.** We only want half of our Torus for a handle; change the **From** value to **90** and the **To** value to **-90**. Now, switch to the **Coordinates** tab and move **Torus** up to about **80** in the **Y** position. This value can vary slightly based on how high you pulled up the slope on your lid. Reduce the Scale **Y** to **.75** so it's a little shorter. Double-click on its name in the **Object Manager** and change it to **Handle**.

16. I like to add small details to make it seem like the handle is attached a little more securely. Add one more **Cylinder** object and change its name to **Bolt**, and adjust the properties in the **Attribute Manager** to have **Radius** of **4**, a **Height** of **1**, and change its Y Position in the **Coordinates** tab to be **81** and **15** in the Z Position. Click on its **Caps** tab and check the box to activate **Fillet**; this will round off the edges. Now, take your cylinder in the **Object Manager**, hold down the *Ctrl* or *command* key, and then click-and-drag it away. As you release the mouse, it will create an exact copy of the **Cylinder** object, so take this one and place it on the other side of the handle by changing its Z position value to **-15**. Now, the handle looks a little more secure, and we have created a simple trash can out of both primitives and polygon objects:

How it works...

We started with a simple cylinder to use as the base for our trash can, and we were able to add the necessary details to make it a more realistic model by changing its subdivision and making it a polygonal object. We learned how to select points, edges, or polygons using different tools such as the **Ring Selection** tool or the **Rectangular Selection** tool. We used the **Extrude** and **Bevel** tools on specific groups of polygons to create the details for the lips and grooves of our trash can. **HyperNURBS** objects provided an easy solution to round the sharp edges of our trash can; it turned our rigid cylinder into a smooth-looking object and much more of a finished product.

Trying different tools

Sometimes it's tricky to decide when to bevel, extrude, move, or scale a selection of polygons with a particular tool. That's why the *Ctrl* or *command + Z* command is your best friend. If the tool you picked didn't get the job done, go back to how you had the object and try something else.

Making backups of your primitives

Once you convert an object to polygons, you lose all those helpful controls you have when the object is a primitive. So, before you convert an object to polygons, duplicate it in the **Object Manager** and deactivate it by clicking on its green checkmark to make it a red X. Now, you have a copy as a last resort if your subdivision turns out wrong, you delete some crucial polygons, or you want to precisely change any of the Object properties and start over. Group all your backups together into one group and label it `Backups` to keep your project clean.

Entering the exact values

When you select a tool such as the **Bevel** or **Extrude** tool, it loads controls in the **Attribute Manager**. You can enter exact values to create specific transformations for your selected pieces. This is handy if you need to make sure you apply the exact same transformation to polygons, points, or sides on different objects. Otherwise, it's completely fine to adjust the eyeball movement with the mouse and see what looks good.

Weighting with HyperNURBS

When you have an editable polygon object inside a **HyperNURBS** object, you can use the Point, Edge, and Polygon modes to push, pull, and manipulate these pieces to create specific details into your object. This is referred to as weighting, where you can finesse fine details into your model. You can start with a sphere and manipulate the geometry to form the ears, eyes, nose, and other features of a character's head. Check out the reference documentation for Cinema 4D for some good examples and strategy when weighting your **HyperNURBS** objects.

What is a NURBS?

NURBS stands for **Non-Uniform Rational B-Spline**. Unless Maxon makes a Cinema 4D trivia game, you probably won't ever need to know that. There are a bunch of NURBS objects that we will cover in this chapter, and basically they require other objects (mostly splines) to generate surfaces and create objects. They are very useful modeling tools and are often the correct choice when creating models, rather than the polygon editing we did in this particular recipe.

Creating from splines – extrude NURBS

One of the more useful NURBS objects is Extrude NURBS, which takes the outline of a spline and extrudes to create solid surfaces. Splines are lines made up of points, and they can be drawn, made from one of the many preset shapes in Cinema 4D, or imported from Adobe Illustrator to create 3D objects from custom designs drawn out in that application. Splines can't be seen when rendered, so we need to combine them with Extrude NURBS in order to make them have surfaces and appear visible in our renders.

Getting ready

Locate the `Fleur_De_Lis.ai` file in the C4D Content Pack and have it ready to go when called for in this recipe.

How to do it...

1. Let's start by looking in our Splines icon inside the Command Palette; it's the backwards looking "S" with the plus sign on it. All of these icons inside correspond to a different shape, which is a result of various settings and mathematical products to determine what your spline actually looks like. For instance, click on the icon for one of the simplest splines: the **Circle**. You'll see an outline and a new item in the Object Manager, but doing a render preview by hitting *Ctrl* or *command + R* will show an empty screen. Splines are just lines; they have no volume or anything that gives them definition for us to see. Click on the **Circle** spline in the **Object Manager** to load it into the **Attribute Manager** and you'll see that it has a couple of properties to determine its shape under the **Object** tab. Just like primitives, these parameters vary according to the shape, for example, the **Circle** has a **Radius** field that will grow or shrink the spline, whereas a **Square** spline will have the **Height** and **Width** setting to make it more rectangular. Change the **Radius** to **300** and check the **Ring** checkbox. We now have a new property, **Inner Radius**, which you should change to **250**. We have created a ring; it's a perfect circle because it's created by the math as a spline object:

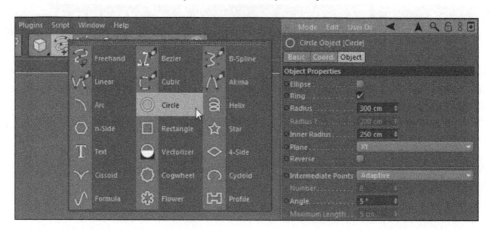

2. Splines are made up of points, but you can't access them without making the object editable. Highlight the **Circle** in the **Object Manager** and press the *C* key to make the object editable. Your ring will still look exactly the same, but the important distinction is that we can now manipulate points on our spline. Click on the **Use Point** mode on the left-hand side of the application in the Command Palette and you'll see little boxes at the vertexes of your splines. Click on each of them and you have the ability to move them anywhere in 3D space using the **Position, Rotate,** and **Scale** tools. Use the **Rectangular Selection** tool, grab the two outermost points on the x axis, then switch to the Scale Tool, and pull the red handle on the Scale Tool outwards (to the right-hand side) and you'll see that our ring is only stretching via those points.

Once again, subdividing is important. If you have too many points on a spline or polygons on an object, moving one or two won't make much of a difference because your shape is defined by so many. A circle spline can be defined by just four points or it can have an infinite number of points. Changing the location of one of the four points on your circle will look different if you were to change the position of one point on a circle with a hundred other points instead. When designing objects, you need to keep in mind how you may need a lesser or a greater number of points or surfaces, depending on what you plan to do with them.

3. Our ring is now an oblong letter O but still has no substance to it. We need to add an **Extrude NURBS** object to our scene to extrude the spline and make it visible. Click on the green cube icon in the Command Palette, which handles all of your **NURBS** options, and click on the **Extrude NURBS** icon. It's added to your **Object Manager** where you have to make the spline a child of the **Extrude NURBS**, so take your spline and drag it below the **Extrude NURBS** in the **Object Manager**, making sure it is not just below it, but a child of it. Your cursor will point downwards with an arrow when you make it a child; it will point straight left if you are simply placing it below **Extrude NURBS**. Once you make it a child, you'll instantly notice that you now have actual gray faces of your oblong ring. You can still manipulate the points on the spline and the shape will change automatically, so try scaling the points out more or less and you'll see the gray pieces stretch with it:

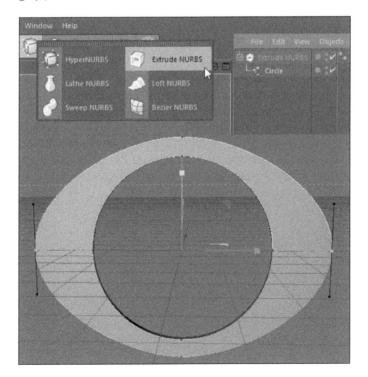

> The **Extrude NURBS** object will take your spline and extend it in any way you specify in the **Movement** setting in the **Object** tab in the **Attribute Manager**. The default is always 20 units in the Z dimension, so it will always extend a spline backwards when it's oriented on the XY-plane. You can set it to go up and down or left and right, based on the other two fields for the X and Y values; it all depends on the orientation of your spline. You can also input negative values to have it extrude the opposite way.

4. If you need simple shapes to work with, Cinema 4D has you covered with these basic splines. But, if you have a shape that is pretty complex and needs to be very accurate, you might want to try importing the spline from Adobe Illustrator or another vector-based design program. The most common use for this is handling a client's logo that is drawn to certain specifications to fit with a company's design and trademark. You should rely on a vector file made with Adobe Illustrator. This is the most important part: save it as an `.ai` file but as an Illustrator 8 file when prompted. It's an old file type that works between all versions of the software. Cinema 4D won't recognize the vector data in any version higher than Illustrator 8, so make sure you save the file in this older format.

5. Open the `Fleur_De_Lis.ai` file, which is already saved as an Illustrator 8 file for you. From inside the **File** menu in Cinema 4D, click on **OK** on the ensuing pop-up window that asks you how to resize your spline. You'll see that the spline of our common symbol is perfectly captured as an editable spline inside Cinema 4D. Sometimes, (as with this one) the placement of your object in Adobe Illustrator causes your spline to import with strange coordinates. To center our spline, highlight it in the **Object Manager** and go up top to the **Character** menu, and under **Commands**, you'll find **Reset PSR**, meaning position, scale, and rotation. Select this command and your spline will snap to the origin directly. Make sure the spline is selected and hit *Ctrl* or *command* + *C* to copy the spline, and then hit *Ctrl* or *command* + *V* to paste it inside the other document with your **Extrude NURBS**. Delete the current spline for our oblong "O" in the **Extrude NURBS** and place the **Fleur De Lis** spline as its child instead. You'll see our more intricate shape is also cut out perfectly, exactly as it was drawn in Adobe Illustrator.

6. **Extrude NURBS** and splines can also be combined to make text rather easily. Go into the spline menu and select a Text spline and add it to your scene. Select it so it's active in the **Attribute Manager**, and click under the **Object** tab so we can change the **Text** field to, say, **Fleur De Lis** and change the **Height** to **100**. Grab the Move Tool from the Command Palette and move the spline from on top of the symbol to above it, holding the *Shift* key so it snaps into place in increments of 10; it's in a good place at about 250 units higher in the Y position. Add another **Extrude NURBS** to your scene; double-click on its name in the **Object Manager** to change its name to **Text** and do the same for the symbol by naming it **Fleur De Lis**, so we can easily keep track of which is which. Place the **Text** spline as a child of the **Text Extrude NURBS** and you'll see we now have some words to match our symbol:

How it works...

The combination of splines used with **Extrude NURBS** is a useful way to extract surfaces from shapes. The splines can be simple from the menu inside Cinema 4D, or brought in from a program such as an Illustrator to represent a more complex design. Using splines allows us to draw or create precise shapes and use that information to generate depth. Without an object such as an **Extrude NURBS**, the splines have no way of being seen by our renders.

There's more...

Splines and NURBS tend to go together. Check out some of the other recipes in this chapter on the Lathe NURBS and the Sweep NURBS to see what else you can create from these wonderful magic lines.

Using MoText instead

If you have the MoGraph module, use the object called MoText instead of the **Text** spline and the **Extrude NURBS** combination illustrated here. MoText gives you way better control over your text and allows you to animate each letter using MoGraph to create interesting text animations that the Text spline simply can't. I only pointed out how to make text here in case you don't have the MoGraph module. Check *Chapter 8*, *The Awesome Power of MoGraph*, for more information on using MoText.

Using Lathe NURBS

Another popular tool from within the **NURBS** menu is the **Lathe NURBS**, which derives its name from the lathe, a tool used in crafts such as woodworking, pottery, and glass work. The tool spins an object around an axis to deform or manipulate it in some way, depending on the craft. I remember using a small pottery wheel in art class as a kid, and this was my first introduction to the Cinema 4D tool that bears its name. It's important to make this connection with the name of the tool to better understand what it's capable of.

How to do it...

1. Start with a new project and immediately switch the viewer from the **Perspective** view to the **Front** view, under the **Cameras** menu option. We want a **Front** view of what we are working on, in this case, to use the tool properly. We are going to use the **Lathe NURBS** to create a pawn on a chess board.

    Whenever you are about to start to model, do an image search on the Internet to see what an object really looks like. There could be multiple variations of it, and you could maybe combine real-life designs together in your 3D project to make something really unique.

2. The key to using the **Lathe NURBS** is to use the Freehand **Spline** tool to draw half of the profile's shape of the object you want to create to the immediate left or right-hand side of the y axis. Click on the Freehand **Spline** tool and do your best with a steady hand to draw the vertical half of a pawn, as if somebody sawed it in half from top to bottom; try to keep all the points on the right-hand side of the y axis. Now, click and select the spline in the **Object Manager** and head down to the **Coordinates** tab in the **Attribute Manager**. Make sure that the X position value for the entire spline is 0.

    Never worry about getting your shape exactly right on the first try. Just get it close and we'll make it work.

3. Now, go up to the **NURBS** icon in the Command Palette and click on the shape that looks like a green vase and is labeled **Lathe NURBS**. It will add the item to your **Object Manager**, and just like the **Extrude NURBS** from the last recipe, we need to drag our spline in the **Object Manager** and make it a child of the **Lathe NURBS** object. Once completed, you'll notice the result immediately. The **Lathe NURBS** object has created a cylindrical object based on the profile shape we drew. It rotates the spline around the y axis in a perfect circle and you get all of the contours you drew with your spline:

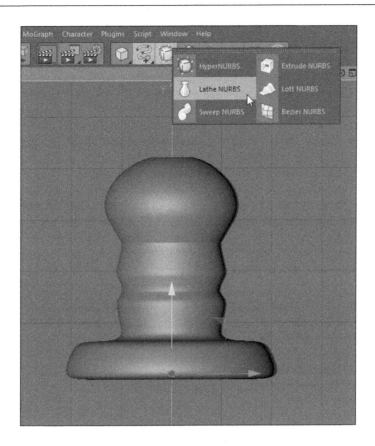

4. Unless you are incredibly gifted with a mouse or tablet stylus, your pawn probably looks terrible like mine. The general shape is there, but it likely needs some work. The general tip when using points (and keyframes too) is less is better. Having fewer points creates smoother and more natural curves between them. It also makes editing a spline much easier when you only have to move a couple of points instead of perhaps dozens.

5. Click on the green checkmark in the **Object Manager** to deactivate your **Lathe NURBS**, so now we will only see our spline. Zoom in on your spline to as close as you can select it in the **Object Manager**. Click on the **Use Point** mode button on the left-hand side in the Command Palette and let's delete any clusters of redundant points. You should have roughly between 10 to 15 points on your spline, which will be plenty.

6. Now that you have the right number of points, the next key is their positioning and the angle of their curves. Switch to the **Rectangular Selection** tool at the top of the Command Palette and drag a box around all of your points on your spline. They are now highlighted in yellow and they should have little black tabs sticking out of them; those are your Bezier handles, which represent the angle and direction of the gradual curve between points on your spline. Right or context-click on an empty spot in your Viewer, and there are a couple of options to highlight here. You have the option to change your selected points to a **Hard Interpolation**, which will eliminate your Bezier handles and make jagged linear segments between points. Sometimes, this is desired, but we want our **Soft Interpolation** (listed right below it), which enables our Bezier handles, if we need to add them. Following them are two useful options for **Equal Tangent Length** and **Equal Tangent Direction**. Click on **Equal Tangent Length** first and then click on **Equal Tangent Direction**. These features even out any extremes in the curves that may have come about as you tried to sketch the perfect pawn on your first try. Toggle the green checkmark on and off so you can see you results when you want and see your spline when you need to make adjustments.

7. Depending on your points, you'll need to tweak their position to get the shape right. You can select them individually with the **Rectangular Selection** tool or switch back to the Move Tool and click on them that way. Once you get the red and green axis handles, you can slide the points up and down or left and right to get a better-looking pawn. With the points highlighted, you'll also get the opportunity to adjust the Bezier handles. Pulling or rotating one handle grabs the other automatically and applies the congruent adjustment, but if you hold the *Shift* key, you can adjust one independently without affecting the other one:

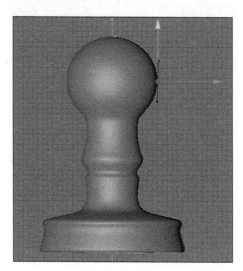

8. The only two points we need to make sure we absolutely get right are the points that are supposed to be lined up exactly with the y axis. These pieces are the middle points in the Lathe creation of our pawn, and they extend to far beyond the y axis or not far enough to it; you'll get weird-looking overlaps or gaps when you apply the **Lathe NURBS**. Select just the top point on the spline in the Viewer and look down in the **Coordinate Manager** under the **X position** field. Enter a value 0 in this field and then press *Enter*, and the point will snap to the Y axis automatically, leaving it perfectly in the middle. Repeat this step for the point at the very bottom, so they are both lined up exactly in the middle.

9. For our points representing the curved areas of our pawn, the **Soft Interpolation** works great. But, we need our pawn to have a flat edge along the bottom, so it can rest on a chessboard evenly. This is an easy adjustment to make. Simply click on the other point on the bottom of your spline; the one furthest away from the y axis on the bottom. Even it up with the other bottom point, either using the **Coordinate Manager** or by dragging it in the viewers so they have the exact same values. Now, with the point selected, turn your Bezier handle so it's parallel to the X axis, which should create a flat edge along the bottom but maintain a curve where the pawn begins to shape upward. You should now have a much better-looking pawn with the adjustments you made to the shape and position of your points on the spline.

10. Reactivate your **Lathe NURBS** object if you haven't already, and check out the chess piece you created.

How it works...

The **Lathe NURBS** tool takes a spline that we draw on one side of the y axis and creates a 3D object based on its profile, rotating it around the y axis in a circle. We switched to the **Front** view right away because this is the best view for using the tool, as you can see the exact profile you are drawing and with no differences in perspective. The objective is to first draw the general shape and then eliminate any redundant or unnecessary points, thereafter adjusting and finessing their position and curves using their Bezier handles. We can adjust the points as much as we need to get our object just right.

There's more...

It's hard to tell how big your object will be by just drawing a spline, so make sure early on in the process that your spline isn't going to be too big or too small. Resizing and moving the points will affect the distance of the y axis, which is the whole basis of how shapes are created with **Lathe NURBS**. **Lathe NURBS** include: Cups, bowls, plates, bottles, glasses, bird baths, barrels, vases, missiles, lamps, baseball bats, funnels, light bulbs, pots, and trophies. If it's got a cylindrical shape, try making it with **Lathe NURBS**.

Adding points

If you find yourself needing an extra point somewhere on your spline, you can either context-click or right-click on the spline and select the **Create Point** tool. After this, your cursor changes and you can click on your spline and it will add a point in that spot. It's also found under the **Create Tools** submenu in the **Mesh** menu up top.

See also

There are two more recipes in this book that use **Lathe NURBS**, including the last one in this chapter.

Using Sweep NURBS

The next important member of the NURBS family is the **Sweep NURBS**, which takes a spline path and sweeps a shape across it. It can be used to create very abstract and stylized designs, or it can be used to solve very practical modeling issues. The file for this recipe has a simple setup where a **Sweep NURBS** object is really the only way we can achieve our effect. We'll also get introduced to the handy Spline Mask feature in Cinema 4D.

Getting ready

Open the `Plug.c4d` file from the C4D Content Pack to use with this recipe on **Sweep NURBS**.

How to do it...

1. The objective here is to create a cord that travels from the plug on the back of our text labeled "Plug" over to the plug that is attached to the electrical outlet. Cords are usually long and skinny and have many different bends and twists throughout. **Sweep NURBS** will give us the ability to dictate where our cord will travel and what the shape of the cord will be. **Sweep NURBS** requires two splines to work properly: a spline to define the path that will be swept, and a spline to define the shape that is applied to the swept path. So, in this case, one spline will define the path of our cord from plug-to-plug, and another spline will create the actual shape that our cord possesses across its distance.

2. Start by changing the **Perspective** view in the Viewer to the **Top** view. Like we learned in the previous recipe, drawing splines tends to be much easier when you are only working in two dimensions and not three, so switch between views so your view has a 2D perspective instead. In this view, we only want to draw the path of our spline from plug-to-plug. Select the **Freehand Spline** tool and draw a path that leads from one plug to the other; make it so it's not perfectly straight and has a few bends in it. Once you draw your path, delete the redundant points like in the previous **Lathe NURBS** recipe, so you only have a few points to work with (aim for about four to eight in this exercise). Zoom in to the Viewer and select points by hitting the Use Point mode button on the left-hand side of the Command Palette, and select the Move Tool up towards the top. Make sure the end points of your spline are close to the bases of your plugs-in order to properly define where our cord starts and ends:

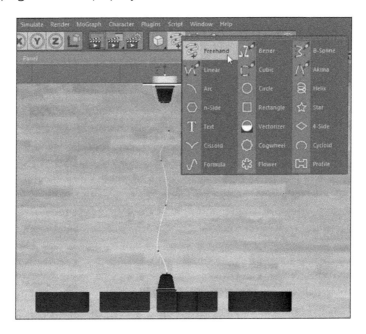

3. Now, switch from the **Front** view to the **Right** view in your Viewer. This is where we need to adjust the height of our spline's points. Switch from **Point** mode to **Model** mode, so click on the gray cube with the orange outline in the Command Palette. Bring the entire spline down so that the endpoints are even with both plugs using the Move Tool on the whole spline, and not just any one point. With the spline now even with the plugs, we need to add some variation to the height of our spline between the points. Because we are looking at a direct profile view of our spline, we will not be able to change any of the curves we drew that moved from left to right in our top view; we will only add some variation to the height of the points on our spline. Click-and-drag some of the intermediate points towards the floor, so they appear as if they are resting just above it. A little variation in the height of each point will create a more interesting and realistic cord.

4.   Now that the path of the cord is determined via a spline, we need to create another spline to determine its shape. Cords can come in varying shapes, and the beauty of the **Sweep NURBS** is you can switch out any spline for another and your cord will take the shape. Let's make our cord look like it's made of two wires with a rubber casing around it. Deactivate the **Room** group with the traffic light so it doesn't get in your way, then switch the Viewer from the **Right** view to the **Front** view, and then go to your spline menu in the Command Palette and click on the **n-Side** spline. This spline tool is used for creating polygons with a set number of sides. The default six sides are fine, but we need to shrink down **Radius** to a much smaller value of **5** and click on the checkbox to activate **Rounding** and change its **Radius** to **2**.

5.   To get the effect of having two wires in our cord, we need to create another instance of the **n-Side** spline and combine it with the other. For this, we'll need the **Spline Mask** tool, which is a useful tool for combining or subtracting splines from one another. It's very similar to the **Pathfinder** tool in Adobe Illustrator, if you've ever used that, and it results in a new single spline resulting from our two original splines. So, take your **n-Side** spline inside the **Object Manager** and drag it while holding the *Ctrl* or *command* key to make a copy of it. Now, take one copy of your spline and move it by **4** units in the position **X** value in the **Attribute Manager** under the **Coordinates** tab, and then do the same for the other **n-Side** spline, but do it for **-4** units instead. This should result in our two splines barely overlapping in the middle.

6.   Click on the icon in the Command Palette featuring the **Array** object; it's a white cube surrounded by six green cubes. Inside, you'll find the **Spline Mask** tool; add it to your project. Now, take your two **n-Side** splines and move them below the **Spline Mask** as children. The **Spline Mask** assigns each of the two splines as either the **A** object or the **B** object. In the **Attribute Manager** under the **Object** tab, you can control what the **Spline Mask** does with the two splines; you can create a union between them, subtract one from the other, or create a spline from the intersection of the two. We want ours to remain on the default **A union B** setting, and you'll notice that our splines are now connected in the middle where they were slightly overlapping before. Double-click on its name and rename the **Spline Mask** to **Cord Shape**.

7.   A **Spline Mask** object works just like a regular spline with our NURBS objects. Click on your **NURBS** icon in the Command Palette and select the icon with the sweeping tube for the **Sweep NURBS** to add it to your scene. Now, take the **Path Spline** and the **Cord Shape** splines and add them under your **Sweep NURBS** object as children. The order in which you place them will determine whether you get your cord to look right. The spline to determine the shape of your sweep goes above the spline to determine your sweep's path. So, the cord-shape spline mask should be above your path spline. You'll notice that your cord now exists; it's a double-wire cord that leads from the Plug text and into the outlet. If the rotation of your cord appears off and it's misaligned, don't worry; just switch on **Enable Axis Modification** by clicking on the button with the orange two-way arrow on the left-hand side of the Command Palette. Now, grab the **Rotate** tool from up top and highlight your cord-shape spline mask in the **Object Manager** and zoom back and rotate the blue band by 90 degrees in the Viewer, while holding the *Shift* key to snap in place. This changes the alignment of the axis and corrects the rotation of your cord shape:.

8. If your cord is too high or low so that it doesn't appear on the ground properly at times, you can still adjust the points on your path spline to make it fit whichever way you want. Just make sure you disable the Enable Axis Modification button, then Use Point mode to modify the individual points, and finally, adjusting their position and Bezier curves where needed. Apply the material labeled Plug in the **Material Manager** at the bottom of the screen to your **Sweep NURBS** object in the **Object Manager** (check out *Chapter 6, A Material World*, for more on materials):

How it works...

Our cord is an easy-to-make product of the **Sweep NURBS** tool. It allowed us to draw something that slinks and bends and sweeps along whatever path we want it to. We simply drew our path to determine where we wanted our cord to go, and then used a **Spline Mask** tool to create a unique shape for our cord. There are many other useful techniques out there involving the **Sweep NURBS**, which you can use to create much more sophisticated objects than just a cord, but this recipe shows you what a practical solution it can provide.

The **Sweep NURBS** comes with a cool pair of parameters for **Start Growth** and **End Growth**. These features can be animated in the **Attribute Manager** to make them appear as if your sweep is growing or tracing along your spline. Use this parameter if you ever want your sweep to appear as if it is growing or being written on the canvas.

Modeling with Loft NURBS

The last NURBS tool we'll cover in this chapter is the **Loft NURBS**. **Loft NURBS** uses multiple splines as children to create a stretched surface that fits the profile of all the splines contained within. Think of it as a **Sweep NURBS**, but with multiple splines modifying the shape of the sweep over a fixed distance. In this recipe, we are going to create a flathead screwdriver using a few different splines and **Loft NURBS**, and you'll see how useful **Loft NURBS** can be when modeling an object that has many different kinds of contours.

How to do it...

1. Let's start with the handle for our screwdriver in a new project. Click on the **Splines** icon in the Command Palette, select the **Circle** spline, change its **Radius** in the **Attribute Manager** to **25**, and rename it as **Base 2**. Now, take this spline and hold down the *Ctrl* or *command* key and click-and-drag two new copies of this spline in the **Object Manager**. Rename one to **Base 1** and the other to **Base 3**, so you have three copies of the same spline.

2. Take your **Base 1** spline and reduce its **Radius** to 20 in the **Object** tab, and then switch to the **Coordinates** tab and change its **Z** position value to **-10**. Then, take it in the **Object Manager** and slide it above the **Base 2** spline so it's the first object in the sequence, and make sure that the **Base 3** spline is below both of them. Now, switch to the **Base 3** spline and change its **Z** position value to 10 in the **Coordinates** tab. Open the **NURBS** icon in the Command Palette, click on the **Loft NURBS** icon, and then place the splines as its children in an ascending order; that is, **Base 1**, **Base 2**, and **Base 3**.

3. The **Loft NURBS** has created an extruded shape based on the spacing and contours of our three splines. Let's add an indented grip to our handle to really see the **Loft NURBS** work its magic. Open the **Splines** menu again and select the **Flower** spline. In its **Object** tab, change the **Inner Radius** to **15**, the **Outer Radius** to **25**, and the **Petals** to **7**. Switch to the **Coordinates** tab and move it to **10** in the **Z** position, so it's even with **Base 3**. We then place it as a child of the **Loft NURBS** and make sure it's below the three circle splines. Now, hold the *Ctrl* or *command* key and drag a copy of the **Flower** spline and move this instance to **150** in the **Z** position; make sure it's the bottom child in the hierarchy. You should now see our handle with some grooves in its grip. Change the name of these two splines to **Grooves 1** and **Grooves 2**.

4. To complete our handle, we need to simply repeat the same shape we have at the base of the handle at the top, so it appears symmetrical. Select your **Base 1**, **Base 2**, and **Base 3** splines in the **Object Manager** and hold the *Ctrl* or *command* key and drag copies of them below the two splines creating our grooves. From top to bottom, rename these three splines to **Top 1**, **Top 2**, and **Top 3**. For **Top 1**, change its **Radius** to be **25** under the **Object** tab and then change its **Z** position to be **150**. For **Top 2**, just change its **Z** position to be **160**. **Top 3** needs a **Z** position of **170**, but reduce its **Radius** to **20**. We have essentially taken the curved base of the handle and applied the same look to the top of the handle, and it reveals the grooved grip in the middle.

5. Highlight the **Loft NURBS** object in the **Object Manager**, and then click on the **HyperNURBS** icon in the Command Palette while holding down the *Alt* or *option* key. This will automatically make it a child of the **HyperNURBS** object and it will smooth out some of the contours around the caps and grooves, giving it a better-looking result. Now, select the **Loft NURBS** object and load the **Caps** tab in the **Attribute Manager**. Change the **Start** and **End** options to be **Fillet Cap**, and then change both the **Steps** values to **10** and both the **Radius** values to **5**. Click on the checkbox for **Constrain**, and you'll have some smooth-looking caps on the top and bottom of your handle. Double-click on the name of the **HyperNURBS** and rename it to **Handle** in the **Object Manager**:

6. Now, let's make the head of our screwdriver. This will be a separate **Loft NURBS** object that uses the same method for creating the handle. Start with a new **Circle** spline, reduce its **Radius** to **5**, and adjust its **Z** position to be **170**. Hold the *Ctrl* or *command* key, drag another copy of this spline in the **Object Manager**, and change the **Z** position of this object to be **310**. Rename this one to **Middle** and the previous spline to **Base**, and make sure the **Middle** is below the **Base** in the stacking order in the **Object Manager**.

7. To flatten out the tip, we are going to need a **Rectangle** spline so our screwdriver becomes pointed instead of round. Grab a **Rectangle** spline from the menu and change its **Z** position to **370** and shrink its **Width** and **Height** settings way down in the **Object** tab; the **Width** should be **10** and the **Height** should be **3**. Rename this spline as **Flat 1** and use the shortcut to create a copy directly below it; press the *Ctrl* or *command* key and drag and rename this to **Flat 2**. Move this one slightly forward in the **Z** position, so it resides at **390**.

8. We need two more **Rectangle** splines, so hit the **Ctrl** or **command** key again and drag two more copies below the **Flat 2** spline. Rename them to **Wide 1** and **Tip**, respectively. The **Wide 1** needs to be at **400** in the **Z** position and have a **Width** of **13** in the setting under the `Object` tab in the **Attribute Manager**. Now, take the **Tip** spline and slide it to **420** in the **Z** position, but reduce its **Width** down to **5**. Add a **Loft NURBS** object and place these splines in this stack order as children of the **Loft NURBS** and rename the **Loft NURBS** object to **Head**.

9. We are almost there; we have just one small tweak to make. When our **Loft NURBS** goes from our **Middle** circular spline to our **Flat 1** rectangular spline, there's a bit of a twisty kink in there. To put it simply, take your **Middle** spline, load its **Coordinates** tab in the **Attribute Manager**, and change its **R.B** rotation value to **-45**, so it twists your screwdriver correctly. Now, you can add this model to your toolbox:

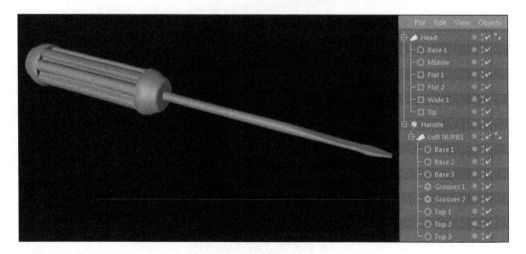

How it works...

We created a flathead screwdriver using just some simple splines and **Loft NURBS**. The variety and spacing of our splines determines the shape created by the **Loft NURBS**, and we are able to mold and blend different shapes together to make them look like they are a piece of one solid construction. Picture our screwdriver's handle being cast in a rubber mold and coming out with those contours and grooves. The flat head of the screwdriver starts out round and cylindrical but tapers smoothly into a flat point for use with that specific type of screw.

There's more...

Use some different splines and turn this flathead screwdriver into a Phillips screwdriver.

Punching holes with Boole

So far, all the methods in this chapter have shown you how to generate or create new geometry and surfaces on your models. What if you want to do the opposite? What if you want to subtract from a model, creating things such as holes, crevices, and dents instead? The **Boole** object is the key to removing parts and pieces of your 3D model inside Cinema 4D. This recipe will show you how to cut out a hole in a model of a birdhouse.

Getting ready

Follow along with the `Birdhouse.c4d` file from the C4D Content Pack with this recipe.

How to do it...

1. This is a relatively simple model, made with a few primitives and **Extrude NURBS**. The problem is we want our birdhouse to be able to, you know, house birds. Right now, there is nowhere for our birds to enter and build a nest. The Boole object takes two objects, and depending on how you set them up to interact, it can eliminate the surfaces of one object based on the size and shape of the other. It's the easiest way to eliminate specific geometrical shapes in your object. We want to drill a hole right in the front of our birdhouse.

2. Add a **Cylinder** object to the scene from your **Primitives** menu in the Command Palette. Set the **Orientation** to **-Z** and adjust the **Radius** to be **20**. Your cylinder is overlapping with the birdhouse and this is exactly what we want at the moment. How and where we position the cylinder to intersect with the birdhouse represents the area we want eliminated.

3. Add a **Boole** object, found inside the **Array** icon in the Command Palette, to your scene. It works in a similar manner to a **Spline Mask**, relying on an **A** and a **B** object to determine what will get cut out. Place both, the entire **Birdhouse** group and the **Cylinder** object, as children of the **Boole** object. Make sure the **Birdhouse** group is on top and the **Cylinder** object is below it. You should see a hole the same size as that of our cylinder punched into our birdhouse:

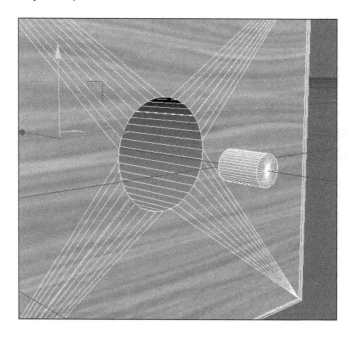

4. There are two issues with our **Boole**. The first problem is that our cylinder isn't in the right spot; it's eliminating the area where our perch is, and it's also coming out the other side. To fix this, we need to adjust the position of the cylinder in the **Coordinates** tab of the **Attribute Manager** to be 40 in the position **Y** and -40 in the position **Z**. Now, the hole is positioned correctly and is only occurring on one side.

5. The second issue is the type of hole our **Boole** is creating. If you look inside the gap created by our **Boole**, it has essentially acted like it drilled a hole in a wooden block, shaped like a birdhouse. It needs to be hollow inside, so birds can get in. There's a simple setting for this: if you select the **Boole** object and load its properties into the **Attribute Manager**, you see the **Boolean Type** under the **Object** tab. It always defaults to **A subtract B**, meaning it takes the first object (object **A**, our Birdhouse) and subtracts the second object from it (our cylinder, the **B** object). Switch the **Boolean Type** to **A without B** and you'll see a different type of Boole where our object appears hollow inside, which is much more suitable for a birdhouse:

How it works...

The **Boole** object is perfect for eliminating a specified shape from existing surfaces. We were able to carve a perfect circle out of the side of our birdhouse, which would be extremely difficult using regular subdivided geometry. You simply place the object you want to use as the shape to cut out in **Boole** with the object you want to cut it from, and it does the rest. There are also a couple of **Boolean Types** that can create different results from the intersection of our two objects, which is the key to creating a hollow birdhouse with the **A without B** setting.

There's more...

Switch the **Boolean Type** to each of the four kinds available; check out how it affects your birdhouse differently.

Similar to Spline Mask

The **Boole** object works very similar to the **Spline Mask**, which is why they are grouped in the same spot in the Command Palette. If you can make your shape by subtracting a few splines and using **Extrude NURBS**, you will find that it's another alternative to using the **Boole** object.

Hide new edges

If your **Boole** object creates new lines that are cluttering up in your model when selected, click on the **Hide New Edges** box under the **Object** tab to hide the new subdivision, just so you'll be able to see your model a bit better.

Increase subdivision if needed

If you use a **Boole** object to punch out an object that has a lot of intricate details, you may need to increase the subdivision on your other object to get a better-looking cutout. If there isn't enough geometry to handle cutting out a particular shape, the hole made by the Boole may look a bit jagged and rough around the edges.

Using the Atom Array tool

The **Atom Array** tool is a bit of a one trick pony, but it's a very good trick. An **Atom Array** object takes any object you place below it as a child and converts it to sort of a skeleton of its subdivision. It places spheres at the vertexes and lines connecting each of them to create the sort of balls and stick models you used in chemistry class. It's very useful for creating things such as cages that would otherwise require a lot of separate pieces and work to position them properly. In this recipe what we are going to create is the timeless classic, the hamster wheel, using primarily the **Atom Array** object.

How to do it...

1. Let's start by creating the main part: the wheel. We'll need a **Cylinder** object from our **Primitives** menu in the Command Palette. In the **Attribute Manager**, change its **Height** to **25** and its **Orientation** to **-X**. Now, go up to the icon for the **Array** object in the Command Palette, open it up, and find the pyramid-shaped ball and stick icon; that's our **Atom Array**. Now, take your **Cylinder** object and add it as a child

underneath the **Atom Array** in the **Object Manager**. You should instantly see that the faces of our cylinder are gone; they've been replaced by a bunch of spheres and lines connecting them. Select the **Atom Array** object to load it into the **Attribute Manager** and change the **Cylinder Radius** (the connecting pieces) and the **Sphere Radius** (at the each vertex) to **0.5**:

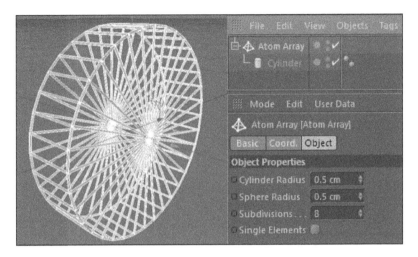

2. We have something that sort of looks like a Ferris wheel. The problem is our hypothetical hamsters could never get inside this wheel for any exercise. Turn OFF the **Atom Array** object in the **Object Manager** by clicking on the green checkmark. Select the **Cylinder** object and hit the *C* key to convert it to polygons. We'll need to delete one side of our wedges so that it's not caged in by our **Atom Array**. Hit the button for **Use Polygon** mode in the Command Palette and then go under the **Selection** menu and click on the **Ring Selection** tool. Click on one wedge so it will automatically select them all. We then hit the *Delete* key. Make sure you use the **Point** tool to also highlight and select the point in the middle of the side where you just deleted all your polygons, otherwise you'll just have a floating dot when your **Atom Array** is active. If you turn the **Atom Array** back on, you'll see that the whole side is now open for our hamster to enter. Double-click on its name and rename the **Atom Array** to **Wheel**.

You can eliminate the caps on a cylinder and a few other primitives under the **Caps** tab. Click on the checkbox for **Caps** to deactivate them. In our case, we need them on one side and not the other, so we turn them on, but it's useful to know that this is a way to deactivate them without converting them to polygons and deleting them.

3. Now, we just need to create a stand for our wheel to be supported on. For this, we are going to use **Sweep NURBS**. Switch to the **Left** view, go to your **Splines** menu, and then select an **n-Side** spline in the Command Palette. In the **Attribute Manager**, change the **Radius** to **60**, the **Sides** to **3**, and check on **Rounding** while adjusting its **Radius** to **5**. Now, switch to the **Coordinates** tab and enter a value of **-45** in the position **Y** field and **-15** for the position **X**, change the **R.P** rotation value to **90**, and lastly lower the scale **Z** to **0.8**, so that we have a triangle with rounded corners for our stand:

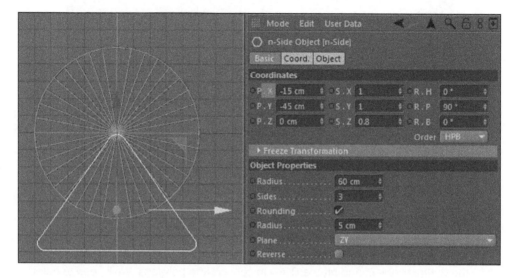

4. Our support base needs to have a portion going along the bottom, so let's add a **Rectangle** spline to the scene and change its parameters to have a **Width** of **40** and a **Height** of **90**; it's **Plane** should be **XZ**. Check on the box for **Rounding** with a **Radius** set to **5**. Move it down to **-70** in the **Y** Position and **5** in the **X** Position under the **Coordinates** tab. Change the Viewer back to **Perspective** view, so you can see your new spline better.

5. Now, select both the **n-Side** and **Rectangle** spline in the **Object Manager**, hit the *C* key, and make them editable. Now, we want to add a **Sweep NURBS** from the Command Palette to sweep our base with a **Circle** spline. Add the **Circle** spline and change its **Radius** to **0.5** so it's very small. The issue is that **Sweep NURBS** work with one spline defining the shape and the other defining the path, but we have two splines for our path. No problem; we can combine our two splines into one by selecting them both in the **Object Manager** and going under **Mesh** up top, then under the **Conversion** submenu, and hitting the **Connect + Delete** command. It has fused our splines together into one, so now place it as a child of the **Sweep NURBS** object and place the **Circle** above it as a child as well. Now, you'll see that our combined spline is being swept, and we have a base for our hamster wheel. Nudge the **Sweep NURBS** object over 1 unit in the **X** Position, so it's up against our wheel, and rename it as **Base**:

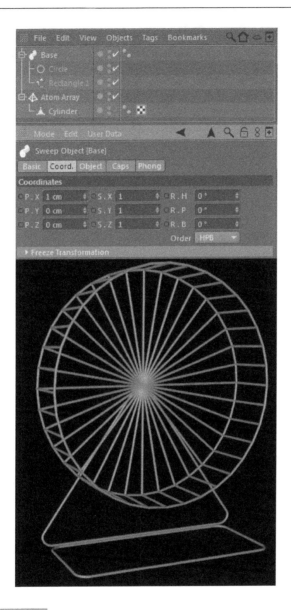

How it works...

Using the **Atom Array** tool was an excellent way to pull off this hamster wheel because it quickly creates most of the model for us without much work at all. Our cylinder was subdivided properly, essentially, in the beginning; all we had to do was delete one side of our polygon in order to open up one side. Then, we used a couple of tools to create a unique-looking spline to serve as the path for our **Sweep NURBS** wheel's base.

Best modeling advice – just go for it

Here's the best way to become a better 3D modeler: pick any object you can think of and work to recreate it in Cinema 4D until you are satisfied with the result. Look at the images of the object you intend to create and break it down into simpler shapes. There is a solution for creating anything in 3D, and the best way to get better at designing is by pushing yourself to gradually design more sophisticated objects. The end result is what's important, and in this recipe, we are going to use many of the topics we've hit on to design a microphone. If you ever need a 3D model of a microphone, then that's just great. You'll have one right here! Regardless, you should strive to become familiar with the tools we'll use so that your skills can transfer over to whatever else you'll need to design one day. So, let's just go for it.

Getting ready

I included a sample of the `Mic_Complete.c4d` file in the C4D Content Pack just so you can see the final model if you get stuck anywhere.

How to do it...

1. I mentioned earlier that it always helps to do an image search online to see what the object you are aiming for looks like. There are dozens of different types of microphones, and we are going to model a standard-looking stage microphone, so search for that to get a better idea of the components. Let's start with the head of the microphone, where the sound would actually get picked up. Usually, microphones have a round head, so start with a **Sphere** primitive from the Command Palette and change its **Radius** to 50 in the **Attribute Manager**.

2. Microphones also have a weaving grid pattern over them that screen out the components inside. The easy way to recreate something like this would be through our **Atom Array** tool. Take your **Sphere** object and rename it as **Head** in the **Object Manager**, and then click-and-drag a copy of it by holding down the *Ctrl* or *command* key while you do it. Now, add an **Atom Array** object to your project, and place the copy of your **Head** object as a child of it in the **Object Manager**. Rename the **Atom Array** to **Head Screen** and change the **Cylinder Radius** and **Sphere Radius** to **1**, so that they are smaller.

3. This is the effect we want; the problem is that microphones don't have screens that look like the pattern we have right now. This is not a problem, because the **Sphere** primitive that is a child of our **Atom Array** has a setting to redistribute the segments in different patterns. Click on the child of the **Atom Array** object to load it in the **Attribute Manager** and check out the **Type** setting under the **Object** tab. It defaults to **Standard** and usually that's fine, but if we change it to **Icosahedron**, you'll get a much better pattern for our microphone. This form of a sphere has an even distribution of its segments and doesn't have smaller segments at the top and bottom, and the bigger ones towards the middle; they are all equal. Increase the number of **Segments** to **44** so that there is less space between them:

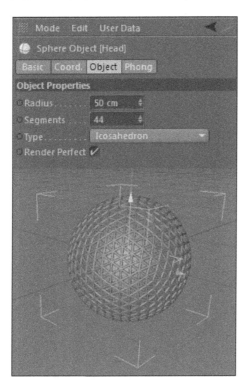

4. Now, add a new primitive, a **Tube** object, and change its settings to be **51** in the **Inner Radius**, **53** in the **Outer Radius**, with a **Height** of **10**. Check the box to enable **Fillet** and make sure the **Radius** is 1 unit. This adds a small band across the middle of the head; it's where you could unscrew the top half of the head and would connect the two halves. Double-click on its name and rename it as **Ring**.

5. Next, let's focus on the shaft of the microphone. This is your perfect opportunity to use **Lathe NURBS** to create a cylindrical handle for our microphone. Switch your camera to the **Front** view and position the Viewer so we have enough room to draw below the top of our microphone. Keep proportions in mind. If you've checked out a few images of microphones, you should have a general idea what a handle looks like, and there is no absolute answer for this as each one is a little different. Start on the y axis and draw half of a profile of your microphone with the **Freehand Spline** tool; it should intersect slightly with the base of the head portion:

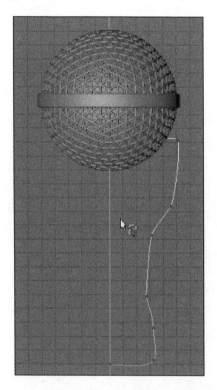

6. Make sure your Spline has all its position coordinates set to 0, and set the spline's values to 0 in the **Coordinates** tab in the **Attribute Manager**. Now, click on the button to **Use Point** mode from the left-hand side of the Command Palette, hit *Ctrl* or *command + A* to select all the points, and use the Move Tool to slide them as close to the y axis as possible. Now, start deleting the points you don't like. Use the Move Tool to reposition your points and use the context menu with commands, such as **Equal Tangent Length** and **Equal Tangent Direction**, to get nice-looking Bezier handles. Adjust your curves and points to get a nice-looking profile.

7. Hide the two **Head** primitives and the **Ring** by clicking on their green checkmarks to deactivate them, so you can see the top of your spline. Take the points closest to your y axis and enter an **X** position value of **0** in the **Coordinates Manager** below, so that they are perfectly even with the y axis. Now, take the other points at the top and bottom of your spline and even them out with their adjacent points on the Y axis, so the top and bottom of your mic doesn't have a slope. Make sure they have the same **Y** position value in the **Coordinate Manager** so they are even vertically, and you'll have a handle that is straight at the top. Follow these same steps for the two points at the base of your microphone, so that you have two points that are even and create a flat bottom with their Bezier handles.

8. Add a **Lathe NURBS** object to your project and name it as **Handle**, make your spline a child of it in the **Object Manager**, and then reactivate the two spheres for the **Head** of your microphone. Now that you have seen the way your microphone handle connects, you have the chance to keep adjusting your points to make your curve even better. Toggle the **Lathe NURBS** on and off with the green checkmark and the red **X** while you use the Move Tool to adjust the position of points, as well as the **Point** mode to select points and adjust their Bezier handles even further.

9. Now, let's duplicate your **Ring**; select it in the **Object Manager** and hold the *Ctrl* or *command* key and drag it to make another copy. Let's put it where our handle and head meet. All this depends on how your microphone looks, but I moved mine down to **-40** in the **Y** position; yours should be right around there too, but tweak the number so it looks best on your model. Now, under the **Object** tab of the model, change the **Inner Radius** and **Outer Radius** to be much smaller; whatever value gets your ring meeting the edge of your microphone. My values were **37** for the **Inner Radius** and **39** for the **Outer Radius**. Make sure your **Fillet** remains and has a **Radius** of **1**:

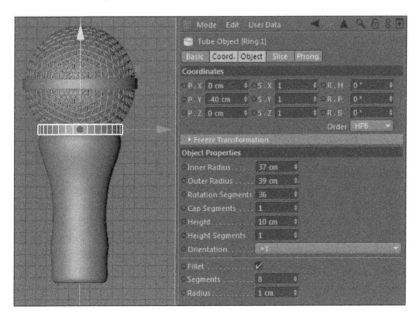

10. Our microphone is looking good, but it needs a plug at the bottom so it can receive power. All we need to do is duplicate our **Lathe NURBS** handle and adjust the spline to be shorter and at the base of the handle. Hold the *Ctrl* or *command* key and make a copy of your **Lathe NURBS** handle and rename it as **Plug**. Deactivate both **Lathe NURBS** objects so you can only see the splines.

11. Switch over to the **Front** view if you aren't there already, and take the spline that is a child of your **Plug** object and use both the **Model** mode and the Move Tool to drag it to the base of the handle; make sure you are moving the whole spline and not just a selected point with **Point** mode. Once it's right at the base, switch back to **Point** mode and select all the points that are below the top two points on your spline and drag them close to the top, so that our spline is much shorter. Select any points that have their Bezier handles going haywire and right-click or context-click on and select **Soft Interpolation** to reset the handles back to normal. The points on the right-hand side need to be moved closer to the y axis so that the width of this **Lathe NURBS** object is smaller than the bigger handle above it. Keep adjusting all your points so that they are in the right spots with the right Bezier curves, and the end result should be that you have almost a smaller version of the handle above it; this will be the connector where we plug in an XLR or another type of cable to get some power.

12. The plug doesn't do any good if we don't have a cord coming out of it (we aren't going to take the wireless microphone shortcut either). Take your **Freehand Spline** tool and draw a fairly straight line, but give it a little curve so it's got some character, from the base of your plug to a decent way down below your mic. You know the drill: delete any points that you don't need, fix any funky curves, and make it so our cord doesn't have any strange kinks in it. Now, add a **Circle** spline to your scene and reduce its **Radius** to about **4**. Now, add a **Sweep NURBS** object and rename it **Cord**. Place your two new splines as children of it, with the **Circle** spline defining the shape on top and the **Spline** defining the path below it. This should make a nice cord for your mic; make sure that the point at the top of the cord is centered with the base of the plug so that it looks like the cord is coming out properly.

13. Depending on the use of this microphone, it may need a mic flag to indicate what news or broadcasting company it belongs to, so let's make one for kicks. The mic flags are usually cubic or triangular, and since a triangular mic flag requires more work to make it, let's pick this one. Go to your **Splines** icon and grab an **n-Side** spline. Change its **Radius** to **75** and the number of **Sides** to **3**, so that it's a triangle. Check the box to activate **Rounding** and enter a value of **2** for the **Radius**. Now, let's grab an **Extrude NURBS** from inside your **NURBS** icon in the Command Palette and place the **n-Side** spline inside it as a child. Under the **Attribute Manager** for your **Extrude NURBS**, change the **Movement** to **60** instead of **20** in the **Z** dimension. Then, switch it over to the **Caps** tab and activate the **Start** and **End** settings to have a **Fillet Cap**. Change both their number of **Steps** to **10** and their **Radius** to **2**. Now, finally switch over to the **Coordinates** tab and change its **R.P** value to be **-90**, so it's now facing the right way on our microphone. Thereafter, change the **Y** position value to be **-50** so that it's on the right spot.

14. Looks good, except if you rotate and check out the underneath portion of the **Mic Flag**, you'll see that it is completely flush with the handle of the microphone. Mic flags have to have a wider opening on the base so that they can be slid on and off the microphone. The intricate details like these can make a good model into a great model, so let's fix this. Add a **Boole** object to your scene and rename it as **Mic Flag**. Now, add a **Cylinder** primitive to your scene, change its **Radius** to **30** (if this is too thin or thick, come back and change it), and slide it down in the **Y** Position so it's intersecting with the entire **Mic Flag**—a value of **-40** should work. Now, place the **Cylinder** inside the **Mic Flag**, **Boole**, as a child, then add the **Extrude NURBS** object as a child as well, making sure it's above the **Cylinder** object so the right **Boole** orientation is applied. Now, if you check out the base of the **Mic Flag**, you'll see that the **Mic Flag** has an opening cut at the bottom, which looks much more realistic:

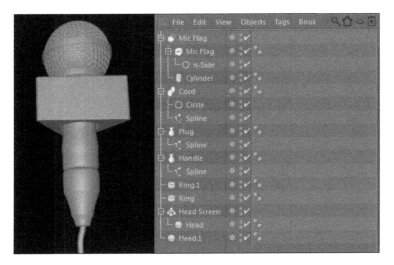

How it works...

So, we have a microphone now, and all it took us was a few different kinds of primitives, a bunch of different splines, an **Atom Array**, a couple of **Lathe NURBS**, a **Sweep NURBS**, and one **Extrude NURBS**, combined with a **Boole** object. Piece of cake! I tried to design a model that combined just about everything we covered in this chapter into one model, and I came close. The point is that you need plenty of different components to get better-looking and more complicated models. There is no icon in Cinema 4D to click on and design a microphone, so learning the fundamental tools is the only way you'll be able to create anything that's pretty specific or has a particular style to it.

There's more...

Hey! We didn't attach anything to that cord...try plugging it into an amplifier or an audio board if you want to go crazy and model some more.

The other chapters will make it even better

Models can get even better-looking with the right kinds of materials and lighting. Check out *Chapter 5, Let there be Lights* and *Chapter 6, A Material World* for those topics, and once you complete them, come back and make this microphone even better-looking.

Getting to grips with sculpting

Digital sculpting is a more intuitive technique than modeling with polygons, subdivisions and hypernurbs. It can be compared to taking a lump of clay and shaping and refining it until you get the shape you want.

Sculpting, like all forms of modeling, takes a bit of time to get used to but it is a lot of fun once you get going. It also really helps to use a graphics tablet.

Sculpting relies on using a very fine mesh (that is, lots and lots of polygons), once we have sculpted our object we can then bake it to a lower density mesh using shaders so we can have a very light and flexible object with lots of detail when rendering.

Getting ready

In this recipe we're just going to have a play around with some of the sculpting tools and get a feel for the workflow. It's a little different to other modes of modeling so it's worth getting familiar with.

Just create a normal sphere (from the **Object** menu) and then press C to make it editable. Now, go to **Layout** and select **Sculpting**. Now, simply press the subdivide button three times and you're ready to begin.

How to do it...

1. Select the **Pull** brush from the big sculpting menu which runs down besides the viewport. Put your mouse over the sphere and hold down the left mouse button whilst you draw some strokes. You should be able to see the surface of the sphere changing. If you can't see any change you may need to adjust the **Pull** brush settings. Simply increase the size and pressure of the brush from the tool attributes panel and then try again. You should be able to see the surface of the sphere changing:

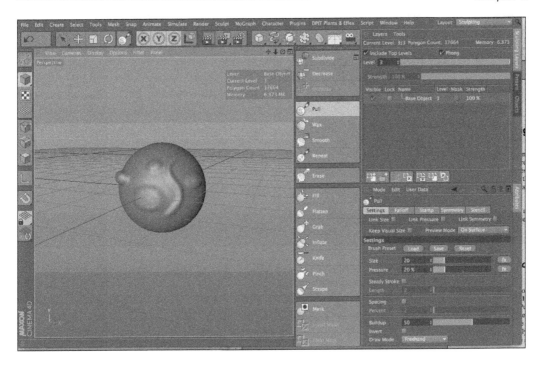

2. If you press the *W* key you can see the mesh of your sphere, you'll already notice that it is quite dense. Try pressing the subdivide key again and you'll see that the mesh is subdivided again. The more times you subdivide the mesh the more detail you will be able to paint onto the sphere. But, also the more of your computer's memory it will use. You can see the number of polygons and the amount of memory the sculpted object is using at the top of the sculpting palette.

3. You should play around with the sphere and try out all the different brushes and try adjusting the settings. It's best just to experiment and get a feel for the tools. Try different shapes and don't be afraid to try things out.

How it works...

Sculpting works by creating a very dense mesh on top of your more simple geometry. We then use a selection of intuitive tools to literally sculpt our polygons into whatever forms we desire.

There's more...

We've only just begun to look at sculpting so naturally there's a lot more to get to grips with, but really we've covered the general principles quite well so far. I recommend you try and play around with the different brushes and really get a feel for the sculpting tools. It's a bit like a pencil, a simple tool with limitless possibilities! The quality of your final sculpts will depend a lot on your artistic and observational level of skill and your technical expertise. Fortunately, these can all be improved by simply playing around! Try to model some things you see around you. Set yourself tasks. But don't be put off by it if you don't get the results you want straight away. It does take time and perseverance but it's extremely satisfying once you start to be able to make the thoughts in your head take on a three dimensional form!

Sculpting a head

In this recipe we're going to be sculpting a head! But don't worry it's not as difficult as it sounds. We're taking what we've learnt in the previous recipe and applying it to a practical task. And don't worry too much if your first effort isn't quite the Venus De Milo. These things take practice!

Getting ready

You should have a feel for the basics after playing around with your sphere. Now, we're going to look at sculpting a head. You won't have to model the base mesh of the head yourself, thankfully Maxon has included some base meshes for us to work on to.

Create a new document and open the Content Browser (**Windows | Content Browser**). Go to **Presets | Sculpting | Base Meshes** and select **Generic Head Bust**.

How to do it...

Now, make sure you're in sculpting mode (**Layout | Sculpting**) and select the head geometry (select the object tab on the right-hand side of the screen and select **mesh**, you may need to expand the generic head bust null object). Once you have done this, make sure you click on the **Sculpting Layers** tab so you can see what you're doing!

Now, as we did with the sphere click on **Subdivide** four times. Now, we can begin to model the head, this is what we're trying to do. Remember, you won't get it exactly the same as I have, so just try and follow along and have fun:

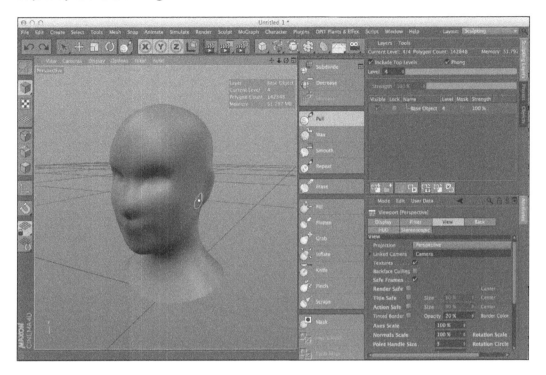

We're going to try and make our generic male head into a kind of monster, a big ugly brute. It's always a lot easier to make something ugly than beautiful so here we go.

Stage one – roughing out

The steps for this are as follows:

1. If you put on **Symmetry** and select **X (YZ)** then you'll see that whatever you do to one side of the head will be mirrored symmetrically to the other. This can be a useful timesaver especially in the early stages of sculpting.

2. Let's use the **Grab** brush to pull the chin out. Make sure it's nice and big. Push the forehead back and pull the eyes closer together. He should be starting to look really mean now!:

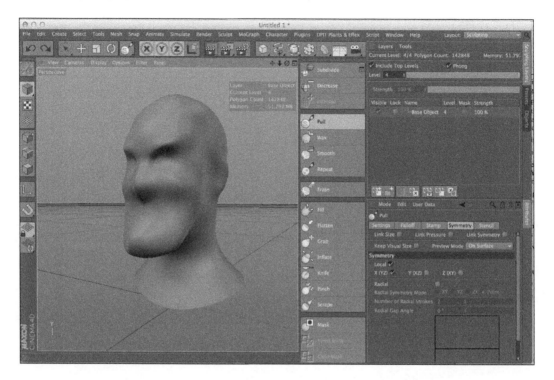

3. Switch to the **Pull** brush and just begin working over the whole object. Adjust the size and pressure of your brush until you feel like you have a good handle on the brush. Remember to keep moving your view around. (Try using the shortcut buttons **1,2,3** as you drag your cursor across the viewport.) This will help you understand what's happening in 3D space.

4. Try using the inflate brush to make his nose more bulbous!

5. Try thickening out his neck, make it very muscular sinewy!

6. You can use the **Command** button when painting to smooth out your model.

7. Now, select the **Knife** brush but be careful with this one! Begin to cut out behind the ear and create deep folds in the model. You can really begin to form the structure of your head. Remember to keep smoothing out the details you don't like.

8. Keep switching between the tools until you have something you're happy with. It doesn't have to be super detailed yet, we're just trying to sketch out the basis for our object. We'll add more detail in *Stage two*:

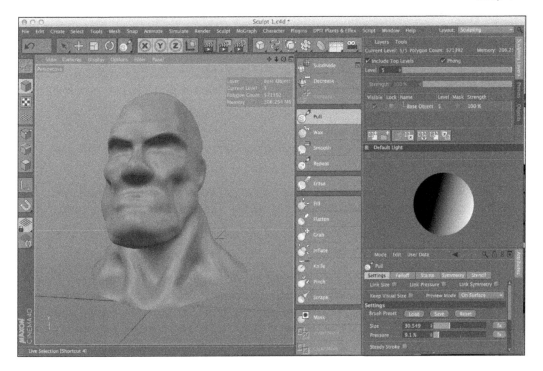

If you're modeling something complicated like a human head it can really help to have a reference. So use an image search to pull up a few images which you can refer to whilst sculpting. It may sound obvious but it is a very useful technique and you should try to get into the habit of using a reference.

9. On the tool attributes you can select **Link Size and Link Pressure**. This means that as you change between different types of sculpting brushes you can keep these attributes the same. This can save you some time.

10. A Steady stroke will help keep your brush strokes smooth, although it will give you less control.

If you press *command* while using a brush, its effect will be reversed.

Middle mouse button + drag left/right (or *Shift + Ctrl*): Adjust brush size.

Middle mouse button + drag up/down (or *Shift + Ctrl*): Adjust brush pressure.

Otherwise, the following key combinations can prove to be very useful:

Ctrl: Switches the respective brush to an inverted mode (mesh will be raised instead of lowered and vice versa).

Stage two

Now, we want to add some more detail but before you subdivide again let's have a look at the layer menu. Sculpting layers are similar to those in applications like Photoshop. We can add new layers and experiment a bit on them. If we don't like the final result we can simply discard the layer and start again. You can add as many layers as you like and also put them into folders and merge them.

So, now let's subdivide again but first click on the add layer button. It sometimes helps to look at your mesh to see how detailed the deformations are. If you press *W* you can see the wireframe.

If you like you can increase the number of subdivisions of your object until you have the detail you need. Be careful though, if you put in too many subdivisions then it may slow down or even crash your computer.

Now, let's start adding some real detail.

Add a new layer and then let's choose one of the sculpt brush presets. Go to the presets in the content browser. Navigate to **Presets | Sculpting | Sculpt Brush Presets | Noise** and select **Noise_02** by double clicking on it. You'll notice that an image has been loaded into your pull brushes stamp options. Now, begin to add some detail to the skin, maybe some stubble and just general texture:

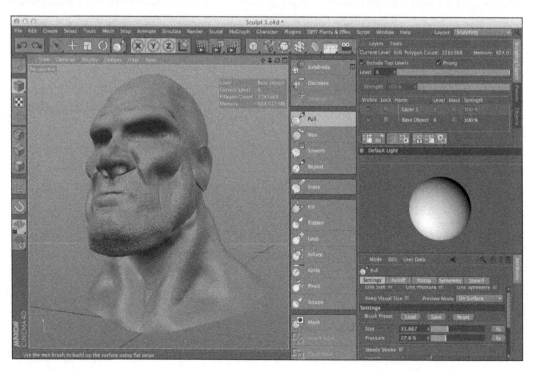

Try exploring the different types of noise and then look even further at all the preset brushes you can use for sculpting. If you want to just try things out, just create a new layer and play on that. If it's not to your liking then just delete the layer and try something new. It's about having fun and experimenting.

Stage three – baking

Carry on playing with your head until you're happy! Now, we're going to bake it. This means we're going to apply all the complex geometry to a more simple mesh. This means it uses a lot less of your computer's resources and makes your workflow a lot more flexible:

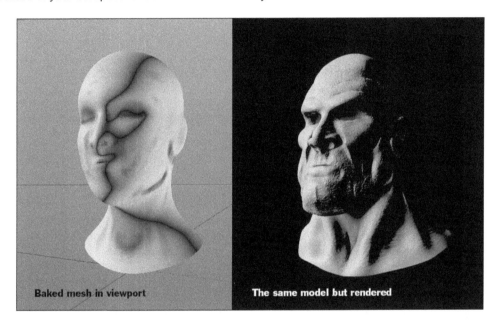

Baked mesh in viewport   The same model but rendered

Press the **Bake Sculpt Objects** button which you'll find at the bottom of your sculpting brushes.

Firstly, you must choose where you wish to save your baking textures. Then, set the **Width** and **Height** of your texture. This defines how much detail will be in your final model. Let's set it to **2048 x 2048**. We can ignore the other options for now but remember all you have to do to understand them is right-click on the option and go to **Show Help**.

Now, let's switch over to the **Options** tab. Check the **Displacement** box. And now, just press **Bake**!

It may take a few minutes but once it's done switch to the **Standard** layout (**Windows | Customization | Layouts**) and you'll see your original mesh with the sculpt tag on and a new mesh with a new texture on it. Hide your original mesh (using the traffic lights). In your Viewer window you'll see that the mesh looks like it did before you sculpted it but fear not! Render to the active view (*command + R*) and boom! There's your high resolution sculpt applied to a light and flexible low resolution mesh.

You can also choose to apply your Displacement texture to a higher density mesh and bake things like Ambient Occlusion. To bake to a higher density mesh just increase the level of your target object with the baking options. To bake the Ambient Occlusion make sure that you have it turned ON in your render settings (see *Chapter 5, Let there be Lights*) and ticked in baking options.

If you model your own objects you may find that the baking process does apply the sculpting textures correctly. This is probably because your texture mapping (or UV mapping) hasn't been applied correctly. You should be able to fix this by choosing the **Cubic** function from the **Optimal Mapping** drop-down in the baking options. You'll learn more about texture mapping, UV's, and projections in *Chapter 6, A Material World*.

If you don't want to bake your head, I mean it does sound kind of painful, then you can select your sculpt tag and activate the **Freeze** checkbox. You may also wish to tick the **Allow Deformations** tick box as well, so that you can apply deformers and animate your head.

Sculpting is great fun and a really intuitive way to model but don't expect to create the Venus De Milo on your first attempt. It takes a little while to get the feel of how the brushes work and to really understand the baking process.

How it works...

We've already discussed how sculpting works in the previous recipe but now we've also covered the process of baking. As we've seen baking takes all the detail of the mesh and stores it in the newly created texture tag, thus allowing us to more easily carry out a number of processes, such as animation and rigging, which would be almost impossible with a high resolution mesh.

The displacement and normal maps created by the baking process store the complex mesh coordinates in the form color information within the texture channels in the shader. Open one of these in an image viewer and you'll see what I mean!

There's more...

As you develop sculpting skills really you'll just be getting a feel of the different tools and improving your hand eye coordination. If you really want to get good at sculpting characters you should look up some websites or good books on anatomy. If you want to model a tree trunk then get loads of reference imagery, really try and observe the patterns in the tree grain. Really try and get under its skin, or bark in this case.

As you you begin to feel more confident you'll begin wanting to create your own brushes and stamps. You can use textures from your own photography or that you find online and edit them in Gimp or Photoshop to really define what kind of effect you want to have on your sculpt.

But observation and knowledge of your subject really will improve your results. The more you understand your subject on every level, the better job you'll be able to do sculpting it.

Hypernurbs and modelling

You may notice that when you subdivide your objects it looks very similar to the way the hypernurbs object changes your mesh. Well you're right, it does do a very similar thing. As you get more advanced you can begin to create low polygon objects which when subdivided create very elegant sculpting meshes.

3
The Deformers

In this chapter we will cover:

- ▶ Getting started with the Taper deformer
- ▶ Animating with deformers: Bend
- ▶ Custom italics with Shear
- ▶ Over-animation with Squash and Stretch
- ▶ Making an asteroid with FFD and Displacer
- ▶ Unconventional animations with deformers
- ▶ Breaking objects with deformers
- ▶ Using Spline Wrap versus Sweep NURBS
- ▶ Applying the Collision deformer

Introduction

I'm not sure if the deformers sounds more like a washed-up rock band from the 80s or some sort of obscure comic book series about mutants. In actuality, deformers are handy tools that allow you to manipulate the shape and structure of the objects you model, without affecting the object permanently. Calling something "deformed" isn't really the nicest thing you can say, but it has a positive connotation inside Cinema 4D. The deformers are very useful and can help you pull off the right kind of alteration or animation inside your project.

In the last chapter, we explored modeling and learned how to edit and alter the structure of polygonal objects, and once we changed the structure of the object, it remained that way, unless you retraced your steps via the Undo command.

You should be encouraged to explore modeling beyond just modifying simple primitives, but with deformers, you have the luxury of applying specialized transformations such as bends, shearing, and tapering, without actually changing the structure of your object. This offers tremendous flexibility because they can alter your objects in special ways that would be much more difficult using the standard selecting and editing of points, edges, and polygons we covered.

There are almost 30 different deformers in Cinema 4D, and they all have special skills. There are some deformers you'll use often and some you probably will never find a use for. We'll learn how some of the most practical ones work and how you can apply them to your designs.

Getting started with the Taper deformer

Some of the deformers are very basic, like the **Taper** deformer. It takes an object and applies a transformation to it to appear narrower at one end than the other. In this recipe, we're going to take a **Cube** object and turn it into a coffee table using a couple of tools and the **Taper** deformer.

How to do it...

1. Start with a new project and create a new **Cube** object from inside the **Primitives** menu in the Command Palette. In the **Attribute Manager**, reduce the **Size Y** value down to 10 units so it's much shorter. Now, change the **Segments X**, **Segments Y**, and **Segments Z** values to **10**, which will divide our **Cube** object into smaller pieces on each of the faces.

2. We are going to edit the polygons of this object; so with the **Cube** object still selected, press the *C* key to turn the object from a parametric primitive into a polygon object. Double-click on its name in the **Attribute Manager** and change it to **Coffee Table**.

3. Now, go in the **Cameras** menu inside the Viewer, and pick the **Bottom** view, so we can select the right polygons in the easiest way possible. Select **Use Polygon mode** on the left-hand side of the Command Palette, and click on each square in the four corners of our object while holding the *Shift* key so they are selected in orange.

4. Now, flip back to the **Perspective** view and go up to the **Mesh** menu, and select the **Extrude** tool from inside the **Create Tools** submenu. Instead of clicking-and-dragging to extrude, enter a precise value of 50 in the **Offset** field of the **Attribute Manager** so that those selected polygons are extruded out to become the legs of our coffee table.

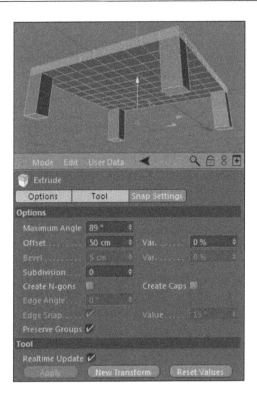

5. You should realize that we now have the required shape for the most plain and boring coffee table in the history of coffee tables. It would be much more interesting if we could taper each leg so that they have a little character to them. We can apply four separate **Taper** deformers to our **Coffee Table** object to give the legs a more interesting shape.

6. A key to using deformers lies in the subdivision of your object. Most deformers tend to create more interesting results when your object is made up of a sufficient number of polygons. The top of the table has enough polygons, but notice our legs are just one simple polygon on each side; and that won't cut it for this deformer.

7. Switch to the **Front** view inside the **Cameras** menu in the Viewer, and zoom in on your table. Now, switch to the **Rectangular Selection** tool at the top of the Command Palette, and uncheck the box in the **Attribute Manager** that says **Only Select Visible Elements**.

8. Now, take the tool and click-and-drag inside the Viewer so that the right leg of your table is completely surrounded by the box, and therefore, gets selected with orange when you release the mouse. Then, do the same on the other side for the other leg while holding the *Shift* key to add to the selection. Because we unchecked the box for selecting only the visible elements, the polygons behind it are selected too, so we actually have all four legs selected.

9. Now, go up to the **Mesh** menu, and look under **Commands**. You'll find the **Subdivide** option, but don't click directly on the text; click on the small black window icon to the far right-hand side of the text. This opens a separate window where you can enter a value 3 in the **Subdivision** field, and then click on **OK**. We now have many more polygons to work with, and it will look much better when we apply our deformers.

Whenever you see these black window icons in the menu, know that clicking directly on the text will quickly apply the default settings for whatever item you select, and the window icon opens the actual editing window where you can make specific adjustments.

10. The **Deformers** menu is the icon in the Command Palette indicated by the purple piece of elbow macaroni. Head inside, and select the **Taper** deformer. Deformers work by applying themselves to the object you want to deform as a child in the **Object Manager**. So, take the new **Taper** object, and drag it below the **Coffee Table** object until it snaps into place as a child as shown in the following screenshot:

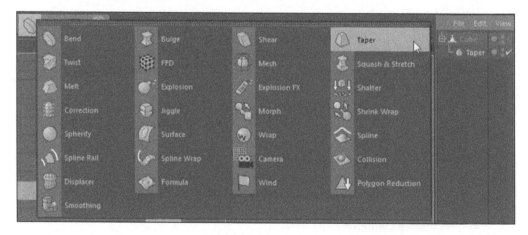

11. The default settings do nothing for us, so click on the **Taper** deformer in the Object Manager to load it into the **Attribute Manager**, and change the **Strength** value to **50%**. This applies a taper effect to the entire table because the **Bounding Box**, the purple cage around your deformer that illustrates how far the effect reaches, is set so large. Reduce the three fields for **Size**, corresponding to the **X**, **Y**, and **Z** dimensions, down to **50** each. The **Taper** deformer has shrunk, but it's still affecting our whole table.

12. Change the **Mode** setting for the deformer to **Within Box**, which confines our deformation to only the area inside our purple bounding box. We can now position this box to get a targeted deformation on just our table legs. Switch from the **Object** tab to the **Coordinates** tab in the **Attribute Manager**. Change position X to **90**, Y to **-30**, and Z to **-90**. Our deformer is now hovering over one of the legs, and is affecting just that part of our table. Change the **R.P** value to **-180**, and now the taper will be thinner at the bottom and wider at the top. Switch over to the **Object** tab again and check the box for **Fillet**, and you'll see our leg now has a nice pleasing curve to it.

13. We can add multiple deformers to the same object, so take your **Taper** deformer in the **Object Manager** and hold the *Ctrl* or *command* key, and drag three other copies of it as children of your coffee table. This way, you can keep exactly the same settings, and just adjust the coordinates of the other three deformers to fit to the other legs. The easiest way to do this is to take one of the new deformers, and invert either the Position **X** value or the Position **Z** value to get it to switch across the table to another leg. If you invert both the values, the deformer will head across to the other leg diagonally. It's a very simple way to get the coordinates exactly right, and also place a deformer in each corner of the table. When complete, you should have the same exact **Taper** deformer applied to each of the four legs, giving a much more interesting look to your coffee table as shown in the following figure:

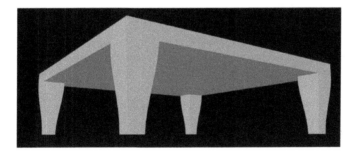

How it works...

The **Taper** deformer is very straightforward, and serves as a good starting point for the chapter. It deforms your object so that one end is thinner than the other, just as the name would imply. We applied four versions of the same deformer to affect just the legs of our coffee table. The deformers gave the table a little more style without much hassle.

There's more...

See? Non-destructive is great! The beauty of deformers is that we can change the look of our object without permanently changing the look of our object. If you change your mind about what your table legs should look like, just remove the deformer and it's back to normal. If you choose to edit and delete polygons to try and get that particular look, you'll have only the Undo command to save you.

I'd group these deformers together

Like I said, if there was a rock band called the deformers, these would be core members of the group: **Bend**, **Bulge**, **Shear**, **Taper**, and **Twist**. Test them all out; they all have the same kind of properties, and apply their deformations in similar ways. They are very straightforward and typically get used more often than many of the other deformers.

Animating with deformers: Bend

In the last recipe, we used the **Taper** deformer to change the structure of a cube to turn it into a coffee table. But, our coffee table is a stationary object that doesn't do anything. We can use deformers as part of animations, and their unique effects can help create the exact kind of movement you're looking for. This recipe will use the **Bend** deformer to create a better-looking animation for the spring in our jack-in-the-box.

Getting ready

Use the `Jack_in_the_Box.c4d` file in the C4D Content Pack with this recipe.

How to do it...

1. Press the **play** button in the Animation toolbar and watch the happy face bounce up and down on the spring. The spring is bouncing for you already, but it would make for a more interesting animation if we had this spring moving in different directions, not just straight up and down. The **Bend** deformer is the perfect solution for this. It is actually the default deformer, so if you just click on the purple icon in the Command Palette, it will be added to your scene.

2. Open the **Jack in the Box** group in the **Object Manager** and examine the hierarchy of this object. We need to place the **Bend** deformer inside the **Head and Spring** group so that it only affects those objects and not the rest of the pieces, such as the box and the handle. Place it as a child inside the **Head and Spring** group, at the top of the group ahead of the **Spring** and **Face** objects.

3. With the **Bend** object highlighted in the **Object Manager**, head to the **Coordinates** tab in the **Attribute Manager**, and change the **Y** position value to **-225** so that the **Bend** deformer is at the base of our spring. Now, switch to the **Object** tab, and change the **Strength** setting to **25**. You should immediately notice the purple box in the Viewer is now bending along with our spring, and the head attached to it.

4. The key to getting some good movement is animating the **Angle** value of our **Bend** deformer. Go to frame 0 and set a keyframe with value 0 on the **Angle** field; press *Ctrl* or command-click on the black circle next to the property to do so. Now, go to the last frame, frame 112, and change the **Angle** value to **359** degrees and set a keyframe so that the angle of our **Bend** deformer will shift **360** degrees throughout the length of our animation. Also, check the box at the bottom for **Keep Y Axis Length**. Now, play back your animation and check out the spring in action; it moves and behaves much better with the **Bend** deformer attached to it as shown in the following screenshot:

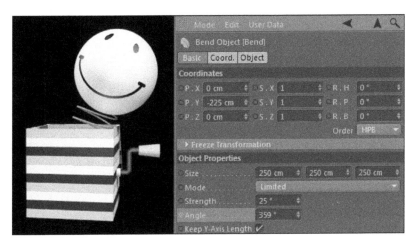

How it works...

The spring in this jack, inside the box, was only bouncing up and down to start with, but with the help of the **Bend** deformer we were able to shift and move it in different directions, and it behaved more playfully. By placing the **Bend** deformer inside the group with the Head and the Spring objects, it affected only those objects. We animated the angle property to have the spring apply the bend at different angles; this makes it look like our happy face has some weight to it, and the result is a nice-looking and fluid movement.

There's more...

Did you notice that I used the **Taper** deformer from our last recipe? I made the handle on the crank, which had a tapered shape to it, instead of being just a plain **Cylinder** object.

How did I make it bounce?

I made the spring bounce in the beginning without any keyframes using XPresso. Check out *Chapter 9, XPresso Shots*, and then come back and find the code inside the project that made that animation quite effortless.

See also

▸ Check out the recipe *Unconventional animations with deformers* in this chapter for another animation example with the **Bend** deformer.

Custom italics with Shear

There have been a few times where I've been working with a font that has no oblique style to it. Programs such as Photoshop have a way to force oblique styles on fonts, but Cinema 4D has no such feature with their **Text** splines or **MoText** objects. This recipe shows you a handy use of the **Shear** deformer to force the italicization of your text in Cinema 4D.

How to do it...

1. Create a new **Text** spline from the Command Palette, and then pick any font you want to work with (even if it is in italics, use a normal style for this exercise) in the font menu. I'm going to use a font called Ostrich Sans. Enter `Cinema 4D` in the **Text** field, and then add a **Shear** deformer from the Command Palette to your scene. Place it as a child of your **Text** spline.

2. There are only a few properties to change, so load your **Shear** object into the **Attribute Manager**, and look into the **Object** tab. Change the **Strength** value to **70**, and watch how your text now has an italic look to it. Reduce the **Curvature** to **0%**, so that there's no bend in the shear. We don't need to worry about the **Size** fields, since we can just change the **Mode** from **Limited** to **Unlimited**. This way, the effect has no boundaries, and it will be applied over the entire length of our text, no matter what word we put in there.

3. Go up to the **NURBS** icon in the Command Palette, and select the **Extrude NURBS** object, place the **Text** spline as a child of the **Extrude NURBS** object, keeping the deformer as a child of the spline. Now, we have an actual text, and it's italicized just like our spline as shown in the following screenshot:

How it works...

The **Shear** deformer can turn our **Text** splines into italics very easily. This is a quick setup for creating italic text, which is helpful in case your spline is no longer parametric or you perhaps imported it from Illustrator and you can't change it. We can also control the degree of the italicization of our text; increasing the **Shear** value will give us a steeper level of italics than maybe your selected font offers. This recipe didn't try to reinvent the wheel, just point out a practical use for the **Shear** deformer.

There's more...

If you have the MoGraph module, and I hope you do, please do this tutorial with MoText instead. I only present the spline method in case any reader doesn't have it, but always use MoText instead.

See also

- ▶ Check out where I got the font "Ostrich Sans" from in case you like the look of it: http://www.theleagueofmoveabletype.com/fonts/18-ostrich-sans

Over-animation with Squash and Stretch

If you are like me and you tell people you're an animator, they tend to think that you draw cartoons for a living. I can't draw very well at all; all my animating comes from keyframes, Bezier curves, and math equations, which don't sound quite as fun as doodling with cartoons. However, Cinema 4D has one particular deformer that has a fundamental technique for animating moving objects in any medium: Squash & Stretch.

Getting ready

This recipe uses the `Bouncing_Ball.c4d` file in the C4D Content Pack.

How to do it...

1. Check out our project, which has a simple animation of a red ball bouncing on a floor before coming to a complete stop. If you play the animation, our ball appears stiff and rigid; it feels lifeless. We can use the **Squash & Stretch** deformer to fix this. Add it from the **Deformer** menu in the Command Palette, and place it as a child of the **Red Ball** object in the **Object Manager**. Its coordinates need to be lined up with the ball properly, so load the **Squash & Stretch** deformer in the **Attribute Manager**, switch to the **Coordinates** tab, and change the **Y** position value from -125 to 0 so it's centered around the ball as shown in the following screenshot:

2. Switch to the **Object** tab in the **Attribute Manager** and locate the **Factor** setting. This is the key parameter for making the ball squash when it hits the ground and stretch when it rises up. You are simulating it building up and then expelling energy. When the **Factor** value is at **100**, the ball is perfectly normal. When it goes above 100, it stretches. When it goes below 100, it squashes.

3. The ball is keyframed to bounce every 10 frames, so our Squash & Stretch movements should match these intervals. Because the ball starts out by bouncing high before slowly dying down, the effect should be greater in the beginning than at the end of the animation.

4. Move to frame 15 when the ball is approaching the ground for the first time. Set a keyframe for **Factor** to be **100**% by holding the *Ctrl* or *Command* key, and clicking on the empty circle next to the property in the **Attribute Manager**, then move to frame 20 and lower it to **50**% and set a keyframe.

5. Now, move to frame 30 when it peaks again, and set a keyframe for **Factor** to be **130**%. This completes one cycle of Squash & Stretch, so let's go with the flow and do the rest. Move to frame 40 and change the **Factor** to **85**% and set a keyframe, and then set another one at frame 50 for **115**%. Now, at frame 60, set a keyframe to **90**% and then to **110**% at frame 70. The last set is a very slight deformation: set a keyframe for **Factor** of **95**% at frame 80, and then **105**% at frame 90, then return the ball to its normal state by setting a keyframe for **Factor** to return to **100**% at frame 100.

 Notice the diminishing values we entered. The idea here is the ball should lose energy over time and eventually come to a rest, so the jumps in our factor values become smaller throughout our animation and get closer to 100%, which is our normal state.

6. Play your animation and you'll see a ball bouncing much more playfully as it goes up and down the cycle thanks to our **Squash & Stretch.**

7. There's one more tweak to make. Switch the Viewer to the **Front** view in the **Cameras** menu and play the animation. You'll notice the ball doesn't quite reach the floor on the bounce. Because it is being squashed it actually becomes shorter than it was when it was animated; the keyframes set in its **Y** position from before no longer work properly. No problem; we can adjust this rather quickly.

8. Switch to the **Red Ball** object in the **Object Manager**, and then locate its Coordinates tab in the **Attribute Manager**. Move to frame 20 in the Animation toolbar, when the squashed ball should meet the floor first. Grab the green axis handle in the Viewer, and using the Move Tool, just slide the ball down so it meets the edge of the floor; a move of about -9 in the **Y** position. The keyframe dot is now yellow in the **Attribute Manager**, meaning you changed the value but didn't set a new keyframe for it. Press *Ctrl* or command-click on the yellow dot to turn it red and set the new value for it. Now, move to frame 40; the next time it should hit the floor, and repeat the process of keyframing with a value of **-2** units instead. Move to frame 60 and this value should be a little less, like **-1**. Then, do it just once more at frame 80, with a slight move to **-0.5** in the **Y** position. Now, the ball reaches the floor each time it's squashed, and we've completed our bouncing ball animation as shown in the following screenshot:

How it works...

The **Squash & Stretch** deformer lets you add the fundamental animation principle to our ball, by applying its name to the type of movement we want to achieve. We took a bouncing ball and made it look like it was actually bouncing by adjusting the Factor setting on the deformer. It was very stiff-looking before, and now it appears to be more playful (with energy and life), which a parametric primitive doesn't really have with the help of a deformer like **Squash & Stretch**.

See also

▶ Check out *12 Basic Principles of Animation* and incorporate the discussed movements to make your animations better: http://en.wikipedia.org/wiki/12_basic_principles_of_animation

Making an asteroid with FFD and Displacer

Let's continue the trend of manipulating parametric primitives with deformers. In this recipe, we are going to use two new deformers, the **FFD** and **Displacer**, to change the shape of a perfectly round sphere to turn it into a lopsided and jagged-looking asteroid. The deformers are perfect for this kind of modeling because an asteroid has no set shape, and we can try a variety of different adjustments to the shape without making any permanent changes to the object.

Getting ready

Locate and open the `Asteroid.c4d` file in the C4D Content Pack and use it with this recipe.

How to do it...

1. Our project consists of a star field background and perfect **Sphere** primitive, with our asteroid material already applied to it. No asteroid has ever appeared to be a perfect sphere, so we're going to use two deformers designed to shift the shape of objects. The first is the **FFD** (**Free Form Deformation**). Locate it in the **Deformers** menu inside the Command Palette, and add it as a child of the **Asteroid** object inside the **HyperNURBS** object in the **Object Manager**.

2. **FFD** creates a 3D cube surrounding the object, with grid points that you can move around that affect the shape of the parent object. In the **Attribute Manager**, change the three **Size** fields from **300** to **200** so the cube is smaller, and increase the **Grid Points X**, **Gird Points Y**, and **Grid Points Z** from **3** to **5** so that there are more points for us to manipulate.

3. From here we go from sphere to asteroid. Switch on the **Use Point mode** button on the left-side of the Command Palette, and click on any of the vertices of the purple cage, indicated by black intersecting points. Once selected, you should have the red, green, and blue axis handles (if not, select the **Move Tool** at the top of the Command Palette). And, you can grab these handles to manipulate the position of the point. You'll see the sphere immediately starting to move with the point, because it's following the cage around our **FFD**. Try moving multiple points in different directions and you'll see it really start to transform. Keep going until each point has been modified from its original position, and you have a unique shape for your asteroid as shown in the following figure:

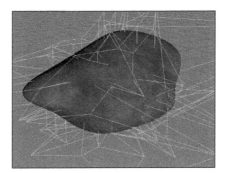

4. The next deformer is the **Displacer**, and it's primarily used for applying a grayscale pattern over your subdivided object, and displacing the polygons based on the pattern you picked. You can get some pretty interesting results, depending on what you use as the source for your displacement. We can use this tool to make the surface of our asteroid appear more uneven and rocky.

5. Locate the **Displacer** in the **Deformer** menu, and apply it as a child of the **Asteroid** object, placing it below the **FFD**. Head to the **Attribute Manager** and change the value for the **Height** setting to **-7**, so our displacement will create holes and craters (there are several different ways to accomplish this).

6. This next recipe deals with a few topics from *Chapter 6, A Material World*, our chapter on materials. Switch to the **Shading** tab, and click on the small triangle button next to the **Shader** option, and select the **Noise** option, which loads a pattern that will cause displacement over our object. Click on the big bar labeled **noise** to open the options for the **Shader**.

7. Change two of the options here: the **Global Scale** down to about **80%**, and the Contrast up to about **50%**. Now, select a different pattern from the **Noise** menu. Pick **Blistered Turbulence**, which makes a nice rocky pattern across our asteroid; it now looks better since it's not so smooth.

8. You now have a unique asteroid that is still technically a parametric object. We can change all of the previous settings to get an entirely different-looking object as shown in the following screenshot:

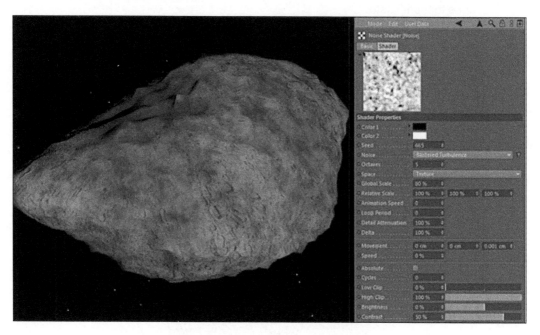

How it works...

The combination of **FFD** and **Displacer** gives us a great way to change the look of our sphere and turn it into a better-looking shape for our asteroid. **FFD** creates a surrounding cage that allows us to shift points around and have our sphere move with them. **Displacer** creates a bumpy pattern for our asteroid that makes it look more natural and not so smooth. We can deactivate or delete the deformers and be right back to where we started, without permanently altering the structure of the original object.

There's more...

Look at *Chapter 6, A Material World*, on materials to get examples about how to use the displacement channel to create different alterations of the surfaces of your objects.

Trying a landscape object instead

Instead of this method, you may want to try creating a landscape primitive and checking the box in its object properties for spherical. You'll get some bumpy terrain on the spherical shape, but no specific controls for deforming it; you'll only be able to cycle between random seeds.

Unconventional animations with deformers

Sometimes with a deformer, there's more than meets the eye. Because each formula has many unique properties, we can animate to go along with their conventional properties, such as their coordinates, you can find alternate uses for them than their names would suggest. In this recipe, we'll take a look at the **Bend** deformer again, and find a way to use it with some extreme values, and come up with an animation that seemingly goes beyond creating a simple bend.

Getting ready

Open the `Blueprint.c4d` file from the C4D Content Pack and use it with this recipe.

How to do it...

1. The objective with this file is to take the blueprint document that is flat on the table. Roll it up, and then unfurl it back to being flat on the table. As we've noticed throughout the chapter, deformers are great for altering the state of objects, so we will be creating an animation with our blueprint starting in the altered state and then returning to its original state.

2. We'll need a **Bend** deformer, so add one from the Command Palette, and place it as a child of the **Blueprint** object. The **Blueprint** object is a **Plane** primitive; select it in the **Object Manager** and take a look at its settings in the **Attribute Manager**. It has a **Width** of **800** and a **Height** of **600**, but note the heavy number of **Width Segments** and **Height Segments**. Each property is set high to **200** because we want our blueprint to be very flexible so it can unravel very smoothly, so the high subdivision is necessary.

3. Load the **Bend** deformer into the **Attribute Manager** and change its size properties to be **5**, **800**, and **600** respectively. Now, we want to change the angle in which the transformation occurs, not necessarily in the **Angle** setting in the **Object** tab, but in the **Coordinates** tab under the **R.B** setting. The **Angle** setting rotates the deformer only around the Y axis, so change the **R.B** setting to **90** so our deformer will bend around our paper properly.

4. So, our purple cage that signifies the bounding box of our deformer pretty much exactly surrounds our blueprint, with a tiny bit of wiggle room above and below the document. Try adjusting the **Strength** setting inside the **Object** tab, and watch how the paper behaves. Very low values will cause the paper to gradually bend, for which the deformer is named, but extremely high values will exaggerate the effect to create our roll.

5. Select a value of **-2880** in the **Strength** field, a very high number, and watch how our paper is now rolled up perfectly. 2,880 is 8 times 360, or eight full rotations around that same point which creates an object so bent that it becomes rolled up.

6. Go to frame 10 and set a keyframe for the **Strength** field to be -2880. Then head to frame 60, and set a keyframe for the **Strength** to be 0 and play your animation. The blueprint unravels, but it doesn't roll out exactly like we want, but this can be remedied by animating the **X** position property of our **Bend** deformer. If we create some movement left to right with our deformer, we can create the effect like our blueprint is being rolled by an invisible hand.

7. Jump to frame 10 and switch to the **Coordinates** tab of the deformer, and set a keyframe for the **X** position value to be **0**. Now, jump to frame 60, and enter a value of 800 for the **X** position, and set a keyframe. Now, switch back to the Object tab, and change the keyframed value at frame 60 for the **Strength** field from **0** to **-1440**. Enter the value in the field, and then press *Ctrl* or command-click on the yellow dot next to the property to set a keyframe for the new value. This value will keep our bend much tighter as it passes through, since the animation will technically only unravel halfway.

8. Play your animation and you'll see our blueprint now rolls out to reveal itself, all from some extreme values and keyframing the right parameters in our **Bend** deformer as shown in the following figure:

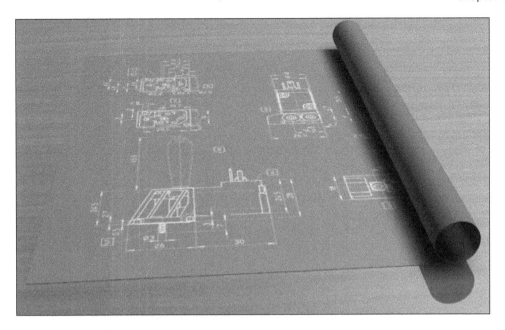

How it works...

Think this as a hidden talent of the **Bend** deformer. We simply applied it like we did in our jack-in-the-box recipe, but we altered its properties much more to fit with what we were trying to accomplish with our rolling blueprint. We adjusted the properties so our strength value curled up our poster into a tube, and we animated it moving over the desk. Since we moved the position of the **Bend** deformer so it was no longer surrounding our blueprint, the document turned into its normal state without any deformation. Try using extreme values and adjusting the position and rotation of your deformers when they are attached to their parent objects; you may come across some unexpected but useful results.

Breaking objects with deformers

There are several deformers you can use to destroy the very same objects you spend your time creating in Cinema 4D. They are **Explosion**, **Shatter**, and **Explosion FX**, and they all do pretty much the same thing: break apart your object based upon its subdivision. We're going to use the **Explosion FX** deformer to create the effect of a bullet passing through a glass orb and shattering it to pieces.

Getting ready

Open the `Bullet_Shatter.c4d` file and use it for this recipe. It's set up and ready to go for you already.

How to do it...

1. Take a look at the project. If you play the scene in the Animation toolbar, you'll see a bullet streak through the scene, and pass through a floating glass sphere. We want to destroy our sphere as the bullet makes contact with it. The right deformer for this is **Explosion FX**, astutely labeled as a stick of TNT dynamite in the **Deformers** menu inside the Command Palette. Add it to your scene and place it as a child of the **Glass Sphere** object. By default, your sphere gets its pieces scattered throughout the scene, so we'll need to adjust the parameters in the **Attribute Manager** as shown in the following figure:

2. There are a lot of settings to tweak, and there's not just one combination of numbers we can use to get a good shatter effect. Let's start with the **Coordinates** tab. We need to move our **Explosion FX** to the left-hand side where the bullet enters, because right now, it's blowing up our **Glass Sphere** from right in the center. Change the position **X** value to **-225**, so it's no longer at the origin.

3. Now, switch to the **Object** tab, which only has one setting for **Time**. This value is indicated by the green circle around the center of the deformer. When it's at **0%** the explosion hasn't started, and when it reaches **100%**, it's fully complete. The other settings we will adjust next will control how our pieces fall, but this is crucial for timing purposes to match the shatter up with our bullet.

4. Let's keyframe the **Time** value to work with our bullet passing through. Head to frame 28 in the Animation toolbar, and change the **Time** value to be **0**, and hold the *Ctrl* or *command* key, and click on the black circle next to the property in the **Attribute Manager** to set a keyframe. Now, scrub to frame 120, and change the **Time** value to **100**% and set another keyframe, so the shatter occurs from frame 28 to 120. If you scrub through your animation, you'll see the bullet start to shatter the sphere at frame 40 when the bullet starts passing through.

5. Our animation works, but it looks terrible right now. Switch to the **Explosion** tab in the **Attribute Manager** for the **Explosion FX** deformer. Here's where we need to make a bunch of adjustments. Start under the **Explosion** subheading and change the **Strength** field from **1000** to **5**, and increase **Decay** and **Variation** to **50**%. Move three fields down to the next **Variation** setting, and increase this all the way to **100**%. Reduce **Blast Time** to **100** and the next pair of the **Decay** and **Variation** fields to **50**%. Finally, change **Blast Range** to **750** and **Variation** to **100**%. These tweaks aim at making our explosion less intense and keep our pieces closer together, while adding a little variation to the way they disperse.

 My values are not commandments. So, experiment with different values in different settings and watch how they affect your sphere. Trial and error is a great way to learn.

6. Switch over to the next tab labeled **Cluster**, and change **Thickness** to **1** so our glass shards aren't as chunky. Change **Density** to **500**, then **Min Polys** to **1**, and **Max Polys** to **3**. These last two settings will control how many of our polygons will stick together; meaning no more than three polygons are allowed to clump together with these settings.

7. Switch to the **Gravity** tab, and reduce **Acceleration** to **0.6** and **Variation** to **50**%. This small value will make our pieces much smaller because this animation is timed to look more like a slow-motion shot with a high-speed camera. Increase **Range** to **1500** and then switch over to the **Rotation** tab and just change **Speed** to **50**. We are almost done.

8. I left the default subdivision on for our **Glass Sphere**, showing you what the **Explosion FX** bases the shattered pieces on, however our object is subdivided. The default settings are really bad for our effect because there are so few pieces and they are all squares. Select **Glass Sphere** in the **Object Manager** and change the number of **Segments** in the **Object** tab of the **Attribute Manager** to **60**. Now, switch the **Type** to **Icosahedron** so that the subdivided pieces become triangles, which look more like a glass shard than the default standard setting. Now, playback your animation and you'll see our bullet pass through and break our sphere, and the glass pieces fall to the ground as shown in the following figure:

How it works...

The **Explosion FX** deformer takes an object and shatters it to pieces based on the object's subdivision. Our scene was set up, and we had to match the shattering of the sphere to the movement of the bullet. We timed our deformer to shatter in sync with the bullet passing through the left-hand side of the sphere, and then adjusted the parameters to make our glass pieces shatter in a more pleasing fashion. The materials and lighting have been set up for you as well; press *Ctrl* or *command + R* to do a render preview and check out the result.

There's more...

Explosion and Shatter are really just simpler versions of **Explosion FX**. They have significantly less properties and don't give you the more advanced controls that **Explosion FX** does. They also break apart subdivided objects, but they are too watered down to pull off an effect like this.

Using Spline Wrap versus Sweep NURBS

In the previous chapter, we learned how to use **Sweep NURBS**, which allowed us to draw a path with a spline, and define the shape that gets swept along that path. There's a similar tool inside the deformers called **Spline Wrap**, which takes a specific object rather than a spline and aligns it along the path of the spline. In this recipe, we'll learn some features available in **Spline Wrap** that aren't available with **Sweep NURBS**, so you can better discern which tool to use in the future.

Getting ready

Open the `Spline_Wrap.c4d` file and use it for this recipe.

How to do it...

1. In this recipe, we're going to create a twisting ribbon animation that will pass right in front of our camera and act as an interesting transition we can render out. Inside this project, I have drawn the spline path that we'll use for this recipe so that we can all be on the same page. The ribbon will pass right in front of the camera with the right settings.

2. The **Spline Wrap** works by taking an object and stretching it along a specified spline path. So, let's add a new **Plane** object to the scenes in the **Primitives** menu in the Command Palette. In the **Attribute Manager**, change the **Height** to 40 and the **Orientation** to **-Z**, and increase **Width Segments** and **Height Segments** to 100. We will need a high subdivision because our ribbons will need to flow evenly along our path. Next, rename this object as **Ribbon** inside the **Object Manager**.

3. Now, go into your **Deformers** menu, and click on **Spline Wrap**. Now, just like every deformer, place it as a child of the **Ribbon** object. Add a **HyperNURBS** object to your project, and place the ribbon as a child of that object; this will smooth out the curves of the ribbons we will add later.

4. Nothing happens, because we need to indicate what spline to use with our deformer. So inside the **Object Manager**, click on the spline labeled **Path**, and drag it into the Spline field inside the **Attribute Manager** for **Spline Wrap** deformer. Automatically, our **Ribbon** object has traced along our spline. Inside the **Attribute Manager**, change the setting under **To** from **100** to **25**, which limits our wrapped object to only going 25 percent of the way along our spline. This setting is similar to the **End Growth** value on a **Sweep NURBS** object.

5. Here's where we explore some features you won't get with a **Sweep NURBS** object. Make sure your playhead is at frame 0 and change the **Offset** value to **-50**, and set a keyframe for the value in the **Attribute Manager**. Now, move to frame 90 and change the **Offset** value to **100** and set a keyframe for this new value. Play your animation back and you'll see the ribbon fly around the shape of the path, starting from off camera and passing right in front.

 The **Offset** value can go to a value below **0%** and above **100%**, so in theory your object can be wrapped beyond the spline. **Sweep NURBS** can't do this; you can only sweep along the predetermined spline.

6. So, we have the animation of our **Spline** done already, but there are some other features to explore inside the **Object** tab of **Spline Wrap**. Un-twirl the subheadings for **Size** and **Rotation** to reveal a pair of graphs we can use to alter the look of our ribbon. Under the **Size** graph, grab the blue dots that represent the start and end points for the curve, and try sliding them around. You can also hold the *Ctrl* or *command* key, and click on the line to add more points. You'll notice that the look of your **Ribbon** object is affected depending on what kind of curve you make. Create a graph that has a curve with the start and end points at the bottom, with the rest of the graph arching up the middle (you can click on the line to add new points). This creates a ribbon that is tapered at the ends based on this new curve.

7. Now, do something similar for the **Rotation** graph, but create a linear graph that slopes downward from left to right. This will twist the **Ribbon** object along the path. Now, for the next graph that is labeled as **Spline Rotation**, create some interesting curves with peaks and valleys, there's no right or wrong answer. This graph dictates where the spline will twist in relation to its position on the spline, where the regular **Rotation** graph twists the actual object based on the curve.

8. Our ribbon is very smooth and can benefit from the **Displacer** deformer, which can help create some wrinkles and creases that will make our ribbon appear more like it's made of cloth or fabric. Add a **Displacer** from the **Deformers** menu and place it as a child of the **Ribbon** object, above **Spline Wrap**. Load it into the **Attribute Manager** and change the **Height** value to **25** in the **Object** tab, and then switch over to the **Shading** tab. Load a **Noise** shader into the **Shader** field, and then click on its name field to edit its properties. Change **Noise** to **Wavy Turbulence**, and increase the Global Scale to a very high value, all the way to **2000**. This has applied a bit of natural-looking creases to our ribbon, so now it's not as rigid as before.

9. Place your **Ribbon** object inside a **HyperNURBS** object to smooth it out. Play your animation back and you'll see our tapered ribbon zip around the frame. Pass the camera while twisting. All this started with a simple plane object, and it became a very twisty-looking ribbon thanks to **Spline Wrap** and **Displacer** as shown in the following figure:

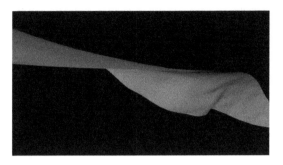

How it works...

Spline Wrap is similar to **Sweep NURBS**, but it has a few great features that are not available inside **Sweep NURBS**. We took a standard plane object, and ran it along the length of our spline. By using the Offset property, we made it fly through our scene along our spline with just two keyframes. Then, we manipulated the curves of graphs for Size and Rotation, giving our ribbon twists and turns. Finally, we added a Displacer, which we set to create a more fabric-like feel to our ribbon. These features aren't available in **Sweep NURBS**, so this kind of animation requires this great deformer to pull it off.

Applying the Collision deformer

A new deformer was introduced in Cinema 4D release 13 called the **Collision** deformer, which simulates an interaction between two objects colliding with each other. This is one of the more complicated deformers and its inclusion into this new version of Cinema 4D opens up quite a few possibilities within the application. In this recipe, we are going to create the effect I often see in mattress commercials, where a bowling ball is dropped on a mattress with a wine glass on it, and the wine glass is undisturbed by the bowling ball. The mattress is soft and deforms the shape of the bowling ball, but the glass doesn't spill, providing the ultimate selling point for clumsy, tired, bowling wine-enthusiasts.

Getting ready

Open the `Bowling_Ball_Bed.c4d` file from the C4D Content Pack and check out the setup.

How to do it...

1. Inside the project, you'll find a nice bed with a bowling ball hovering over it. If you play the animation from the Animation toolbar, you'll notice the ball is dropped and eventually comes to rest on the mattress. Well, it's actually in the mattress right now. We want to replace the lousy, intersecting animation with one that better represents reality; the mattress should work with our bowling ball and look like a soft, forgiving surface.

2. Before we do this, let's use the **Displacer** once more, this time to make our mattress look a little better. Open the **Bed** group and find the **Mattress** object, then go to the Command Palette and load in a **Displacer** from the menu and make it a child of **Mattress**.

3. Under the **Object** tab in the Attribute Manager, change **Height** of your **Displacer** to **2**. Now, switch over to the **Shading** tab, click on the triangle button under **Shader**, and find the **Tiles** option under **Surfaces**. With the **Shader** properties loaded, change **Pattern** to **Waves 1**, and you'll see our mattress now has a wavy pattern to it, one that you may find in certain types of mattresses.

4. The waves are affecting our mattress, but we want to change the **Direction** option from vertex **Normal** to **Planar**, and then switch the new **Orientation** option to **+Y**. Now, the displacement is going upwards, and not popping out the sides of our mattress.

5. Now, locate the **Collision** deformer inside the Command Palette, and add it to your project as a child of the mattress, right below our **Displacer**. Now, make sure it's loaded in the Attribute Manager, and take a look at the **Colliders** tab. We have an option for **Solver Objects**, where we need to drag our bowling ball into this field so the **Collision** deformer knows we want our mattress to interact with it.

6. If you play the animation, you'll see that our ball deforms the mattress with one hiccup. During the initial impact, our bowling ball quickly jumps inside the mattress, and pops back out. This can be fixed by changing the setting from **Intersect** to **Outside (Volume)** under the **Solver Object** setting in the Attribute Manager. This will tell the deformer to keep the bowling ball outside the mattress at all times.

7. Play the animation once more and you'll see a brand new issue—the mattress is folding inwards at the edges when our deformer reacts to the ball. This issue is an easy fix under the **Falloff** tab for our **Collision** deformer in the Attribute Manager. Change the **Shape** field from **Infinite** to **Sphere**, and a small yellow cage will appear around our ball. This controls how far the deformation can reach, and all the transformations will occur inside this outlined sphere. Change the three **Size** settings from **100** to **200**, just to give our bowling ball a little breathing room.

8. Our animation looks good; the mattress sinks with our bowling ball when they collide. One setting we can adjust is under the **Object** tab, listed as **Restore Shape**. The lower this percentage is, the slower your object is to return to the normal state. So, reduce this value to **20**, and watch how the mattress keeps the indentation long after the bowling ball collides. This is a better look for a mattress; the material shouldn't be so springy as shown in the following figure:

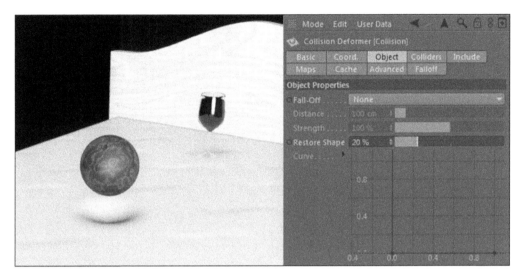

How it works...

We were able to create the effect of a bowling ball sinking into a mattress with the help of the new **Collision** deformer. The deformer allows you to take an object, and have its shape affected by the presence of another object. Instead of our bowling ball intersecting with the mattress like before, the mattress adjusts automatically to the contour of the ball, and returns to normal when it rises back up. Without this deformer, this would be tricky to pull off and requires a lot more work.

There's more...

Notice how the headboard and base of the bed frame which are just the **Cube** objects but they have **Bulge** deformers to make their shape a little less ordinary.

4
Cameras are Rolling

In this chapter we will cover:

- ▸ Keyframing cameras
- ▸ Moving a camera along a path
- ▸ Locking cameras down with the Protection tag
- ▸ Using target cameras
- ▸ Adjusting focal lengths
- ▸ Matching your camera to footage
- ▸ The Physical tab
- ▸ Creating a handheld-style camera
- ▸ Setting up stereoscopic cameras
- ▸ Camera calibration
- ▸ Using the Motion Camera tag
- ▸ Simulating a chase scene
- ▸ Getting to grips with the Camera Morph tag
- ▸ Complex camera moving with the Multi Morph tag

Introduction

Think of a memorable photograph off the top of your head.

There's a good chance you picked a historical photograph from a famous or notable event. It's also likely you picked a photo that occurred at some point in time and somewhere in the world where you were not present. If you weren't there to see the event, how come you instantly recall the image ahead of everything else that resides in your head?

We've been photographing scenes and subjects since the 1800s; the goal to using any kind of camera to capture any kind of image is still the same—to capture a composition of what the lens is pointed at in a particular way. When you look at the pictures, videos, or films, you are experiencing the image through the eyes of the person who captured it, and the particular way they wanted it to be seen and interpreted.

One of the goals of 3D design is to create the optimal image that you can imagine for your particular project. You have complete control over the look and placement of objects, lights, materials, and everything else in your scene, and that is especially true for the camera. The camera in Cinema 4D ultimately controls how people will see and interpret your final image.

Keyframing cameras

If you create a diverse and interesting 3D scene, the odds are you are going to want your camera to navigate through it and not just sit in one spot. We are going to start off this chapter by learning how to keyframe our cameras and have them change their position and angles over the course of our timeline. This is a basic technique you'll use constantly in Cinema 4D.

Getting ready

Open the `Keyframing_Cameras.c4d` file in your **C4D Content Pack** and use it with this recipe.

How to do it...

1. Our scene is a simple setup with a **Figure** object in the middle of the scene posing for us. Start by placing a **Camera** in your scene, found in the **Create** menu under the **Camera** tab, or inside the Command Palette indicated by the icon of the movie camera. Click on its name in the **Object Manager** and label it something descriptive called **Keyframe Camera**.

Whenever you add a new camera or if you end up working with multiple cameras, you need to make sure that you have the correct camera activated in the Viewer, instead of the Default Camera. The Default Camera exists in your scene before you add any other cameras and it cannot be keyframed. So, if you want to control the movement of your camera, you need to add your own camera to have it selected in the Viewer.

2. Select the **Cameras** menu in the Viewer, and mouse over to the **Use Camera** option and click on the **Keyframe Camera** object that you created so that it is checked. The view will not change, but now the Viewer will represent the changes in position and rotation made to your camera, and not the Default Camera. You can also click on the small square box with the plus sign on it in the **Object Manager**; it's next to the traffic light, and when it turns white it means that the camera is the active camera in the Viewer.

3. Set the position and rotation properties of the camera to zero in the **Coordinates** tab of the **Attribute Manager**. You can just enter zero values manually or use the **Reset PSR** command we learned earlier, found in the **Character** menu under **Commands**. Hence, we are starting with a camera that has no tilt to it, and it's positioned exactly at our origin. You should have noticed by now that the Viewer has shifted with these new values, because we have changed the position of our camera.

4. Take a look at the Animation toolbar and take note of the icons inside the three red circles. These icons can control the keyframing of our cameras (and any objects for that matter) when we change our views and move along in the timeline.

5. Move the camera up in the Viewer using any of the techniques learned in *Chapter 1, The Fundamentals*, so that the camera is framing our subject just above the waist. Now, with the playhead at the very beginning of the timeline, click on the red icon farthest to the left of the three with the image of the key inside it; this is the **Record Active Objects** command and it will set a keyframe for all our important coordinate properties in the **Attribute Manager**. Look at how all have a red dot filled in next to their values, meaning that they are keyframed. Now, scrub the playhead forward to frame 60 and then move your Viewer back, so we can see more of our subject and then hit the red keyframe icon once again. If you play your animation in the timeline from the beginning, you'll see that you have created a camera move; the camera moves backwards and reveals more of your subject over time.

How it works...

The **Record Active Objects** button in the Animation toolbar is a quick way to set the keyframe information for your camera and in whichever frame your playhead is currently positioned at. Setting two keyframes moves our camera from one point to another in our scene over time. You could also set the keyframes manually in the **Attribute Manager**, like we learned in the first chapter, and similarly, the set **keyframe** button works for other objects too, not just cameras.

There are cleverer camera setups to be made—keep moving along within this chapter.

Automatic keyframing...do it at your own risk

The middle button in that red group of three enables automatic keyframing. Some people choose to use this, but it also tends to cause headaches if you forget whether it's active or not. Basically, it will set new keyframe values whenever you change your camera view; you can move to new positions in the timeline and change the view, and the keyframes will automatically be set for you. Try it out and see if you like working with it—just remember to turn it on and off when you want to use it.

Moving a camera along a path

You have the ability to draw a spline that represents the path you want your camera to travel, and then dictate the amount of time it takes to complete the movement. This is what you want to do when you want to travel through your scene and focus on multiple objects or alter the perspective throughout your timeline.

This recipe shows how to use the **Align to Spline** feature to control the movement of your camera.

1. In a new project, create a new camera via the icon in the Command Palette. In the Viewer, go and change back to **Default Camera** and turn off your created camera. Next, you should switch the view of your scene from **Perspective** to **Top** under the **Cameras** menu in the Viewer. You are now looking directly over your scene, without altering the perspective of your created camera.

> The Default Camera is good for viewing your scene in different views without messing up the look of the camera we are actually going to animate. Get in the habit of switching between your actual camera and then using the Default Camera to view your scene in a different perspective. Or better yet, select a view that has multiple cameras on-screen, so you can work with your Default Camera while still seeing your scene from your main camera.

2. Under the **Primitives** tab in the Command Palette, pick three different primitives and scatter them in three random places in your scene so that your objects create a triangle. You can use the zoom feature if you can't see all your objects. Click-and-drag them to different spots in 3D space using the **Move Tool** so we can move our camera around each of them in space. The exact position of each is not important, just as long as they are spread out from one another.

3. Click on the **Splines** icon in the Command Palette and select the **Bezier** option. You can now click to add points and drag your mouse to extend the bezier curves; the further you drag the mouse, the smoother the curve will be. This line will represent your camera's movement, so draw the spline such that it passes in front of all three of your objects. Make sure you don't get too close to your three primitives; else they will not fill the frame tastefully.

 The movement will be much smoother if there are fewer points; too many points will cause your animation to look jumpy and jittery.

4. Because we switched to work in the **Top** view in **Default Camera**, our points will only move in the **X** and **Z** dimensions. You can't move the points higher and lower, so you must switch between camera views in order to adjust the height (**Y** position) of the points on your spline. Using the **Left** and **Right** camera views will allow you to adjust the height, but not the length in the **X** dimension, and the **Front** and **Back** views will allow you to adjust the height and the length, but not the depth. As noted before, try out different camera views using **Default Camera** so you can see your scene in these useful perspectives. Adjust the **Y** position of your points in the **Left** or **Right** view so the spline now has a few peaks and valleys.

 Once again, the **Perspective** view is one of the worst views to use when editing the position and rotation of points, because it presents the image at an angle that can mislead your eyes in terms of where the points are lined up. Think of the multiple flat views laid out in an architectural blueprint that provides more technical and accurate views of an object. Use the orthographic views (the Top, Bottom, Left, and Right views) when manipulating points, rather than the **Perspective** view.

5. Now, switch back your view to your created camera and turn off **Default Camera**. Highlight it in the **Object Manager** and slide a little over to the **Tags** menu. Then, under the **Cinema 4D Tags** submenu, select **Align to Spline**. A tag like this places a small icon next to the selected object in the **Object Manager**, where you can select it and open up the tag-specific options.

6. Take your spline in the **Object Manager** and drag it into the **Spline Path** field in the **Attribute Manager**. Once inside, the camera snaps into place at one end of your spline. You have now tied the camera's position to the path you drew for it to travel.

7. Adjust the values in the percentage slider labeled **Position** in the **Tag** properties. You will see that your camera is moving to different points on your spline. The tag works by setting the end points of your spline as **0%** for the start and **100%** for the end, and in everything between. The camera moves between the start and end points, thereby traveling along the spline when keyframed.

8. To complete the movement, set a keyframe at the start of your timeline with the **Position** value at **0%**, move to the end of the timeline and set the value to **100%**, and then set a keyframe. Play back your animation to see your camera move along the spline you drew.

How it works...

Instead of keyframing the position and rotation of the actual camera, we can control how our camera moves by manipulating just the shape of the spline. You can set as many keyframes as you need to move your camera through the completion of your path, and simply sliding them along the timeline allows you to speed up or slow down your camera move.

There's more...

Tweak the spline to get your camera move just right. You can keep moving the points along the spline, or you can use the Move Tool to select the entire spline and move it around that way. Get your camera to pass in front of all the objects in your scene and have them fill the frame nicely. You can also adjust the rotation properties in the **Coordinates** tab for the camera in the **Attribute Manager**.

Not just for cameras

The **Align to Spline** tag can be used on any object, in case you want to control the path that an object or a light moves along.

The Tangential checkbox

You are going to leave the **Tangential** option unchecked in the **Align to Spline** tab. This will align the camera's movements tangentially along the spline, depending on which axis you pick in the **Axis** drop-down menu at the bottom. This is more useful when you are aligning objects to a spline, as you may want time to face a specific direction throughout the movement, but it's not very practical for cameras.

See also

▶ Refer to the *Using target cameras* recipe for another example of using the **Align to Spline** tag

Locking cameras down with the Protection tag

If you would compare the last recipe involving moving cameras with the **Align to Spline** tag to moving an actual physical camera with your hands or on a Steadicam, then this recipe shows you how to place your camera firmly on a tripod and walk away from it.

Once we get a camera positioned where we want, we don't want to have to worry about bumping the scroll wheel on your mouse or accidentally switching camera views and losing your nice scene composition. This can happen by accident and frustrate you in the midst of a deadline, and it can be easily prevented.

How to do it...

1. Start by adding a **Cube** primitive to your scene from the Command Palette. Then, click once on the **Camera** icon in the Command Palette to add a camera to your scene. Switch to it in the Viewer under the **Cameras** menu and the **Use Camera** submenu, making sure that we are no longer on **Default Camera**.

2. Let's say this is the perfect angle and you don't want to lose this shot. Highlight the camera in the **Object Manager** and then click on **Tags**, followed by the **Cinema 4D Tags** and **Protection** tag. A small orange and black "no sign" appears to the right of your camera in the **Object Manager**. This shows that the **Protection** tag is active.

3. Try moving your camera in any way discussed in *Chapter 1*, *The Fundamentals*. Nothing happens: your camera is frozen in place and your shot is preserved. Click on the **Protection** tag in the **Object Manager** to load it into the **Attribute Manager** and you'll see plenty of options for the tag, which is all new in release 13. You have the ability to pick which parameters the tag protects. Uncheck the boxes for the **X**, **Y**, and **Z** values under the **P** group (P for position). Now, try moving your camera. You will be able to move the camera's position, but if you try rotating it, it remains locked.

How it works...

The **Protection** tag is a useful feature that helps preserve your camera shots by making sure you don't adjust the viewer accidently and ruin your composition. When you are working with multiple cameras, sometimes you can lose your place and forget which one is active and you inadvertently move it and regret the move you made.

There's more...

This feature has been highlighted because many of the recipes in this book feature the tag. I set up many projects to have specific camera angles so you can follow along with the same images in the book, so be aware of the tags and don't get frustrated if you can't change the look in the Viewer.

Protection for all

The **Protection** tag can be used on objects too; in case you need to make sure they don't get accidentally nudged or moved. You can still edit an object's properties, and not just the position, rotation, or scale.

Undo view

If you do mess up with your camera view, there's always a way to get it back. In the Viewer under the **View** menu, there's an **Undo View** command, which will revert your view to how it was before you just moved it. This is a convenient fix, but the **Protection** tag is the ultimate way to prevent any issues with altering your camera's perspective.

You can always keyframe

If you keyframe the position of your camera, it will automatically jump back to the keyframe values, even if you change the view. Because you have specifically told Cinema 4D when you want your camera with these keyframes, it will always revert to this spot until you set the new keyframes and tell it otherwise. Also, you have to keyframe all the position and rotation values too for this to work, because a change to a value that is not keyframed will not revert to any specific value, so be careful.

Using target cameras

In Cinema 4D, you have the option to have your camera target a specific object in your scene, and it always remains fixed on it regardless of how the camera moves. Because we are designing objects with three dimensions, it makes sense that we learn and develop camera movements that can display our objects from every angle. This recipe demonstrates how we can easily create a camera that can rotate around an object and display the object from any angle we choose throughout the entire movement.

How to do it...

Be sure to check out the first recipe *Keyframing cameras* in this chapter, because it builds upon that technique. Then, open the `Target_Camera.c4d` file from the C4D Content Pack to use with this recipe.

1. We'll be recreating the famous shot from the movie, *The Matrix*, where time slows to a crawl and the camera completely circles around Neo as he dodges some bullets, remaining fixed on him the entire time. Instead of creating a regular camera, hold down the **Camera** icon in the Command Palette and select the second option for **Target Camera**. Select your **Target Camera** by switching to it from **Default Camera** in the Viewer. By default, **Target Camera** behaves just like a regular camera, but that will change in a few steps. When you create **Target Camera**, you actually create three things: a regular camera, a tag that turns it into a target camera, and a **Null Object** named Camera.Target.1 as a default object for it to focus on. Delete the Camera.Target.1 object from the **Object Manager**, as we won't be using it.

2. Now, we need to create the circular path for our camera to travel around. This is a perfect use for our **Align to Spline** tag, so highlight your camera in the **Object Manager**, click on the **Tags** menu, go under **Cinema 4D Tags**, and select the **Align to Spline** tag.

3. The camera is going to take a circular path around the subject, so we obviously need a **Circle** spline to outline this path. Click and hold down on the **Splines** icon in the Command Palette and select the **Circle** spline option. The spline is good, except that it has the wrong orientation by default, and we need to adjust the **Plane** value. Under the **Object** tab, in the **Attribute Manager** for the **Circle** spline, change the **Plane** value from **XY** to **XZ**. This will align the spline with the proper orientation towards our figure. Adjust the **Radius** to **1200** cm so it is a much larger circle, and our figure will fit into the shot.

4. Next, you need to select the **Align to Spline** tag on your camera in the **Object Manager**, and then drag the **Circle** spline into the **Spline Path** field. Your camera is now aligned to your spline, but it's not really locked in on anything in particular.

5. Our camera is aligned to our spline, but we won't be animating the **Align to Spline** tag like we did in the recipe *Moving a camera along a path*. The **Position** value in the **Align to Spline** tag only goes from **0%** to **100%**. This doesn't do us any good if we want to move in the opposite direction or perhaps make more than one rotation. Going from **0%** to **100%** allows for only one clockwise rotation. We are going to animate the actual **Circle** spline instead so that we can have control over the direction and amount of loops our camera travels.

6. Select your **Circle** spline and look under the **Coordinates** tab in the **Attribute Manager**. Set a keyframe for the **R.H** value at the beginning of your timeline. 360 degrees represents one full revolution, so move to the very end of your timeline and change the rotation value to 360 and set a keyframe. Play your animation and you will see that the camera circles around one time. But, the problem is our camera isn't focused on our subject.

7. Click on the **Target** tag, which is the little target crosshairs in the **Object Manager** on your camera. In the **Attribute Manager** under the **Object** tab, you'll find the empty **Target Object** field, where you can simply drag **The One** from the **Object Manager** into the field and watch as your camera instantly locks onto the target and follows it throughout the length of the animation. You may now unplug yourself from the Matrix.

How it works...

The target cameras allow you to fix the position and rotation of your camera to an object in your scene. This way, whenever you move the camera, it will remain focused on the object you specified. It can work separately from the **Align to Spline** tag, but the combination of the two tags helps us create the exact camera move we were looking for.

There's more...

Experiment with changing the coordinates of your **Circle** spline to get some more interesting camera rotations. Try animating the **Y** position value of the **Circle** spline, and you can move between a bird's eye and a worm's eye view of your figure, while focusing on the center of it. Try adjusting the **R.P** value and you can get an interesting tilt to go with your rotation instead of it being flat.

Pans and tilts

Using a target camera and animating the **Null Object** is a good way to simulate pans and tilts, instead of animating the actual camera. Just specify a **Null Object** to be your **Target Object**, and the camera will stay in one spot and follow the target object if you animate the null position from left to right or from up and down. Think of it as a camera on a tripod, and it's following whatever you are aiming it at.

Adding the target manually

If you create a camera and decide later that you want it to be a target camera, just look for it under the **Cinema 4D Tags** menu and add it manually; it will work the same way.

Linear keyframes for loops

To get a proper looping animation, you'll need to have keyframes with linear interpolation features. Click on the actual keyframe in the Animation toolbar at the first frame when you have the **Circle** spline selected in the **Object Manager**, and change the **Interpolation** value from **Spline** to **Linear** in the **Attribute Manager**.

Adjusting focal lengths

In Cinema 4D release 13, the camera settings were overhauled and we now have new features that give us better control like we see in actual cameras. The next two recipes deal with these features, though this one shows how to adjust the focal length of your cameras in order to compress or exaggerate depth. Just like in actual photography, picking the right focal length and lens is crucial to getting the right look for your image.

Getting ready

Use the `Focal_Lengths.c4d` project with this recipe so you can follow along.

How to do it...

1. Start by adding a new camera to the scene and switching to it in the Viewer instead of **Default Camera**. Adjust the camera coordinates so that the **X** and **Y** position values and all the rotation values are at **0**; set the **Z** position value at **-1500**. Now, take this camera and duplicate it by clicking-and-holding the *Ctrl* or *command* key and dragging the mouse up or down to make a copy on release. Add a **Protection** tag to each camera so they don't move, and rename one camera to **Short Focal Length** and the other to **Long Focal Length**.

2. You'll find **Focal Length** under the **Object** tab of the camera in the **Attribute Manager**. The default focal length is pretty average at **36** mm, and you can often leave it at its default and get a good result. But, let's create two different focal lengths for cameras that are in the exact same position and see how drastically it changes the look of your scene in Cinema 4D.

3. Under the **Object** tab in the **Attribute Manager** for the **Short Focal Length** camera, click on the **Focal Length** menu and select **Wide Angle**, which changes the **Focal Length** value to **25**. Then, switch cameras in the **Object Manager**, so the **Long Focal Length** camera is active in the **Attribute Manager**. Switch the **Focal Length** setting to **Tele**, which is a very big value of **135**.

4. In order to see both cameras at once, change it to **2 Views Stacked** inside the **Arrangement** options, under the **Panel** menu in the Viewer. Activate the **Short Focal Length** camera in one window, and then the **Long Focal Length** one in the other, under the **Cameras** menu. Make use of **Use Camera** in each of the two views:

5. Keep in mind that these cameras are exactly at the same position, but the images look completely different. The camera with a shorter focal length allows us to see more of the cubes with the text appearing small. Also, note the distortion of the cubes that are closer and towards the edges. The camera with a larger focal length has our shot zoomed in way too tight in our text, and it appears that there are far fewer cubes in the scene.

How it works...

This exercise hopefully showed you that it's important to not only adjust the position of your camera, but the focal length as well. A scene with many objects scattered about may require a camera with a shorter focal length, while a larger focal length will allow you to compress and focus on a particular object.

There's more...

Cinema 4D cameras can mimic real cameras, so check out some photography sites for tips on how to compose your scenes and adjust your cameras. The following site from Envato has tons of helpful tips and tutorials for photography and accompanying software:

`http://photo.tutsplus.com/`

Matching your camera to footage

Let's say you create an object in Cinema 4D, and you want it to appear as if it is a part of another piece of footage or a still photo. So, you want to use 4D to make something 3D, and then have it mixed into something that is 2D. That just about covers every dimension you can have. This recipe shows you how to prepare a camera setup to match the look of a still photograph, so the elements you design in Cinema 4D will appear like they belong in the footage you'll be making a composition of.

Getting ready

Use the `Oak_Alley` photograph provided in the C4D Content Pack with this recipe. The image is in 16:9 (aspect ratio) for use in a 1920 x 1080 HD format, so you should change your composition to be in this resolution as well. Go to the **Render** menu and click on the **Render** Settings. Under the **Output** tab, load the preset for **HDTV 1080 29.97** under the **Film/Video** options. Your frame will now have a 16:9 aspect ratio. Whether you use stills or a video, the process laid out in this recipe is the same.

How to do it...

1. Start by creating a new camera and switching to it instead of the **Default Camera** mode. Next, you'll need to create a background object that will serve as a back wall for our scene. Look in the **Create** menu, and then under **Environment** you'll see **Background**. Click on it and add this into your scene.

2. The background object requires a material on it, otherwise it's invisible. So double-click on the empty space in the **Material Manager** and a new material will be created. Double-click on the material, and in the **Color** channel, you'll need to load the `Oak_Alley.jpg` image into the **Texture** field. Click on the small ellipses bar on the left or the bigger bar in the middle; each one will allow you to cycle through your computer and load the image into the **Color** channel from the C4D Content Pack.

When loading an image into a channel, Cinema 4D will always prompt you with the following:

This image is not in the document search path. Do you want to create a copy at the document location?

What it is asking you is if you want Cinema 4D to copy the image to a newly-created folder, in the same directory as your project. Once confirmed, it connects this file via a relative reference to the created folder, instead of an absolute file located in a specific spot, somewhere else on your hard drive. Select **Yes** if you plan on collecting a lot of images and perhaps moving the file from computer to computer. This will help Cinema 4D know where your files are through looking in the same directory as the project file. Hit **No** if you'd rather just keep one copy of the image on your computer and refer to it from its original spot. It all depends on how you are working on a particular project.

3. Now, you have the image loaded into the material. So, drag the material from the **Material Manager** to the **Background** object in the **Object Manager** and release the mouse over it in order to place the material on it. Your Viewer should now be filled with the image, and the background will remain in the same place, regardless of where you move and position the camera.

4. The goal now is to match the perspective of your Cinema 4D camera to the perspective in which I took this photograph. We need to move the camera into a spot that lines up the floor grid in the Viewer with the ground in the photo. This is the process of matching camera shots in Cinema 4D to real-life photos and footage. By creating and aligning floors, planes, and ceilings with the perspective and edges in our photo, we can make the camera project our 3D objects as if they are in front of the camera, filming our image:

5. In the camera's **Coordinates** tab, keep the **X** position at **0**, but move the camera back in the **Z** position to **-2000**. Now, place a **Sphere** object in your scene from the **Primitives** palette. The sphere will be placed at the origin, and moving the camera closer towards it in the **Z** dimension will make the object appear closer to the camera.

6. Next, we need to make adjustments in order to line up the floor plane in our Cinema 4D scene to that of our photograph. These adjustments will be made to our camera's **Y** position value, as well as to our rotation values. You'll notice a grid that's projected as a floor in the **X** and **Z** dimensions. This is ideal for matching our perspective with the ground in our scene. If the grid does not appear in your scene by default, you can activate it in the Viewer window by clicking on the **Filter** menu and selecting **Grid**.

7. The grid should be placed even with the ground in the photo, so that the lines on the grid are parallel with those in the photo, such as the rows of bricks on the sidewalk. Move the camera up higher in the **Y** position to a value of **92**. Next, you can slightly tweak **R.H** to a very small value of **0.3**, and **R.P** should have a value of **1**. This is a good alignment for our scene, which will vary from photo to photo or video to video, but the process remains the same.

8. The last step to get an even more accurate setup is to adjust your camera settings to match the lens to the actual camera lens. I took this photo with the focal length set to **42** mm. Simply go to the **Object** tab in the **Attribute Manager** of your camera and change the value of **Focal Length** from the default **36** to **42**. It's a slight change, but will provide more convincing renders if the photo or video was shot with special lenses, such as a wide angle or telephoto lens.

How it works...

Use the grid to line up as if it was the ground or the floor in your photo or video. It can also represent a ceiling if the footage was taken from a lower angle. Add **Plane** objects and make them perpendicular to your floor if you need to represent walls. Basically, you are trying to mimic the camera that was used in real life to capture your image, so add the faces of the room or environment where you can match them up with the footage you shot. Getting the coordinates and the camera settings as precise as possible will help you build a more convincing scene.

There's more...

This example used a still photograph, which could also be a video shot on a tripod. The point is the camera is not moving and the perspective is not changing. Matching a camera in Cinema 4D to a moving camera is much trickier. You'll need to learn more about 3D camera tracking in order to get your objects to match up with a camera that changes position and angles on your footage. SynthEyes is a software application capable of handling 3D camera tracking, and it can be used in conjunction with Cinema 4D and other programs.

[To download SynthEyes and get going with its tutorials, you can visit `http://ssontech.com/synovu.htm`]

Don't render the background

When you render your scene with your objects matched up to your camera, you don't actually want the background to be rendered with it. You'd much rather composite your render on the top of the original image in a program, such as Photoshop or After Effects. Once you are ready to render, go to the **Basic** tab of the **Background** object in the **Attribute Manager** or just use the traffic light to change **Visible** in the **Render** setting to **Off**, and then render your scene with an alpha channel so you can composite it elsewhere.

See also

▸   See the *Projecting shadows* recipe in *Chapter 7, Rendering Strategy* to animate our sphere rolling through our scene and also how we can get shadows to project on the ground to make it more realistic with multipass rendering. Save this project for later use.

The Physical tab

Each camera in Cinema 4D now comes with the new **Physical** tab in the **Attribute Manager** in release 13. These features streamline the previously clunky process and make your cameras behave like real cameras in 3D projects. Within the **Physical** tab, we can control all the features to help create a realistic depth of field, motion blur, and more with our cameras. This recipe shows you how to adjust all the settings in order to get more than ever before out of your cameras in Cinema 4D.

Getting ready

Open the `Card_Table.c4d` file and use it while you work through this recipe.

How to do it...

1.   Check out the setup we have here. It's a camera close-up of a card table, and when you play the animation, a pair of cards slides in front of the camera. The camera is set to the **Portrait** setting, giving it a focal length of **80** mm for a more shallow focus. Switch your camera over to the **Physical** tab in the **Attribute Manager** and you'll notice the options are mostly grayed out. Click on the checkbox for **Movie Camera**, and then open the **Render Settings** window from the Command Palette or via the **Render** menu under **Edit Render Settings**. You'll see the drop-down menu in the top-left corner, which is used for setting our renderer to **Standard**.

However, we need to switch that to **Physical** in order to take advantage of all the new features in our camera. Also, check the boxes for **Depth of Field** and **Motion Blur**. Lastly, change the **Sampling Quality** value from **Low** to **Medium**.

2. Let's start by getting our depth of field up and running. The setting we'll want to adjust is **F-Stop** in our **Physical** tab. The F-Stop on real cameras adjusts the aperture, or how much light is let into the camera. The smaller the F-Stop is, the smaller the depth of field will be, which will result in a selective focus that can draw attention to certain objects of the scene. Lower the **F-Stop** value to **f/2.8**, then switch to the **Object** tab, and take a look at the ways we can define where our focal plane is.

3. The **Focus Distance** value is a set distance you want to define for the focal plane width, so you can tell the camera at what distance to focus on and also about all the objects that will be out of focus in the front and behind. Or, you can drag-and-drop an object into the **Focus Object** field, and it will automatically adjust and focus on that object. Drag the **Deck of Cards** group from the Object Manager and drag it into the **Focus Object** field. You then do a render preview by hitting *Ctrl* or *command + R*. Depending on how fast your computer is, you'll get a rendered sample of your scene in a few seconds. The deck of cards at the back should be the objects in focus, while the dealt cards and the chips should be blurred out:

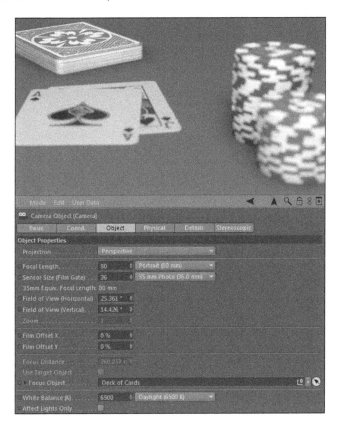

4. I'd rather have the dealt cards in focus, with the other objects slightly out of focus. Remove the **Deck of Cards** group from the **Target Object** field by clicking on the small arrow on the right-hand side of the field and then clicking on **Clear**. Switch to the **Default Camera** mode in the Viewer from inside the **Cameras** menu under **Use Camera**. Rotate the active camera around so you can see the cone of your other camera. Make sure the playhead in the Animation toolbar is on a frame towards the end, where the cards are dealt, and are sitting in their final position. Now, let's adjust the **Focus Distance** value manually to a value of **200**. You'll see the end of the plane jump. Move over on top of the two dealt cards. If you switch back to your main camera and do a render preview with *Ctrl* or *command + R*, you'll see the two dealt cards and the $1 chips that are with them are in focus, and the deck and $5 chips are out of focus because they lie further away from the focal plane we assigned:

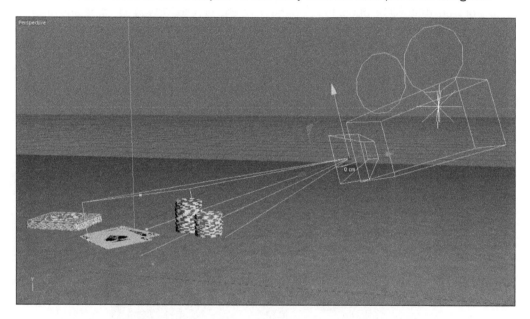

5. Now, let's figure out how to apply motion blur to our animation. Move to frame 55 while the Jack of Spades is in motion. Because we checked on the **Movie Camera** box, our motion blur is controlled via the **Shutter Angle** setting. Movie cameras have two shutters that rotate and capture images. The shutter angle is the gap between the two shutters, and the larger the angle, the more motion blur gets captured. However, increasing it will also cause the shutter to become overexposed, because more light will be entering, so make sure the **Exposure** checkbox is deactivated to eliminate this issue. The **Shutter Angle** value is set to **180** and that will give us a solid motion blur. We don't need to increase it to notice the result. If you do a render preview, it won't matter. This is because the motion blur is not displayed in the Viewer. We'll need to render to Picture Viewer instead, which can be activated by pressing *Shift + R*. The Picture Viewer will pop the open angle; you'll get a frame with your motion blur on the playing card as it slides across the table:

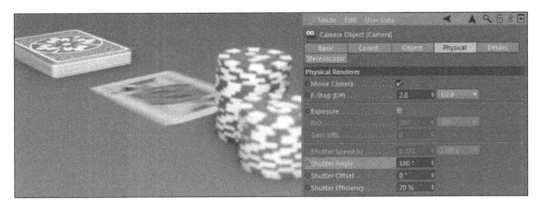

How it works...

We were able to get realistic camera effects, such as the depth of field and motion blur, by using the **Physical** settings in our camera and in the **Render Settings** too. By enabling these features, we were able to get a nice, shallow focus by adjusting the **F-Stop** value and positioning the focal plane on our two dealt cards. We activated motion blur in **Render Settings** and had control over it via our **Shutter Angle** value. Our final image contains both these effects and results in a more interesting-looking image.

There's more...

These new features are great, and are head and shoulders better than the methods used in the previous versions of Cinema 4D to add depth of field and motion blur. But, they will increase your render times for certain, and all these effects can be added in a finishing program such as After Effects. Check out *Chapter 7, Rendering Strategy* for some examples of multipass rendering to see how much more flexible your project can be by adding these effects after you render out of Cinema 4D.

More effects

There are a few other effects you are able to add via the **Physical** tab, such as vignetting, chromatic aberration, and lens distortion. These can all be added after you render in After Effects as well.

Rack focus

Set a **Null Object** to be your **Target** object, and animate its position within the depth of your camera shot. This will simulate a rack focus, where your focal plane will change during a shot and bring different objects into focus over time.

Creating a handheld-style camera

The cameras we've created so far have all been controlled by keyframes, aligned to splines, or have had specific values assigned to them. This recipe takes us in a different direction and creates a camera with randomly-controlled movements. We're going to use this technique to simulate a boxer's point of view from his/her corner, or better yet, a boxer who is headed into the twelfth round and is in a world of hurt.

Getting ready

Use the `Boxing_Ring.c4d` file in the C4D Content Pack that was provided for this recipe.

How to do it...

1. Start your scene with a new camera and name it `Boxer POV`, switch to it from the **Default Camera** mode, and set the camera's position and rotation values to be in the red corner facing the blue corner in the **Coordinates** tab for the camera in the **Attribute Manager**. These values work for our setup: position **X** at **110 cm**, **Y** at **100 cm**, **Z** at **-110 cm**, **R.H** at **45** degrees, and **R. P** at **-10**:

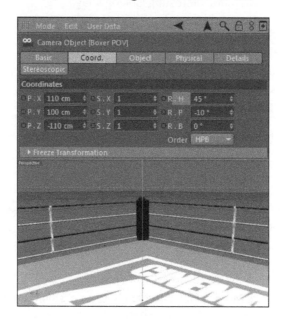

2. To simulate the look of a boxer's point of view who is seeing stars, we're going to need a lot of constant movements in all directions. Rather than tediously keyframing a complex camera movement like we did before, we're going to let Cinema 4D do the work for us.

3. Select your camera in the **Object Manager**, go to the **Tags** menu, and under **Cinema 4D Tags**, select the **Vibrate** tag. This tag will cause whatever object it is applied to, to shake randomly to the specifications you give for the position, rotation, and scale.

4. We want our **Vibrate** tag to randomize just the position and rotation values of our camera. The moment you click on the checkboxes next to **Enable Position** and **Enable Rotation**, the camera will jump and move to a new spot in the Viewer. If you scrub through the timeline, you'll see that our camera is now shaking back and forth, but it doesn't give us a great look for our stunned boxer, so we're going to have to adjust our values.

A lot of the time, when we use expressions or formulas to drive animations rather than keyframes, we rely on two variables: frequency and amplitude. They may not always be explicitly called this, though these two parameters are often the main ingredients for creating a successful expression-driven animation. Amplitude is the maximum value that your expression can draw values from. Frequency is the rate at which your amplitude values are cycled. The higher the amplitude, the more drastic are our movements. The higher the frequency, the more often our movements occur

5. By enabling the position and rotation values on our **Vibrate** tag, we now have control over their frequency and amplitude. By entering the right values, we can make it look like our boxer has taken a few shots; whether punches or alcohol, either one works in this case.

6. The first thing you notice is that the frequency is too high; our boxer is shaking his head way too fast. Reduce the **Frequency** values for both position and rotation from **2** to **0.5**, so it's now moving four times slower. Click on **Play** in your timeline and you'll see this is a much more realistic movement.

7. Right now, our boxer is only shaking from side-to-side; that's because our amplitude values only have data in the **X** position and the rotation **H** values. The three values are not labeled that way, but correspond to the same order you would see in the **Coordinates** tab (**X**, **Y**, **Z** and **H**, **P**, **B**). Of the position values, the **X** dimension should remain the most dominant, as his head is likely to move strongly from side-to-side rather than up and down (**Y** dimension) or forward and back (**Z** dimension). Add a value of 10 to both the **Y** and **Z** values for our position amplitude, so that there's a slight movement in all directions. Now, from our boxer's point of view, it looks like he is wobbling in all directions, but the side-to-side movement in the **X** dimension remains the most noticeable and dominant trait.

8. The rotation amplitude values are where we make our boxer really look out of it. The default value in **H** is good at **30**, which pivots his head from side-to-side, and shows off more of the ring making it appear like he can't focus on what's right in front of him. The **P** rotation value can be increased up to about **15**, which simulates him tilting his head up or down. The **B** value is the fun one; it gives a Dutch angle effect, which acts as a sideways tilt and makes it seem like his neck can't support his head. Use a value of **20** here and play back your animation. Then, give some much needed words of encouragement to your fighter before the bell rings.

How it works...

The **Vibrate** tag randomizes the position and rotation values of our camera at our determined magnitude (**Amplitude**) and rate (**Frequency**). This gives the effect that our boxer is on the ropes without using any keyframes, which is the key thing for an animation taking all day or 10 minutes.

There's more...

There is a valuable set of tools out there for Cinema 4D called **CSTools** by Chris Smith that have some similar prebuilt cameras which can help you create a similar handheld look. Check out his `CS_DocuCam` and `CS_ActionCam` files, which use **XPresso** to create a more complex camera setup, complete with a control panel to adjust the camera movements. And check out *Chapter 9, XPresso Shots*, which will teach you how to create more complex projects like these.

Visit `http://circlesofdelusion.blogspot.com/` to download CSTools for free from Chris' site.

Got some good vibrations

The **Vibrate** tag works on anything, not just cameras, so you can just apply it to any object and watch it move and shake.

Keyframe your values so that they can change over time

What if you want your camera movement to start slow and finish fast? Easy, you just need a couple of keyframes in the right spot. If you set the **Frequency** and **Amplitude** values to **0**, your animation will not vibrate. So, set a keyframe at the beginning of your timeline when the values are at zero, and go to the end and increase your values to the values you desire; also set a keyframe. You have now animated the frequency and amplitude, so your vibration will start out really slow and ramp up to the maximum value by the end.

Keyframes first

The **Vibrate** tag has a glitch if you add keyframes to the object value after the tag has been applied. I recommend drawing a path for your handheld-style camera and using the **Align to Path** technique to control the path and rate at which you want your camera to move. Then, just apply the **Vibrate** tag to the spline instead of the camera so that not only does your camera travel along your path, but the path itself bounces and is randomized instead of the camera.

Random Seed equals infinite possibilities

The **Vibrate** tag has a **Random Seed** value, which is common throughout a lot of different properties and objects found in Cinema 4D. **Random Seed** is a number that replicates the exact pattern every time the same values are entered and applied to the same object. Simply change the **Random Seed** value and you change the pattern in which your object moves. It will follow the same constraints set by the amplitude and frequency, but change the randomness and give you a similar yet different movement.

Setting up stereoscopic cameras

There's been a steady increase in the amount of 3D media developed in recent years, and Cinema 4D has responded by creating stereoscopic cameras in release 13. This new feature allows you to generate stereoscopic content right in your Cinema 4D projects, and you can instantly see the 3D projection in action. This recipe introduces the new features and shows you how to turn your 3D scenes into actual 3D designs.

Getting ready

Use the `3D_Glasses.c4d` file in the C4D Content Pack with this recipe. If you have a really basic pair of anaglyph glasses like the ones the model is wearing, try them out with this recipe.

How to do it...

1. Our scene is already set up; all we need to do to get stereoscopic images is to go up to the **Camera** palette in the Command Palette, click-and-hold on the icon, and grab the **Stereo Camera** option to get started. Now, switch to this new camera under the **Cameras** menu in the Viewer; you can find it under the **Use Camera** submenu. Nothing will change because we need to adjust our Viewer to activate stereoscopic effects. In the Viewer, under the **Options** menu, toggle on the **Stereoscopic** switch towards the top of the menu; your composition should change right away. Our Viewer is showing us an anaglyph image by default.

Any camera can be turned into a 3D camera. Under the **Stereoscopic** tag in the **Attribute Manager**, the **Mode** option for regular cameras is set to **Mono**. Switch it to **Symmetrical** and you'll turn it into a stereoscopic camera.

2. Select the camera in the **Object Manager** and switch over to the **Coordinates** tab in the **Attribute Manager**. Set the camera to be positioned at **0** in the **X** position, **150** in the **Y** position, and **-600** in the **Z** position. Eliminate all rotation values as well so that all the three settings read 0. Now, switch over to the **Stereoscopic** tab, whose settings control how your stereoscopic image is captured.

3. Just look over a few important settings. The **Eye Separation** setting should almost always be kept at a small value like the default **6.5 cm**. It represents how far apart the average pair of eyes is from each other, so it's best to leave that alone. The **Show All Cameras** checkbox is handy, when enabled, and we can see both the left and right-hand cameras in the Viewer when looking at our setup from another camera. It will also help by showing the **Zero Parallax**, **Near Plane**, and **Far Plane** objects in the Viewer as well.

4. Now, switch from your stereoscopic camera to the **Default Camera** mode in the Viewer. Position **Default Camera** so that you can see the cones projecting from your stereoscopic camera rig. With the **Stereoscopic** tab loaded in the **Attribute Manager**, change the **Zero Parallax** from **1000** to **600**. You'll notice the middle plane in your cone jump right up against the figure holding the 3D letters. **Zero Parallax** is set to be even with the projection, meaning that it's the screen which you are viewing the 3D image. Objects in front of this plane will appear to pop out in front of your screen with the right glasses, and the objects behind the plane will appear further back in your screen. Objects that are even with the plane will appear to have the same depth as the screen. Change the **Auto Plane** settings from **Manual** to **90**, which represents a safe default setting for our eyes to observe our stereoscopic image. Our plane is set so our figure object will appear in front of the screen coming towards the audience.

5. In order to see our final stereoscopic image, we'll need to activate the **Stereoscopic** options in the **Render Settings** dialog. Click on the icon of the orange film slate with the gear in the Command Palette to open **Render Settings**. Click on the checkbox for **Stereoscopic** and check out the settings available. The **Calculate Stereoscopic Images** menu allows you to render multiple individual channels for your image, so you can create more sophisticated renders outside of Cinema 4D. We want ours to remain on **Merged Stereoscopic Image**. The **Mode** setting is put to **Anaglyph**, which renders a red and cyan image for each eye and works with the basic 3D glasses I mentioned earlier. **Additional Parallax** can increase the stereoscopic effect if you enter a higher value here, but it's usually fine by default.

6. If you hit the icon directly to the left of **Render Settings**, you'll render your image to the Picture Viewer and you'll have a sample frame of your stereoscopic image. The figure that's holding the 3D text appears to pop off the screen when viewed with simple anaglyph glasses:

How it works...

The new stereoscopic camera in Cinema 4D release 13 allows you to create stereoscopic renders that appear to pop off your screen. When activated in our camera and Viewer settings, we are able to preview our stereoscopic scene and make adjustments to the camera rig that captures 3D objects in 3D. We adjusted the **Zero Parallax** plane to make our figure holding the 3D letters pop towards us when viewed with anaglyph glasses.

There's more...

There are many more sophisticated setups possible when using the stereoscopic cameras in Cinema 4D. You can optimize the 3D animation for more specific and sophisticated glasses, and adjust your camera to mimic more creative setups. This is a brand new feature in Cinema 4D and is valuable to learn as its use becomes more popular in TV and film.

Configuring the Viewer

If you go under the **Options** menu in the Viewer and select **Configure**, you'll find a **Stereoscopic** tab that contains the same kind of options available in the **Render Settings** dialog. Adjust these to get a different look inside the Viewer.

Camera calibration

Camera calibration allows us to put 3D objects into real world images. The **Camera Calibration** tag allows Cinema 4D to work out the camera angle and focal length used in a picture and match it within the program. That way we can realistically place our own objects into the scene.

For example, in this scene I used the **Camera Calibration** tag to place some abstract 3D objects in the scene:

How to do it...

Firstly, create a new camera by clicking on the camera icon or select it from the menu.

1. Now, right-click on **Camera** in the **Object Manager** and the **Camera Calibrator** tag from **Cinema 4D tags**. You can now see all the settings for the camera calibrator in the attributes window.

2. Firstly, we want an image to calibrate. Click on the dots at the end of the **Image** field and then browse to room.jpg in the content pack. You should see the image in the perspective Viewer.

3. We help calibrating the image by selecting the perspective lines from within the image. These allow **Cinema** to work out the vanishing points and then from there, the camera angle and focal length values are known.

4. Now, switch over to the **Calibration** tag and click on **Add Line.** We need to align the line with one of the horizontal lines in the picture. So, drag one end of the line to a horizontal edge and then the other, so that it's nicely mirroring the angle of the line. Now, click on the line until it turns red. You'll see in the **Attribute Manager** that the line is now representing the X axis. Continue doing this for all the clear horizontal lines you can see. Four or five should be enough.

5. Let's do the same for the vertical lines. Add another line and align it to any clear vertical edges. Now, *Shift* + click on it until it turns green. This tells the program that it's an edge parallel to the y axis. Keep adding until you have three or four.

6. Let's add in the z axis lines. Just follow the same process but now choose the edges that move away from the camera. Make sure to *Shift* + click on them until they turn blue.

7. Now, all that we have to do is drop in a pin at **Add Pin**. This will be the center of our world grid. Drop it into the corner of the room. All the camera calibration fields should now be green or yellow indicating that they have been solved:

8. Now, let's click on **Create Background Object**. This will do just what it says but the background object will have our room image applied to it. Now, you can simply add any object and it will appear in the correct perspective within the shot. Try adding a cube, for example. You'll notice that as you move it around it appears to move within the scene.

How it works...

Camera calibration works by analyzing a 2D image (usually a photograph) and then trying to deduce various characteristics of the camera through this information. These characteristics include the focal length, orientation, and position of the camera. This is pretty clever stuff but the more information we can give the calibrator the better. That's why it really helps to know the measurements of various items visible in the shot.

There's more...

The **Camera Calibration** tag is very useful in some situations but it is designed for still imagery rather than for moving images. You could use it for filmed footage but you'd have to make sure that the camera doesn't move at all. If you do want to track shot footage, then you can use programs like PF Track, Bijou, or SynthEyes but these are fully-fledged 3D tracking programs. If you don't have the budget for that, then I recommend trying out The Foundry's Camera Tracker plugin for After Effects. It's much cheaper than other programs mentioned and will work pretty well for most users. It has also got a free trial period, so give it a go!

Limitations

Camera calibration works best for images with lots of straight and parallel lines such as buildings or room interiors. You will find it much harder if there are no straight lines, for example, an image of some trees in a field. You can try and estimate where the lines would be, but obviously the results will not be so accurate.

You should try and avoid any images with lens distortion or that which use fish-eye lenses or tilt shift lenses.

Tips to help calibrate better

You can make your calibration much more accurate if you know the measurements of some of the objects in your scene. For example, if you know the length of the sideboard to be 125 cm, then you can enter that value into the **Known Length** field in the Attributes/Calibrate field as you add a line to it.

If you want to make it look as if the elements you've added are really in the scene, then you'll need to try and duplicate the lighting. Try and match how the room is lit and use shadow catchers to increase the realism of your scene. We'll cover some of these concepts in *Chapter 5, Let There Be Lights*.

You can also create the basic geometry of your scene and use the **Create Camera Mapping Tag** to project the image onto that geometry. Simply drag your newly created tag onto your geometry. You can then move your camera around and create your own realistic camera moves within the scene. This is a more advanced technique but if you feel confident with what we've covered so far, you may want to begin exploring it.

Using the Motion Camera tag

Motion Camera is a powerful new tag which can help you simulate real world camera movements. It can help simulate all those things which make a camera look realistic which are sometimes lacking when you animate a CG camera. It actually creates a virtual camera person and can give them attributes like footsteps, headroll, and even overshoot the focus!

The **Motion Camera** tag can either follow a spline or can be used on top of an existing camera. We're going to be mainly looking at the spline based application of this tag but once you understand that, you can easily apply it to the existing camera moves that you've created.

How to do it...

In this recipe, we're going to have a quick look at the main parameters of the tag, and try and get a feel of how it works. We'll then move on to the next recipe to try it out in the field!

Go to **Create | Camera | Motion Camera**. This will set up a basic motion camera scene for you:

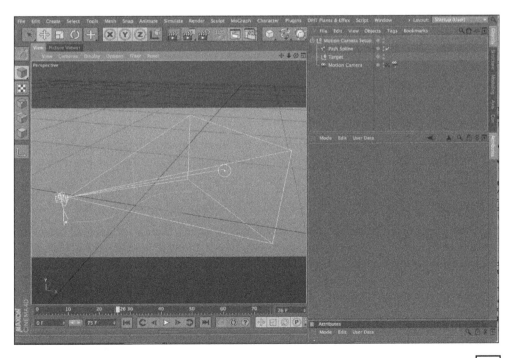

You can see that we have a spline along which our camera will move a camera, a camera person, and a camera target. If you look at the **Animation** settings in the **Attribute Manager** for the **Motion Camera** tag, you'll see that **Cinema** has already entered the objects into the correct fields. If you look through Motion Camera (**Viewport Menu | Camera | Use Camera | Motion Camera**) and click on **Play**, you'll see that the camera is moving naturally and gently.

1. If you adjust the slider **Camera Position**, you'll notice our camera rig moving along the spline. Simply set a keyframe at frame 0, move the time along to 75 frames, set **Camera Position slider** to 100, and then set another keyframe. Click on the little target icon beside the camera and you will see that the camera is now moving and that we're focusing on the target. So far so good!

2. We can control the basic alignment, rotation, and positioning of the set up in the **Rig** tab of the **Attribute Manager**. It's fairly straightforward to adjust the height and the parallax (or offset) of the camera. You can also adjust the rotation of the camera.

3. Now, let's add in some banking to make our move more dynamic! Check the **Enable** box in **Automatic Banking** and set it to **5**. When you play the animation, the camera tilts realistically with the motion.

4. We can also create a new target for our camera by dropping in a new null object at **Create | Object | Null**. Move it reasonably close to the original target object and then select the **Motion Camera** tag and then the **Animation** tab. Drop the new null object into the **Target A2** field.

5. You will notice that a new option has become available now. This is the Target Pos A1 <-> A2 slider which enables us to choose how much we look at each target. You can enter targets into the B1 and B2 fields also and then mix them all up.

6. Switch to the **Motion** tab of **Motion Camera** in the **Attribute Manager**. Now, increase the **Footsteps Intensity** value to **80**% and click on **Play** again. You'll see that our camera now jiggles up and down in an attempt to simulate our camera person's footsteps.

7. It doesn't quite feel right just yet. So, turn the **Frequency** value down to **0.4**. You can also play with the scale to affect how much the camera moves on each step.

8. You can, of course, add some values to the **Head Rotation** and **Camera Rotation** sliders. These add some random movement into the various parts of the camera rig.

How it works...

The **Motion Camera** tag works by taking a normal camera and then adding lots of secondary movement to it. These movements are meant to simulate the kind of behaviors you'd see if you used some real hand-held footage. A lot of these secondary movements are things you could keyframe by hand, but it would take a really long time to do so. With the tag, you can make amends quickly and cleanly.

Simulating a chase scene

In this recipe, we're going to animate a camera that zooms through a series of buildings chasing a red cone. Don't worry, it'll make sense when we open up the scene. We're going to get some really nice fluid, flowing, and dynamic movement which feels really organic and hand-held.

We're going to add some motion camera dynamics to a pre-existing camera move. Open `Chase.c4d` from the content pack.

How to do it...

Click on **Play** and watch the scene from the top viewport. You'll see that the camera (runCam) follows the linear spline through the buildings. Now, we want to make this more dynamic and natural, like someone is running through the buildings.

1. Add a new camera and name it `Motion Camera`. Now, add the **Motion Camera** tag. This can be found by right-clicking on the camera or going to the **Tags** menu in the **Object Manager**. Select the **Motion Camera** tag from **Motion Camera**.

2. Drag the runCam into the **Base** link field on the **Rig** tab of **Motion Camera** in the **Attribute Manager**. Click on the checkbox for **Override Rig Dimensions**. What we're doing here is using our original camera as a base, and allowing it to use some of the motion camera functionality.

3. Switch to the **Dynamics** tab and set **Damp Rot** to **80**%. Now, when you play the animation back, you'll see that rotation at the corners has been smoothed out. You can switch the mode to **Spring** if you want to create some whip and bounce in the movement. Simply add some **Inertia Rot** to the slider.

4. Again add in **80%** of **Intensity** into the **Footsteps** slider in the **Motion** tab and set the **Frequency** to **0.1**.

5. You can also add a little banking by using the **Automatic Banking** parameter in the **Animation** tab. Set it to **0.3** and set the **Dampen** value to **9%**:

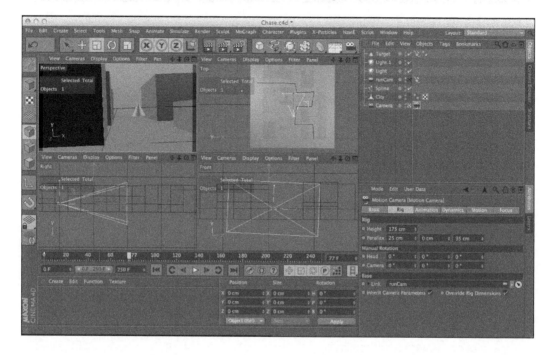

This setup should give you quite a pleasing and natural camera move based on a very simple animation setup.

There's more...

There's a lot to play with in the motion camera. You can mix between splines and target objects, and even activate the chase function which is a lot of fun and can be very useful. But, it's best just to have a play and see what works for you.

Getting to grips with the Camera Morph tag

The **Camera Morph** tag allows you to seamlessly transit between two or more cameras. Its power lies in the ability to set up multiple cameras, with exactly the framing you want, and then simply morph between them. It can be a lot less fiddly than doing it by keyframing or attaching your camera to a spline. You can even morph between moving cameras or cameras using the Motion Camera tag.

Getting ready...

In this recipe, we're going to have a quick look at using the **Camera Morph** tag and just get a feel of how it works. It's quite a simple tag but it's definitely worth having a look at this simple recipe to understand the basic principles. Open `Camera.Morph.c4d` from the content pack.

How to do it...

1. You'll see there are two cameras set up in the scene: one is animated and the other is stationary. Now, create a third camera and apply the **Camera Morph** tag to it. (Go to the **Tags** menu in the **Object Manager**. Select **Motion Camera** tag from **Camera Morph**):

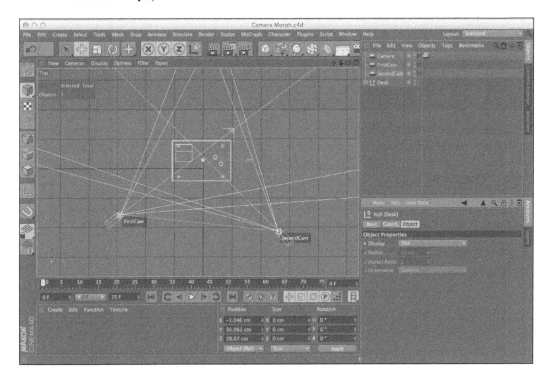

2. Now, drop **FirstCam** into the **Camera 1** link field and **SecondCam** into the **Camera 2** link field.

3. Animate the **Blend** slider to be **0%** at frame 0 and **100%** at frame 75, and look through your newly created camera. You'll see it morphs seamlessly between the two cameras.

How it works...

You should see that the **Camera Morph** tag simply interpolates between your two selected cameras. It is much the same as setting two sets of keyframes for the position and rotation of the camera, so why use it you may ask? Well, it's simply because it's a nice workflow. You can keep your two key positions up in your scene the whole time. You can then look through your cameras and tweak them easily without having to set more keyframes. Basically, it's nice and clean!

There's more...

You can also decide which elements from your original cameras you want the morph camera to inherit. You do this in the **Morph Tracks** tab. Simply tick which attributes you want to take from your set up cameras. If you want to control your **Focal Length** value independently through keyframes, then simply uncheck it.

Complex camera moving with the Multi Morph tag

The **Multi Morph** option allows us to use more than two cameras to define our motion. Set up as many cameras as you like and drop them into the **List** link field. Your morph camera will blend through each position. The **Multi Morph** option is a natural extension of the **Camera Morph** tag.

You can tweak how the camera interpolates between each camera with the **Interpolation** dropdown menu.

How to do it...

1. Drop in another two cameras into the scene we created in the previous recipe.

2. Put the cameras in some interesting positions and get nice shots lined up by looking through them.

3. Now, switch the **Source Mode** in your **Camera** tag to **Multi Morph**. This will open up a list field for you to drop your cameras into.

4. Then, drop all the cameras you want to use into the list field. Make sure that you put them in the order you want them to run through them.

5. You'll see that these new cameras have been incorporated into the camera move! It's a pretty neat way of creating complex camera moves.

6. You can tweak the way the cameras move by adjusting the **Interpolation** field to one of the three presets.

How it works...

The **Multi Morph** option works much the same way as the Simple Morph option. It simply interpolates through the various cameras we drop into the **List** field.

There's more...

You may notice a little tickbox named Stabilize. Well if you tick this, it will make your camera align its own up vector with Y. This can be useful, but by ticking this box it also allows you to drop another object into the Stabilize Object field. With this, you can now control the Banking rotation of your camera with another object. Simply drop a null (or whatever you want) into this field and keyframe the Banking (B) rotation of the object during the duration of your animation. You'll notice that you get a nice Z roll or banking movement with your camera.

5
Let there be Lights

In this chapter we will cover:

- ▶ Picking the right type of light
- ▶ Exploring shadow types
- ▶ Applying volumetric lighting
- ▶ Hot and cold – adjusting the temperature of the light
- ▶ Lighting specific objects
- ▶ Applying Global Illumination
- ▶ Lighting using the Luminance channel
- ▶ Lighting with Sky objects

Introduction

Having good lighting can turn an amateur photo into a professional photo. Photographers have countless tools such as shades, reflectors, and soft boxes to create the ideal lighting situations for their subjects. They don't just round up their models, products, interiors and the like, and start snapping away. They carefully calculate things such as what time to take the photo, what part of the image needs more light than the others, and what direction should the shadows fall. However, in Cinema 4D, you have the ability to add, position, and modify lights that seem suitable, in order to get the best-looking image.

This chapter will explore recipes that deal with the lighting. We'll learn what each type of light does, how to cast and control shadows, and how to light scenes beautifully without using the typical light objects in Cinema 4D. There's a wealth of techniques that can be borrowed from real-world photography to use within the 3D world, and you'll find that having the right lighting will make your work jump from amateur to professional, faster than the speed of light. Well, maybe not that fast, but reasonably quick.

Picking the right type of light

Stop! Look around and think about all the different light sources, lighting you right now. As I write this at my desk, I'm being lit by the sun coming in from outside, a small lamp I have on by my desk, and the glow of my computer monitor. Light can come from so many different sources, and each source has their own unique properties that differentiates them from each other. The sun is going to provide a much different kind of light than a flash light, so Cinema 4D is equipped with several different kinds of lights for getting the right look you are going for. Here's a rundown of them.

Getting ready

Open the `Light_Types.c4d` file in the C4D Content Pack and use it with this recipe.

How to do it...

This recipe explains how the different types of light work in Cinema 4D; we won't be creating anything too breathtaking. There are three scenes contained in three groups: **Omni Light**, **Spot Light**, and **Area Light**. We will be adding a specific light to each scene to discover the different ways to light our scenes, and we will discuss some other important settings available when creating lights.

1. Let's start with the most basic light, **Omni Light**. Its name is indicative of its distribution; it emits light evenly from one point outwards in all directions. Think of it as a basic incandescent light bulb, which casts light all around it in every direction (except for the base where it's screwed in). So, if we open our **Omni Light** group, we have exactly that; a light bulb with the words **Omni Light** circling around it.

2. Click once on the **Add Light Object** icon up top in the Command Palette, it will create an **Omni Light** object, by default. The setting as to what type of light you are using is found in the **General** tab of the light in the **Attribute Manager**, under the aptly named **Type** setting. Drag the light in the **Object Manager**, so it is a child of the **Bulb** group; this way, when you move the bulb around, the light will also move with it, as it's now part of the group.

 You can change the types of light whenever you want under the **Type** drop-down menu; you don't have to create a specific one and keep it that way forever.

3. The light can be positioned just as any other 3D object. Make sure you have the **Use Model mode** option and Move Tool icons selected in the Command Palette, and then slide the position of the light down towards the center of the bulb, so it will have a value of **100** in the Y position under its **Coordinates** tab. Remember, you can hold the **Shift** key while you drag to get values that snap to intervals of 10:

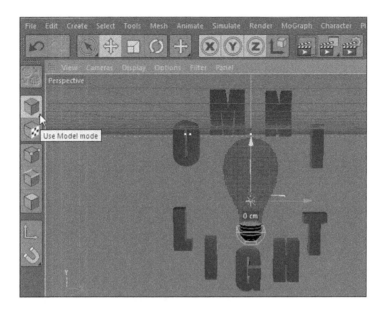

4. If you do a render preview by hitting **Ctrl + R** or **command + R,** you'll see what this **Omni Light** lighting has done. It's emitting in all directions from our bulb and it's casting light on our text, which is located slightly behind the bulb. Notice, how the extrusion of the letters receives the light, and how the sides of the letters that aren't directly exposed are dark. This illustrates the illumination path of the **Omni Light** lighting. Toggle this light OFF and deactivate it by clicking its green checkmark in the **Object Manager**; this way, you can see how it affects your scene without doing a render.

5. Let's turn OFF our **Omni Light** group by deactivating it, so switch the traffic light to two red dots to make it inactive in the Viewer and then in our render. As you made **Omni Light** a part of the group, it is deactivated along with all the other objects in the group. Now, do the opposite for the **Spot Light** group, and make it active by removing the two red dots so we can see our scene, for that, these two dots should appear gray. I have already set up this one with **Spot Light** and with shadows, so we can see exactly what this light does; you will only need to make one adjustment to it.

6. The **Spot Light** type is a directional light that shines in the direction you specify. It comes from a point and shines outward based on its **Cone Angle** value, revealing as much or as little in its path. Perhaps, think of the most famous spot light, the Bat-Signal; it's a light that shines only in the direction Commissioner James Gordon points it; that is, toward the sky, and it doesn't illuminate everything around it like the Omni-Light.

7. By default, the **Spot Light** lighting points forward in our scene along our Z axis. The **Spot Light** object inside the group is currently pointed upward, with a value **90** in **R.P.** Bring this value down to **0** in the **Coordinates** tab, or use the Rotate Tool to actually rotate your light forward in the Viewer; either way you'll reveal the text in our scene once the spot light is pointed forward.

8. The light cuts out a circular path of brightness that illuminates the background plane and our text. Under the **Details** tab for our light, change the **Outer Angle** value to **50** first, and then to **10** secondly, to test how this works. The value of **50** lights up nearly the entire plane, as now our light cone has expanded much wider, and the value **10** now creates a very narrow light source that barely reveals anything in our scene. This **Outer Angle** setting holds the key to how much your **Spot Light** actually illuminates in your environment. Set it to **35**, so we can see all of our text, and do a render preview to see the spot light in action:

 I activated the shadows in the lights that are already in place; they do not come on when you create a light by default. If you want to learn about how to apply shadows, head to the *Exploring shadow types* recipe, later in this chapter.

9. Now, deactivate your **Spot Light** group so we have an empty Viewer, and then switch on the **Area Light** group so it is now the active part of our scene. This setup has a small room with a **Figure** primitive in it and a hole cut out of the wall representing a window. The **Area Light** is already placed in the scene with shadows activated, so you only need to worry about its placement.

10. The **Area Light** emits light outward from the sides of its surface, which can be defined as any number of 2D or 3D shapes found under the **Details** tab of the **Light** properties in the **Object Attribute Manager**, by changing the **Area Shape** option from the default selection of **Rectangle** to **Disc**, **Line**, **Sphere**, and many others. As a rectangle, the light area is 2D and will emit light out from both sides in a rectangular pattern. This mimics the light cast by a defined shape like a TV screen, or in this example, the light pouring in from a rectangular window.

11. Take the **Area Light** object and rotate it **90** degrees in the **R.H** value in its **Coordinates** tab to make it parallel to the wall cut with the window. Now, change its **X** position so that it is lined up with the gap for the window, which should give you a value of **500**. Go under the **Details** tab and change the size of our **Area Light** object to **300** in both the **Size X** and **Size Y** fields; this way, it is the same size as our window.

12. Render a preview and notice how the light behaves. It directly emanates into the room from the surface of the rectangle, and casts shadows on the left side of the wall. There is no light spilling onto the right wall above or below the window, because the pattern of the light is defined by the shape of the area light. Change the **Area Shape** option from **Rectangle** to **Cube**; your render preview will now light up the right wall because the cube has a shape with faces aiming the light in that direction:

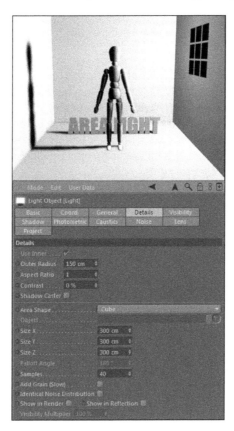

13. Those are the available types of light, and some of them have unique properties, but the two common parameters with all lights you should familiarize yourself with are **Intensity** and **Falloff. Intensity** is found under the **General** tab for the light properties, and is very straightforward. The higher the intensity, the brighter the light. You can make the **Intensity** value as high as you want, but the default **100%** is usually bright enough, and if you add multiple lights to your scene at **100%** intensity, you'll get an overexposed image, so adjust this value on your lights accordingly.

14. **Falloff** is another important parameter to account for when setting up your lights. **Falloff** has to do with how intense your light is based on the distance an object is away from it. In reality, light follows **THE INVERSE SQUARE LAW**, which states, **"The intensity of the light is inversely proportional to the square of the distance the object is away from it"**. Here's a chart that can help illustrate this concept with some sample distances:

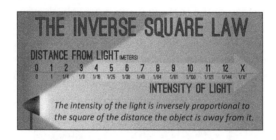

15. Looking at this curve, we can tell that light tends to fall off pretty drastically at first, but then much more gradually as the distance increases. By activating the **Falloff** parameter to **Inverse Square (Physically Accurate)**, our lights no longer extend way beyond their reach with a linear brightness; this creates a more pleasing light distribution over longer distances. The other **Falloff** types (**Linear, Squared, Inverse Square Clamped**) can achieve interesting visual results as well, but **Inverse Square** is the most accurate for real lights.

16. Note the **Radius/Decay** value here, as it can be adjusted to have the light fall off closer or farther away from the source, which is ideal when positioning light in a scene, especially an interior. Try adjusting this **Radius/Decay** value for the **Area Light** setup, and note how different values can allow the light to reach the walls or cover them in darkness:

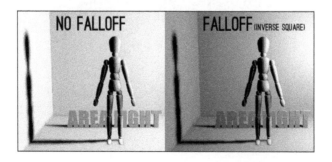

The other light objects	Description
Target Light	A special type of spot light that is added to your scene with a **Target** tag already on it, so it can remain directed to any particular object you specify within the tag.
Infinite Light	Casts your light in one direction from every point in your scene, regardless of where objects are positioned. The light source has no defined origin, and all objects are lit the same way.
IES Light	Stands for **Illuminating Engineering Society**, and it's a very realistic light that can be adjusted to have photorealistic illumination and falloff. Manufacturers of lights have specific settings that can be loaded into these lights to get the right look for their specific type of light.
Sun Light	A light source that can be customized to create sun light occurring at specific times from specific coordinates.
Square Spot	Same as a regular **Spot Light**. It just uses a square instead of a circle for its shape.
Parallel	A one-way directional light that casts rays along the z axis by default, and they can be rotated to do so in any direction. They are designed to cast light as if they are originating from very far away.
Parallel Spot	Similar to a regular spot light, but it doesn't originate from a point and create a cone; it merely casts light as a cylinder with both ends being the same size.
Square parallel spot	Same as the **Parallel Spot** light, it just uses a cube shape instead of a cylinder.

How it works...

In Cinema 4D, we have several different types of lights to work with, most notably the **Omni Light**, **Spot Light**, and **Area Light**. Their key properties, such as their position, rotation, intensity, and falloff determine the way in which they illuminate the scene. The three lights used in this example are the kinds of lights you are going to use the majority of the time. As you will find out later in the chapter, there are a few other ways to light your scene, so you'll never be short on options in your arsenal.

There's more...

Keep going with this chapter; there're more options to light your scenes than just traditional lights. A combination of various sources can make far more beautiful renders and make your designs more sophisticated.

Turning off the default light

You can create a scene and, without adding any lights, your scene is lit. How can this be? Cinema 4D starts you off with the **Default Light**, and it's bad. Your scene will never look good by relying solely on the **Default Light**. *Ever!* The **Default Light** is ON until you add some light to your scene. To turn it OFF, go to the **Render Settings** panel in the **Render** menu, and click on **Options** and you'll find a checked box with **Default Light**. Uncheck it to deactivate it.

The Inverse-Square explained

Check out this article on **photo tuts+** that will give you a photographer's perspective on how the Inverse-Square Law works in great detail:

http://photo.tutsplus.com/articles/lighting-articles/rules-for-perfect-lighting-understanding-the-inverse-square-law/.

I have seen the light

As a designer, it's your job to determine what kind of light you need to set the tone for your work, so always be thinking about things like the mood and emotion of your design. Lighting with lots of shadows and contrast can create more drama and impact, while keeping things bright and evenly lit can come off as clean, professional, and positive. Try to picture where your objects belong and what kind of sources would be lighting them in real life. Chandeliers, desk lamps, stadiums, and torches, all give off different kinds of light, so picture how they uniquely look and interact with objects in real life and try to recreate it in Cinema 4D. Use the Internet as a resource for finding diagrams of photography setups and lighting tips that match the look and feel of your scene.

Exploring shadow types

Shadows add to the realism of your renders in Cinema 4D. In everyday life, we expect to see shadows cast by objects when they block a light source, so enabling our lights to cast shadows is a no-brainer. There are a few different choices in terms of what type of shadows you want to render in your scene, and this recipe gives the details of each type.

Getting ready

Open the Beach_Shadows.c4d file from the C4D Content Pack; we'll be working with this small setup to judge the differences between shadows.

How to do it...

1. If you render a quick preview with *Ctrl + R* or *command + R*, you'll notice right away how unrealistic this scene is without shadows. The idea of having an umbrella at the beach is to block the sun so you can sit in the shade created by the shadows. The scene is lit by a light high above, representing the sun at about 12 o'clock, so the shadows should be cast directly underneath our umbrella.

2. Click on the light in the **Object Manager** labeled **Sun** and locate the **Shadows** option under the **General** tab. Besides the default option of **None**, there are three types of Shadows to choose from: **Shadow Maps (Soft)**, **Raytraced (Hard)**, and **Area**.

3. You are likely to select **Shadow Maps (Soft)** for the majority of the time to add shadows to your scene. They are simulated grayscale images that are calculated and softened based on the light intensity and uniformly applied to your scene where you have objects casting shadows. These shadows can have nice blurred edges that appear in reality when a light source is diffused and is not very intense. They are least memory-intensive, so they render the fastest of the three choices, and their quality is flexible. The size of the **Shadow Maps** option can be increased to obtain better results; this will cause render times to increase as well.

4. Select the **Shadow Maps** render option and preview your render. You'll now see relatively quickly that the **Shade** text is now blanketed in actual shade cast by the umbrella. The shadow is dark and intense but softens along the edges:

5. The edges of your shadow map look fine from far away, but switch cameras from the **Main Camera** option to the **Edge Detail** camera in the Viewer under the **Cameras** menu, and then do your render preview. The edges look a little worse the closer we get to them, which can be problematic when your camera angle requires a detailed shot with shadows being cast:

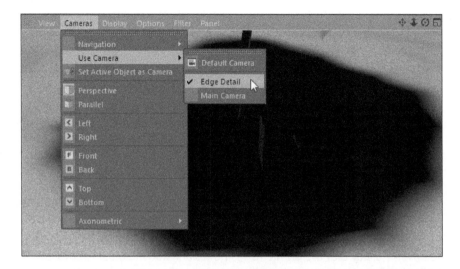

6. You can adjust the quality of your **Shadow Maps** object by going under the **Shadow** tab and selecting a higher resolution for **Shadow Map**. The default is **250x250**, the lowest setting, and it goes up to **2000x2000** or enables you to enter a custom value. The higher the resolution, the more memory is used to calculate the **Shadow Map**, so if your scene is filled with shadows and you have a high-resolution shadow map, your computer may lag and slow down:

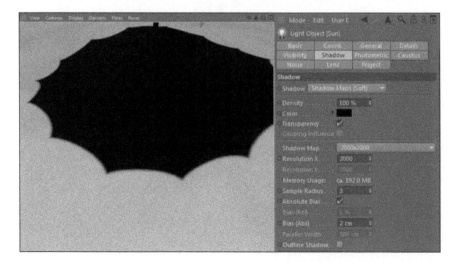

You can also increase the **Sample Radius** option to get more accurate edges for your **Shadow Map**.

7. **Raytraced (Hard)** shadows, in all honesty, you'll never likely feel the need to use the **Raytraced (Hard)** shadows option. Select this option as the **Shadow** type under the **General** tab and do a render preview. Compared to **Shadow Maps (Soft)**, the edges on this version are razor sharp; there's no softening whatsoever. The edges of your geometry cut and cast a perfect shadow onto the other objects. These can be used in very precise scenes for architecture or other technical models, but they aren't very realistic. Also, they tend to take longer than the more pleasing-looking soft shadows:

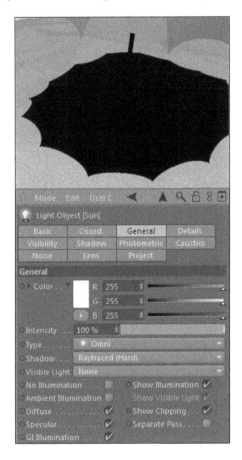

8. **Area** shadows can result in the most realistic shadows of the three choices, but they also take the longest to render, by far. They have softer edges like **Shadow Maps (Soft)**, but they factor in distance between lights and objects to vary the intensity of the edges. If Object A is very close to Object B and the casting shadows, you'll get much more intense shadows than if they were farther apart.

9. If you select the **Area** shadow and do a render preview, you'll see a little more variation in the shadow edges than the **Shadow Map (Soft)**, because the landscape varies and the **Area** shadow is calculating this into the render. You'll notice a little noise that can occur using **Area** shadows, but you can eliminate this using the quality controls under the **Shadow** tab by increasing the **Accuracy** setting, as well as both the **Minimum Samples** and **Maximum Samples** drop-down. Increase **Minimum Samples** to **100** and **Maximum Samples** to **150**, and then do a render preview and check out the result. Notice the softer edges that seem to contour better with the sandy terrain:

The **Area** shadows increases your render time, but they can provide a more realistic and higher-quality result in a lot of cases. I recommend testing your render to see if you get a noticeable quality increase with area shadows versus shadow maps, and if you can afford to add the extra time on the render. These are the kinds of decisions you get to make as a 3D artist.

How it works...

Of the three options you have to add shadows to, **Shadow Map (Soft)** is going to be your best choice, the majority of the time, because it renders fast and can look pretty realistic when the quality is adjusted. **Raytraced (Hard)** is an unnatural style to use, but could be used for more technical-looking renders. The **Area** shadows can provide even more accurate shadow details, but their long render times make it a less-likely choice for complicated scenes and longer animations.

Applying volumetric lighting

In most instances light is invisible: we don't see the light but we know it's there. However, there are times when we want our light to appear to have volume, like if we were creating spotlights at a concert or car headlights shining forward. Light can be visible in instances like this where we have something like a smoke, fog, or rain in the atmosphere. So let's learn how to activate visible light in this recipe, where we will be creating a flashlight shining in a dark room.

Getting ready

Open the `Flashlight.c4d` file in the C4D Content Pack and use it with this recipe.

How to do it...

1. First, let's take a look at our scene. It's a small room with a flashlight in the center, and there is a circuit breaker panel on the wall. Let's simulate that the power has gone out and we need to use our flashlight to find it. Start by turning down the **Intensity** option of the light labeled **Ambient Light** to something very small, such as **10**%; this will give us just a tiny amount of light so we won't be working in complete darkness.

2. In order to simulate the light coming from a flashlight, we will use a spot light because it will be directional and we can point it somewhere specific. Click-and-hold on the **Add Light Object** icon in the Command Palette and add a **Spot Light** object to our scene, then move the spot light into the grouped object labeled **Flash Light** in the **Object Manager**. This way, when we move our flashlight, the actual light will be connected and moved as part of it too. Lower its **Y** position down to **-200** and rotate it towards the sky by entering **90** in the **R.P** field in the **Coordinates** tab of the **Attribute Manager**. The light is now originating from inside the flashlight.

3. The light is active, but we can't see it. We can change that by going under the light's **General** tab in the **Attribute Manager** and changing our settings on the **Visible Light** menu. It defaults to **None**, but it comes with three other options: **Visible**, **Volumetric**, and **Inverse Volumetric**.

4. The **Visible** setting makes the entire scope of your light visible, and it passes light through any objects in your scene; it isn't obscured by any 3D surface. Select this option for your spot light and do a render preview by hitting *Ctrl + R* or *command + R*, and you'll see that there is light inside our flashlight, but it's spilling out from the side. This is not what we want. We want the housing of the flashlight to direct the light outwards for a more realistic look.

5. The **Volumetric** setting is the key to this issue; it factors in the objects in its path and blocks the light accordingly. Select the **Volumetric** option and do another render preview, and you'll notice right away that this is exactly what we want: the light cone is emitting based on the width of the flashlight and not pouring out of the geometry:

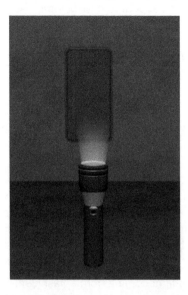

6. **Inverse Volumetric** is exactly what it sounds like, it applies a volumetric light, and then inverts it so that light emits from where it normally gets blocked. So, instead of the shadows being created by light being obscured, that part becomes the actual light being emitted. This can create some cool light-ray effects when done properly, but we want to use the **Volumetric** setting for this recipe.

7. So, we have our volumetric light emitting from our flashlight, and it's created a cone that we can now point our circuit breaker panel to. You're probably thinking the cone is way too short, and you are certainly correct. However, we can lengthen it by going under the **Visibility** tab in the **Attribute Manager** and increasing the **Outer Distance** option to a much larger value like **4000**. Now, the light cone extends way further and will reach our back wall easily.

8. Next, go under the **Details** tab and shrink the **Outer Angle** value to **20**, so that the cone of the light doesn't spread far beyond the visible light cone. Next, take the entire **Flash Light** group and rotate it **-90** in the **R.P** setting in the **Coordinates** tab. Now, it's pointed right at our panel. Render a preview and check out the result. You can see our light cone shining towards our back wall and illuminating the circuit breaker panel. Switch cameras from the **Front Camera** to the **Overhead Camera** to see the full cone from above, and you can get the full effect of our volumetric light:

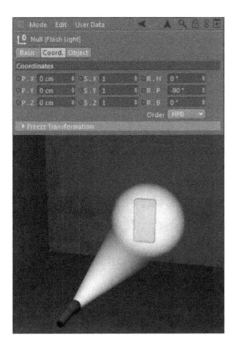

9. Let's take this a step further and actually demonstrate how this light is actually volumetric and not just visible. There's an object titled **Flash Light Text** in the **Object Manager**, and it's inactive. Activate it by changing the red traffic light dots to green or the default gray to turn them on. I positioned a piece of text that says **Flash Light** that appears backwards, in the same spot as our flashlight. Select the **Flash Light** group and change its **Z** position in the **Coordinates** tab to **-1500** to bring our flashlight further back so they aren't on top of each other.

10. Change the **Shadow** setting in the **General** tab to **Shadow Maps (Soft)** so we can now cast some shadows on our wall. Do a render preview and you'll now see that our text is casting a shadow on the back wall and blocking our volumetric light:

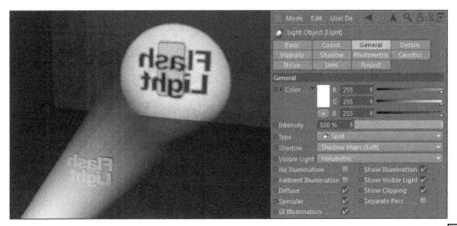

11. The visible light will cast shadows as well, but they don't get blocked by 3D geometry. To prove this, I've supplied a reverse camera, so switch from the **Front Camera** to the **Rear Camera** in the Viewer. In this view, we are close to our text with the flashlight coming from behind and backlighting our text. Switch the **Visible Light** from **Volumetric** to **Visible** and do a render preview. It will look as if a soft, glowing fog has descended on our scene. To get a true backlit effect, switch **Visible Light** back to **Volumetric** and render that preview to see a much more interesting-looking effect. We now have light rays splitting from behind our letters since the **Volumetric** setting is causing our visible light to be blocked by the geometry in its path:

How it works...

Cinema 4D has different settings for making our light visible, and the **Volumetric** setting is the most commonly used group. The **Volumetric** lighting is a popular effect that makes it appear as if your 3D objects are blocking part of your light source. Our flashlight cone is visible and is blocked by our text that casts shadows onto our wall. The two other settings could be useful in some instances, but this effect creates visible light and can make some nice backlighting visuals when applied behind our 3D objects.

There's more...

Check out the **Noise** tab under the **Light Object** settings in the **Attribute Manager**. This can create varying density to your visible light, so you won't have a perfectly clean light cone if you so choose. It can even be animated so that you can simulate smoke or dust moving through the light. Also, try the **Dust** and the **Dithering** settings under the **Visibility** tab to add a little noise to the light; it may help prevent banding in your renders.

Hot and cold – adjusting the temperature of the light

If you have a background in photography, you'll know that different lights have different color temperatures; therefore, they can illuminate a setting to appear warmer or cooler. Lights with lower color temperatures (measured in degrees Kelvin) cast light that appears more orange or yellow, while lights that have higher temperatures give off a colder tint that appears blue. Certain scenes should have a light that feels warmer or colder, and by changing the temperature of the lights in Cinema 4D we can create a tone within our 3D environment. Cinema 4D has multiple methods to cast colored light on your scene, which can result in a more realistic and pleasing image.

Getting ready

Open the `Warm_Wine_Scene.c4d` file in the C4D Content Pack. We are going to use this scene to demonstrate three different ways to warm up the tone of our wine bar.

How to do it...

Start by opening the project and picture yourself at a nice little outdoor Italian wine bar in Tuscany approaching dusk. You're outside, so the orange-red setting sun is going to be your light source. The objects in this scene are mostly red, orange, brown, and yellow. This scene is begging to have some warm light added to it, and we will learn three methods for doing so:

- Adding gels
- Coloring the light
- Adjusting the color temperature.

Adding gels

1. If you've ever been in a studio or production facility, you may know how gels work. Basically, they are a special type of plastic that is placed over a light designed to tint the light a different color. It's how you make a sunset scene occur when you are shooting in a basement. Cinema 4D works similarly, by placing a material over the light with a specified color, we can make the light change colors.

2. Look in the **Material Manager** and find the material named **Warm Gel**. We will discuss materials in depth in *Chapter 6, A Material World*, but just know that this material acts as a somewhat transparent tint to place over our light.

3. Place the warm gel material on the lights in the scene, and hit *Ctrl + R* or *command + R* to do a quick render preview. You'll notice the light is tinted in the render, but the colors stay true to their materials when editing in the Viewer. Your scene should feel warmer now with the gel on it. This takes care of method number one.

Use this method when you have multiple lights in your scene. That way you can make one adjustment to the material and have it apply the same effect to all the lights in your scene at once, instead of making changes to them individually.

Coloring the light

This method is probably the easiest and most straightforward way to adjust the temperature of your scene. Each light has a color control under its **General** tab. Delete the gel materials off your lights from the last part of the exercise, so we are back to the normal white light. Use the slider to adjust your color values for both lights to the same numbers as in the last method: **255** in the red, **207** in the green, and **187** in the blue. You'll notice right away that the color of your scene in the Viewer shifts to be warmer without rendering, such as with the gels. Render your scene and preview your result, and feel the warmth.

Adjusting the Color Temperature

Our third method for warming our scene is to simulate actual **Color Temperature** measurements within our light controls. Adjust your light color from the last exercise so all three color values are set to **255** for white light. Twirl down the small black triangle to the left of the word color to open the **Use Temperature** checkbox. Select this box and you'll see an immediate difference to the tone of your scene. A default **Color Temperature** value of **3,600** gives off a very warm tint, but this is a little strong. If you enter a temperature value of **6,500**, you'll see your scene revert back to the typical default white light. Take note, that the **Color** option of the light automatically jumps according to the value you type into the **Color Temperature** field. Enter a value of **5000** and you'll see that this value is reasonably close to the values we entered in the previous two examples.

Whichever way you choose is an acceptable method to adjust the color temperature of your lights. They all end up yielding a similar result. The goal is just to give off a warmer light, not just strictly plain white light when the scene calls for something warmer or colder:

How it works...

Our wine scene feels much more natural with our tinted light, and the result can be achieved using any one of our three methods. Notice, how the orange picks up nicely on the lighter parts of the scene such as the cheese and the wine label. The light is not as bright when we tint our scene, because it is slightly closer to black now than the pure white light, but this can be fixed in any number of color-correcting methods after rendering your file. As is the case here, simulating actual light temperatures and sources can only help make your scene look more convincing.

There's more...

Try cooling our scene instead by adjusting our color values to yield a light blue. It doesn't look particularly good in this instance, but it's the way to go if you are modeling a scene that deals with technology, an office setting, a laboratory, or a cold winter to name a few. Pick the right temperature based on the setting of your scene.

Fix it in post, always!

The idea here is to get your color and tone as close as possible for visualization purposes. Your final enhancements should be made in compositing programs such as After Effects and Photoshop; they help you get your scene as close as possible before rendering out from Cinema 4D. Cinema 4D has some fine-tuning capabilities, but other programs are much better suited to get your image absolutely perfect in terms of brightness, contrast, and saturation, so just try to be close and touch it up after you render.

Gauge your temperatures

If you would like to learn more about how color temperature works with different types of light, check out the following website for a handy chart that lists what kind of lights register at what temperature http://www.schorsch.com/en/kbase/glossary/cct.html.

Where did that Ivy come from?
The Ivy Grower 1.2 plugin for Cinema 4D is available for free at:
http://www.kuroyumes-developmentzone.com.

See also

Be sure to check the recipes on **Global Illumination** and using the **Sky** objects; we will make this render look much better than it does in this recipe, later in the chapter.

Lighting specific objects

One of the unique features about lighting in a 3D application such as Cinema 4D is you can apply lights to your scene and select specific objects to receive, or not receive, light from any particular source. *Think about how awesome that is for a second!* There's no way you can possibly pull this off in real life; you can't open your refrigerator and tell the light inside only to illuminate food you think tastes good or only food you should be eating while on your diet. Whatever is in the path of light gets illuminated here in the real world, and a photographer often has to go to great lengths to try to dodge and burn, which is the process of adding or removing light from specific objects or parts of the composition. Lucky for you, with the 3D designer we have options in Cinema 4D that allow us to achieve this rather easily.

Getting ready

Use the `Beach_Shadows.c4d` file from the C4D Content Pack that was utilized in the earlier recipe about shadows. If it's still open and you didn't save over it, revert it back to its original point by going into the **File** menu and selecting **Revert to Saved**.

How to do it...

1. Start by selecting the light labeled **Sun** and applying **Shadow Maps** as the shadow type in the light's **General** tab. Hit *Ctrl + R* or *command + R* for a render preview of our beach scene, and you'll see our shadows and how dark and unrealistic they appear. When you go to the beach and put up an umbrella, it doesn't shroud you in complete darkness like your current render looks. The **Shade** text should be darker because of the shadows, but not pitch black like it is now. We are going to add another light that will brighten just our **Shade** text and fill in those dark shadows with a little more light.

2. Add a new **Light Object** by clicking on the Light icon in the Command Palette. This creates an omni light at the origin of our scene, which fits nicely right under our umbrella. Double-click on its name and change it to `Fill Light 1`. Check to see what our new light has done to our shade by doing a render preview, and you'll see that it has almost wiped out all of our shadows, completely:

3. Let's do two things to improve this effect immediately. Slide the light forward towards the camera by giving it a **P.Z** value of **-50**, just so that it is lighting the face of our text. Then, we are going to need to crank the intensity of this light down; it's way too bright. So find the light's **Intensity**, which is set to **100%** in the **General** tab and reduce it to about **30%**, then do a render preview. Our scene looks much better now; we can see the detail of our text while it remains in the shadows:

4. However, this fill light that we added is now brightening everything in the scene, and in my opinion the underside of the umbrella now appears too bright. You can kind of tell that it is being lit from underneath by the light under the umbrella, and it should be somewhat darker since no direct light should be able to get to it. Therefore, let's use a versatile feature of 3D lighting in Cinema 4D to exclude this part of our umbrella from being lit too brightly by our fill light.

5. Select your new light in the **Object Manager** and select the **Project** tab of the light in the **Attribute Manager**. The default mode is set to **Exclude**, followed by an **Objects** list that is empty. So, by default, the light isn't excluding anything and is lighting all the objects in the project. If you switch the mode from **Exclude** to **Include**, the light basically becomes inactive because no object is included in the list. Leave it on **Exclude** for this exercise.

6. Go to your **Object Manager** and find the **Umbrella Top** and the **Supports** objects inside the **Umbrella** group and drag them into the **Objects** field. We have now selected specific parts of a specific group to not receive any illumination from this light. Meanwhile, if you view a render preview, you'll see that everything except the underside of the umbrella remains lit by our fill light:

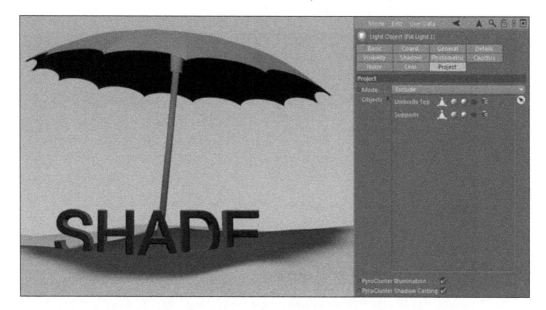

7. The underside of the umbrella looked too bright before, but now compared to the rest of our scene it looks too dark. We can use a different light to find a middle ground between these two extremes, and this light will only brighten up the umbrella and nothing else using the **Include** setting.

8. Take your fill light and duplicate it in the **Object Manager**, but holding *Ctrl* or the *command* key and dragging to another spot in the **Object Manager**. Rename this light as **Fill Light 2**. Because we copied it we will have the same exact settings, but with a few minor tweaks it will behave exactly the opposite.

9. Firstly, adjust the **Intensity** (of this light) to just **15%** to reduce the amount it will fill in. Next, go to the **Project** tab and instead of excluding the **Umbrella Top**, flip it to include the **Umbrella Top**. Now, we are using the feature to light only the umbrella top, and our preview will now look much better, because the underside of the umbrella doesn't appear quite as dark as before, and this is a much more realistic result:

How it works...

You can pick and choose what objects you want to be lit by your lights when designing in Cinema 4D. By setting up and positioning fill lights, we can brighten areas that seem too dark when hidden in shadows. Lights can be set to include or exclude objects; therefore, you can mix numerous objects and numerous lights to get very specific lighting results.

There's more...

You can achieve a similar effect by adjusting the **Density** setting in the **Shadow** tab of a light object. Start with this base scene again and lower the **Density** value of the **Sun** to a value like **70%**, and you'll get a look that is closer to what we did with the fill lights.

Turning a positive into a negative

Another unique feature of Cinema 4D is that lights can have a negative intensity value; hence they can subtract light from a scene. All you do is add a light object and set the **Intensity** to a negative value; you can remove light from certain areas of your scene if you need to.

See also

Check out the next recipe, *Applying Global Illumination*, to see how to get the best looking lighting and shadows in Cinema 4D.

Applying Global Illumination

Setting up these basic lights and shadows will only take your renders this far. To get the best interaction between your lights and the objects, you'll want to activate **Global Illumination**, which is a feature of 3D software that simulates the concept that objects are lit not just by lights, but by the light rays bouncing off all objects around your scene. **Global Illumination** is quick to set up and complicated to adjust, but often it has the power to greatly enhance the quality of your lighting. This recipe is an overview of what **Global Illumination** does and how it can help you in your 3D design.

The following example will mimic a studio setup with a subject being filmed on a green screen. If you have ever done any keying with video footage that was shot on a green screen, you would have probably encountered a light spill. A light spill is a reflection of the surrounding area on the subject you are trying to film. In this green screen scenario, it can be hard to eliminate this spill because the surrounding screens take the visible light that is making them green and reflects it back out, where they seem to bleed into other objects that are also slightly reflective. There are several tools and techniques for doing **Spill Suppression** in the other programs, but instead we are going to use Cinema 4D to intentionally create some light spill to simulate this real-world concept.

Getting ready

We are going to use the GI_Green_Screen.c4d file for this recipe.

How to do it...

1. Hit the render preview command, *Ctrl + R* or *command + R*, and check what our setup is going for here. It's a subject being shot on a green screen holding two objects with reflective surfaces, and the shadows come from two lights with a low-quality **Shadow Map** setting:

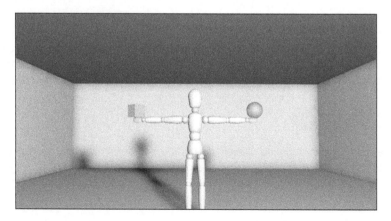

2. Switch cameras in the Viewer to the camera labeled **Spill Suppression**. This will give us a closer look at the edges of our subject. Now, do a render preview from this camera angle and you'll notice that the back of our subject is covered in dark black shadows with no direct light, and the sphere the subject is holding is reflecting the green screen behind it to some extent. In some instances, this light setup may suit you just fine, but applying **Global Illumination** will enhance the quality of the lighting and shadows in your scene by reflecting the light off all the surfaces in your scene and combining them together:

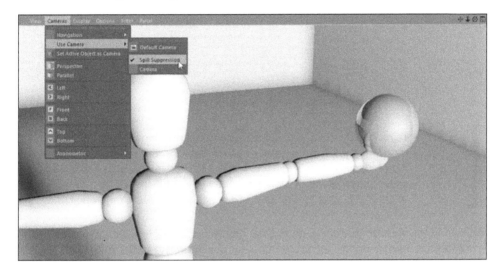

3. Switch back to the original camera view and then navigate to the **Render Settings** inside the **Render** menu. Click on the **Effects** button on the left-hand side and find **Global Illumination**. Selecting this option gives you a checkbox with many options that we don't necessarily need to touch; they come preconfigured. Now, go back to your scene and hit the render preview command.

4. During the rendering process, you'll notice a different-looking scene as Cinema 4D cooks up your image. Once your image has been previewed, you should notice two things. First, our render took much longer than before, and second, our green screen setup now looks much better:

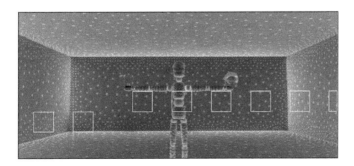

5. Notice, how more evenly the light is distributed. That's because GI (short for **Global Illumination**) fills in crevices and corners where light technically gets blocked directly, but it can still receive light from an indirect source:

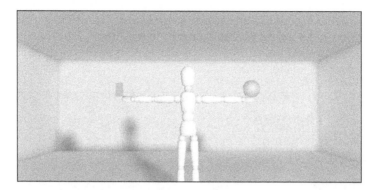

 Think back to our previous recipes with the beach umbrella. The area underneath our umbrella should receive some indirect light from the sand. The sand should reflect some light upwards and fill in our shadows, which can be accomplished by using GI. Go back and add it to your render after this recipe and note the difference.

6. Our shadows look much smoother than before, as the GI has sampled our image and provided more accurate measurements for our **Shadow Maps (Soft)** to be generated with. Notice, how smooth the edges are and the even density that exists across the entire shadow. The image is also much brighter because the light rays bouncing around the room are providing indirect light, thereby increasing the overall brightness of the render.

7. Switch the camera in the Viewer to the **Spill Suppression** camera, and then render a new preview. Notice, how the shadows on the back of our subject are now much less harsh and have a hint of green spilling on them. GI is taking the rays from our surrounding green screen and applying them to our subject. The following is a much more realistic look, and it simulates a light spill that exists to an extent in any kind of studio shoot such as this setup. Take note of our reflective sphere as well; the green spill is much smoother and well-blended compared to what it was without GI:

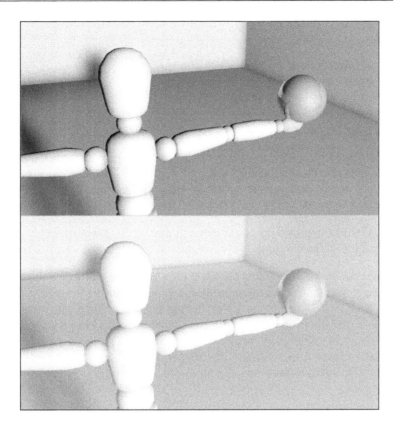

8. Replace the green material with the blue material to view the same process take place with a different color. The surrounding color is reflected and blended with the other objects in our scene.

How it works...

Global Illumination is an effect to add to your render that can simulate how light doesn't just flatly emit from a source in a scene, but rather interacts with all the different objects and surfaces. The result is a much more realistic render, at the expense of render time. **Global Illumination** can be applied to any scene, but it shouldn't be applied to every scene. Take note of how much longer a single frame takes to render with GI turned on. If each frame takes ten times longer to render with GI, then your entire render will end up taking ten times longer. Frames that have more geometry and detail take longer as well, so it becomes a decision if the improvement in the lighting with GI is worth the greatly increased render time.

There's more...

The **Global Illumination** settings are very scientific and complicated. You can often just apply the defaults and feel content with the results, or maybe reduce the settings such as **Stochastic Samples** and **Record Density** to still get GI interaction but speed up your render. If you want to know a bit more about what some of the options are to adjust GI parameters, the following is a brief rundown.

If you're using GI for animation then you may notice some flickering. This maybe because your **Stochastic Samples** and **Record Density** are set too low or sometimes it is nothing to do with those settings. You can try using the **IR + QMC (Camera Animation)** or the **IR + QMC (Full Animation)** settings in the **GI Mode** but be warned, the renders will take a very long time.

As a rule, I try and use the lowest settings I can and then build up values until I get a result I'm happy with. Often the default settings are too high, and thus take too long, for a lot of uses.

Irradiance Cache mode (**IR**) and **Quasi Monte Carlo** (**QMC**) are the two sampling methods that can be used to generate **Global Illumination**. IR is a newer method used since Cinema 4D release 12, and QMC represents an older method used in the previous versions of Cinema 4D. The settings under the **Irradiance Cache** tab can be increased to get a more accurate render, or decreased to render your image faster. It's a form of give-and-take that you'll have to test out in your individual scenes as it varies depending on your project. Similarly with QMC, you can increase the **Sample Count** to get a more accurate render, with the trade-off being that it takes longer.

You don't need to know how a car is built in order to drive it, and you don't need to know all the precise scientific processes behind the GI algorithms to get a good render. The defaults are set for a reason: they provide a better render with considerations given to keeping your render times, acceptable. For example, if you are taking photographs, you can get great photos with your camera set to its automatic settings, but for professional-quality photographs you'll probably need to fine-tune the camera's settings.

There could be a whole chapter filled with dense, technical information about **Global Illumination**, though we're just going to remain basic and only apply it when we need it. If you want to read an incredibly detailed overview of **Global Illumination** in Cinema 4D, check out this link to an excellent article by Michael Vance: `http://mvpny.com/R11GITutorial/R11GITutorial_Part1.html`.

Ambient Occlusion

There's an option in Cinema 4D called **Ambient Occlusion**, which can help add some realism to your renders. **Ambient Occlusion** helps simulate the way light falls in small details, gaps, and creases where objects meet each other. Simply activate it in **Render Settings** in the same way you activate **Global Illumination** and you'll notice a pleasing difference. You can take down the **Minimum** and **Maximum** samples if you wish to decrease your render times.

This will make the effect grainier so you'll have to judge how far you push this. You can even change the color of the **Ambient Occlusion** if you wish on the gradient slider. The effect will be subtle but can help you add sophistication to your images. Feel free to increase the maximum distance if you wish to spread it further.

You should really try and experiment with **Ambient Occlusion** and get a feel of how it adds to a render. You can also apply **Ambient Occlusion** within a **Shader**. Simply go to the channel in your Shader you wish to load it into and then flip down the **Texture** menu and go to **Effects/ Ambient Occlusion**. All the same settings that are in the render settings are accessible. The advantage of loading it into a Shader is that your render times should be quicker as you're selectively applying it rather than adding it to your whole scene. You should load it into your diffusion channel but you can be more creative and load it into a **Luminance** channel.

But, as always, don't be afraid to play around with it and really crank the settings.

Lighting using the Luminance channel

Our last recipe showed that you don't even need light objects to light your scene in Cinema 4D. You can emit light from any object if you apply a material with a value in the **Luminance** channel. This recipe shows how you can model and simulate actual light sources instead of simply relying on Cinema 4D's basic light objects to illuminate your scenes.

Getting ready

Open and work with the `Candle_Flame.c4d` project file for this recipe. We are going to be lighting candles.

How to do it...

1. Our scene consists of the word **Candles** behind five evenly-spaced candles with no flames to light them and with **Global Illumination** activated. If you do a render preview with *Ctrl + R* or *command + R*, you'll see complete darkness. That's because **Global Illumination** disregards the default light, and we have nothing else providing light. We need something to light our scene, so we are going to do it by candle-lighting.

2. Start by deactivating our **Candle** group in the editor and the renderer, so we can have some space to work in. Then, add a **Cone** primitive, rename it to **Flame**, and reduce its size to have a **Top Radius** of **0**, a **Bottom Radius** of **10**, and a **Height** of **40**. Click on the **Caps** tab and check the boxes to enable the **Top** and **Bottom** caps, and then reduce the **Bottom Height** to **10** and **Radius** to **20**. You should have something that resembles a very smooth candle flame, though we need to add a little movement and variation to it so it behaves naturally like a real flame.

3. We are going to add two different **Formula** deformers to our flame so it dances around a bit. Click on the **Deformers** icon in the Command Palette and find the **Formula** deformer and add it to your **Object Manager**, and then drag the deformer so it's a child of your flame. Now, reduce the size of the deformer by clicking on its **Object** tab in the **Attribute Manager** and reduce the size in each dimension to **40**; this way, the effect is applied to a more concentrated area.

4. Their default formula is a little intimidating; it reads **Sin((u+t)*2.0*pi)*0.2**. If you are allergic to math, have no fear, we won't need to delve into the construction of this formula. We are only concerned with the last number, the **0.2** value that controls the frequency of our formula. Change this value from **0.2** to **0.1** and note how the flame wiggles slower now.

> Whenever you see a formula that looks confusing and doesn't seem to make any sense to you, resort to trial and error. Changing the default numerical values will most likely affect the amplitude or frequency of the transformation being applied by your formula. It won't ruin your animation just to test it out.

5. This alters our flame in the Y dimension; now let's do the exact same transformation for our X dimension. Select your **Formula** deformer in the **Object Manager** and hold *Ctrl* or the *command* key and drag to make a copy. Place the deformer as a child of the **Flame** object just like the first one. Now, under the **Object** tab in the **Attribute Manager**, change the **Effect** drop menu from **Y Radial** to **X Radial**. It's that simple. Now, our flame is moving in the X dimension as well. Place this entire group of objects inside a **HyperNURBS** object to smooth out our flame, and rename it **Flame:**

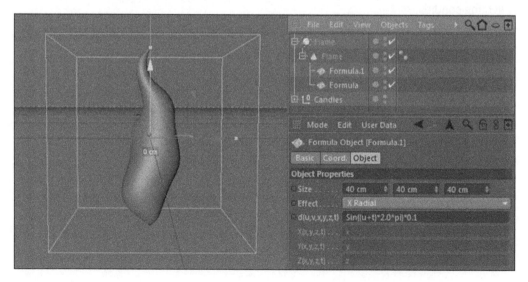

6. We now have a **Flame** object for use with our five candles. Highlight the **Flame** object inside the **Object Manager**, go under the **Tools** menu up top, and move under the **Arrange Objects** submenu hitting **Duplicate**, next. In the **Attribute Manager**, you have an option for the number of copies to make. Enter a value **4** in the field, because we already have one as our original, and then open the newly-created group. Bring in the original flame, so we have a group of five.

7. Next, activate the **Candles** group so we can see them again, and then align a flame on top of each of the candle wicks by switching between various views such as the **Top** view and the **Left/Right** views. Slide them into place by moving them with the Move Tool and holding the **Shift** key so you get nice even values. They should all have a Y position value of **60** and a Z position value of **175**. One flame should be at **-450** in the X position, one at **-225**, one at **0**, one at **225**, and one at **450**.

8. Our flames should now be in place on each candle, but we want to add a little bit more random movements to each one so they don't appear the same. Pick one flame and add a **Vibrate** tag to it, under the **Cinema 4D tags** menu inside the **Object Manager**. Enable all the position and rotation parameters by clicking their checkboxes. For position, enter a value **2** for each **Amplitude** field, and also leave the default value of **2** for **Frequency**. The rotation should be set to **20** degrees in each field with a **Frequency** of just **2**. Preview your scene in the timeline and you'll see the flame will now dance around a bit more than before.

9. Now that we have this random movement programmed to our satisfaction, we can simply copy the tag to the other four flames by doing our *Ctrl* or *command* key click-and-drag. Once on our flames, enter a different value for each tag under the **Seed** field so that they will all take a slightly different pattern under the same parameters. Feel free to test out each **Seed** value to find your favorite; it only goes up to infinity so take your pick. I recommend **7,349,451**, it's perfection.

10. So, now each flame dances slightly differently in place, let's have it give off some light now. Double-click on an empty spot in the **Material Manager** to create a new material. Uncheck the default **Color** and **Specular** options, and click on the **Luminance** channel. The **Luminance** channel gives your material the power to illuminate; it gives off light from whatever object it's placed on.

11. Click on the triangle button in the **Texture** field and find the **Gradient** option to add to our **Luminance** channel texture. Set the gradient type to **Circular**. Instead of the default black and white colors, change the left-hand side color value to orange, leave the right-hand side value as white, but double-click on the gradient to add another knot towards the middle, and apply a bright yellow color to it. Click the checkbox on the left-hand side menu for the **Glow** channel, and add a glow to our material. You should drop down the **Outer Strength** field from **500** to **100** so it's a little more subtle. Name this material as **Flame**.

12. This material is going to emit an orange and yellow light from wherever we place it, which you'll have probably guessed will be our flames, so place the material on each one of the flames. **Global Illumination** uses the information in the **Luminance** channel and applies it to the other objects in your scene. If you do a quick render preview, you see our Global Illumination being applied; our scene is now lit by candles:

13. The default settings don't really light up our candles and the text enough, so we can increase the amount of light the flames give through **Global Illumination**. Open up the **Flame** material in the **Material Manager** and click on the **Illumination** option all the way towards the bottom of the left-hand side menu. Towards the top, you have options to allow your material to generate or receive more GI. Increase the **Strength** option under **Generate GI** to 1000%, for the flame. Then, switch to the **Text** material and under its **Illumination** options increase the **Receive GI–Strength** option to **500%** as well. This will boost the amount of light received from our flames by the text in the scene and the amount of light given off by our flames.

14. Do a new render and see how our scene is now exclusively lit by candles. No light objects were required:

How it works...

The **Luminance** channel allows you to generate light from a material and place it on any object in the scene. **Global Illumination** needs to be active for you to see the light to emit from your objects and light up your scene.

There's more...

This is incredibly useful when lighting scenes with light sources that need to be seen by the camera, such as our candle flames. Think of other objects you can easily model and have their **Luminance** channel to be your light source for the environment; a bank of fluorescent light bulbs, glow sticks, neon signs, and sirens to name a few.

More flicker to your flicker

The only thing I would add to this would be to have the intensity of the **Luminance** channel rise and fall to simulate the light dancing. You can learn the skills to pull this off in *Chapter 9, XPresso Shots*.

Lighting with Sky objects

Now that we've learned how to apply **Global Illumination**, we can discover yet another way to light your environments inside Cinema 4D. Using **High Dynamic Range** (**HDR**) images as a material on a **Sky** object can provide all the light we need inside Cinema 4D. It works great in scenes with reflective surfaces because we can use actual HDR photographs to light our scene that will appear in our reflections. This eliminates the need to position and set up lights; we just need to rely on the HDR image to distribute light among our scene.

Getting ready

Open the `Warm_Wine_Scene.c4d` again. We are going to light this image with an HDR image. Revert to the original image by hitting **Revert to Saved** in the **File** menu of the project.

How to do it...

1. Our wine scene is currently lit by two point lights; we no longer need these because we are going to use an HDR image for our lighting, so delete the light objects from the **Object Manager**. Next, go inside the **Create** menu, into the **Environment** submenu, and find **Sky**. This adds a **Sky** object, which is essentially a sphere wrapped around your entire project environment. You'll have to switch OFF the main camera to see it because we are in tight on our wine bar. It just appears as a gray background, so we need to add a material to it.

2. Double-click on an empty spot in the **Material Manager** to create a new material. Open the material and name it HDR Sky, and deselect the **Color** and **Specular** channels. Now, check the box next to the **Luminance** channel and let's load our HDR image into the **Texture** field. Click on the ellipses button and navigate on your computer to load our HDR image in the C4D Content Pack; its filename is DH-ITALY06SN.hdr. Next, take the material and apply it to our **Sky** object by dragging it from the **Material Manager** to the new **Sky** object in the **Object Manager**.

3. We need to activate **Global Illumination** in order to see the optimal effect of our HDR image, so go into your **Render** menu and select the **Edit Render Settings...** option. Then, hit the **Effects** tab on the left-hand column and check on **Global Illumination**.

4. In this case, our camera blocks out the **Sky** object so we don't need to worry about it being seen by our camera, but be sure to check out *The Compositing tag* recipe in *Chapter 7, Rendering Strategy*, because this is crucial for scenes where we don't want our sky to appear yet still lighting our scene. To get the optimal render lighting with an HDR object, **Global Illumination** should be activated. Do a render preview; it should take a bit with our GI turned on, but the result will be much nicer than our recipe from earlier where we lit our wine scene without GI.

5. As you can see, we are illuminating our 3D scene with just an image and nothing else. The beauty of this HDR image is that it's an actual setting in Italy, providing a realistic source of light and surrounding for our scene. Note the reflections in the bowl, wine bottle, and glasses; you can see them reflecting parts of our HDR image, which are highly useful when you want the scene to appear to be taking place in a particular environment. The wine scene looks significantly better when rendered with an HDR sky and **Global Illumination**, rather than just a simple light setup. The increase in render times is completely justified:

How it works...

An HDR image contains far more light and color information than regular compressed images such as JPEGs. By adding these images to the **Luminance** channel, Cinema 4D takes these images and applies them as light when our material is applied to the **Sky** object. With minimum setup and some **Global Illumination** effects, we have a great-looking render with well-distributed, unique lighting and actual images in our reflections.

There's more...

The best part about using this HDR image was that it was a scene from Italy, and it fit in perfectly with the scene that was built. There are tons of resources for HDR images on the web, to download for free or purchase. A quick query on any search engine will give you ample resources. You can build a nice collection of images that can be used to light your exterior or interior scenes. HDR image lighting is a quick alternative to using traditional lights and can often achieve far superior results. The images in the C4D Content Pack were provided by Dosch Design; they have many great HDR image packs and other useful design tools available at http://www.doschdesign.com.

Creating your own HDR

If you are into photography and have the right equipment, you can create your own HDR images and use them with minimal problems in Cinema 4D. Check out this site for more info on HDR photos: `http://www.hdrsoft.com/resources/dri.html`.

And, there's even a software where you can create your own images without actually taking any pictures. Check out the program, HDR Light Studio, at: `http://www.hdrlightstudio.com`.

Some of your renders will benefit from adding **Ambient Occlusion**. Mentioned earlier in this chapter, it adds finer details to your shadows and gives you some more realistic-looking shading in tighter areas and crevices in your scene. It can be added under the **Render Settings** window from inside the **Effect** tab. This scene benefits some from adding **Ambient Occlusion;** note the better shading inside the holes in the cheese. But be careful, render times will sky rocket by adding this in conjunction with **Global Illumination**. Sometimes your project will benefit from using one, the other, or both. You'll have to test it out and see if the effects are worth the wait:

See also

Check out the *The Compositing tag* recipe in *Chapter 7, Rendering Strategy*, which has some more helpful information when using HDR images to light scenes.

6
A Material World

In this chapter we will cover:

- ▶ Using an Alpha channel to model
- ▶ Using video as materials
- ▶ Using multiple materials on one object
- ▶ Using Shaders
- ▶ Make adjustments with the Layer Shader
- ▶ Using different Projection methods
- ▶ Reflective materials with the Fresnel Shader
- ▶ Creating a glass material
- ▶ Adding relief – Bump and Displacement channels
- ▶ Applying Subsurface Scattering

Introduction

If you look at an object and ask yourself, "What kind of material is that made of?", you tend to define it as an actual material like wood or plastic, but in Cinema 4D, we have to be more specific while designing materials to apply to 3D objects and scenes. Instead you have to ask yourself, "How would you describe the look of this object?", "Is it shiny?", "Does it have bumps or dents in it?", "Can you see through it at all?"

Think about the home improvement stores, they are loaded with all sorts of products that are composed of different materials. The paint aisle is a sea of colors, filled with swatches of similar shades, so you have to decide to paint your bedroom in Soft Winter Eggshell, Light Bone, Snowy Beige, or, you know, white. There are so many different types of wood and wood stains to use on your projects; you have to decide between oak, pine, mahogany, and cherry, because they all have a slightly different look and feel. I'm certain there have been couples who have ended relationships because of arguments stemming from whether the knobs on the kitchen cabinets should be Aged Bronze or Rustic Copper.

We care about the way things look, so we fuss over all the details when it comes to the materials that we use in our home improvement projects. Inside Cinema 4D, we are no different. The possibilities behind creating materials are literally endless. You have the ability to mix different colors, shaders, and textures in multiple channels to create a unique-looking style every single time. We can create everything from dirt to metal to alien skin, and everything in between, and we can change the look over and over until we are completely satisfied.

There are a few core recipes to learn about materials to unlock a wealth of potential in your material designs. We are going to focus on some of the main channels that you'll use most often and figure out how to achieve some specific results when applying them to your 3D objects.

Using an Alpha channel to model

If you are a user of **After Effects** or **Photoshop**, you probably understand the concept of an **Alpha** channel, it's a grayscale image used to define transparency, where 100 percent white indicates full opaqueness, 100 percent black indicates fill transparency, and the gray values in between represent varying levels of transparency. You can use this information and apply it to materials, and end up saving loads of time, creating 3D objects with bitmap images and a corresponding **Alpha** channel, rather than tackling the task using actual 3D modeling tools. This recipe shows us how we can easily apply an **Alpha** channel to a piece of geometry and end up with a 3D object.

Getting ready

Locate the `Maple_Leaf.png` and `Maple_Leaf_Alpha.psd` files in the **C4D Content Pack**; we will be using them in this tutorial.

How to do it...

1. Start a new project and add a new material in the **Material Manager**; name it **Maple Leaf**. Uncheck the **Specular** channel, then in the **Color** channel, click on the **Texture** button and navigate to the `Maple_Leaf.psd` image found in the C4D Content Pack, and load it as the texture.

> Please note the size of the image, its **1000 x 1000**, so it's a good idea to make any objects that we are going to apply it to, proportional to the ratio to avoid any distortion.

2. Create a **Plane** primitive and leave it on the default **400cm** by **400cm** to match our image's proportions. Change the **Orientation** option of the plane to **-Z** so it stands upright.

3. Apply the **Maple Leaf** material to the plane and see what happens. Even though our image is a PNG with the colored leaf isolated on its own layer without a background, Cinema 4D has disregarded this and applied a black background around our leaf.

4. We need to define the **Alpha** within the material of the **Maple Leaf** object to cut out our leaf on the **Plane** object's geometry as follows:

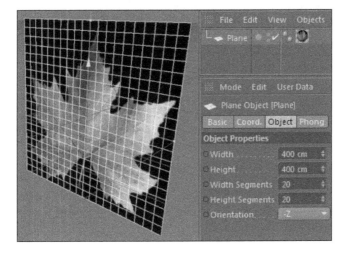

If you ever import a texture on a primitive and it appears upside down, just flip the orientation from the positive value to the negative value, or vice versa.

5. Reopen the material and check the box for the **Alpha** channel, then under its **Texture** field find the `Maple_Leaf_Alpha.jpg` file and load it into the channel. The white part of the image is the leaf, and the black part is the area around the leaf that we want to cut out. You notice that the preview icon has gone from the default shaded sphere to a cut out version of our leaf, and if you take a look at the plane in our scene, the black edges are gone; we now have a leaf defined by an **Alpha** channel, as shown in the following image:

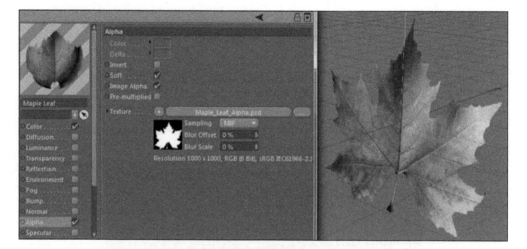

 If you forget which part should be white and which part should be black, don't worry. Just click the **Invert** checkbox to flip between the two options if you got them backwards.

6. But, we have a new problem, our leaf is as flat as paper; it has no life to it. If we want it to have some texture and contour to it, we need to apply it to an actual 3D object. So, delete our boring flat **Plane** object and add a **Landscape** primitive to the scene, and change its **Orientation** to **-Z**. The **Landscape** has relief and contains plenty of actual 3D geometry for our leaf. Rename the **Landscape** object to **Leaf**.

7. Take the **Maple Leaf** material and apply it to the **Landscape** object, and then uncheck the box that says **Borders At Sea Level**; that way, the edges won't be perfectly flat. Now, we have a leaf that would bend and crumple like a dried and falling leaf:

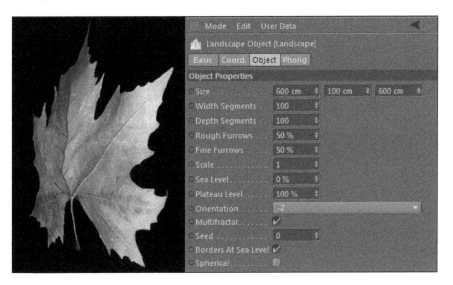

How it works...

By defining our leaf using an **Alpha** channel, we are able to use a real image of a leaf with its precise coloring and texture, and turn it into a 3D object. The process of modeling and texturing the actual polygons of a **Maple Leaf** like this would be very time consuming, and with a little prepping of our **Alpha** image, we can use the material to cut through the heavy work and create a leaf object in minutes.

You could take maybe 10 images of leaves with their **Alpha** values, and apply them all as different materials. Then, you could apply each of them to as many different **Landscape** objects as you wish, while changing their individual **Random Seed** values. Now, you have plenty of different leaves with different patterns and shapes without any heavy lifting.

Using video as materials

You're not just limited to still photos as textures in your materials; you can easily implement video as a material and apply it to a 3D object. There are a couple of details to take note of that are unique to video, but this recipe shows how to apply a video file as the main source of your material.

Getting ready

Locate the `Screen_Saver.mov` file in the C4D Content Pack for this scene, and open the `Computer_Monitor.c4d` file for us to use as our starting point for this recipe.

How to do it...

1. So let's say we have a computer monitor that has been inactive for a while; we need to activate the screen saver. We've got a separate screen saver clip that we want to be applied as footage inside our 3D scene; all we need to do is get it inside our monitor.

2. Let's start by adding a **Plane** primitive to our scene and rename it as **Screen**. It's important to pay attention to the **Height** and **Width** of our plane, as it needs to have the proper aspect ratio of our video file, otherwise it will appear distorted when applied to our object.

3. The `Screen_Saver.mov` file is a **1280 x 720** image, so let's change our plane to be **720** units high and **1280** units small, and what do you know, it fits perfectly inside our video frame like someone planned it that way.

4. Change the **Orientation** to **-Z**, so it faces the right way, and rename it as **Screen.**

5. Create a new material by double-clicking on the empty space in the **Material Manager** and name it **Video**. Next, go into the **Texture** field and find where the `Screen_Saver.mov` file is stored in the content pack and load it into the channel.

6. Apply the material to the **Screen**, and you'll see that a frame of video is now live on screen:

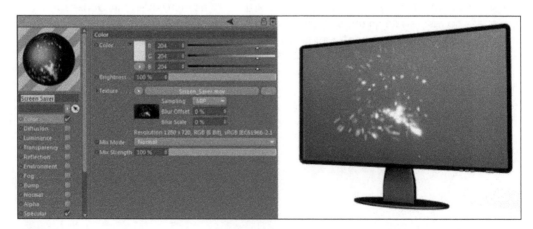

7. However there is one issue, if we scrub through or play our timeline, we don't have any motion on our screen. The video is loaded; you can do a test render preview on a different frame and you'll see the screen load a different part of the movie file. By default, Cinema 4D doesn't let you see the movie play in the Viewer, but we can turn this on by opening the **Material Editor** for our video material and going almost all the way down to the bottom to the **Editor** options on the left-hand side. In these settings you should check on the first parameter that reads **Animate Preview**; now our video will play if we move through our timeline.

How it works...

Videos are loaded just like still images into the **Color** channel, and they can be applied to 3D objects. Once applied to our screen, our video is part of our 3D environment and it will behave as part of our video monitor. We can enable the video to play in our Viewer via the **Animate Preview** checkbox in the **Editor** setting of our material.

There's more...

There are some video controls available for your texture inside the **Material Editor**. If you click on the video file in the **Texture** field, you'll find a new window that has an **Animation** tab at the top. Inside that tab, you can change several video parameters for playback as your texture inside Cinema 4D. The **Mode** setting controls what your clip does after it finishes playing one time. You can set it to **PingPong** to have it start playing in reverse until it reaches the beginning, causing it to go back and forth like a game of ping pong. Or, you can set it to loop and have it play from the beginning over and over again each time it finishes. You can also adjust the in and out points of your clip under the **Timing** field. I wouldn't recommend relying on these to make fine adjustments; it's not the most intuitive set of controls. You should use a program like **After Effects** to cut and time your footage before bringing it into Cinema 4D, so it plays exactly how you want it to.

Calculator 4D

The fact is, Cinema 4D can do math much better and faster than you, so learn this tip and use it on any parameter that accepts numbers as the input. You can enter a math equation into any numerical field, and Cinema 4D will do the math and yield the correct result. This is very useful when trying to keep objects proportional like our video screen. Let's say you want to have a screen with a video that is 1280 x 720 and fitting properly on it, but you can't have that big object because it won't be properly scaled in your scene. Simply enter **1280** and **720** in the **Width** and **Height** fields, respectively, then enter something like `1280/5`, and Cinema 4D will automatically change it to 256, which is 1280 divided by 5. Do the same for the **Height** field and you get 144, or 720 divided by 5. This is a quick way to resize images and keep them proportional.

Available in more than just color

You don't have to use video just in the **Color** channel; it can be loaded anywhere else where there is a **Texture** field. For example, you could animate a black and white image, render it out as a video file, and load it into the **Alpha** channel of a material and apply it to an object. The video file would appear to cut out the geometry, based on the differences between black and white in your video.

Using multiple materials on one object

Sometimes you can luck out as a designer, and you only have to apply one material to an object and it looks perfect. But at other times you may end up creating a model that has multiple different colors, textures, and surfaces that can't be universally applied via just one material. In cases like this, we have to be aware of a couple of techniques that can be used to apply different materials to the same object.

Getting ready

Open the `Bullseye.c4d` file from the C4D Content Pack for this project.

How to do it...

1. Start by checking out the two objects in this scene. We have an **Extrude NURBS** object creating our **Bullseye** text, and we have a Disc primitive behind it. We are going to apply red and white colors to both objects; the text will become two-tone and the disc will become a **bullseye** target.

2. Let's start with the text. If you use an **Extrude-NURBS** object (and other **NURBS** objects) to create an object from a spline, you can create what are called **Caps and Rounding**. **Caps** correspond to the faces of your object; in our case it would be the actual shapes of the letters. The **Rounding** of the edges is created when you apply a **Fillet** to create different kinds of dimension and bevels to your object. By default, under the **Caps** tab of the **Extrude-NURBS**, our **Start** and **End** Caps are set to **Cap**, but instead go ahead and change it to **Fillet Cap** and reduce the **Radius** to **3cm**. Now, our text has a bit of a beveled edge, and we can apply specific materials to parts of these elements, so you can get text or any extruded object with more than one color material on it.

3. Let's start by applying the red material to our **Bullseye** object, which will turn the whole text red. Highlight the newly-created texture tag and look at the options in the **Attributes Manager**. The second field from the top, which is under the **Tag** tab is **Selection**, this is where we can specify where to apply this material.

4. The Caps of the **Extrude-NURBS** object can be selected by typing **C1** or **C2** in the **Selection** field. **C1** corresponds to the front face and **C2** is for the back. Enter **C1** in the field, and you'll see that now just the front of the text is red; the rest is the default gray material.

5. Change the **C1** to **R1**, and now the red color is applied to just the rounding. You can add multiple **Texture** tags to the same object and specify a different material for each Caps and each Rounding.

6. Reset the tag back to **C1** so the red is just on the front cap. Now, take the white material and apply it to your **Bullseye, Extrude-NURBS** object. Once you apply both, the white material dominates the red and the whole object becomes white.

7. You need to adjust the order in which the **Texture** tags appear. The tags are applied from left to right, so the ones on the left are applied first and the ones on the right are applied last.

8. Switch the positions of the tags by clicking-and-dragging the red onto the right of the white one, so it is essentially on top. Now, the red selection made to the cap is placed above the rest of the text that is covered by the white material.

9. But what if your object doesn't have Caps and Rounding? If it's a polygon object, we can apply selections to certain groups of polygons, and use specific materials on them.

10. Highlight the **Target** object, which is a **Disc** primitive, and observe the subdivision of the object. It's a circle that has 60 rotation segments that look like pie slices. The key to applying materials to specific polygons is getting the subdivision accurate to how we want the materials to appear on the object.

11. If we want to make this a red and white striped target, we'll have to increase the number of disc segments in the **Attributes Manager** to a higher number like **7**, so we have some rings within the target to work with. Once you have some rings, convert it to a polygon object by highlighting it in the **Object Manager**, and hit the **C** key.

12. Sometimes, you may need to create your own specific subdivisions using tools like the knife to get exactly the shape you want.

13. Apply the red material to the **Target** object, so it's all solid red. Now, go to the **Select** menu and grab the **Ring Selection** tool. This is handy for grabbing groups of polygons that appear in a circular pattern in different dimensions.

14. Hover over the outermost ring of polygons and click on it to select the whole ring. Now, while holding the **Shift** key, click every other ring so that your rings alternate from being selected and unselected. You should have four rings selected, including the innermost group of polygons that represent the dot in the center.

15. Go back under the **Select** menu, and go almost to the very bottom and find the **Set Selection** option. This has applied a **Selection** tag, represented by an orange triangle, next to your **Target** object in the **Object Manager**. Under the **Name** field, enter the word Red, which is a helpful habit when you have multiple tags that you need to organize.

16. Now, apply the white material to your **Target** object, which should turn the whole **Target** object white, so you will need to shuffle the **Texture** tags so that the red texture is to the right of the white texture.

17. Now, with the **Target** object highlighted and loaded into the **Attribute Manager**, drag your small orange triangle for the **Selection** tag, and place it into the **Selection** field for the red material. The red material is now only applied to the polygons that you selected from before, and the **Target** object has alternating rings of color.

How it works...

The **Selection** field inside any **Texture** tag allows us to apply specific textures to our Caps, Rounding, or selected groups of polygons. These methods allow us to apply more than one material to specific parts of a polygon object. The **Set Selection** command assigns your selection of polygons to a specific group, which you can load into the **Selection** field of any applied material.

There's more...

This example uses **Extrude-NURBS**, because it is the easiest to see and demonstrate. But, **Sweep-NURBS**, **Lathe-NURBS**, and **Loft-NURBS** also have this feature to apply **Fillet Caps**, in order to get Caps and Rounding.

Caps and Rounding come automatically

If you convert an **Extrude-NURBS** object to a polygon object by hitting the C key, it creates multiple polygon objects; some are labeled as a Cap, some are listed as Rounding. This makes it even easier to apply specific textures, because now the pieces are completely separate objects. However, once you convert this to polygons, remember that you will lose the ability to adjust the settings available to the object as an **Extrude-NURBS**, so get the **Depth** and **Fillet** settings right before you do so. When we complete this recipe, convert your **Text** to an editable polygon and select the different objects in the new group, so you can see them highlighted in the Viewer and know what they correspond to.

Using Shaders

Instead of loading an image as a texture inside Cinema 4D, we can use Shaders to simulate the look and feel of certain textures and patterns. Shaders are what we would call procedural textures, meaning that they are determined by formulas and different input parameters that we specify. Cinema 4D is equipped with many kinds of Shaders that can help you generate the kind of material you want right inside Cinema 4D, rather than relying on images outside the application.

Getting ready

We are using the `Bathroom.c4d` file from the C4D Content Pack for the remaining recipes in this chapter. The bathroom is modeled and labeled for you already, so you can focus on just the materials. Everything is organized into different groups, so just position your camera on the area where we will be focusing on during each recipe. Also, disable groups that become distracting or block your view, especially the walls, then enable them when we need them as a part of our scene.

How to do it...

1. We are going to create three different materials with Shaders–a pattern for the towels, wallpaper for the walls, and a marble pattern for the sink countertop. Start by double-clicking on an empty spot in the **Material Manager** to create a new material, and name it **Towel**.

2. The best thing about using Shaders to texture something like a towel is that there is no right or wrong answer for how a towel should look, and we can try many different Shaders and get many different looks all within Cinema 4D, until we find the one we like.

3. Deselect the **Specular** channel in the **Material Editor**, so we only have the **Color** channel active. Under the **Color** channel, click on the small button with the triangle to the left of your **Texture** field to reveal our choices for shaders.

4. As you can see, there are tons of options to pick from, but we are going to look under the **Surfaces** submenu and find **Tiles**. **Tiles** is one of the most useful Shaders, because it can generate many useful patterns with a variety of shapes:

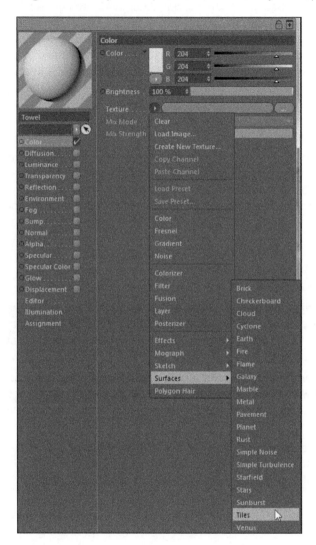

5. With the **Tiles** Shader now loaded on our **Towel** material, we have a red and gray square pattern. Apply it to your material to both towels located within their **Towel Rack 1** and **Towel Rack 2** groups, and then observe how ugly our towels now are. Maybe you found them in the clearance aisle and they were a bargain, but we can make a nicer-looking pattern than this one just using the **Tiles** Shader as follows:

6. In the **Tiles** Shader, there's a **Pattern** menu where you have all the patterns that you'll ever need to pick from. The default **Squares** is good for making a chessboard, but switch it from **Squares** to **Scales 2** instead. Now, we have a red and blue sideways fish scales pattern. Adjust the **Global Scale** down from **100%** to **25%** so the whole pattern becomes smaller. Also, adjust the **Orientation** from **U** to **V** so our scales map vertically along our towel.

7. Check out the preview in the Viewer and you'll see how much better this looks than the default, but the key to making it better is in the colors. The **Tiles Color 1**, **Tiles Color 2**, and **Tiles Color 3** fields, control which groups of scales correspond to which color. Let's take each of these three colors and make them all look more similar, instead of having such contrasting values; let's make this towel be sort of a yellow-gold color.

8. For **Tiles Color 1**, set your color values to **213** red, **176** green, and **88** blue. For **Tiles Color 2**, pick the values **246** for red, **212** for green, and **82** for blue. **Tiles Color 3** should be close to the others, with **197** for red, **165** for green, and **91** for blue.

9. Check out a preview of your towel and notice how much nicer it looks. Just tweak the **Bevel width** value to be **5%** and then set the **Grout Color** to **180** for red, **161** for green, and **37** for blue. Now, the towel looks like an actual towel and not like a circus tent with the defaults, and we did it all within the **Tiles** Shader:

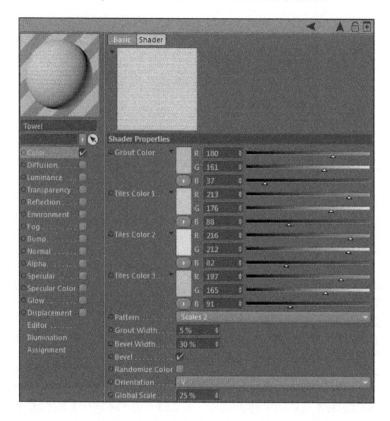

10. Let's use the **Tiles** Shader to apply a striped wallpaper pattern to our walls. Take your **Towel** material and hold the *Ctrl* or *command* key and drag it inside the **Material Manager**, so we can easily duplicate it, and rename it as **Wallpaper**.

11. Apply the material to the **Wallpaper** group within the **Walls** group. Change the **Projection** option from **UVW** to **Cubic** (more on this later in the chapter), and notice how our scales don't look too bad on here either, but we want a totally different look on our walls.

12. Go inside the **Tiles** Shader in the **Wallpaper** material, and change it from **Scales 2** to **Lines 2**. Now, we have a striped pattern on our walls with different shades of yellow. The yellow is a bit much, so let's go with a nice peaceful blue for our stripes.

13. Just like the **Tiles Color** option for our towel, we need to switch all the swatches to change the color of our wallpaper stripes. For the **Grout Color** option, enter **210** for red, **226** for green, and **252** for blue. For **Tiles Color 1**, enter **231** for red, **242** for green, and **255** for blue. For **Tiles Color 2**, change the red to **239**, the green to **250**, and the blue to **252**. And finally for **Tiles Color 3**, enter **250** for all three to make something very close to pure white. Check the Viewer, and you'll see we now have some nice striped blue wallpaper.

14. Let's check out a different Shader that we can use for creating a marble pattern for our sink counter, which is cleverly named **Marble**. Create a new material and name it **Marble**, and then load the Shader into the **Texture** field; it's under the **Surfaces** submenu just like the **Tiles** Shader. In the blink of an eye, we now have a nice-looking **Marble** pattern, so apply it to the **Sink Counter** object and the **Counter Extension** object in the **Sink Counter Mirror** group, and see the result. By default, the **Marble** Shader creates a marble pattern with a black and white gradient. Let's tweak the colors inside the Shader's properties to have a little less contrast. Double-click on the black knot and change it to a light gray with its red, green, and blue values equal to **208**. Do a render preview and you'll notice the light, subtle marble pattern on the counter, as follows:

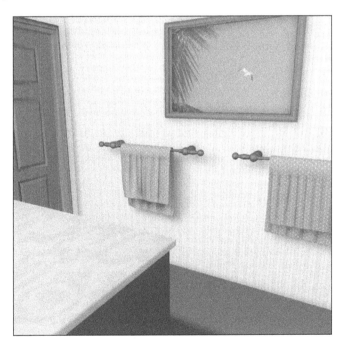

How it works...

Different shaders can generate different patterns that we can use as textures in our materials. Within Cinema 4D, we were able to create three different materials to use on different objects in our scene. Using shaders allows us to make real-time adjustments and observe the results as we go, as well as having an infinite number of combinations and possibilities to create unique materials.

There's more...

Don't you think that the towel looks a little smooth? Check out the *Adding relief – Bump and Displacement channels* recipe in this chapter to make a more convincing-looking towel.

Make adjustments with the Layers Shader

When buying wooden furniture, you usually have the choice between several different stains or finishes. They all have the same texture that we recognize as wood, but you start wondering if you should get it stained in oak, pine, natural, cherry, mahogany, or espresso. The **Layers** Shader is a unique tool that serves like a miniature version of Photoshop within Cinema 4D. You can stack and blend different textures, as well as make enhancements to their colors and levels' information.

Getting ready

We are using the Bathroom.c4d file still, and we are loading the Wood.jpg file as a texture, so make sure you have it ready to go.

How to do it...

1. Let's create the wood texture in our new material. Double-click in the Material Manager to create a new material and rename it Wood. Now, in the Color channel, use the Texture delta (the little triangle) to flip open the options, go down to Surfaces and select Wood.

2. Now, click on the button that says Wood and you'll see the options. You can stick with the default settings, or you can have a play around with the color by manipulating the gradient interface. Or, you can choose from the preset list of different woods, for example you could pick Pinewood for a nice light grain. This is a nice Shader (and much improved in R14) as it not only simulates the grain of the wood on the surface but simulates the rings you see if you cut through a real piece of wood. Feel free to adjust the settings until you have a nice wood texture you're happy with.

3. Take the **Wood** material and apply it to the following objects in the Cabinets group–**Left Door**, **Right Door**, **Cabinet Construction**, and all six of the **Drawers** objects located within their respective left and right groups. Each one should have a separate **Texture** tag. Outside of the **Cabinets** group, apply the material to the **Picture Frame** object inside the **Picture** group.

4. With a texture like wood, you need to offset the patterns in the wood on individual objects so they don't appear like one continuous texture, or in this case, like they have the exact same pattern. The cabinets would be cut from different pieces, so they would have a similar texture but different patterns.

5. Use the **Offset U** and **Offset V** in the **Texture** tag for each object to slightly offset the material applied to each wooden object. You can also attach negative values to the **Length U** and **Length V** to flip the materials in different directions to come up with a seemingly different pattern. These methods allow you to get different wood patterns for all your objects by using just the one material.

6. Once you've offset the individual tags, do a render preview with *Ctrl* or *command* + *R* to see our wood in our scene. Notice how the patterns in the wood from drawer to drawer are all different-looking, yet they still come from the same texture. If you were designing this bathroom in reality, you'd have to make a decision on whichever stain of wood you want and stick with it; changing it constantly would be expensive and time consuming. But by using the **Layers** Shader, we can switch between multiple colors of wood on the fly to see what we like best:

7. Under the **Color** channel, click on the small button with the triangle to the left of your **Wood** texture loaded in the **Texture** field to reveal our Shader options. Look towards the bottom and select the **Layers** Shader. Nothing has changed in our scene or our material, but now the **Texture** field has the value **Layers** in it. Click on the **Texture** field, and we are now inside the **Layers** Shader, where our bitmap image of wood has been transferred.

8. Inside here, we can add many more layers that can consist of more bitmap images, all of our Shaders, as well as a variety of effects to enhance our image. To the right of the name of each layer, we have blending mode options, as well as an opacity slider. This is where we can tweak our image inside Cinema 4D and have it updated on our material automatically, without having to leave Cinema 4D and adjust the file in another program such as Photoshop.

9. Let's change the finish of our **Wood**. Click on the **Effect...** button and select **Hue/Sat/Lightness**, which will give us control over the color and tone of our **Wood** texture. We want to remove all the color information from our **Wood** and add our own color separately, so set the **Saturation** to **-100%** to create a grayscale version of our **Wood**. Next, click on the **Shader...** button and apply a **Color** Shader to supply our new color information:

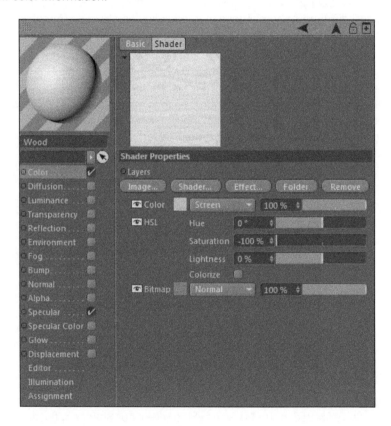

You could just select the checkbox that says **Colorize** to remove the color information, and allow yourself to color the **Wood** object right there with the **Saturation** slider and the **Hue** wheel. But, it's much easier to visually find the color you are looking for with **RGB** sliders than by using different saturation percentages and sifting through different degrees on the **Hue** wheel.

10. Click on the **Color** square to find our **RGB** sliders, and pick a light tan color that resembles a pine finish; try color values **223** for red, **166** for green, and **72** for blue. To get back to the **Layers** Shader, you can click on the back arrow towards the top-right corner of the **Material Editor**. Now, we have our color, we just need to blend it with the wood layer as follows, so change the **Blending** mode from **Normal** to **Screen**, and you'll see that we have a light-colored **Wood** texture now loaded on our cabinets:

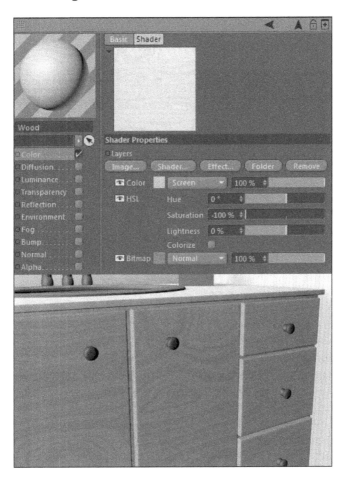

How it works...

The **Layers** Shader brings in the functionality of a program such as Photoshop within our **Material Editor**. We can make on the fly adjustments to our textures to see how they look within our scene, instead of loading and applying new textures just to see what you like better. We were able to remove the color information from the original wood image and then apply the new color to our wood with a simple **Color** Shader and blending mode adjustment.

There's more...

The **Layers** Shader gives you the ability to be non-destructive with your image, meaning you can leave the original image untouched while just applying adjustments to it. You can add or remove the effects as your taste changes, instead of saving over the actual image every time you want to change the look of a texture like wood. This is a good design habit, because you don't want to end up losing the original state of your image.

Using different Projection methods

It's easy to apply a material that is just of a solid color or some pattern that can appear in any state on your object. But, sometimes the shape or contours of a 3D object can distort a texture that has images, text, or shapes on it. Therefore, you have to be able to switch between different **Projection** methods in order to get the textures to appear correctly on your object. The recipe will introduce you to different **Projection** methods and techniques to apply specific images as textures without distorting them.

Getting ready

Look in the C4D Content Pack for the following images: `Shampoo.psd` and `Tissue_Box_Pattern.jpg`, for use inside our `Bathroom.c4d` file.

How to do it...

1. If you create primitives or **NURBS** objects in Cinema 4D, they come equipped with **UVW Coordinates**. UVW Coordinates take the width (U) and height (V) of a flat image texture and contours it across the object. The W coordinate is the depth information used when shaders are applied. When your 3D object has UVW Coordinates, the **Texture** tag sets the **Projection** method to **UVW Mapping** by default. This method sticks the texture to your objects, so your texture shifts properly without any transformations or deformations to your object. But, what if your object doesn't have UVW Coordinates? Or your texture doesn't look right with the default UVW Coordinates?

2. Locate the **Shampoo Bottle** group in your **Object Manager** and activate it; look for it in the shower basket. It's a **Lathe-NURBS** object for the bottle and a **Cylinder** primitive for the **Caps**, which already has a material on it. We want to apply a custom label to this bottle to make it look like an actual product, so it needs to have logos and markings on it, instead of just being a plain, boring, unmarked bottle. The label is created already, so create a new material and load the Shampoo.psd file into the **Texture** field of the **Color** channel. Rename the material as **Shampoo Label**.

3. Apply the **Shampoo Label** material to the bottle and note what happens. The **Texture** is applied sideways up the length of the bottle with **UVW Mapping** as the **Projection**, which may look ok for some products, but we want our label straight on as it was designed in Photoshop:

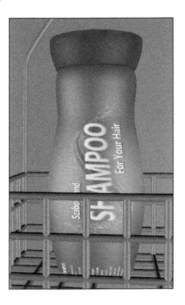

4. Delete the **Texture** tag from the bottle, and then convert the bottle to a polygon object by highlighting it and pressing the **C** key. You should notice that a new tag appeared with your bottle by converting it from a **Lathe-NURBS** to a polygon object; it's a black and white tiled icon that is a UVW tag, which takes the UVW information from the **NURBS** object and transfers it to the polygon object. Take the **Shampoo Label** material and add it to the bottle again, and you'll notice that the material is applied the same as before, because the UVW Coordinates are still there, now in the form of the tag.

5. Sometimes, you may end up needing to texture objects that don't have UVW coordinates, so **UVW Mapping** is not an option. Delete the UVW tag from the bottle and watch what happens, the material is now out of sorts, and using **UVW Mapping** option is no longer useful now, so we'll need to switch **Projection** methods.

6. Switch the **Projection** method from **UVW Mapping** to **Cylindrical**. Since the bottle has a cylindrical shape, this **Projection** method will apply a **Projection** that fits the material most accurately to the object. You may need to rotate your camera around to find the label, but you'll find that our label now appears on our bottle in the correct orientation. The only problem is that it is stretched incorrectly. Right-click or context-click on the **Texture** tag and select the option **Fit to Object** so the material will resize to be proportional with the object. Change the **Offset U** value to **57%** so that the label will rotate around and have the logo facing outward:

 The **Length U**, **Length V**, **Offset U**, and **Offset V** are key controls for resizing your textures and making small adjustments to get them lined up the way you want.

7. Now, we can use the current texture setup to set new UVW Coordinates for our bottle that will accurately apply the material to our bottle instead of the sideways version that we got before. Right-click or context-click on the **Shampoo Label–Texture** tag and select the **Generate UVW Coordinates** option. A new **UVW** tag is created, and you can reapply the **Shampoo Label Texture** and have the label placed in the right orientation. Any adjustments you made in the **Length** and **Offset** fields will need to be added again, so adjust the **Offset U** option to **57**% again.

8. The next object to texture is the tissue box. There are two tissue box groups that appear identical, but the difference is in the way materials are applied to them. One object is based from a simple **Cube** primitive, the other is a **Rectangle** spline combined with an **Extrude-NURBS** object to create a cube.

9. Create a new material and name it **Tissue Box**, and find and load the `Tissue_Box_Pattern.jpg` image into its **Color** channel. Make sure both **Tissue Box 1** and **Tissue Box 2** groups are active and visible in the editor, then open both groups and apply the material to just the **Box** object in both groups. Notice how the pattern is distributed differently on both:

10. **Tissue Box 2** is created with an **Extrude-NURBS** object, and as a result our texture is mapped all wrong. Keep in mind that an **Extrude-NURBS** doesn't work exactly like geometry, so their UVW Coordinates are thrown off compared to the exact same shape made with a **Cube** primitive. The **Caps** of our **Extrude-NURBS** has the dots of our pattern, but they are stretched incorrectly, and the extrusion between the **Caps** is just our blue color stretched out and filling in the space.

11. We need to pick a different projection than **UVW Mapping**. In this case, our box is a perfect candidate for **Cubic** projection, so switch the **Projection** mode over and notice how the pattern now maps better onto the box, yet it still isn't perfect. It's stretched just a little bit too far vertically because it's applied to a **Boole** object that makes up our **Box**, but we need to apply the **Texture** tag to the actual **Extrude-NURBS** object named **Box**, which is a child of the **Boole** object. Switch the tag over and then right or context-click on the **Texture** tag and select **Fit to Object**. If it prompts you to include sub-objects, hit **Yes**, and now you'll see our material fits exactly like it does on the other tissue box:

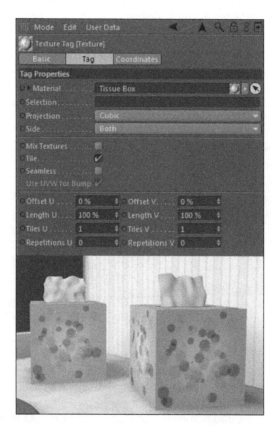

How it works...

Sometimes, the textures you apply to 3D objects don't fit properly the moment you apply them. It all depends on how the objects were designed and modeled. If the object has UVW Coordinates, **UVW Mapping** is applied and it may or may not give the best look for your texture. We can delete and generate new UVW Coordinates based on a better **Projection** mode. Primitives and **NURBS** objects apply textures differently with their UVW Coordinates, even when they are shaped the same. Switching the **Projection** mode and applying it to the correct object can help you get the result you are looking for.

There's more...

Try enabling the **Texture Axis**, located on the left side of the Command Palette. It's the cube icon with the checkerboard pattern on it. You can use it to reposition textures on their objects by clicking-and-dragging on the applied texture.

Projections come with instructions

The **Reference Documentation** for Cinema 4D has good diagrams of how the different **Projection** methods apply your materials to objects. Do a search for **Projection** and you'll find the illustrations and see exactly how materials get applied when you switch to different methods. Some of the modes such as **Spatial**, **Frontal**, and **Shrink Wrapping** are very specialized and limited in their use, so the guide can give you some background information on them if you'd like to see what they are capable of.

Reflective materials with the Fresnel Shader

Many of the materials that you will create need a reflective quality to them in order for them to look convincing. Surfaces like glossy plastic, shiny metal, and good old-fashioned glass all have a reflective nature, so adding this quality to them in Cinema 4D is crucial to our designs. This recipe will show us how to use the **Fresnel** (pronounced *Frah-Nell*) Shader to achieve realistic reflective behavior in our materials.

Getting ready

We are also going to keep using the `Bathroom.c4d` file from the C4D Content Pack. Our bathroom is getting close to being complete.

How to do it...

1. Before we even create a reflective material, it's important to understand where reflections come from. Reflections don't come from the object that you want to appear reflective, they come from the environment around the object you want to appear reflective. You need to have items in your scene that can be reflected; where there are other objects, lights, or HDR images in a **Sky** object, you need something for the material to reflect. Simply activating the **Reflection** channel and putting it on a 3D object won't do you any good. You need to build a complete scene or apply several lighting objects in order to generate good reflections. Our bathroom scene has plenty of objects and lights to generate reflections, so we are ready to go.

2. We are going to apply a shiny silver metal texture to a few objects in our scene. Create a new material called **Metal** in your **Material Manager**. Open the **Color** channel and change the color values to **127** for each color slider to make a middle gray. Now, go to the **Specular** channel and change the **Height** to **100**% and the **Width** to **40**%; this will produce bright highlights for our metal.

3. Now, activate the **Reflection** channel and your material preview should change to a shiny sphere. Apply the **Metal** material to your **Faucet** group and check out the result with a render preview. Notice how intense the reflections are; the metal on the faucet should be reflective, but this is way too shiny for the brushed metal style that we are going for, as shown:

4. This leads us to the **Fresnel** Shader. The **Fresnel** can be loaded into any channel, but it works best with the **Reflection** channel. It simulates the natural tendency of reflections to be more intense and noticeable when an object is seen at an angle. On objects with contours and rounded surfaces like our faucet, this is particularly noticeable.

5. In the **Texture** field of the **Reflection** channel, click on the triangle button to add a shader and select the **Fresnel** shader. It loads a shader that has a black and white gradient. Now, adjust the overall color of the **Reflection** channel to **175** for each **R**, **G**, and **B** values, and increase the **Blurriness** value to **5**%, so the effect is not quite as intense but still strong. Switch back to your scene and now check a new render preview of your faucet. Notice how much smoother the reflections seem, they fall off gradually and get more intense on the spots that we aren't facing directly, all thanks to the **Fresnel** Shader:

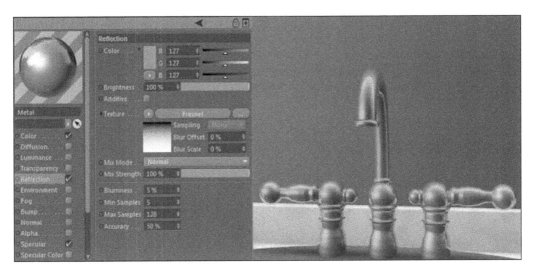

 The left side of the gradient in the **Fresnel** Shader corresponds to the surfaces faced at an angle, and the right side is for the surfaces faced towards the front. The default **Fresnel** gradient is black on the right and fading to white on the left. So, the gradient works like an **Alpha** channel if you think about it. The right side is black, or transparent in **Alpha** terms, so it's allowing the more intense reflections to come through, and the left side with the white is blocking our reflections from being too intense when seen from the front. You can change the intensity of the **Fresnel** effect by adjusting the white and black knots to different grayscale values and also picking a different option under the **Render** drop-down menu. You can get some unusual-looking reflection patterns by adjusting the default values.

6. Lastly, we are going to add some diffusion to our metal material. Diffusion will darken certain areas of your material based on the light and dark areas of the texture. This simulates slight irregularities and imperfections caused by dirt, smudges, or any type of noise that you may find in a material. Metal is rarely perfect with any dirt or scratches on it, so adding this can increase the realism of your material.

7. Activate the **Diffusion** channel and load the **Noise** Shader into the **Texture** field, and leave it on the defaults. Make sure that the **Affect Specular** and **Affect Reflection** boxes are checked on, and reduce the **Brightness** aspect of the channel to **80%**. Lastly, change the **Mix Strength** value to **30%** to make the overall effect more subtle. Now, the metal has just a little bit of diffusion on it, giving it a more believable look for our brushed metal.

8. Now, add these materials to the other metal objects in our scene–the **Bath Towel Racks**, the **Shower Head**, the **Shower handles**, the **Shower Frame**, the **Shower Basket**, the **Knobs** group for the **Cabinets**, the main **Door Knob**, the **Sink Ring**, and the **Toilet Flush Handle**. Do a render preview and you'll see that these objects have a more realistic look applied to them instead of just the plain gray default material, and they all match, since they are coming from the same material:

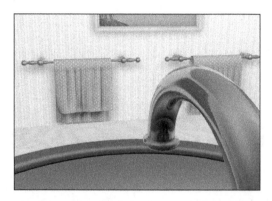

9. Now, for a special object in the scene–the mirror. A mirror reacts differently than the other reflective objects. Its reflections are seen from any angle, regardless of where we are standing. Apply the **Metal** material to the **Mirror** group, and then activate our **Mirror Man** object in the scene, who is trying to check out his reflection to make sure he is looking sharp. Now, switch cameras to the **Mirror View** camera, which is looking over the shoulder of our **Mirror Man** object.

10. Do a render preview and you'll notice that the mirror is not reflecting anything, because it has the **Fresnel** shader attached to it, so it's making our reflections disappear when we look at our object from the front. The mirror is perfectly flat unlike our curvy faucet, so we get absolute reflectivity anywhere in our view:

11. Create a new material and name it **Mirror**. Set the **Color** channel to pure white, deselect the **Specular** channel, and activate the **Reflection** channel. Now, replace the **Metal** material on the mirror with the **Mirror** material. Do a render preview and behold, he is no longer a vampire, he has a reflection:

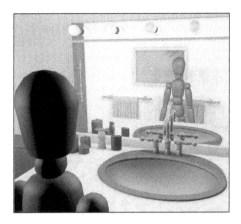

How it works...

There are two keys for getting good reflections in Cinema 4D, the **Fresnel** Shader and the environment available for reflecting. The **Fresnel** Shader simulates how reflections tend to be less intense when we are facing them straight on and become more intense when they appear on our objects at an angle away from us. The environment around the object is crucial as well, because if there is nothing to reflect, your material won't have anything nice to bounce back to you.

There's more...

A vast majority of materials out there have some reflective quality to them. Go back and apply proper reflections to any objects, such as our plastic shampoo bottle or marble counter top that should generate reflections. Mix up the reflective values of different materials; try reducing the **Mix Strength** value of the **Fresnel** Shader and the **Brightness** level of the **Reflection** channel to get less intense reflections on certain objects.

Designers prefer objects with curves

Nature doesn't produce flat objects; we do. Reflections always look nicer when your object has more curves, contours, relief, dimensions, nooks, crannies, and so on. Build these into your objects and you'll get more interesting reflections. If you have to use something simple like a **Cube** primitive and still want it to be reflective, add a **Fillet** to the edges so there's a slight curve instead of a sharp edge.

Use real textures for real results

Sometimes metal isn't perfectly polished and brand new like we see on our faucets. Think of the old tools in your garage or your car that desperately needs to be washed. If you want to simulate metal that has got some grunge and life to it, you should download a texture of actual metal that has scratches, rust, dirt, or any other kind of characteristic that you want on it. Using a real metal texture with the **Reflection** channel will make a more realistic-looking surface than using something perfectly smooth and clean with just a gray color in the **Color** channel. This goes for any other texture that you want to simulate. Using a real image of a texture can make your designs look like they are made of something real instead of just binary code.

Reflections are a render hog

As you probably noticed with this exercise, you should be prepared to wait longer for your final renders once you add reflections to your scene. Rendering objects with reflections requires more analyzing by Cinema 4D and higher anti-aliasing for accurate results. I would love to add some **Global Illumination** to this scene to fill in some dark shadows that are created by our overhead lights, but a scene like this with tons of reflections and **Global Illumination** might take more time than you have available.

Creating a glass material

Glass is a tough material to master. It's clear and transparent, so we shouldn't be able to see it, right? Well what it lacks in color value, it more than makes up for it in refraction, reflection, and specular properties. There are a lot of little things to iron out when creating a good glass material, and in this recipe we are going to learn the steps to create a fragrance bottle to put on the counter of our bathroom sink.

Getting ready

If you skipped the earlier recipe on the **Lathe-NURBS**, go check it out to get the hang of the process back in *Chapter 2, Super Modeling*. We are going to put this in our `Bathroom.c4d` file, but I'd recommend creating the bottle in a new project and just pasting it on once we are done.

How to do it...

1. The good thing about a fragrance bottle is that there is no specific shape that we have to follow. Do a search on the web for images under "fragrance bottle" and you'll find a number of starting points for a design. We will be using **Lathe-NURBS**, so our bottle is going to be cylindrical, curved, and rounded. Start with the Freehand Spline tool, and switch your camera to the **Front** view. Using the y axis as a midpoint for your glass, draw the general cross-section shape of a bottle. If you aren't satisfied with a rough sketch of your shape, undo your drawing and try again until you are satisfied with the look.

2. Keep in mind, the proportion of your bottle compared to the other objects in your scene. Zoom in with your camera to draw a smaller spline; otherwise, your fragrance bottle will need to be measured in gallons not ounces.

3. Use the techniques that we learned earlier by making our **Lathe NURBS** objects and the **Freehand Spline** tool. Once you draw a shape you can work with, click on the button on the left-hand side of the Command Palette–the **Use Point** mode, and use the *Delete* key to remove any redundant and unnecessary points from your spline, and adjust the remaining points in the position where they can create the look of half a fragrance bottle.

4. Line up the points on the edge of the y axis or as close as you can to the Y axis, or simply select each individual point and enter a value of **0** in their **X** position value, located in the **Coordinates Manager**, and hit *Enter*.

5. When your spline is satisfactory, add a **Lathe-NURBS** object and make the spline a child of it. Rename it as **Fragrance Bottle** and check out the look of your shape. Make sure you like what the **Lathe NURBS** object has created for you; if not, you can go back and tweak the points on your spline.

6. This next step is important, because if you don't follow it, your glass won't behave properly once you apply the material. Right now, your glass bottle has no thickness, because the **Lathe-NURBS** object takes just the segment created by your spline and doesn't bevel, extrude, or widen your surface at all. You need to create the thickness in the shape of your spline, otherwise your glass won't behave properly, because even if it's really thin, glass has a thickness to it. If you were to apply a glass material to this right now, the reflections would flip upside down and you'd be wondering what's wrong with your material, when in fact it's the object causing the trouble.

7. We have to work with our spline again, so deactivate the **Lathe NURBS** object so that it's easier to see the spline. Select your spline in the **Objects Manager**, and create a copy by holding the *Ctrl* or *command* key and drag the spline into your **Object Manager**. Now, take the spline and slide it over **Use Point** mode again and adjust the points on your new spline so they line up evenly in the Y dimension with the original spline.

8. Make a copy of this new inner spline and repeat the process again; rename it as **Liquid Spline** to keep track of it. This is going to be the liquid inside our bottle, so bring the top points down and inside the second spline, delete them if you have to, so that this **Lathe-NURBS** object won't be as high up as the **Lathe-NURBS** object that corresponds to the bottle, so it appears as if the liquid has been used.

9. Now, select the outer two splines in the **Object Manager** and find the **Connect Objects + Delete** option in the **Mesh** menu under the **Commands** submenu, and we've turned two splines into one. Rename the spline as **Bottle Spline**, then remove the **Liquid Spline** from inside the **Fragrance Bottle**, and add its own **Lathe-NURBS** object called **Liquid**. Reactivate the **Fragrance Bottle** object and you'll notice it won't look very different. But this saves us an extra step now, when we apply our glass material.

10. Next, you need to create a cap for our **Fragrance Bottle**. Your bottle will likely be different-looking than mine and have a different size, so you'll have to just use your own settings to get the result to fit on your own bottle. Feel free to make a more interesting one with another **Lathe-NURBS** object, but two primitives with a low **Fillet** value checked on in the **Caps** tab will do the trick just fine. Just stack a wider one at the bottom and a thinner one on top, and you have a **Cap**. Group them together with *Alt* or *option* + *G*, and rename the group as **Cap**. Group the entire set of objects together and call it **Fragrance Bottle**, then copy and paste it into your Bathroom. c4d file.

11. Place the **Fragrance Bottle** group on the counter top in your scene, next to the other bottles. My coordinates are **190** in **X**, **-40** in **Y**, and **-175** in **Z**, but you can position it anywhere you want. Make a new material in the **Material Manager** and name it **Glass**. Open it in the **Material Editor**, and let's adjust the two channels that are already selected: **Color** and **Specular**. Set the **Color** value to pure white so that it is **255** for the red, green, and blue values. Now, go under the **Specular** channel and adjust the **Height** of the **Specular** to **100%**, making the highlight very bright. Then, make the **Width** smaller to about **10%**. Also, tweak the **Inner Width** to **20%** so the highlight is a little sharper.

12. Different kinds of glass can have different kinds of specular highlights. Make the **Height** value really high to get very intense ones, and the **Width** value high to get very smooth ones that are distributed over the entire surface.

13. Glass has a reflective nature to it, so we need the **Reflection** channel to be active. Inside the channel, we are going to apply our **Fresnel** shader from the previous recipe so that the reflections fall off more naturally. Click on the triangle button to list our Shaders and select **Fresnel**. Click on the **Fresnel** button so we can adjust the gradient it uses. Make the knot that is currently white to middle gray; just drop the **V** (for **Value**), which sets the color down to **50%**. For the black knot, make it a dark gray with a **V** value of **10%**. By having these settings not at full white and black values, the **Fresnel** effect is lessened and not as intense.

14. The most important channel needed in our glass material is the **Transparency** channel, which is what makes glass behave like glass. Activate the channel and our material preview will seemingly disappear except for our bright specular highlights. Our material is now transparent, but in order to behave like glass or other transparent materials, it needs refraction. Refraction is when light is bent while passing through a material like glass, but it also occurs in transparent materials, notably water. Refraction causes the bend and distortion that we see when we look through a glass object, and it's the key for making believable glass in Cinema 4D. Change the default **Refraction** value of **1** to **1.52**, which is now the refractive index for normal glass.

15. Apply the glass material to your **Fragrance Bottle** object, and apply your **Metal** material from before to the **Cap** group. Do a render preview to see the result. You now see the area behind the bottle with a bit of distortion from our refraction, and our glass is also reflecting the bathroom scene around us slightly.

16. Our bottle doesn't have to be clear glass, however. Go back into the **Transparency** channel of the glass material and drop the **Brightness** value down to **80%**. Then, go back into the **Color** channel and change it to a dark blue, with the values of **20** for red, **35** for green, and **120** for blue. Now, our bottle has a tint of blue and a little more style to it.

17. The liquid inside can be tinted and made transparent too. Make a new material called **Liquid** and apply a simple blue color to the **Color** channel, something like **0** for red and green, and **150** for blue. Deactivate the **Specular** channel and activate the **Transparency** channel, increase the **Refraction** to **1.2**, and change the **Brightness** to **50%**.

18. Apply the material to the **Liquid, Lathe-NURBS** object that is inside our **Fragrance Bottle**, and now the liquid is blue and transparent. Change the **Color** and **Brightness** settings of the different channels in the two materials, and you can get some very different-looking bottles and fragrances:

How it works...

The **Transparency** channel lets us create transparent materials like glass inside Cinema 4D. By combining it with reflections and specular highlights, we can make a glassy, shiny bottle that is transparent and lets us see through it, revealing what's inside. You can tint it with different colors, so you can get a glass that simply isn't just clear.

There's more...

There are more kinds of transparent materials than just glass, which means that different materials are going to have different refraction values. Here's a handy table that gives you the refraction value of every transparent material you can think of:http://jag4d.com/ior.html.

Adding relief – Bump and Displacement channels

Part of the process of making the perfect 3D model is the concept of imperfection. There are many surfaces in the world that aren't perfectly flat or smooth, whether by nature or design. Think in terms of the carpet on your floor, if every fiber was the same height and angled uniformly towards the ceiling, it would look strange, wouldn't it? Many surfaces have divots, dimples, relief, and all kinds of bumps to make them unique, and as a result are incredibly difficult to model using basic tools to tweak geometry. There are two channels in the **Material Editor** that we can use to apply very structured or natural kinds of relief to our objects without modeling, the **Bump** channel and the **Displacement** channel.

Getting ready

Keep using the `Bathroom.c4d` file from the C4D Content Pack.

How to do it...

1. First off, both these essential channels aim to accomplish the same task of adding fine detail to your materials. They both use grayscale values to generate the pattern in which you want to displace your object. But the **Bump** channel doesn't change the actual geometry of an object that it is applied to; it just creates the look that it does when rendered. The **Displacement** channel has the ability to deform the actual geometry using **Sub-Polygon Displacement** (available in the Cinema 4D Visualize and Studio packages) option, so you can get more realistic results. Both channels can be useful, and we will do the examples in our scene with each.

2. Let's take our **Shower Doors** objects and make a frosted glass material instead of just plain old regular flat glass. Create a new material and name it **Frosted Glass** for starters. Make the **Color** channel pure white and leave the **Specular** channel on its default settings. Next, activate the **Transparency**, **Reflection**, and **Bump** channels. For the **Transparency** channel, we want our glass to be transparent, but not fully transparent; it should have a slight tint to it, so change the **Brightness** value to **80%**. The **Reflection** channel only needs to be reduced to **25% Brightness**, and turn up the **Blurriness** to **5%** so the reflections won't appear too sharp in the glass.

3. Activate the **Shower Man** object and deactivate the **Mirror Man** object. Place the **Shower Glass** material on the **Shower Doors** object. Do a render preview and note how we have a slightly tinted glass, but it's perfectly flat and completely boring:

4. So, let's fix that with our **Bump** channel, which is the key to our frosted glass effect. In the **Bump** channel you only control the **Strength** and the **Texture** of your displacement, and frankly that's all we need. Click on the **Texture** field and load in the **Noise** Shader. The **Noise** Shader is incredibly useful, because it can simulate different patterns of random noise with an infinite amount of combinations. It can be used to create things like dirt, sand, dust, glitter, and a myriad of other surfaces; it's one of the most useful shaders. Click on the **Noise** shader loaded in the **Texture** field, and let's change the values to make our pattern look like that which would displace the glass properly for our shower door.

5. Under the **Noise** drop-down menu, you have all sorts of different types of noise that are generated with specific random formulas. Take the time one day to sample them all and see how many different looks you can get from the simple concept of noise. There really aren't many wrong answers here; numerous **Noise** patterns will provide the kind of bumpy glass we are trying to create. Let's pick the **Naki** version, and decrease the **Global Scale** value down to **20%** so that it appears finer on our door. Do a render preview and notice how the glass becomes deformed in our preview, and the visibility of the **Shower Man** is obscured by our **Bump** texture:

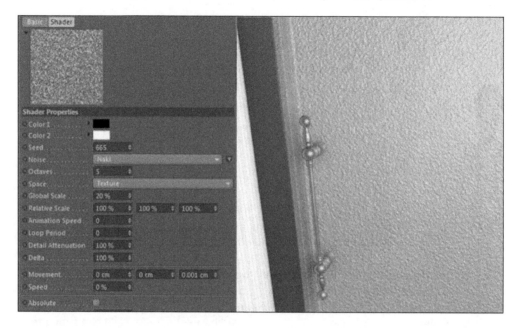

6. Using the **Bump** channel is an easy way to add surface detail to an object, but it has its limitations. It doesn't actually deform geometry, so you'll notice little drawbacks like your shadows won't take the shape of the **Bump** map, or the shadows cast upon your object won't contour to this fake geometry. Stick to **Bump** channels when you need to add surface detail like our door detail, and try the **Displacement** channel for more complex surfaces.

7. Let's create a tile surface for the floor and shower. Start with a new material and name it **Tiles**, and enable the **Displacement** channel. For the **Texture** field in the **Displacement** channel, we are going to load in the **Tiles** Shader, and by default it will load the **Squares** pattern, which is exactly what we need. Under the **Shader** properties, we need to change the colors to grayscale colors to get the type of displacement we want. Change the grout color to middle gray, with **R**, **G**, and **B** values at **127**, so that there is no displacement from the grout at all. Then, make both **Tiles Color 1** and **Tiles Color 2** pure white so that they are displaced forward or upward at the maximum value. Then, change the **Grout Width** and **Bevel Width** to **2%** each, and increase the **Global Scale** to **200%**.

8. Now, go back to the **Displacement** channel option and lower the **Height** value down from **5** to **1**, and check on the box that enables **Sub-Polygon Displacement** so we can properly deform our surfaces.

9. Next, we can conveniently copy the **Texture** field in the **Color** channel by clicking on the arrow button and selecting **Copy Channel** from near the top of the drop-down menu. Now, go into the **Color** channel and hit the arrow button next to the **Texture** field and select **Paste** channel. This command will take the exact settings in our **Tiles** Shader from the **Displacement** channel and apply them to our **Color** channel, so now we have a white tile with gray grout in between. Change the **Grout Color** value to a gray value that is closer to white; try **233** for the red, green, and blue values:

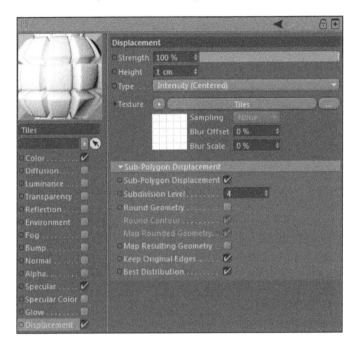

10. Apply this material to the **Floor**, **Right Tile**, **Left Tile**, **Back Wall**, and **Bottom Step** objects in the **Walls** group. Turn OFF any objects that are getting in your way, or switch camera views and do a render preview. There are a few things wrong with our tiling that we'll have to fix. Notice how the tiles on the floor and the sides of our shower aren't square, or lining up properly. This is because we have their **Texture** tags set to **UVW Mapping**, and its tiling is based on the shape of our surfaces, which aren't perfectly square.

11. The easiest remedy for this is to select all the **Texture** tags of the objects you applied the **Tile** material to by holding down **Shift** and clicking on them in the **Object Manager**, then the **Attribute Manager** will load all of their shared properties, and just change the **Projection** value from **UVW Mapping** to **Cubic**. And now, our tiles are all square and lined up correctly on each surface:

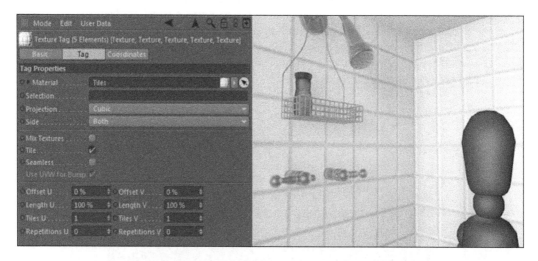

12. But, let's take a closer look at our **Floor** object. It looks like our tiles are a little off; they appear to be backwards, and their extrusion looks like it is going the wrong way. It actually is going the wrong way, and this is due to how our bathroom was modeled. I created the walls by starting with a large **Cube** primitive, converting it to a polygon object and adding the objects inside it. So technically, we are looking at the inside of the cube, and the displacement is going outside the cube. There's a simple fix to flip the orientation of the surfaces, so they will displace the opposite way; it has to do with aligning **Normals**.

13. **Normals** are the information assigned to polygons to designate which side is the inner or outer surface. This comes into play when you are assigning information in the **Displacement** channel, or using certain modeling tools. Since Cinema 4D looks at our **Floor** and **Back Wall** objects and thinks this is the inside of a cube based on their **Normals**, the displacement is sent in the opposite direction, which is completely outside our bathroom.

14. In order to fix this, we simply need to highlight our **Back Wall** and **Floor** objects, and find **Reverse Normals** under the **Mesh** menu and the **Normals** submenu. You won't notice the change until you render a preview, and now you'll see our tiles are headed in the right direction as follows:

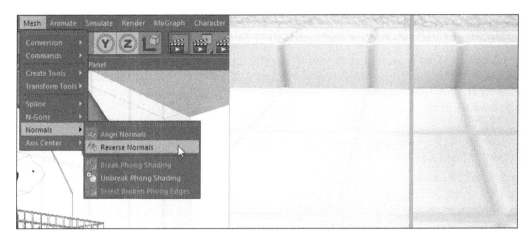

15. Let's also use the **Displacement** channel once more to create a better-looking towel. Right now, our towel is way too smooth and looks nothing like an actual towel. Go to your **Towel** material and activate the **Displacement** channel, and add a **Noise** Shader to the **Texture** field. Change the pattern to **Sema**, and make the **Global Scale** very small, down from **100%** to **5%**, so we can get some fine fibers on our towel instead of big clumps. Lastly, just check on the **Sub-Polygon Displacement**, reduce the **Height** to **1**, and do a render preview. You'll see the towels now look like they are made of softer cloth, instead of being perfectly smooth like before:

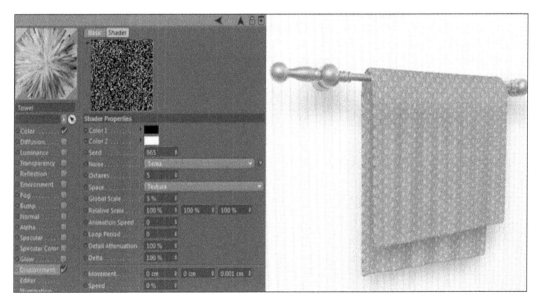

How it works...

The **Bump** and **Displacement** channels offer different options for adding relief to your 3D objects. The **Bump** channel works well to add detail to surfaces, but the **Displacement** channel creates deformed geometry using **Sub-Polygon Displacement**, so we get an actual manipulation of our model in our renders.

There's more...

Take note of how we can activate and deactivate the **Displacement** channel in order to turn a tiled floor back into a plain floor. Don't waste time modeling rows of floor tiles; you may want to change it later on. Use the **Displacement** channel, because it doesn't permanently affect the geometry of your model.

Adding details adds to render time

Wow, did those renders take a while? Yes, **Bump** and **Displacement** channels will add to your render times. The giant transparent glass doors with reflections aren't helping either. Make enough time for longer renders when using these features.

Applying Subsurface Scattering

Cinema 4D R14 features better upgraded results with **Subsurface Scattering**. This effect is used to create slightly transparent materials that can both scatter and absorb light across the object that it is applied to. It allows light to pass through certain parts of the object, the thinner areas, to give the effect that the material isn't 100% opaque. This effect will help create a variety of realistic-looking materials. We are going to use Subsurface Scattering to create two materials: porcelain for some bathroom fixtures and wax for some candles.

Getting ready

Our bathroom is about to be finished. Use the `Bathroom.c4d` file for this last recipe in the chapter.

How to do it...

1. Let's start by creating a porcelain material to use for our sink and toilet fixtures first. Double-click on an empty spot in the **Material Manager** and make a new material and name it **Porcelain**. Under the **Color** channel, change the **R**, **G**, and **B** color values to **250** each, so they are almost pure white. Now, activate the **Luminance** channel, and click on the triangle button next to the **Texture** field, and find the **Subsurface Scattering** option under the **Effects** submenu.

2. Click on the effect to load it into the **Texture** field to open up its options. It has a presets menu that you can use as a starting point, but **Subsurface Scattering** can be effective using the default values. The **Color** settings define the color on the interior, which is what gets revealed when the light is penetrated based on the **Path Length** option. The lower the **Path Length** value, the faster the light is absorbed and there's less penetration.

3. Apply the **Porcelain** material to the **Toilet** group, **Sink** group, **Sink Lip** group, and the **Sink Ring** object. Hit *Ctrl* or *command + R* to do a render preview, and you'll see the material in action. The **Toilet** object has a better dispersion of shadows than if it didn't have any **Subsurface Scattering**. Activate the **Reflection** channel of the **Porcelain** material. Apply a **Fresnel** Shader to the **Texture** field, and reduce the **Brightness** and the **Mix Strength** values both to **20%**. Now, we have a nice glossy-looking **Porcelain** material for our bathroom. It looks much cleaner and whiter with this effect added to the **Luminance** channel:

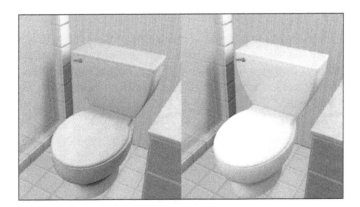

4. Let's create a different material for the candles on the counter. Create a new material and call it **Wax**. Change the **Color** in the **Color** channel to a light yellow, with values of **230** for red, **235** for green, and **170** for blue. Now, activate the **Luminance** channel and load the Subsurface Scattering effect into the **Texture** field again. Under the **Color** settings, change the **RGB** value to be **255** for red, **200** for green, and **150** for blue to give us another shade of yellow for the light that is allowed inside our material. Reduce the **Path Length** to **3**, and apply this material to the **Candles** objects inside their groups. Also, find the **Wick** material in the **Material Manager**, and place it onto each of the three wicks, and place the **Flame** material onto each of the flames:

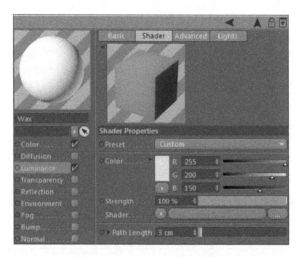

5. Now, let's set the mood and turn OFF the **Lights** group entirely and rely on our candles to light the scene. Use the traffic light to deactivate the **Lights** group, then go to the **Render Settings** window and activate **Global Illumination**, so our flames objects will light our scene using their **Luminance** channels. Do a render preview to check out the result.

6. Notice how the inside of the candles absorbs some light, giving you the illusion that they aren't fully opaque. **Subsurface Scattering** is the perfect effect to add to your **Wax** material. Without it, your candles receive no light from the flames lighting them and they don't look very realistic:

How it works...

The **Subsurface Scattering** effect is good to use for certain materials that you want to allow light to penetrate the surface to an extent. We used it to make a **Porcelain** and **Wax** material for some objects in our bathroom, but the effect has far-reaching uses for other materials that can simulate skin, liquid, plastics, and more. In our bathroom we saw how it can provide better lighting on our surfaces for the toilet, sink, and our candles.

Note on SSS.

The **Subsurface Scattering Shader** is a powerful and deep Shader which has lots of settings which will help you refine the exact effect you need. The built-in help files provide an excellent background to effect so if you wish to dig deeper simply right click any setting and go to show help

There's more...

Our bathroom is finally complete. You may not care for the design, but that's ok; feel free to change anything to get your own unique look with a totally different set of materials. Here's a sample to show you how different you can make a scene look, just by changing the materials:

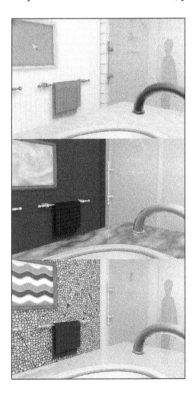

7
Rendering Strategy

In this chapter we will cover:

- ▶ Render settings overview
- ▶ Creating a batch of renders
- ▶ Previewing renders with Render Region
- ▶ Comparing different renders
- ▶ Using anti-aliasing effectively
- ▶ Exploring the Physical Renderer engine
- ▶ The Compositing tag
- ▶ Setting up multi-pass renders
- ▶ The External Compositing tag and After Effects
- ▶ Projecting shadows

Introduction

I had a professor in college who taught several interesting technology classes, and one particular course was aimed at examining how computers are viewed and used in modern society. A prevailing topic of the course was the idea of how we put way too much credit into data and information created by computers and how frustrating computer errors can be largely attributed to the owner. My professor would point out that computers only do what we tell them to, meaning that the output that we get from them is the result of the input we humans give them.

You aren't a real designer until you've stared at a progress bar that's trickling along like sand down an hour glass. Waiting on renders can be agonizing, but sometimes it's our own fault. You should have noticed in the previous chapters that our scenes are becoming more complex with things like lights, shadows, materials, reflections, and transparency. The combination of these elements has caused your render previews to take far longer than before. Most of us don't have supercomputers processing our scenes, so you have to understand long renders come with the territory of complex design.

Part of being a good designer is not just to design a beautiful scene or object; it's designing your project to render as effectively as possible. Time is money, and if you spend twice as long waiting on renders, you are being less efficient than you could be. For example, you may render a scene and it takes one minute to render your preview frame. One minute is not a long time to wait by itself, but what if your animation is 10 seconds long? That's 300 frames, or 5 hours of rendering at the aforementioned rate.

What if you could easily cut that down to four hours? Or may be to just two and a half? Every minute counts when you are trying to maximize your productivity. Rendering in Cinema 4D hogs your computer's resources and slows down your system, it's not recommended that you use any other system-intensive applications while rendering. So it's important to learn plenty of tricks and tips for not just rendering your final file, but previewing your renders so you only need to render your file one time because you know you got it right.

This chapter will explain all the important aspects of rendering; our ultimate goal is to get your images and animations out of Cinema 4D as fast and good-looking as possible. You are responsible for telling your computer what kind of image it should render. Don't yell at your computer if your image looks terrible or is taking forever to render; it's simply following orders from the boss, and that's you.

Render settings overview

The decisions you make when setting up your renders should be the result of the consideration between how long you need your render to take and how good you want your image to look. The render settings window has most of the controls you will need to optimize your render. This recipe is an overview of the most crucial options available when rendering, and how adjusting them can help you juggle the speed and quality of your renders.

Getting ready

Use the Glass_Spiral.c4d file from the **C4D Content Pack** for this recipe. It's a simple project for this warm-up exercise; you just have it open to follow along and make a few adjustments along the way.

How to do it...

We have a simple scene with some floating glass shapes and a camera slowly moving towards them. Let's say our animation is complete as it is, so now let's get the file ready to render properly:

1. Open the render settings, which is found in the **Render** menu or activated with the shortcut of *Ctrl* or *command + B*. A window should pop up with a column on the left-hand side that has all of our parameters to control how our render looks. Let's break down the categories and highlight some of the most useful features found in this window.

2. The **Save** option is checked by default, meaning that if you render this image, Cinema 4D will look to save this file somewhere on your computer. Files are rendered in Cinema 4D via the Picture Viewer, which displays what our render looks like as well as the progress of the total render. By unchecking the box next to **Save** (either within the menu or outside the menu in the left-hand column), we can render to the Picture Viewer without creating an actual copy of the rendered file somewhere on our computer. This is alright to do when you are just testing renders out while gathering all the information available through the Picture Viewer. Leave the box checked so we can save our file.

3. The **Save** options are mostly used to control what kind of file we want to render and where it will end up. Click on the ellipses button next to the empty **File** field and find a spot on your computer where you'd like to save your renders from this book. Name the file `Glass_Spiral_Render`, and then click on **OK** to go back to the **Render Settings** window to see our complete path loaded into the **File** field:

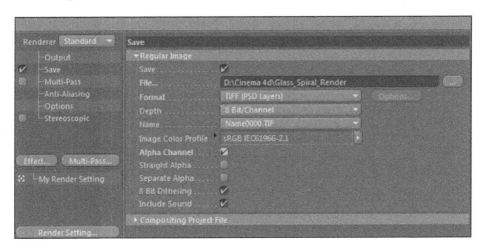

4. The **Format** drop-down menu contains all sorts of different file formats that we can select as the file type we want our render to ultimately be. Each file has its own special attributes; I use TARGA or TIFF as my format quite often, which is a setting that creates an image sequence consisting of separate files for each frame rather than one movie containing them all. For this exercise, let's just select QuickTime movie so we have a simple playable file at the end.

Rendering an image sequence instead of a movie file has its advantages. You can easily render parts of the sequence as a frame range in case you need to perhaps change a certain section without having to start over and do an entire new movie. Think if there's a power outage, your computer crashes, or maybe you need to stop the render and do something else. If you have half of your frames done when this happens, your computer has saved those frames, whereas the movie file will be incomplete and probably corrupted; it may not even open properly.

5. The **Alpha Channel** checkbox controls whether you want to render your image with the transparency information that exists in Cinema 4D. Otherwise, your image will be rendered over black in areas that have no defined geometry. The **Straight Alpha** checkbox allows you to render your image with a straight alpha channel rather than a premultiplied alpha, which can be useful when using your render in certain compositing projects afterward. With the **Separate Alpha** checkbox activated, Cinema 4D will simultaneously render a grayscale TIFF image sequence that is separate from your actual render, in case you need it for compositing purposes.

6. There are different types of video that have special specifications for resolution, frame rate, and aspect ratio. The **Output** option in the **Render Settings** window has everything you need to customize the specifications of the image you are going to render. At the very top, you have a **Presets** menu that is divided up into different categories for web, video, and print and likely has the right settings already predetermined for you.

7. You can manually adjust all of the important parameters instead. The **Width** and **Height** parameters control how big your render actually is; by default it's in pixels, but you can change it to other units of measurements such as inches if you are creating a document for print. Likewise, the **Resolution** field below it is for changing the DPI, in case you are going to perhaps print a high-quality image of your render. For our image, we want to render this in 1080 HD, so change the **Width** value to **1920** and the **Height** value to **1080**, or select the preset labeled **HDTV 1080 29.97**:

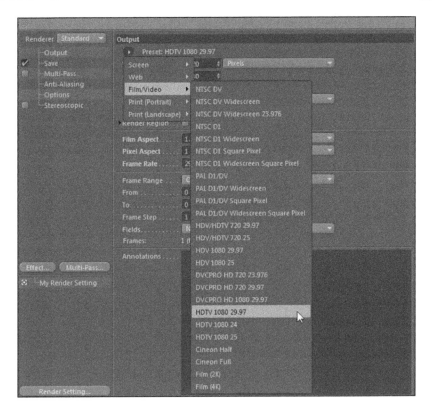

You can save lots of time by rendering a smaller-sized image in case you only need to see a sample of your render. Early on in your project, you don't really need your render to be full-sized yet just to get a general feel for the look and animation, so pick a smaller render size to work with. Take the full resolution value in the **Width** and **Height** fields and enter /2 right after them to divide the values by two. Now, they are exactly half, with the same aspect ratio. You'll spend less time waiting to see what your render looks like.

8. The next group of the **Output** option contains the **Film Aspect**, **Pixel Aspect**, and **Frame Rate** options. The **Film Aspect** option can automatically resize your image to fit within a number of different common aspect ratios. Ours is now listed at HDTV (16:9), which is important to consider when examining your scene in the Viewer because we now have a wider image that is no longer cutting off the edges of our scene as if it was a 4:3 ratio image.

9. If you know you are going to be working in a specific aspect ratio, change the setting in the beginning so it's easier to visualize how much space you are working with on screen. The **Pixel Aspect** option can be switched to accommodate different-sized pixels like those used in DV NTSC, DV PAL, Anamorphic, and a few others. The **Frame Rate** option controls how many frames per second are rendered; this will change the render value but not the actual frame rate in your timeline. To do that, you'll need to go under the **Edit** menu and find **Project Settings**, where the **FPS** field has the actual frames per second that your timeline will use. This is important because it affects the timing of your keyframes and data in your timeline, so it's wise to set this to the proper rate before you start animating.

10. The last group under the **Output** settings controls how much of your timeline you are actually going to render. The **Frame Range** option has several settings to choose from; **Current Frame** will only do the frame in which the playhead is currently positioned. **All Frames** does the entire length of the timeline, and **Manual** allows you to set specific start and end points using the **From** and **To** fields. **Manual** allows you to render just a portion of your scene if need be. Set the **Frame Range** option to **All Frames** so we can render the full 90-frame animation of our glass spiral.

11. Under **Options** we find all sorts of, well, options, that we can adjust, activate, and deactivate in order to change the quality and speed of renders. Many of your projects can use the defaults and they will suit you just fine. But, here's where you can make some wide, global changes to how your project looks in its final render.

12. The top options are checkboxes for **Transparency**, **Refraction**, **Reflection**, and **Shadow**. By deactivating these, we could simply remove all instances of each from our renders, which saves a lot of time if we want to render something quick and don't want to wait on some heavy transparency or reflections to render. Uncheck the **Transparency** box and do a render preview with *Ctrl* or *command + R* and you'll see how quickly the scene renders with the transparency deactivated. If you have lots of complex materials, you can easily deactivate these render-hogging properties right here instead of individually inside each material, and you'll get to preview your scene much faster:

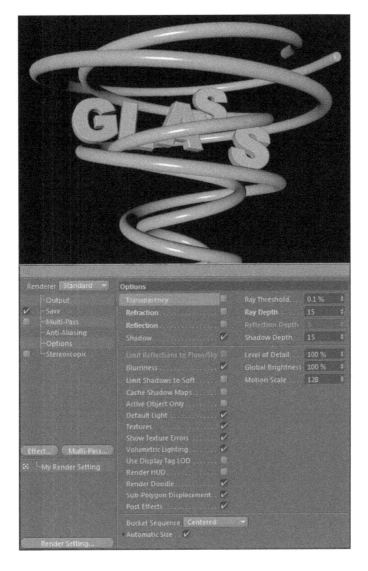

13. The other noteworthy settings under **Options** are the **Ray Depth**, **Reflection Depth**, and **Shadow Depth** options. These settings all behave similarly; in complex scenes can require higher depth settings than the defaults. Rays are used in Cinema 4D to bounce off objects and surfaces to send back information to the renderer. The setting for **Ray Depth** is used to calculate the number of times a ray is allowed to bounce within the scene, thus affecting the levels of transparency in our render.

14. Do render previews with the default level of **Ray Depth** set to **15**, check back on the **Transparency**, **Refraction**, and **Reflection** boxes from the last step, and take note of how long the scene takes. Mine took 34 seconds on my computer. Now, reduce the **Ray Depth** option from **15** down to **6** and do another render preview. Visually the renders are pretty close in quality; you probably wouldn't notice a difference just by looking at them. But this render for me took 21 seconds, which in an animation that runs 10 seconds or 300 frames long would save an hour of waiting during our render time, just from tweaking our **Ray Depth** setting:

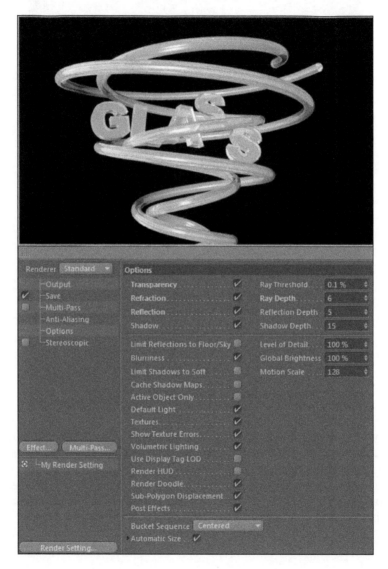

You may need to increase **Ray Depth** if you have a lot of transparent materials and surfaces overlapping. Creating complex transparent objects like a crystal or a diamond will require more rays to bounce so all of the transparent surfaces are accounted for. Long render times will be *unavoidable*.

15. Now that we've sifted through most of the important render settings, we can go ahead and render our file. Hit the **Render to Picture Viewer** button or *Shift + R* to render our glass spiral scene. You can actually wait for the render to finish and see Cinema 4D do its job, or you can move on to the next recipe and keep learning some more effective rendering methods.

How it works...

We went over a lot of the important and influential render settings that change the speed, quality, and format in which we render. There's plenty more to go over within the **Render Settings** window; we skipped a few topics that deserve their own recipes throughout this chapter. This was a good overview and warm-up exercise, and we can now move on to some more advanced techniques to help grow your rendering knowledge.

There's more...

This was just an appetizer; there are plenty more recipes to be learned in this chapter about how to properly render files in Cinema 4D. Keep going!

Don't be tempted with effects

The **Effects** button in the left-hand column has some very tempting goodies to try and add to your rendering effort to enhance your project. Stop right there and step away from the effects! You should ignore most of them and do your post adjustments in another program such as After Effects or Photoshop. Effects like color correction, glow, and highlights should not even be bothered with in Cinema 4D; they will only add to your render times. Effects should be applied in another application after your render is done so that you can add effects that are non-destructive and not embedded into your actual image. You'll never get the perfect render straight out of Cinema 4D, so just get it as close as you can and use other programs to make adjustments and add any effects as you please.

Creating a batch of renders

A good way to utilize your computer is to have it set up to render multiple files consecutively, that way you don't have to physically activate the render each time. This is called **batch rendering**, and it's useful because you can leave your computer for a long stretch of time but still keep the computer productive. Instead of rendering just one file and heading home from work, you can render multiple files and have your computer working overnight while you are enjoying your free time. This recipe shows how to take advantage of the fact that computers can work overtime without us having to.

Getting ready

Use the `Batch_Render.c4d` file for this recipe in the C4D Content Pack.

How to do it...

1. Batch rendering in Cinema 4D works by loading actual C4D files into the Render Queue, where they are sequentially rendered based on the render settings you specify in each project. If we have one file like our `Batch_Render.c4d` file, we need to save copies of this file and load them separately into the Render Queue.

2. Play this animation in the timeline and see what we have. It's a 90-frame animation of a **Figure** object doing some incredible jumping jacks, with three cameras in total in the scene doing different moves. We are going to render a QuickTime movie for each camera angle, so make sure **Camera 1** is selected and active in your Viewer. Now, go to your **Render** menu and select **Render Settings**, and under the **Save** options you need to specify a spot on your computer where to save these three renders. Make a new folder called `Batch Renders` and save this render as `Batch_Render`, and make it a QuickTime movie for playback:

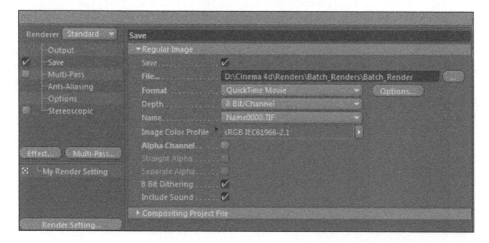

3. Next, go to the **Render** menu and select **Add to Render Queue** (you can save the file if prompted), and your file is set to render with our specified settings. But, inside the Render Queue, we are able to import other project files or switch between cameras in our current project. Go to the **File** menu in the Render Queue and select **Add Current Scene**, then select the new instance of your project and pick **Camera 2** from the **Camera** drop-down menu. You may have to manually append the render name in the **Image** field; make sure it ends in **Camera 2**. Repeat the process and switch the file to be rendered with **Camera 3**. Once they are all in there, go under the **Job** menu and hit **Start Rendering**, and check back in a few minutes to see your rendered files. Make sure they are all separate files, each with a different camera angle.

How it works...

The Render Queue in Cinema 4D is where we set up our computer to render your project file with different camera angles, or different .c4d files altogether. By adding jobs in the queue files we are able to render as many consecutive files as necessary, without activating them individually after one render finishes. As long as the files are entered with different names in the **Output** path, you'll get different renders from different files.

There's more...

If you sleep for eight hours, that means you can set up eight hours' worth of renders to process overnight. Create some different files with different light setups, materials, camera angles, and so on to examine and compare the results when you are fresh the next day. Utilize the entire clock while you are away so you don't have to wait on renders the next day while you are actually awake. This way you will be able to start working immediately and be more productive. Computers only go to sleep when you tell them to.

Give it some space

Make sure you don't create renders that are going to hog all your hard drive space as a batch render. If you only have a few gigabytes of space left, don't queue up files that will exceed that because your renders won't be able to finish while you are away.

Previewing renders with Render Region

Sometimes you don't need to focus on the big picture; sometimes you are only worried about the details. If you have a scene that takes a while to render a preview, you can limit the area in which you preview your image using the **Render Region** tool. There are two versions of the tool: regular Render Region and the Interactive Render Region. This recipe will show you how to use both.

Getting ready

We will be using the `Warm_Wine_Scene_Render_region.c4d` project. It's the same setup from *Chapter 5, Let there be Lights*; with it we will learn to focus only on specific parts of our image to render when previewing.

How to do it...

1. Our wine scene contains a lot of reflections and transparency, so this render will take a bit if we want to preview the whole thing. Start by doing a render preview by hitting *Ctrl* or *command + R* then note how long the render takes to process via the time in the bottom-left corner of the Viewer. Mine took a minute and 20 seconds, which is understandable with all these objects and **Global Illumination** turned on:

2. In order to be efficient, we shouldn't wait all that time if we don't have to. Imagine you are to the point in this scene where you are only focused on how the bowl of grapes looks. We can limit our render preview to only that particular portion of the Viewer using the **Render Region** tool.

3. The **Render Region** tool can be activated under the **Render** menu by selecting **Render Region**. Your cursor becomes crosshairs and you can now click-and-drag to select just a rectangular section of your image to render a preview. Click-and-drag to draw a rectangular box around the bowl of grapes and release the mouse; Cinema 4D will start rendering the portion you selected and nothing else. Once complete, note the time in the corner again that represents how long this portion took. Mine took just 15 seconds to render instead of one minute and 20 seconds for the whole frame.

4. Using the **Render Region** tool is just fine if you only want a one-time preview of your region, or if you are going to check on the rendered state of the image sparingly. But, what if you want to examine the image constantly while you tweak, so you can view the corrections without having to ask Cinema 4D to render each time? You can set up an Interactive Render Region to constantly render your specified area anytime you make a change to a parameter in your scene.

5. Select the **Interactive Render Region** option under the **Render** menu and Cinema 4D will automatically load a box in the center of your screen that renders just the image inside of it. The quality of the renders can be controlled by sliding the small triangle on the right side of the box up or down the height of the box. Place the triangle at the top, which will make our render at the highest quality, then resize the box so it fits over our bowl of grapes. Wait until your region renders and note the time it takes to render in the bottom-left corner. On my computer it took only nine seconds to render the bowl; much better if we are just focusing on this part of the scene:

6. Let's make two adjustments and observe the changes happening live in our scene. First, take the material labeled **Red Grapes** in the **Material Manager** and apply it to your **Grapes** group inside the **Object Manager**. Notice how when you apply the new material, the **Interactive Render Region** tool resets and starts rendering an up-to-date preview. We now have a different flavor of grapes in a different bowl right before our eyes. Apply the **Silver Bowl** material to the bowl object and the region resets and shows us a completely different look for our bowl of grapes:

How it works...

The **Render Region** tool allows us to select just a portion of our image to render in the Viewer, allowing us to focus on specific areas of our scene. We can manually select just a specific area to render one time, or we can set up an Interactive Render Region to constantly update the preview of our image whenever we change parameters inside Cinema 4D. These techniques allow us to save time and focus on specific parts of our image without rendering anything extra, so we can work faster by spending less time waiting on full-frame render previews.

Comparing different renders

Instead of making mental images of what your renders used to look like and comparing them to your current renders, you can observe actual changes firsthand by using the Cinema 4D's **Compare** menu in the Picture Viewer. You can load rendered frames into the Viewer and use a variety of tools to spot differences between two images that are rendered with any differences in lighting, materials, positioning of objects, render quality, you name it.

Getting ready

We will be using the `Warm_Wine_scene_Render_Region.c4d` project again for this recipe. Revert back to the original version if you want to have green grapes again by navigating to **Revert to Saved** in the **File** menu.

How to do it...

1. Our wine scene is modeled, lit, and textured from before, so all we need to focus on is the rendering. We used this scene earlier to demonstrate how to use an HDR image and Global Illumination, so let's try to highlight exactly how having Global Illumination influences our render by using the **AB Compare** feature. Open the **Render Settings** window and uncheck the **Save** box so that our image is not actually saved to your hard drive. Make sure that Global Illumination is applied as an option on the left-hand side. Now, either hit the **Render to Picture Viewer** button in the toolbar or press _Shift + R_. It may take a while with the GI active, so just be patient.

2. The Picture Viewer has a copy of our wine scene once it officially finishes rendering. The column on the right-hand side has all the recent images you've rendered, and this frame from our wine scene should be the most recent one. Now, either context-click or right-click on the image name in the column, or go to the **Compare** menu on top and select **Set as A**. Our image is now loaded and ready to be compared to a different frame:

3. Go back into the **Render Settings** window and deactivate **Global Illumination**, either via the checkbox if it's present or by finding it under the **Effects** menu on the left-hand side of the window. Now, render your scene to the Picture Viewer again, and the wait for this render will be much shorter since the GI is now off. Once finished, the image with GI should be below your first render in the Picture Viewer, so under the **Compare** menu select the option as **Set to B**.

4. Now you have two images, an A image and a B image, to compare in the Picture Viewer. You may have noticed a white line appear in the window, this is the dividing line between our A and B image. You can slide this image up or down, so elect **Swap Vert./Horiz.** in the **Compare** menu to move the slider left to right. Slide the line back and forth and notice the effects of our Global Illumination in image A in comparison to the lack of it in image B:

How it works...

You can set an A image and a B image in the Picture Viewer that will allow you to compare the look and quality of our scene with any changes you make between renders. We can now compare our wine scene with and without Global Illumination (GI), while being able to tell how long the render for each takes per frame. At this point, we can analyze the quality increase at the sake of render time, and we can easily determine if our GI is crucial to getting the final look that we want, or if it can be sacrificed for a quicker render. In this project, the render with GI looked really good but it took forever to render, while the lighting setup we have looks terrible without GI but renders faster. You can either wait a long time for a way better render with GI, or adjust the lighting and try to get a better-looking image that renders faster. You can make tweaks and load in a new image B to compare to the GI version to try and get it to look better.

There's more...

We'll use this **AB Compare** tool again in the next recipe dealing with anti-aliasing.

Do you have the time?

The Picture Viewer has the **History** tab loaded by default in the column on the right, which will detail how long each frame takes to render. Use this information to determine if you need to decrease the quality to get a faster render, or if you can afford to use more intensive settings because it took less time than you anticipated. Render times can vary from frame to frame. The more geometry and objects in a frame there are, the longer the render will take. Make sure you don't assume the render will be quick because the initial frames rendered quickly, but once your animation or scene got more complex the render slowed down drastically.

Adjusting your image inside Cinema 4D

You can also perform basic image adjustments such as **Contrast**, **Exposure**, and **Brightness** as well as basic grading within the Picture Viewer. Simply switch to the **Filter** tab and play with the settings until you get the effect you want. The settings should be fairly straightforward if you're familiar with an image processing program such as Gimp or Photoshop. To save your newly altered result, navigate to **File** within the Picture Viewer menu and select **Save as**. Then choose your preferred format and check the **Use Filter** checkbox:

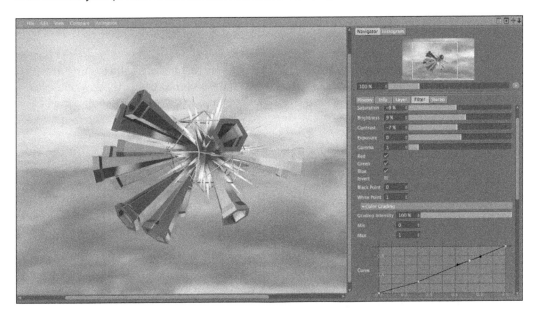

Using anti-aliasing effectively

The objects you create within Cinema 4D are created in a world of shapes, lines, and math. But, when you render them out to your computer, you are creating bitmapped images that contain pixel data, so we have to manage anti-aliasing to get the best out of our renders. **Anti-aliasing** is the process of reducing the rough and jagged edges you find in bitmapped images by dividing pixel information into smaller subpixels, then averaging them to form a smoother result. Balancing and tweaking your anti-aliasing settings are important for creating images that are give and take between results that are high-quality and what renders fast. This recipe demonstrates when higher anti-aliasing is needed and how to adjust the quality settings to get optimal results.

Getting ready

Open the `Anti_Aliasing_Demo.c4d` project from the Cinema 4D Content Pack to use with this recipe.

How to do it...

1. We have a blue background with concentric circles surrounded by blue orbs in our scene. This scene is pretty basic. It will render very fast because the lighting and materials are all pretty simple to start. Open the **Render Settings** window and click on the **Anti-Aliasing** option on the left-hand column and note the default options. The **Anti-Aliasing** setting is set to **Geometry** by default, which eliminates rough edges on the geometry of the objects in your scene.

2. Go ahead and render this scene to the Picture Viewer by pressing *Shift + R*, it will render very fast. Using the **Compare** menu in the Picture Viewer set this frame as the A object for now:

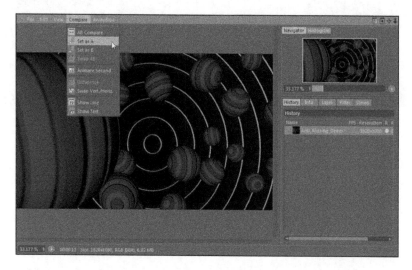

3. Next, go back into the **Anti-Aliasing** options in the **Render Settings** window and switch the mode from **Geometry** to **Best**. Once activated, we have a couple more options that are no longer grayed out. The **Best** setting provides anti-aliasing beyond just edges in geometry—it factors in changes in color, contrast, shadows, reflection, transparency, and more.

4. With the **Best** mode active, render your scene again to the Picture Viewer and then set it as the B object in the **Compare** menu. Now, we have our A object set to anti-aliasing with the **Geometry** setting and our B object set with the **Best** mode. Slide the dividing line to compare between each frame. You shouldn't notice a difference between the two images; the anti-aliasing had no effect when the quality was set to a higher level:

5. When your scene lacks a heavy amount of details in shadows, reflections, and transparency you can leave the **Anti-Aliasing** option set to **Geometry** and you should be fine. But, when your scene becomes more complex you will have to bump up the setting to **Best** in order to get an acceptable result.

6. In the **Render Settings** window, activate the **Transparency** and **Reflection** checkboxes under the **Options** parameters. These features were turned off in your previous renders; now they are active. Now, go into the **Anti-Aliasing** setting and switch the mode back to **Geometry**, and render our scene to the Picture Viewer. Our scene now has more render-intensive materials all over the place, so be prepared to wait a little longer for this one to finish.

7. Select this new reflective frame in the **History** window and set it as the A object in the **Compare** menu. You should notice right away that the reflections seem kind of harsh, but it will be even more glaring when the anti-aliasing is bumped up.

8. So, go ahead and do it: bump the **Anti-Aliasing** feature up to **Best** and render this frame to the Picture Viewer. Load this frame into the B object and slide the divider back and forth, and zoom in close with the zoom control in the bottom-left corner. Notice our image looks better with the higher anti-aliasing:

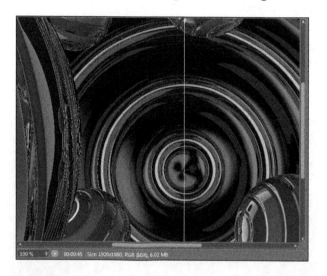

How it works...

The **Geometry** setting for **Anti-Aliasing** is primarily used for simpler scenes. It focuses the efforts on smoothing edges on your geometry and renders very fast. The **Best** mode is required to get acceptable renders when you are dealing with scenes that have more sophisticated materials and lighting. Our reflections were sharp and jagged when rendered with the **Geometry** setting so we needed to switch to **Best** in order to get a better image. Conversely, our original render without any transparency or reflections was not affected at all when we used the **Best** setting, so we could simply leave the default **Geometry** setting active.

There's more...

Check out the *The Compositing tag* recipe to see another useful trick for applying selective anti-aliasing.

1x1, 2x2, 4x4...

The **Min Level** and **Max Level** settings become active in the **Anti-Aliasing** menu when you select the **Best** mode, and these settings control the accuracy of the anti-aliasing with a direct effect on the speed of your render. The numbers represent the amount of neighboring pixels that are sampled around each pixel, with the higher levels potentially yielding more accurate results at the expense of longer sampling and render times.

If you would like to try and get more accurate renders, raise both the **Min Level** and **Max Level** values to higher than the default **1x1** and **4x4**, but if you want to speed up your render while still using the **Best** mode, lower the **Max Level** value down from **2x2** to **1x1**. Use the **AB Compare** tool to check the result to see if it's worth it; sometimes results can be negligible and worth adjusting to improve render times. You may have noticed our render wasn't very clean in a lot of areas. Here is an improved render with the **Min Level** value set to **4x4** and the **Max Level** value set to **8x8** for our anti-aliasing:

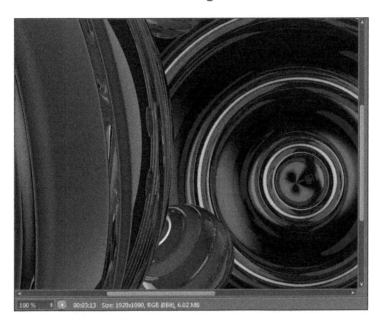

Using the Filter menu

There are several settings under the **Filter** drop-down menu that determine how your image is processed. Each setting has different levels of blurring or sharpening and can give you slightly different results depending on the content of your scene. For scenes with high movement, try the **Animation** setting; it blurs more of your edges when anti-aliasing is applied, which may reduce a flicker when viewed as a movie file. The images it outputs may also look a tad more realistic. Since the edges won't appear as sharp, they may look more convincing like they were shot on an actual camera. Check the *Cinema 4D Reference* documentation for some very detailed notes on all of the **Filter** options.

Exploring the Physical Renderer engine

One of the newer features of Cinema 4D is a new rendering engine called the **Physical Renderer**, which simulates camera effects such as depth of field and motion blur to create more realistic-looking images. We explored the settings briefly in *Chapter 4, Cameras are Rolling*, when examining the **Physical** tab available in cameras. Now, we'll tackle how to use more of the features available in the **Render Settings** window to get some realistic-looking camera effects.

Getting ready

Locate and open the `Bokeh.c4d` file in the C4D Content Pack to use with this recipe.

How to do it...

1. Right now, this project is just a bunch of floating colorful spheres dancing around. Hit *Ctrl* or *command* + *R* to do a render preview, and you'll see a frame of our scene and be very unimpressed. But, with the right camera setup we can turn these uninspiring little orbs into a cool-looking image of bokeh, the photography term for out of focus points of light that are beyond the camera's depth of field, which can create some pleasant-looking images. Think of holiday lights that are blurry in the background when you have a shallow focus on your camera:

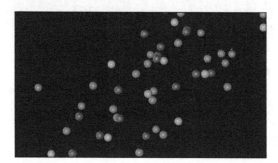

2. The Physical Renderer should only be used when we want to create these kinds of camera effects. If your project doesn't require any sort of effects like depth of field or motion blur, you should stick with the standard renderer. Open the **Render Settings** window and switch the option in the top-left corner from **Standard** to **Physical**.

3. If you do a render preview now, you'll get largely the same image as before; you'll just note that it takes longer. Like I said, the Physical Renderer will likely take longer to calculate your image, so if you aren't using the effects it's designed for, don't bother with it. Select the camera in the **Object Manager** and head to the **Attribute Manager** to examine some of the settings. Under the **Physical** tab the **F-Stop** option has been set to **1.2**, which will give us a lot of blur on our out-of-focus objects.

This leads us to the **Object** tab next, where you'll see that the **Focal Length** option is set to **300** mm or **Super Tele**, and the **Focus Distance** option is **500**, which is far in front of our spheres. These settings will cause our sphere to become very blurry when we activate the depth of the field.

4. Back in the **Render Settings** window, check the box to enable **Depth Of Field**, then hit *Ctrl* or *command + R* to do a render preview. You should immediately see the difference; our spheres are now out of focus and creating these soft blurry dots, or our bokeh. The render takes much longer because it's accounting for the depth of the field, but you're getting a much more interesting image as a result:

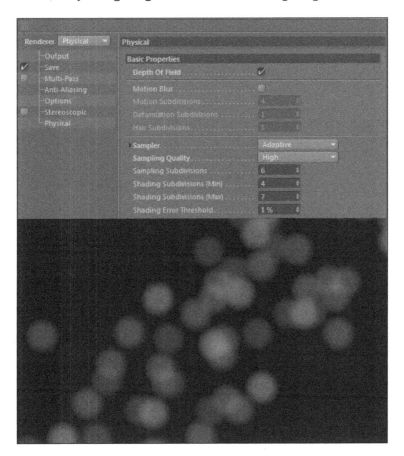

5. The Physical Renderer has different samplers that you can choose to handle your renders. The default is **Adaptive**, which adjusts the renderer to account for more complicated areas when calculating the image. The default **Sampling Quality** setting of **Low** is making our bokeh look fuzzy. Bump it up to **High** and do a render preview. The render will take much longer, but the quality increase will seem necessary.

6. The next sampler to examine is **Fixed**, which offers a high-quality sampling method, but takes longer than **Adaptive** because it doesn't adjust to the areas of your image that need more or less sampling. Switch to the next sampler, **Progressive**, which uses a very different method to arrive at your image using the Physical Renderer. Do render preview with **Progressive** set as the **Sampling Quality** value and you'll notice almost instantly you get a low-quality render, and Cinema 4D will gradually refine it over time. This is useful for seeing a quick, low-quality sample without waiting, so you can make adjustments sooner if you don't like where the render is heading.

7. Set the **Sampler** option back to **Adaptive** and **Sampling Quality** back to **High**. We want to increase the **Sampling Subdivisions** option to **9**, just to try and avoid some of that noise around the edges of our bokeh.

8. Head down into the **Physical** tab of your camera and locate the **Diaphragm Shape** box. Check the box and untwirl the options to examine this feature that is the key for an effect like bokeh. Depending on how many blades the aperture of the camera has, it will affect the shape in which your points of light defocus. Leave the **Blades** set to **6** and do a render preview. You'll notice our shapes are less circular and seem more like hexagons, because the number of blades we defined in the **Physical** tab controls the defocused shape of our particles:

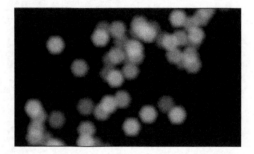

How it works...

The Physical Renderer is a new feature in Cinema 4D that allows us to add creative camera effects to our renders. We took a simple scene with some floating spheres and turned them into bokeh. With the right settings activated on our camera and in our Physical Renderer, we are able to create this cool effect.

There's more...

If you are using the Physical Renderer and have a scene being lit by **Global Illumination**, try using the **Indirect Illumination** setting instead. It's a different method for distributing your light available when you activate the Physical Renderer, and it may give you better results or a quicker render, depending on the scene.

The Compositing tag

We've learned about quite a few tags so far, and now we are finally ready to learn and use arguably the most useful tag of them all—the **Compositing** tag. The **Compositing** tag can control how objects interact with the surrounding scene, and it can affect visually how objects look when fully rendered. This project will try to show all of the useful features of the tag and show you how it's hard not to use it when you are making sophisticated projects and composites.

Getting ready

Load the project file `Rings_Text.c4d` from the C4D Content Pack for this recipe.

How to do it...

1. Check out the animation in the project to start. The word **RINGS** lands in the center of the screen and a row of spinning rings comes by and passes over it. Hit *Ctrl* or *command + R* to do a render preview on frame 60 to see the materials. The text has a reflective metal on it and the rings are made of a transparent glass. The scene is lit by the default auto light, so let's get to work on that.

2. Create a new material in the **Material Manager** and name it as `Sky`. Open the material in the **Material Editor** window and disable the **Color** and **Specular** channels, and enable the **Luminance** channel. Load the `STUDIO_ATM_01SN.hdr` image from the C4D Content Pack into the **Texture** field.

3. Next, create a new `Sky` object for our scene, and load the `Sky` material on it as our light source. Do another render preview and now we have some very interesting reflections going on. But the problem is, our sky is filling our frame, and if we want to be able to composite our text and rings later, we need to remove the sky but still keep its influence in our reflections:

4. This is where the **Compositing** tag comes through. Highlight the **Sky** object in the **Object Manager** and go under the **Tags** menu to Cinema 4D tags and find the **Compositing** tag. In the **Tag** tab, within the **Attributes Manager**, we have an assortment of checkboxes that allow us to enable or disable our object's influence on the properties that cause heavy renders, namely shadows, reflections, transparency, and refraction. Deselect the checkbox labeled **Seen by Camera** and watch how your sky instantly disappears, but do a render preview and you'll see that it is still influencing the text and rings in the scene, while remaining out of sight, which is exactly what we need for compositing purposes:

5. Now, add new **Compositing** tags to both the **Rings** group and the **Text** group. The tag will affect the children equally within the group, so we don't need to apply separate tags for each object. Now, watch how the tags can be used to omit certain objects from the more render-intensive properties.

6. Take the tag on the **Text** group and uncheck the box labeled **Seen by Transparency**. Next, do a render preview and look at how the rings are still transparent, but the text behind them is not visible inside the clear areas of the rings. Now, take the tag on the rings and uncheck the box that says **Seen by Reflection**. Now, your render preview will show that the reflective text is not showing any part of the rings in its reflection. Reset the checkboxes on these two tags back to the defaults; we want to be able to see everything within our transparency and reflections in our render.

7. The other powerful feature of the **Compositing** tag is the **Object Buffer** tab. Object buffers allow us to render mattes for groups of objects we choose, so that we cut out parts of our renders in a program such as After Effects and apply different color corrections and effects to specific parts of our one and only render.

8. Select the **Compositing** tag on our **Rings** group and go under the **Object Buffer** tab and check the first box at the top that says **Enable**. The **Buffer** field with the number **1** becomes active, and you can assign different objects to be included in different buffers with this feature. Leave this as **Buffer 1**, and in the next recipe we will render out the buffers and you'll see exactly how useful it is to have separate mattes that can mask out your image in the compositing stage.

9. Another useful feature alluded to in the previous anti-aliasing recipe is the **Force Antialiasing** option underneath the **Tag** tab of your **Compositing** tag. This feature allows you to apply selective anti-aliasing to objects specified by your **Compositing** tag. For the tag on the **Text** group, check the box to enable this feature, and leave the default settings. We are going to render our text group with this forced anti-aliasing and the rings without.

We are aiming to save time with our render, and the rings will be going by fast with some motion blur applied to them in After Effects, so the accuracy of their reflections and transparency in terms of anti-aliasing is not a concern. I will record how long my renders take with **Force Antialiasing** applied via the **Compositing** tag versus how long it takes to have **Best** anti-aliasing applied to the entire scene.

How it works...

The **Compositing** tag allows us to limit the render-intensive properties of objects it's applied to, thus making it possible to speed up renders. You'll also find times where you will have objects that you wish weren't visible to the camera but still influencing the scene, such as our HDR sky, and you can use the **Compositing** tag to hide the sky but not its impact. There will be times where you need to remove an object from impacting another object's reflection or transparency, or you want to remove the object from receiving Global Illumination or best quality anti-aliasing to speed up your render. The **Compositing** tag allows for ultimate flexibility when try to get your renders just right.

There's more...

Don't stop! Keep on going on to the multi-pass rendering recipe that awaits next. We will see how the **Compositing** tag produces very useful object buffers for use in our compositing stage.

Setting up multi-pass renders

The power of multi-pass rendering lies in the ability to generate several separate files filled with useful information from just one actual render. We can set Cinema 4D to output all sorts of different channels that we want control of in the compositing stage, and by having them as separate images we have all the flexibility we'll need to enhance our image. In the last recipe, we set up two object buffers with our **Compositing** tags, but there's plenty more to configure for our multi-pass render.

Getting ready

Hopefully, you still have the `Rings_Text.c4d` file from *The Compositing tag* recipe open and completed; we are going to be picking up right where it left off. We will also be using Adobe After Effects for this recipe, so be sure to have the program ready. You will also need to make sure the After Effects Exchange plugin has been installed correctly. It can be downloaded from Maxon from the following link:

`http://www.maxon.net/?id=1372`

How to do it...

1. We set up our file to be ready to render the last recipe, so open the **Render Settings** window inside the **Render** menu and let's set up a proper multi-pass render. Check the box next to **Multi-Pass** so we can open the **Save** option and define the path for both our actual image and our multi-pass images. Pick a path on your computer to save the file as `Rings_Text` and create a new folder to keep these renders separate. Activate the checkboxes for **Alpha Channel**, **Straight Alpha**, and then twirl down the **Compositing Project File** options and check the boxes for **Save** and **Include 3D Data**:

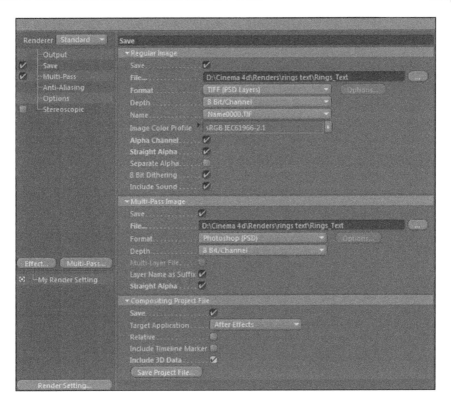

 Cinema 4D will append the end of your multi-pass files to include what channel or buffer it is, so you can just give it a generic name and it will label them automatically for you.

2. The **Output** and **Anti-Aliasing** settings are already configured properly, so all we need to do is click on the **Multi-Pass** button and add the necessary channels for our render. There are tons to choose from and different projects will require different channels. Click to add **Ambient**, **Diffuse**, **Specular**, **Shadow**, **Refraction**, **Reflection**, and **Object Buffer**. Check the **Object Buffer** option and make sure it has the **Group ID** value set to **1**, which corresponds to our **Rings** group. These passes should all be listed in the left-hand column, when we are ready to render, hit the **Render to Picture Viewer** button and wait for your render to complete.

3. When the render finishes, head into After Effects and go to the **File** menu, and find **Import** and select your `Rings_Text.aec` file in your folder for your renders. After Effects imports two folders that contain all your files. Twirl down the folders and check out the contents. Each image sequence is a separate component we specified our multi-pass render to generate.

4. The sequences all have an appended name to let you know what they correspond to. Open the `Rings_Text.c4d` project composition and you'll find a camera and our passes stacked and set to proper blending modes to make a composite image.

5. Drag the **Rings_Text[0000-0120].tif** sequence. This is our main render from Cinema 4D; place it at the top of the timeline. Click the small eyeball to the left to hide it and show the layers below. You will notice that the main rendered image is exactly the same as the composite images layered below it:

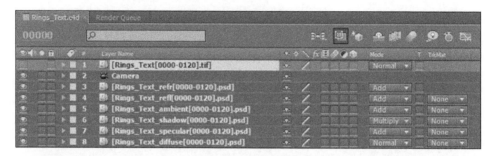

6. The benefit of having separate passes is that we have way easier control over how they look here in After Effects than we do in Cinema 4D. Highlight the reflection pass layer (**Rings_Text_refl[0000-0120]Text.psd**) and hit the **T** key to bring up the **Opacity** control of the layer and reduce it down to **50%**; do the same thing for the refraction layer. You'll see that the reflections are now less intense overall in our composition. So, instead of fussing with the **Brightness** and **Mix Strength** options in our **Material Editor** window in Cinema 4D, we saw our bright reflections change instantly on a fully rendered sample of our 3D scene. From here you can try other effects to enhance and stylize the reflections, like maybe adding a blur to soften them up or adding glows to make them appear much brighter:

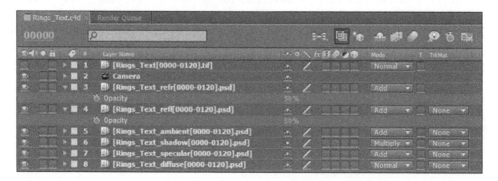

7. Don't forget about our object buffers. Hide all the separate passes by clicking on the eyeball to the left of their layer name and unhide the main render in the timeline. Drop in the file appended with `object_1` and place it directly above the main render in your timeline. We are going to activate what we call a **track matte** in After Effects, where we take either the alpha or luminance value of one layer to define the alpha channel of another. Our object buffers are rendered out as grayscale images and the objects that contained the **Compositing** tag with the buffer activated appear white, therefore defining their shape for us to use in After Effects.

8. Find the **Track Matte** drop-down menu next to the **Blending Mode** options in the timeline, and set our track matte for our main render to **Luma Matte**. This will take the black and white values of our object buffer and apply them as the alpha channel for our main render. Notice that we essentially cut out the rings from our render without actually getting rid of them:

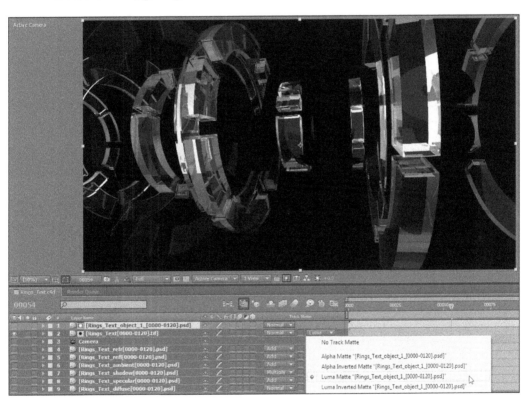

9. We can now pre-compose these two layers so they are seen as one layer with a clearly defined alpha channel. Select them both in the timeline and navigate up to the **Layer** menu and select **Pre-compose** towards the bottom. Name the composition Rings and hit **OK** on the pop-up window; now you have a nested composition containing just the rings from our render:

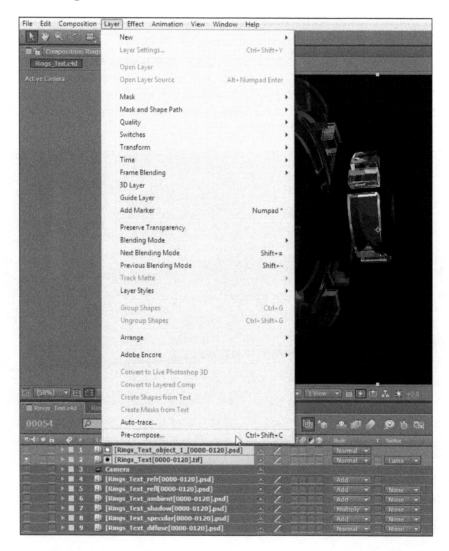

10. Drop in another copy of the main sequence below the **Rings** composition in the timeline, then drop the second object buffer right above it, then set the main sequence's track matte to **Luma Inverted Matte**, which will cut out the opposite image of our **Luma Matte** selection. This cuts out the text from our render, using the inverse colors from the object buffer to define this track matte:

11. Now, select the **Rings** composition and find the **Fast Blur** effect under the **Blur &
Sharpen** group in the **Effects** menu. Change the **Blurriness** value to **50** and the **Blur
Dimensions** value to **Horizontal**, and now you have a motion blur effect on just the
rings, and not the text. The elements defined by object buffers can be customized
with their own unique filters and adjustments, while leaving the other objects in the
same render unaffected:

How it works...

We can set up a multi-pass render to include as many different channels and properties as we
want control of in our composite. We can also include object buffers that we set up with the
Compositing tag that we can use in After Effects as track mattes to define the alpha channels
of specific objects we want to target with effects. Multi-pass rendering allows us to maximize
our ability to control how our image looks by giving us more options than we could possibly want
during the compositing stage. Instead of fussing over the adjustments and waiting to compare
differences between renders in Cinema 4D, we can get the image as close as we can and make
the final adjustments in real time in another powerful program such as After Effects.

There's more...

Check out the last recipe in this chapter on projecting shadows. It's another multi-pass example in case you just can't get enough.

Saves time, not space

You can add as many multi-pass channels as you wish, and it won't take much longer to render your image. It will, however, take up tons of space on your computer, because it is rendering full-frame image sequences for each pass you specify. If you are working in a large image format such as HD video, these files will accumulate and take up much more hard drive space. So make sure you actually want control over that particular pass before you add it to your multi-pass render, otherwise you'll just waste lots of valuable hard drive space. We rendered plenty of channels and didn't touch them in this recipe, so you may want to streamline the amount of passes you use based on the adjustments you anticipate making.

Adobe have recently introduced a new feature to After Effects CC, which somewhat simplifies the compositing process by allowing you to extract the various passes from your Cinema 4D file without having to render all of them out individually. It only works with version R14.042 or later and After Effects CC. There is a lot of good quality information online about how to use Cineware, especially on Adobe TV and Greyscale Gorilla.

How did that force anti-aliasing work out?

In the last recipe, we set the **Compositing** tag on our **Text** group and set it to force anti-aliasing upon this object, while leaving the main anti-aliasing settings for the render set to **Geometry** instead of **Best**. The idea was that we could add a motion blur to our rings in After Effects, so processing best quality anti-aliasing on those transparent rings was only going to slow us down. And it sure did. With the **Force Antialiasing** and **Geometry** combination, my whole project rendered in 10 minutes and 47 seconds. When I turned off the setting and switched the whole composition to render as **Best** instead, it took 20 minutes and 10 seconds. So, basically we cut our render time to half by using the **Force Antialiasing** option; that's something to think about next time you render.

The External Compositing tag and After Effects

Like his cousin the **Compositing** tag, we add the **External Compositing** tag to specific objects that we want to render and behave a certain way in After Effects. But, the **External Compositing** tag extracts different information from our objects in Cinema 4D. It takes the position and rotation of our surfaces and can export them as either null objects or solids in After Effects. This opens up several different possibilities for enhancing our renders in After Effects.

Getting ready

Open the `Animated_Computer_Monitor.c4d` project from the C4D Content Pack to use with this recipe. It's the monitor we applied video to in the last chapter on materials, now it has an animated camera and we are going to use the **External Compositing** tag to do the same in After Effects.

How to do it...

1. We want to be able to project an image on our computer monitor such as the previous recipe, but we are going to do it in a different way instead of applying materials. So, add a plane primitive and rename it `Screen` and change the **Orientation** value to **-Z** so it is facing the right way, and make it **1280** in the **Width** field and **720** in the **Height** field. We don't need to apply any materials to our screen, just two tags.

2. Apply the **External Compositing** tag found under the **Tags** menu in the **Cinema 4D Tags** submenu to your **Screen** object. Under the **Tag** tab, there are only a couple of options, but the one we need to activate is the **Solid** checkbox. This will render a solid object in After Effects to the size we specify in the **Size X** and **Size Y** fields. Change the **Size X** value to **1280** and the **Size Y** value to **720** to match the dimensions of our screen.

3. Now, add the cousin, the **Compositing** tag to the **Monitor** group, and under the **Object Buffer** tab check the box to **Enable Buffer 1**. Open the **Render Settings** window and check the **Multi-Pass** checkbox. Now, under the **Save** options, specify the path on your own computer where you can save the render and multi-pass files from this project in the **File** paths. Name the files `Animated_Monitor` in both fields.

Activate the **Alpha Channel** checkbox and then twirl down the **Compositing Project File** options if you can't see them below, and check the boxes for **Save** and **Include 3D Data**. Next, click the **Multi-Pass** button on the left-hand side and select **Object Buffer**. The default has loaded a buffer for anything with the one buffer active in a **Compositing** tag, which is what our screen has been set to. Your render is now ready, so hit the **Render to Picture Viewer** button and wait for it to finish so we can take it into After Effects to finish working with it:

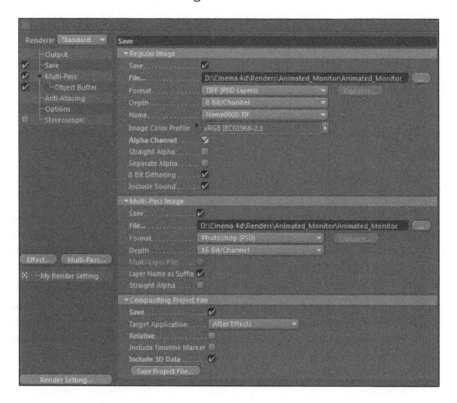

4. When the render is done, open After Effects and go under the **File** menu and find **Import**, then select **Files** and navigate to the spot on your computer where Cinema 4D outputs your render. Select the `Animated_Computer_Monitor.aec` file and it will import all the files and information we need. In the **Project** window, you can now twirl down the folders to see all of our files. Open the main composition and you'll see our rendered movie with our lights and animated camera already in place. The key object is the red Solid layer that is in place where our screen is. We can use the placement of this Solid layer to replace it with any video file we want.

5. Under the **Composition** menu, select the **New Composition** option and load **Preset** with **HDV/HDTV 720 29.97** so we have a composition that is **1280** x **720**. Enter the name as `Screen_Saver`, make 10 seconds or 300 frames as the **Duration** value, and click on **OK** to open the empty composition.

6. Now, go back to the **Import** option in the **File** menu and find the `Screen_Saver.` `mov` file in the C4D Content Pack and load it into After Effects. Place the `Screen_` `Saver.mov` file into the timeline of the new composition we've created, and now switch back to the main composition that came from Cinema 4D.

7. Now, we can take our red Solid layer and replace it with the `Screen_Saver` composition. Simply highlight the Solid layer in the timeline and then hold the *option* or *Alt* key while dragging the `Screen_Saver` composition from the **Project** window on top of the Solid layer in the timeline. After Effects will instantly swap the files, and now our `Screen_Saver` composition is occupying the same space that our Solid layer was. Scrub through the timeline and you'll see that the camera keeps the screen saver applied exactly where it needs to be to track with the monitor.

8. But, we need to fix our edges; the edges of our monitor cuts off the corners of the screen. That's why we rendered the buffer for our screen, so we can use a track matte to define the alpha channel of our new composition. Load in the rendered sequence for your buffer, it begins with `Animated_Monitor_object1`, and place it directly above the `Screen_Saver` composition in your timeline. Now, select the **Luma Inverted Matte** option from the **Track Matte** menu and you'll see the corners are no longer an issue:

How it works...

The **External Compositing** tag allows us to take the position and rotation properties of objects in Cinema 4D and use that information to composite in After Effects. We already learned how to add video as a material within Cinema 4D, but this method is different because it allows you to render out of Cinema 4D just one time, then add, swap, and mix multiple video clips in After Effects where you have far more control over the video. Our `Screen_Saver.mov` clip is nested in a composition, where we could add any new video we choose and have it update automatically as the image on our screen inside our main composition, and we have no more need to render any files within Cinema 4D anymore.

There's more...

We may design our scenes in 3D within Cinema 4D, but as soon as we rendered them out they become flat and 2D. They are nothing more than static movie files placed directly in the center of our composition. After Effects can't look at our pixels in a rendered file and determine what objects are placed where in the scene in terms of depth. That's why the **External Compositing** tag is very useful. We took an object in Cinema 4D and transferred its 3D properties to After Effects where we now have more control instead of it being rendered and flattened within the final rendered image.

Go from After Effects to Cinema 4D

You can also take a file from After Effects and export its camera settings and data into Cinema 4D to work with. It's also available on Maxon's plugin page, available at the following link:

`http://www.maxon.net/?id=1372`

Projecting shadows

You couldn't help but feel a little empty after completing the recipe we did earlier, which involved setting up a camera to match the image we had to the walkway covered by oak trees. I mean, we set up the camera and just kind of left it there, what gives? Here's where we add something extra to the scene by compositing a rolling sphere through our scene. There's quite a few tricks we needed to learn before being able to accomplish this effect, and after learning how to use the **Compositing** tag and multi-pass rendering we can now make a convincing composite and breathe some life into our still photo.

Getting ready

Make sure you do the *Matching your camera to footage* recipe from *Chapter 4, Cameras are Rolling*; we are picking up where we left off at the end of it.

How to do it...

1. So, where we left off we had a camera in the correct position to simulate the vantage point to where I took this photograph. Place a **Sphere** primitive into the scene, reduce its **Radius** value to **75**, increase the **Segments** value to **60**, and move it up in the **Y** position to **75**.

2. Next, create a new material in the **Material Manager** and name it `Sphere`, and open up the **Material Editor** window. Under the **Color** channel, we need to load a marble shader so that our sphere has a texture that we can observe its movement as it rolls. Change the gray knot on the gradient to be more of a blue color: try red to **53**, green to **144**, and blue to **213**. Open the **Specular** channel and change the **Width** value to **30%** and the **Height** value to **80%**:

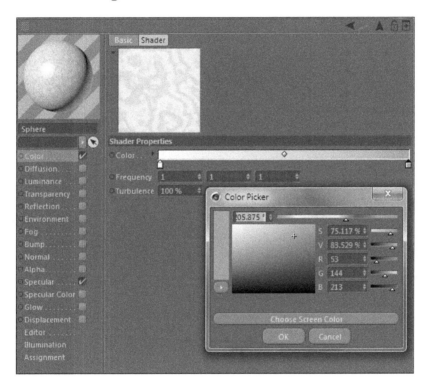

3. Now, we need to activate the **Reflection** channel to give our sphere a little bit of a mirrored quality, and so it picks up some of our scene and feels like it actually belongs there. Inside the channel, load a Fresnel shader and open the shader options to adjust the colors of the gradient. Make the white knot slightly darker, a really light gray with a value of **219** for the RGB values, and then apply this material to the **Sphere** object. Reduce the **Brightness** and **Mix Strength** options of the **Reflection** channel to **40%** each:

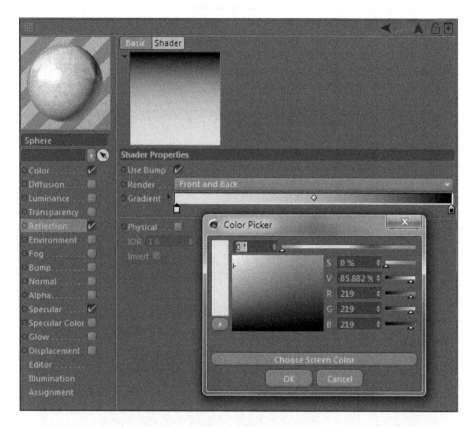

4. Animate the sphere by setting a keyframe for the **Z** position to be **1000** and the **R.P** value to be **0** at frame 1, and then adjusting the **Z** position value to be **-1850** and the **R.P** value to be **720** at frame 90 with two new keyframes. This will bring the sphere towards the camera with two complete rotations to make it appear as if it's rolling forward.

5. Next, we need to add a **Plane** primitive to act as the road surface that our sphere is rolling on. Resize the **Plane** primitive to have a **Height** value of **6000** in the **Object** tab of the **Attribute Manager**. Rename the **Plane** primitive to Road in the **Object Manager**.

6. Now, add a **Light** object to the scene, and under the **General** tab in the **Attributes Manager** leave it to the default **Omni** light and change the **Shadow** type to **Soft**. Then, go to the **Shadow** tab and increase the **Shadow Map** value to **1000x1000**.

Head under the **Details** tab and change the **Falloff** type to **Inverse Square (Physically Accurate)**. Now, adjust the position so it's high in the sky to simulate our sun, so move it up to **3000** in the **Y** position and move it closer to the front of our scene by changing the **Z** position value to **-500**. Do a render preview by hitting *Ctrl* or *command + R* and check out the shadow our sphere is casting on the road; this is going to be the source of our shadows when we composite.

7. Our sphere is very dark. It needs to be brightened up and reflect the surroundings in our oak tree scene. Add a **Sky** object and then place the material with the loaded image onto the sky. The sky has trumped our background, so let's add a **Compositing** tag to it and uncheck the **Seen by Camera** option, so it's hidden from our view. Do a render preview and check out how our sphere now has the scene reflecting on the outer parts of it:

You won't get 100 percent accurate reflections with just a flat image like this, but it's a simple way to add the feeling of the same environment into the reflection. The user has no chance of being able to determine whether these reflections are accurate in a quick animation such as this. They likely won't notice as long as your reflection projects a similar environment.

8. The most glaring thing you should have noticed in our render preview is that the sphere is reflecting the ugly gray floor below it, which is ruining the rest of the reflections in our sphere. Highlight the **Road** object in the **Object Manager** and go under **Tags | Cinema 4D Tags**, and add a **Compositing** tag. Now, under the **Tag** tab, check on the **Compositing Background** box, then take the material we have loaded in the **Material Manager** with our Oak Alley photo on it and apply it to the **Road** object.

9. Highlight the **Texture** tag in the **Object Manager** and make sure the **Projection** mode is set to **Frontal**, and now our **Road** object is seamlessly matched up perfectly with the road in the photograph, and the geometry will accurately reflect the ground into our sphere after you activate Global Illumination. Click on the **Effects** button, in the **Render Settings** window, and select **Global Illumination** and do a render preview to see the reflection of the ground:

10. There's one last step in setting up our scene to add a little something extra that simulates how this sphere would actually look if it were rolling on the road in this photo. Check out the shadows cast by the oak trees in the main photo. There are a few breaks where the sunlight is poking through. If the sun is affecting the lighting of the ground like in the photo, it should affect the lighting of the sphere. We need to simulate these bright spots as the sphere rolls our way, otherwise the final composite may seem a little off.

11. All we have to do to pull off this subtle effect is position a few lights to act as our sun spots and have our sphere get brighter as it passes under the lights. Create a new spot light and rotate it to face downward by changing its **R.P** to **-90**. Now, move it higher in the sky by increasing the **Y** position value to **500**. Reset the timeline to frame 1 and scrub forward and find where the sphere hits a spot of light. The first one should be at about frame 22, so move your light back in the **Z** position to be directly over the sphere when it hits the spot at this time, a **Z** position value of **450** looks about right. Finally, make sure that the light is only affecting the sphere, so under the **Project** tab drag the instance of the Road plane into the **Objects** list so the light has excluded the **Road** object from its illumination.

12. Now, duplicate the light by highlighting it in the **Object Manager** and holding the *Ctrl* or *command* key and dragging it to make a copy. The next sun spot it hits is at about frame 35, so line the new light up with it, give it a **Z** position value of **0**. Copy the light again and go to frame 44 where it gets bright again, and move the new light forward with a value of **-460** in the **Z** position. There's one more small spot we should get at frame 55, so make one last copy of the light and adjust its **Z** position to be **-950**. All these lights will make the effect worth it because they will make your composition more believable, and that's what really counts:

13. Add one last **Compositing** tag to the **Sphere** object and go under the **Object Buffer** tab in the **Attribute Manager**, and check the box to **Enable Buffer 1** and the **Force Anti-Aliasing** box in the **Tag** tab. Now, we are ready to render, so open the **Render Settings** window and let's get this thing ready to go.

14. Start with the **Output** options, load the **Preset** option for **HDTV 1080 29.97**, and adjust the **Frame Range** option to include **All Frames**. Next, under the **Save** options, specify the output path on your computer for this render, name it `Oak Alley`. Check the box to enable **Alpha Channel** and **Straight Alpha** so we can composite this effectively in After Effects.

15. Now, let's set up the **Multi-Pass** options. Check the box on the left-hand column to enable multi-pass rendering and twirl down the **Multi-Pass Image** options. Specify the same file path as before for the **File** field as well.

16. Under the **Compositing Project File** area, check the **Save** box and the **Include 3D Data** box. Now, click on the **Multi-Pass** button on the left to add the proper layers. Within the menu, select the option for **Shadow** and then **Object Buffer**. The buffer has a default level of 1 so we don't need to change it. This will make a separate render with our shadows to composite with, and the **Object Buffer** option will give us a matte to cut out our sphere from the image and isolate it later:

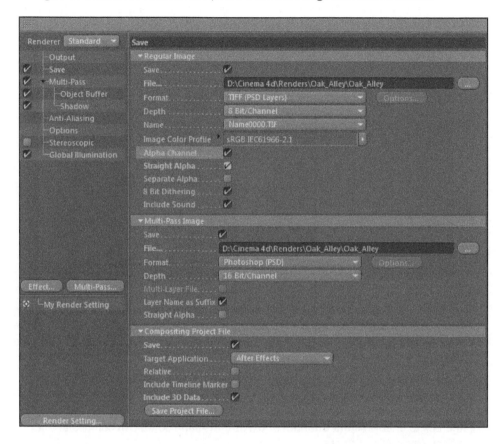

17. The last step is to turn the traffic light on our **Background** object in the **Object Manager** to be inactive in just the renderer by switching it to a red dot. Finally, save your project on your computer as Oak_Alley. We are all set, so hit the **Render to Picture Viewer** button and take a short break while Cinema 4D renders out our file.

18. Once your render is complete, open After Effects and load your composition project file into the After Effects under the Import option in the **File** menu. Also, load in the actual Oak_Alley.jpg image from the C4D Content Pack to be our official background.

19. Untwirl the folders down and examine our rendered files in the **Project** window. Open the `Oak_Alley.c4d` composition and you should see our timeline needs the two image sequences from our `Special Passes` folder, one being our main render and the other being the object buffer for our track matte. Place them in the timeline below the shadow sequence layer, and then hide the shadow sequence layer altogether by clicking on the eyeball on the far left of the layer in the timeline.

20. Keep the object buffer layer above the main render, and switch the **Track Matte** setting of the main render to **Luma Matte**, so it will use the white parts of the object buffer as its alpha channel. This means just our sphere will be cut out of the main image, so our road will no longer appear beneath it.

21. Highlight these two layers and then go under the **Layer** menu and select **Pre-compose**, set the name as `Sphere` and hit **OK** in the pop-up window. Now, they are nested as one image.

22. Now, place the `Oak_Alley.jpg` image as the bottom-most layer in the main composition, highlight it and hit the S key, and resize to have a scale value of **64%**. Now, it's in place as our background again. Finally, we can turn on our **Shadows** layer and make sure the blending mode is set to **Multiply**, so the white areas are knocked out and the darker areas pass through to the other layers, and our shadows are projected onto our background image.

23. We need to make some useful tweaks with several tools found under the **Blur and Sharpen** effects menu in After Effects to complete our composite. For the **Sphere** layer, add the effect **Directional Blur** with a **Blur Length** value of **7** with the default **Direction** value of **0** degrees. This will add a little bit of a blur to our moving sphere to make it seem like it's rolling fast.

24. On the **Shadows** layer, apply a **Gaussian Blur** filter with a value of **11** so the shadow appears to have softer edges. With the **Shadows** layer highlighted, hit the T key to bring up the **Opacity** controls and drop the **Opacity** down to **35%**, so the shadows appear to blend in with the scene and aren't as dark. We now have a nice-looking composite that makes our still photo much more interesting:

How it works...

We set up Cinema 4D to cast shadows to match the simulated movement of our sphere along the ground in our photo. The material we applied to it is slightly reflective, and by adding the right **Compositing** tags to objects in our scene, our sphere picks up fake but realistic-looking reflections that help it blend in properly with our environment. The lighting casts proper shadows onto our floor, and it also simulates the bright spots of the sun poking through the trees to add to the realism of our 3D scene. By setting up the right multi-pass render, we brought the scene into After Effects where we can composite the shadows properly and preform color corrections and adjustments and add the necessary effects to pull off our final composite.

There's more...

We could have just left our image as a frontal projection on our floor and get the shadows cast within Cinema 4D, so why did we bother messing with After Effects? As is the key with multi-pass rendering, we have all the elements separate from each other, giving us more flexibility and control. Let's say you need to adjust the exposure of the background, or change the color of the rolling sphere, or add lots of motion blur to it after you'd already rendered it from Cinema 4D. You'd have to go back into Cinema 4D to adjust it and then render it again. Adjustments in After Effects are made and updated instantly, and you can try different looks without waiting for a different render from Cinema 4D.

8

The Awesome Power
of MoGraph

In this chapter we will cover:

- ▶ MoGraph basics – cloners and effectors
- ▶ Making text with MoText
- ▶ Using selections with cloners
- ▶ Applying deformation with effectors
- ▶ Creating abstract shapes
- ▶ Applying random textures to clones
- ▶ Creating a mosaic
- ▶ Combo #1 – building a 3D logo
- ▶ Combo #2 – dynamic stage lighting
- ▶ Combo #3 – dancing music orb

Introduction

I tend to watch film or television with a critical eye at all times. Whenever some motion graphics come on the screen, I immediately begin analyzing the design. I try my best to figure out what the designer did to pull off the effect. There are times when I know the name of the special font being used. I notice when someone didn't do a good enough job keying their green screen footage. Once or twice, I've even recognized the online video tutorial. The person must have lazily based their entire effect, because it seems all too familiar to something I've seen.

I don't recommend doing this if you can help it. It can be such a pain. I'd often love to be able to shut off my brain and just be entertained by what's on the screen in front of me, but it's a bad habit of mine, or a good habit if you want to recognize what it takes to get quality work on television. If you've ever looked at an animation and have just been stumped as to how they got all those pieces to animate together, or wondered how many people must have set a million keyframes for that design to move like that, it's time you learn MoGraph.

MoGraph is Cinema 4D's motion graphics workhorse. It allows you to create complex projects with similar or different 3D objects and gives you a great control over their transformations, look and feel, their movement, and more. The capabilities of MoGraph are seemingly infinite, using combinations of their special cloners and effectors to effortlessly create 3D designs that require a higher level of control and experimentation.

If your Cinema 4D bundle does not include the MoGraph module, I strongly suggest you find a computer using this module and work through the recipes discussed in this chapter. You can download a free demo on Maxon's website. MoGraph creates animations that wouldn't be possible without it, simply because your hands would shrivel up and fall off your arm from setting so many keyframes. If you don't have it in your bundle, you just might reconsider getting it after these recipes.

The recipes of this chapter will not necessarily blow you away with their level of sophistication, but hopefully provide a base understanding of what is possible using MoGraph. Like I said, there is an infinite amount of possibilities available by learning just the basics. Work through the recipes and you'll be on your way towards creating something on TV that really gets me and everyone else wondering how you pulled it off.

MoGraph basics – cloners and effectors

The power of MoGraph is derived from the way you design and utilize two things: **cloners** and **effectors**. Cloners take objects you specify as clones and arrange them in various patterns and quantities. Effectors are specialized tools that are applied to cloners to modify their look and behavior. In this recipe, we will learn the ins and outs of these two building blocks of MoGraph.

Getting ready

Open the `Cloners_Effectors.c4d` file from the C4D Content Pack, and let's get started.

How to do it...

1. This project file contains an **Extrude NURBS** object for each of the four playing card suits. These four objects are going to be the objects we use with our cloners and effectors. Start by opening the **MoGraph** menu on top and finding the **Cloner** option. Click to add a cloner to your scene, which does nothing but add objects to be cloned. Take each of the four objects and make them the children of the cloner, and you'll see MoGraph begin to stack them upwards.

2. Click on the **Cloner** option in the **Object Manager** to load its properties into the **Attribute Manager**. Now, let's examine the properties under the **Object** tab. The **Count** value is the number of clones that our cloner is making; increase the number from **3** to **12**. You'll see more instances of our card suits going upward, but they are overlapping. This is caused by two settings: the **P.Y** value and the **Mode** setting.

3. The group of settings for our position, scale, and rotation under the **Object** tab controls what happens from one clone to the next. The **P.Y** value by default is **50**, meaning that the next clone will occur 50 units above the previous clone in the **Y** position. Change this value to **100** so that the distance between clones increases and they will stop overlapping. Change the **R.H** value to **45**; now each clone will rotate 45 degrees from its predecessor.

> When the **Mode** value is set to **Per Step**, each clone has the position, scale, or rotation value applied to them in succession. If you switch it to **End Point**, you can set the maximum values in which you transform your clones across the start and the end point.

4. The **Mode** (the first **Mode** setting in the tab) setting is set to **Linear** by default, meaning that the series of clones will occur in a straight line. This is the key setting for getting your clones arranged in a certain way. Switch the **Mode** value to **Radial** and you'll see our suits are now arranged in a circle. Increase the **Radius** value to **500** and the **Count** value to **12** again, and you'll see our clones arranged in a nice circular pattern. The more clones we add, the less space we get between them in our circle:

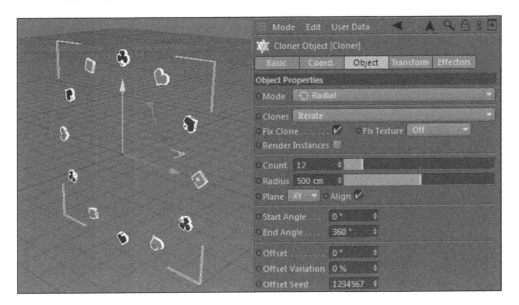

5. Change the **Mode** setting to **Grid Array** and you'll get new options for arranging your clones. The **Count** setting is set to **3** by default, and there are three different fields this time. These fields correspond to the amount of clones in the **X**, **Y**, and **Z** dimension respectively, so you can create a deeper arrangement of cloners than a linear or radial cloner could offer. Adjust the **Size** setting to read **500** in each field, to spread out our clones so that they aren't on top of each other.

6. The drop-down menu for **Clones** is set to **Iterate** by default, meaning that the clones are mapped in the order of how they are listed as children under the **Cloner** option in the **Object Manager**. There are a few other options in this menu, notably the **Random** setting that will create a random distribution of the order of your clones, instead of keeping them in perfect order. Change the setting to **Random** and shuffle through the **Seed** values to get different patterns in the clones among how your playing card suits are organized.

7. The last type of cloner is the **Object** cloner. It takes your clones and can map them onto the geometry of an object you specify. Go up to the Command Palette, load a **Platonic** primitive into your scene, and increase its **Radius** to **1000**. Use the traffic light in the **Object Manager** to make it invisible in both the renderer and the editor. Now, load your **Cloner** in the **Attribute Manager**, change its **Mode** to **Object**, and then drag your **Platonic** shape into the **Object** field and watch how your clones now appear at the vertexes of your shape. You can change the **Distribution** pattern to be something other than **Vertex**. Switch it to **Edge** and you'll get your clones appearing along the sides of your invisible platonic shape:

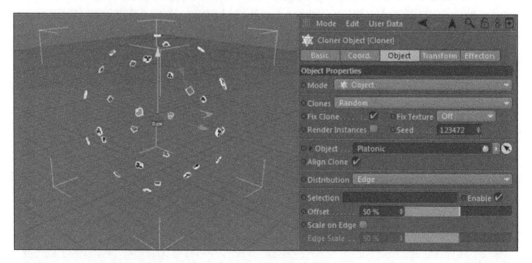

 Make sure the object you are using for your cloner is only invisible, and not deactivated. You can't see either one, but the cloner won't work if the object doesn't have a green checkmark next to it.

8. Cloners are the key to generating many instances of our objects, and we can add effectors to our project to change certain properties of our clones. The most widely used effector has to be the **Random** effector, so we are going to get familiar with it and use it in just about every recipe in this chapter.

9. Make sure you have your cloner highlighted in the **Object Manager**, as effectors apply themselves only to cloners that are selected when they are created (you can apply them separately, but it's just an extra step). Now, go up to the **MoGraph** menu and find the **Effector** submenu that contains an array of effectors, all with special uses. Select the **Random** effector and you'll notice that the clones have shifted around. If you don't see it right away, deactivate the **Random** effector in the **Object Manager** by clicking on the green checkmark.

10. Load the effector in the **Attribute Manager** and take a look at the **Effector** and **Parameter** tabs. These are the main controls for your effector and it's where you change how your clones are influenced. The **Parameter** tab contains a group of **Transform** properties for our position, scale, and rotation settings for our clones. The position group has a value of **50** in each dimension, which is basically saying that our **Random** effector is randomizing the position of each clone within 50 units of its original position in each dimension. Change the values from **50** to **500** and you'll see the clones are now much more scattered. Check the boxes for **Scale** and **Rotation**, activate the **Uniform Scale** function, and then enter a value of **1** for **Scale**. Enter values of **360** for each of the three rotation fields, and you'll now notice that the sizes and angles of your clones have been randomized in the Viewer as well.

11. Switch over to the **Effector** tab and note the **Seed** setting at the bottom. Change this value, enter any number you wish, and you'll get a completely different random distribution. You can cycle through as many numbers as it takes to get the perfect random scattering of your clones (contradictory to the idea of randomness, isn't it? I call it controlled randomness).

12. **Random** mode has several different patterns for applying randomness to your clones. Switch it over to the **Noise** mode and you'll no longer have a **Seed** value to switch, but if you play your scene in the Animation toolbar, you'll notice that your clones are now randomly moving. The **Noise** and **Turbulence** modes generate random motion based on the information you specified in the **Parameter** tab. These are the useful settings that you apply whenever you like to get some random movements without messing around with tons of keyframes.

13. Lastly, the **Strength** setting dictates how strongly your settings from the **Parameter** tab are applied. They are at their full strength of **100**, but they can also exceed this value or be negative as well, and when it's set to zero, the transform settings are ignored.

How it works...

This basic overview hopefully gave you an idea of how things are built within MoGraph. Cloners are constructed to create multiple instances of objects, and effectors are applied to, well, affect the clones in the ways we specify. The cooler stuff you create in MoGraph mixes and matches certain types of cloners and effectors to get unique results. We will go over plenty of other effectors and create some interesting samples with MoGraph in the rest of the chapter. Keep going!

There's more...

The **Random** effector will be used extensively in this chapter because the idea of randomness should be an important component of your designs. A lot of times, things in the real world are rarely perfect and uniform, so using something like the **Random** effector to change the position, scale, and rotation of your clones is a great way to simulate this. Adding randomness to your clones will often make your designs appear more interesting and natural, so more often than not you'll be using it in your MoGraph creations. Get familiar with it.

Making text with MoText

So far, every time we wanted to create text in Cinema 4D, we've used the **Text** spline with an **Extrude NURBS** object to create the surfaces. MoGraph makes it easier with **MoText**—a tool that creates and extrudes text without the help of any other item in Cinema 4D. Using **MoText** instead of **Text** splines lets you combine your text with effectors, allowing you to create dynamic text that moves and acts like any other object would inside a cloner. This recipe will show you how to create a title with MoText and animate it with an effector.

How to do it...

1. Look in the **MoGraph** menu for the **MoText** item and select it to add it to your scene. MoText will instantly create a giant extruded instance of the word **TEXT** by default. Inside the **Object** tab of **MoText** in the **Attribute Manager**, you'll find similar controls to the **Text** spline that we used before. Change the **Height** value to **100** and the **Align** field to **Center**. Change the **Text** option to **MoText**, and pick any font you wish from the **Font** menu.

2. Check under the **Caps** tab. It's time to give our text a little more style. Change both the **Start** and **End** options to **Fillet Cap**, reduce the value of **Radius** down to **2**, and then pick **One Step** for your **Fillet Type**. These controls were previously found inside the **Extrude NURBS** object, separate from your **Text** spline. They are now found directly inside your **MoText** object:

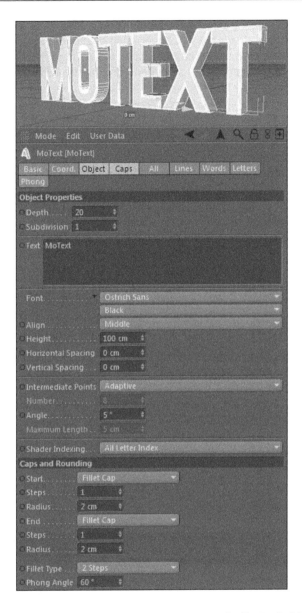

3. We now have a piece of text, and can use any type of effector in MoGraph to manipulate it. With the **MoText** highlighted in the **Object Manager**, go up to the **MoGraph** menu and select the **Plain** effector under the **Effector** submenu. The **Plain** effector is probably the simplest effector there can be; it simply applies a position, scale, and/or rotation transformation to our clones. You should have noticed right away that your text jumped up in the Viewer. That's because under the **Plain** effector's **Parameter** tab, the default setting has value **100** in the Y position, meaning it will scoot all our clones (letters) up in the Y dimension.

4. Change the **R.H** value under the **Parameter** tab to **180**. Now, our letters are backwards because they have all been rotated by the **Plain** effector. Switch to the **Effector** tab and locate the **Strength** setting. Head to the first frame of your timeline in the Animation toolbar and set a keyframe for the **Strength** value to be **100**, then move to the end of your timeline and set a new keyframe for the **Strength** value to be **0**. If you play your animation, you'll see the text start out higher up and backwards, and it will twist down into position. By keyframing the **Strength** setting, we are gradually reducing the effector's impact on the text over time.

5. A unique feature of MoText is the ability to apply effectors to your text to affect just letters, entire words, or entire lines. Click on the **MoText** option in the **Object Manager** and switch to the **Letters** tab. You should see your **Plain** effector inside the **Effects** listing. Highlight the item inside the list and delete it; now our **MoText** isn't being affected at all. Switch to the **Words** tab and drag the **Plain** effector from the **Object Manager** into this empty field in the **Object Manager**. Now, if you play your animation, you'll notice that the entire word is being affected by the **Plain** effector, and not the individual letters. You can specify which effectors influence letters, words, or lines under the labeled **MoText** tabs.

How it works...

MoText combines the previous method of using a **Text** spline and an **Extrude NURBS** object to create 3D text. Since it's a **MoGraph** object, we can use the array of effectors to manipulate the text any which way we want. We set just two keyframes with a **Plain** effector and got a simple rotating text animation, instead of setting many keyframes to move individual letters. We also learned that we can specify to affect the letters individually or perhaps as an entire word.

There's more...

Kerning text is tricky in Cinema 4D, but check out the kernimator as a simple solution for spacing out your characters properly at `http://www.kernimator.com`.

Using selections with cloners

There's a handy feature of MoGraph that is similar to the **Set Selection** feature we used when applying materials. MoGraph allows you to apply your effectors only to clones that you specify with the special **MoGraph Selection** tool. In this recipe, we will apply two different effectors to two specific types of clones in our scene.

Getting ready

Open and use the `Arrows_and_Cubes.c4d` file from the C4D Content Pack with this recipe.

How to do it...

1. Our scene is centered around our **Figure** object with a **Radial Cloner** surrounding it with two types of clones: arrows and cubes. We're going to start by introducing the **Target** effector, which takes our clones and has them point towards a particular target you specify in your scene. Select the **Arrows and Cubes** cloner in the **Object Manager**, go up to the **MoGraph** menu, find the **Target** Effector under the **Effectors** submenu, and apply it to the scene.

2. You'll instantly notice our arrows get flipped the wrong way, and there's a simple remedy for this by checking the **Reverse Heading** box under the **Effector** tab, inside the **Attribute Manager**. With the arrows facing inwards, take the **Figure** object from the **Object Manager** and drag it into the **Target Object** field. You won't notice a difference, but now take your **Arrows and Cubes** cloner and drag the entire cloner upward in the view, so that it's above our figure. You'll notice that the clones are pointing towards the **Figure** object; this is the main use of the **Target** effector:

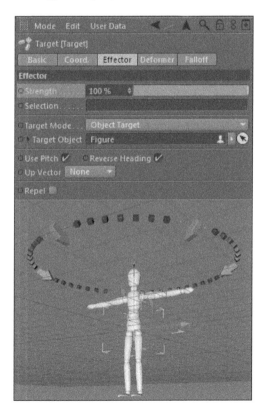

3. But this **Target** effector is affecting all of our clones. Let's say we just want to apply it to the arrows and not the cubes. MoGraph has a selection tool specifically as a remedy to this situation. Return the position of the cloner back to the original spot and then go up to the **MoGraph** menu and click on the **MoGraph Selection** option. Immediately, you'll see a bunch of red squares pop up over your clones in the Viewer, and inside the **Attribute Manager,** you'll find the settings for our **MoGraph Selection** tool:

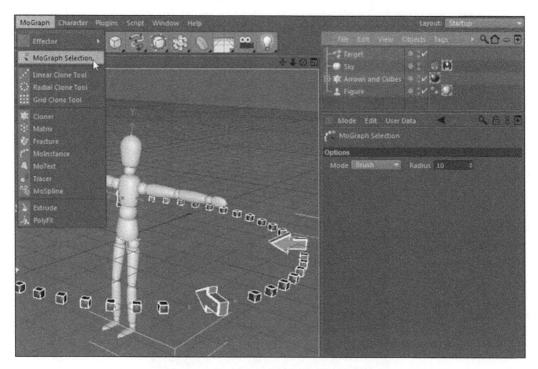

4. I recommend switching to the Top view so that you can see over your clones directly. By default, the **MoGraph Selection** tool works like a brush, with a radius for growing or shrinking the area for making selections. Switch the Viewer to the Top view, so we can see our clones directly overhead. Take the selection brush and click on the boxes that are on top of, and correspond to, just our arrow clones, holding the *Shift* key every time you want to select more than one clone. The dots will turn yellow when selected.

5. There's a tag for our selection options in **Cloner** in the **Object Manager**, which is a red dot surrounded by three white dots. Click on the tag to load it into the **Attribute Manager** and switch to the **Basic** tab, and then change the default **MoGraph Selection** name to **Arrows** instead so that we can identify it. Now, click on the **Target** effector and drag the tag from the **Object Manager** directly into the **Selection** field in the **Attribute Manager** for the **Target** effector.

6. Switch back to the **Perspective** view and move the cloner high above the figure, and you'll see that only our arrows are tilting towards the figure; the cubes aren't anymore. So, we know that the selection is working.

7. Let's take this a step further and apply a new effector to our **Cloner**: the **Formula** effector. The **Formula** effector allows you to create expressions that can be used to drive the changes in position, scale, and rotation of your clones. The default formula is a smooth sine wave function, and for our purposes, it works perfectly. Apply this tool from the **Effector** submenu, inside the **MoGraph** menu up top, and load its **Parameter** tab in the **Attribute Manager**. Uncheck the **Position** box and preview the motion by playing your scene in the Animation toolbar. Your clones are now scaling up and down in a pattern, but what if you wish your arrows to not participate in this movement?

8. We just need to flip our selection and apply it to the **Formula** effector separately. Hold the *Ctrl* or *command* key and click-and-drag your **MoGraph Selection** tag in the **Object Manager** to duplicate it. Change the name of it from **Arrows** to **Cubes** under the **Basic** tab, and then under the **Tag** tab, hit the **Invert** button, which will flip the selection from our previously selected **Arrows** to **Cubes**. Now, select the **Formula** effector and drag the new tag for our **Cubes** into the **Selection** field and watch how your arrows are no longer under the effect of the **Formula** effector.

9. Add a new cloner from the **MoGraph** menu and make your **Arrows and Cubes** cloner a child of it (yes, you can do this; cloners can clone cloners. Did I blow your mind a little right there?). Load the new cloner into the **Attribute Manager** and change the **Count** value to **6** and the **P.Y** value to **110** under the **Effector** tab. Also, increase the **Step Rotation H** value to **180** and switch over to the **Coordinates** tab. Move the cloner down to **-280** in the **Y** position, so the cloner surrounds our figure from head to toe. Notice how the arrows are pointing at our figure, regardless of what level they are on.

10. Apply one last **Formula** effector to create some interesting expression-driven movements to the new cloner. Start by changing the **P X** transformation to **0** and the **P Y** transformation to **100**. Next, check the **Rotation** box and enter a value of **360** for the **R H** field. Then, be sure to check the **Absolute Scale** box; this eliminates the negative values in the transformation by taking the absolute value of the result. Finally, go to the **Effector** tab, twirl down the **Variables** options, and reduce the **Project Time** down to **0.1** to slow down our movement. Now, play back your animation and watch how everything behaves very dynamically with all of these effectors working together to create some interesting motions:

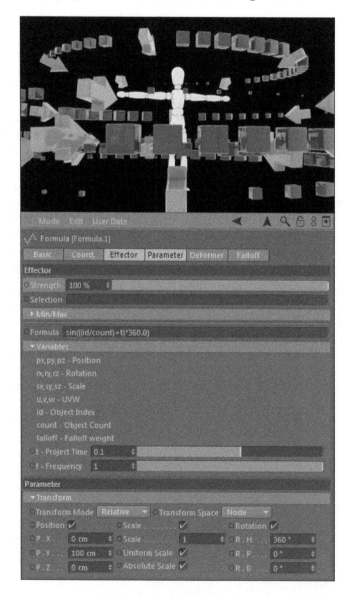

How it works...

You don't have to create different cloners to apply effectors to different types of clones. The **MoGraph Selection** tool is the perfect tool for targeting specific effectors to specific clones. In this instance, we applied the **Target** effector to just our arrows and the **Formula** effector to our cubes, while both were mixed within the same cloner. Instead of creating separate cloners for each kind of clone, we can mix them together and make our selections inside just one cloner.

There's more...

The final result is a lot of moving pieces that move around without any keyframes. Imagine trying to recreate this motion without MoGraph. We can change the items in the **Parameter** tab in each effector and come up with a totally different set of movements for all the objects in our cloners.

Applying deformation with effectors

The effectors can not only be applied to cloners, but can be used to modify single objects as well. This lets you use the abilities of any effector as a tool to modify things like primitives, splines, basically anything with geometry. This recipe will show you how to use effectors as point-level deformers, where their unique characteristics can modify the points of individual objects instead of just affecting cloners.

Getting ready

Open the `Line_Graph.c4d` file in the C4D Content Pack and use it with this recipe.

How to do it...

1. The project opens with an empty axis that we will fill with 3D line graph data. Switch the **Camera** mode to the **Front** view so that we can see our axis head on. Now, grab the **Linear** spline tool and try to draw a straight line about the length of the bottom axis by clicking on a start point and then moving along the axis and clicking on it to make an end point. Select each of the two points and line them up as closely as possible such that they make a line parallel to the x axis in our Viewer. Rename it to `Line` in the **Object Manager**.

2. With your two end points still selected, head to the **Mesh** menu up top and under the **Commands** menu, select **Subdivide** (remember to click on the small black icon to open the value field) and enter a value of **5**. Next, we are going to apply a **Sweep NURBS** object to our line to give it some thickness. Find the **Sweep NURBS** object inside the Command Palette, and then add a **Circle** spline from the **Splines** icon. Reduce the **Radius** of the spline to **2**, and then place it as a child of the **Sweep NURBS** object along with the **Line** spline we drew. The circle should be on top of the line as a child, so it will define the shape of our **Sweep NURBS** object.

3. Now, go to the **Caps** tab of the **Sweep NURBS** object in the **Attribute Manager** and select the **Start** and **End** caps to be **Fillet Cap** with the **Steps** value as **10** and a **Radius** of **2**. Then, switch to the **Object** tab and change the value of **End Growth** to **0** and set a keyframe at the first frame. Move ahead to frame 60 and set a keyframe for the **End Growth** value to reach **100** the other way.

 If your line happens to animate backwards, there's an easy fix for this. With all the points selected on your spline, right-click or context-click and select **Reverse Sequence**, which will flip the direction of your points and tell your animation to go.

4. Go to the **MoGraph** menu up top, select a new **Random** effector, and make it a child of your **Line** spline. So, instead of affecting a cloner, the **Random** effector will now affect just our spline. All we need to do is go under the **Random** effector's **Deformation** tab and select a **Point** value for the **Deformation** tab. You'll notice that our spline has now jumped around and created a jagged line instead of a perfect straight line. Under the **Parameters** tab, change the **Transform** position values to be **0** for **X** and **Z**, and **100** for **Y**. This will scatter our points vertically in a random pattern, and create a trending line plotted on our graph. If you need to move your line up to prevent the line from intersecting the bottom of the graph, you can simply move the **Line** spline in the **Y** dimension.

5. Now, hold either the *Ctrl* or *command* key and drag your entire **Sweep NURBS** object and its children to make a copy, and then do it again so that you have three instances of your **Sweep NURBS** object, creating the jagged line. Rename them as Line 1, Line 2, and Line 3. Now, go up to the **MoGraph** menu and select **Cloner** so that we have a default **Linear** cloner and make your three lines, children of the cloner. Select the **Cloner** option inside the **Object Manager** and go under the **Object** tab in the **Attribute Manager** to change the **P.Y** value to **0** and the **P.Z** value to **150**, so that our lines are now repeating in the **Z** dimension. Scoot your cloner into place along the axis so that your lines are in a good spot on your axis. It all depends on where you drew your line.

6. The cloner is repeating each of our lines but they have the same random **Seed** value and so appear exactly the same. Go under the **Random** effector for two of the three lines, change their random **Seed** value to a different number, and you'll get an entirely different point distribution. Now, take the red, green, and blue materials in the **Material Manager** and apply one to each of your three lines. Go to the beginning of your timeline and play your animation. Your three different lines will start animating and create a colorful 3D line graph, thanks to point deformation and the **Random** effector:

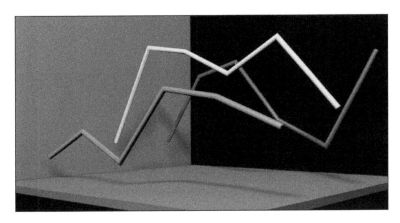

How it works...

MoGraph effectors can be used to affect the geometry of an object based on the setting under the **Deformation** tab. We used the point-level deformation to randomize the **Y** position of our points along the line we drew. Instead of drawing the shape ourselves, we let the **Random** effector create the lines for us, and we can cycle through as many random seeds as we want to get the shape we are looking for.

There's more...

In this example, we used the **Point** setting under the **Deformation** tab, but the other options are useful too. The **Object** setting will affect the entire object that the effector is a child of, and the **Polygon** setting will affect the subdivided geometry of the object.

Creating abstract shapes

So far, we've used MoGraph to clone and animate specific 3D objects, but what if you are in need of a design that is more abstract? Abstract is tough to design, because it's more arbitrary than knowing how to model something definite. Abstract doesn't have a particular look. MoGraph can help you do the heavy lifting and create some very interesting shapes that don't really look like anything, yet they may be exactly what you need.

Getting ready

Use the `Abstract_Mograph.c4d` file from the C4D Content Pack for this recipe.

How to do it...

1. Start this unconventional use of MoGraph by grabbing a **Helix** spline from the Command Palette and then a **Cloner** object from the **MoGraph** menu. Make the **Helix** a child of the cloner and increase the **Count** value to **30**. Look towards the bottom of the **Object** tab for the cloner and you'll see **Step Rotation H**, **Step Rotation B**, and **Step Rotation P**. These values correspond to the amount of rotation that occurs from one clone to the next. Increase these values to an incredibly high amount of **5000** for each.

2. Because we are only using splines as our clones, we have no defined geometry as a result. However, splines can be useful in creating a geometry with the help of a **NURBS** object; in this case, we want to use the **Loft NURBS**. Add a **Loft NURBS** object from the Command Palette and place the cloner as a child of the **Loft NURBS** object. Now, add a **HyperNURBS** object to smooth our **Loft NURBS** object, by making that a child of our **HyperNURBS** object.

3. We have a tightly-wound little bowl of sorts and it's nothing to print out and hang on to the refrigerator as of now. However, as you may realize, every cloner needs a good effector, and we are going to apply the **Random** effector to ours. Highlight the **Cloner** object in the **Object Manager** and add a **Random** effector from inside the **MoGraph** menu.

4. Our shape expands a bit with the default values, but look inside the **Parameter** tab of the **Random** effector in the **Attribute Manager** and increase the position **X**, **Y**, and **Z** to much larger values such as **3000**.

5. Apply the **Reflect** material to the **HyperNURBS** object and do a render preview with **Ctrl** or **command + R**. You'll see a shape that twists and winds in a very unique way; a very dynamic and interesting shape created in no time at all:

How it works...

Our cloner is cloning our **Helix** spline, and the high **Step Rotation** values are twisting our clones. We use the cloner as a source for our **Loft NURBS**, and our **Random** effector comes in and displaces the clones, creating a very complex shape. We can tweak any of the settings we changed to get a different result; change the spline from a **Helix** to a different shape, or simply adjust the random **Seed** value of our **Random** effector to get a completely different result. Here are some examples made from just changing the **Seed** value:

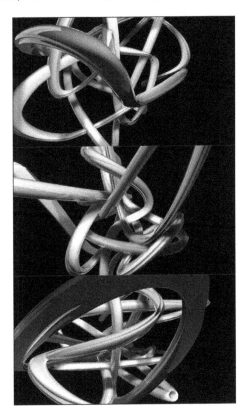

There's more...

Not only can you change the **Seed** value to get different results, but also position the camera in a different spot to get a different perspective on your abstract shape. If you don't like a particular twist or maybe your shape is intersecting strangely, no problem; just focus on a different part of the shape.

Abstract in motion

Under the **Random** effector, change the **Random** mode in the **Effector** tab from **Random** to **Turbulence**, and check the box that says **Indexed**. Watch your shape contort and dance around without any keyframes.

Applying random textures to clones

Eventually, there will be a time when you'll need to map a bunch of different colors or textures across a sea of clones. It will happen, I guarantee it, because it's a common concept and therefore you need to have this technique in your Cinema 4D arsenal. There are several different ways to apply random colors or textures to clones, and in this recipe, we will learn a few methods for pulling off this effect. We will learn two methods for applying random colors, and a simple solution for applying random image textures to clones.

Getting ready

Use the `World_Map.c4d` file in the C4D Content Pack with this recipe.

How to do it...

1. Our project is set up with a spline shaped like a map of the world. We are going to use this shape as an **Object** cloner to have our clones fit among the contours of the map. Start by creating our clone. Go up to the **Primitives** menu in the Command Palette and select **Plane**. In the **Attribute Manager**, change the values of **Width** and **Height** to **10**, and reduce the values of **Width Segments** and **Height Segments** to **1**. We will be dealing with a lot of clones, so we want our subdivision to be as small as possible. Lastly, change the **Orientation** value to **–Z**.

2. Add a cloner to the scene from inside the **MoGraph** menu and make the plane a child of it. In the cloner's settings inside the **Attribute Manager**, change the **Mode** setting under the **Object** tab from the default **Linear** to **Object**.

3. **Object** cloners work by distributing clones across the geometry of the object you designate. In this case, we have a spline, so the clones will simply be mapped along the path, which is not what we want. We want our squares to fill the volume of the map. To fix this, we'll need to add an **Extrude NURBS** object to the scene and make our **World Map** spline a child of it. Rename the 3hExtrude NURBS object as `World Map`. Now, select the **World Map Extrude NURBS** object and switch to the **Caps** tab in the **Attribute Manager**. Change the **Type** setting from **N-Gons** to **Quadrangles** and check the **Regular Grid** option. This will give our **Object** cloner more of a subdivision to work with:

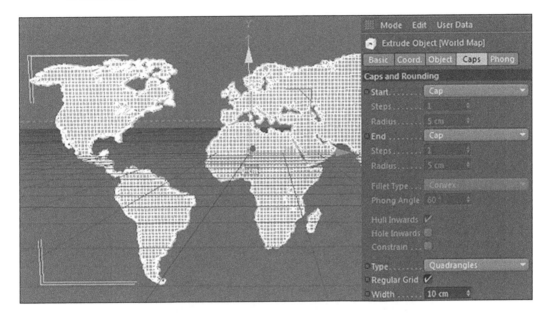

4. Now, take the **World Map** object and make it editable. Press the *C* key with it highlighted within the **Object Manager**, and it will be converted to a **Polygon** object. Unfold the icon for your world map in the **Object Manager** to reveal the two **Caps** objects, which are the newly-created pieces that we can use to map our clones to. Select the **Cloner** option and drag the **Cap 1** object from the **Object Manager** into the **Object** field under the **Object** tab. Change the value of **Count** to **5000**, and then hide the **World Map** object from the Viewer using the traffic light in the **Object Manager**.

5. Let's add a little variation to the clones in terms of their **Z** position, so they are layered slightly. With the **Cloner** option selected in the **Object Manager**, go up to the **MoGraph** menu and pick the **Random** effector. Under the effector's **Parameter** tab, reduce the **X** and **Y** position values from **50** to **0**, and change the **Z** position value to **3**, so that there is a slight offset to all our squares. You'll notice that this gives a nicer feel to all our clones so they aren't all flatly sitting on the same plane:

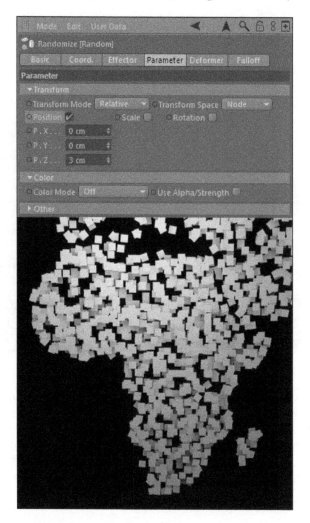

6. Now for the colors, let's say you want to create a colorful map that has squares with all different types of colors. The quickest way to get this result is to go under our **Random** effector, and under the **Parameter** tab, select the **Color** options. Set the **Color Mode** to **On**, and just like that you have a bunch of colorful squares scattered around the world. You can change the random **Seed** value of the effector to get a different distribution of colors:

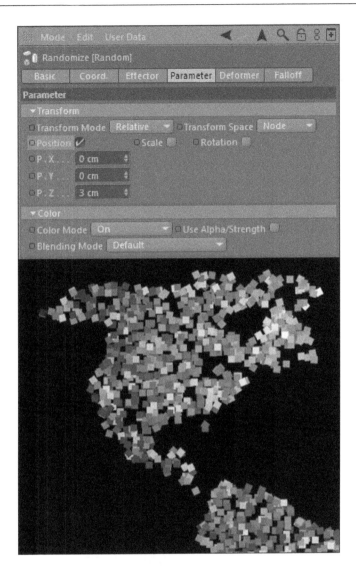

7. The issue with this method is that the color randomization is completely random. What if you want to have a few selected colors repeated randomly over the grid? The key to pulling this off is the **Multi Shader** option, which is a tool available inside the **Material Editor** window.

8. Create a new material in the **Material Manager** and call it **Random**, and double-click on its icon to open it in the **Material Editor** window. In the **Color** channel, click on the arrow button next to the **Texture** field, search down towards the bottom, and look in the **MoGraph** menu to select the **Multi Shader** option. Also, uncheck the box for the **Specular** channel; we don't want any specular highlights on our squares.

9. Click on the big **Multi Shader** button loaded into the **Texture** field to open up the **Shader** options. You have two blank fields where you can add up multiple colors, shaders, or textures, and some buttons to allow adding or subtracting more channels. This is where the Multi Shader gets its name from: you can add many different types of textures to apply to your clones.

10. For **Shader 1**, click on the triangle button to see your list of texture sources and select **Color**. Click on the **Texture** field loaded with the **Color** shader and use the color slider to make the color bright red. Now, you'll have to navigate back to your **Multi Shader** option using the black backwards arrow at the top-right corner of the **Material Editor** window to load another **Color** shader into the **Shader 2** field, and make this one a bright green. Return to the **Multi Shader** settings and click on the **Add** button to add an option for **Shader 3**. Make this as blue color so that we have three color shaders inside our **Multi Shader** settings.

11. Apply the **Random** material to your cloner, and you'll notice that because the **Random** effector is still applied with its **Color Mode** set to **On**, we get our three colors from inside the **Multi Shader** settings, randomly placed on our clones. You may notice that the red color seems to be dominating our grid, and if you cycle through different **Seed** values under the **Effector** tab, you'll see that it seems like red always has a great share of coverage over the clones. Check on the box that says **Indexed** and cycle through some more seeds; the **Indexed** option will completely randomize the **Multi Shader** allocation, which was set to **Color Brightness** inside the **Multi Shader** settings. It always seems to favor the **Shader 1** option when distributing the different shaders, but applying the **Indexed** mode applies a better random distribution over our clones:

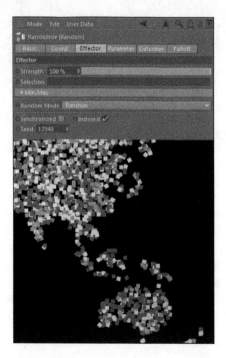

12. Now, here comes a beautiful feature. Let's say you have dozens, or even hundreds of images you want to randomly apply to your clones. The thought of individually loading these images into the **Material Editor** window one at a time makes me cringe; the process would simply take loads of time and be painfully repetitive. The **Multi Shader** setting has a key feature that will eliminate this process for you.

13. Open your **Random** material again, go back inside the **Multi Shader** option and remove each of your channels by clicking on the **Clear** button to start afresh. Click on the **Add from Folder** button, which opens a new window for you to navigate on your computer to load a bunch of files. Under the C4D Content Pack, load the **Random Images** folder and watch **MoGraph** work. All these random photos are loaded into the **Multi Shader** setting and are mapped across all the clones on our map:

14. Let's make this a little more dynamic. Select the **Cloner** option in the **Object Manager** and add another **Random** effector to the scene. Under the **Parameter** tab, change all three position values to be **500** so that they are scattered about the scene. Adjust the **Rotation** values to all be **180** as well.

15. Switch to the **Falloff** tab, where we will create a nice-looking animation to assemble our map from our scattered squares. **Falloff** creates a defined area that applies the transformation of any effector we activate it for, which we can then animate to move through our clones to create a moving zone that selectively brings our clones under the influence of our effector. Activate the **Falloff** tab by changing the **Shape** field to the **Box** field. Adjust the **Size** fields to be **2000**, **500**, and **500** respectively. Now, switch to the **Coordinates** tab and change the **X** position value to be **1000**.

16. Head to the first frame in your timeline and set a keyframe for the **X** position value, then move to frame 60 and change the value to be **3000**, and set another keyframe to tweak the animation. If you play your animation, you'll watch how a bunch of scattered squares become a nicely-constructed map of the world:

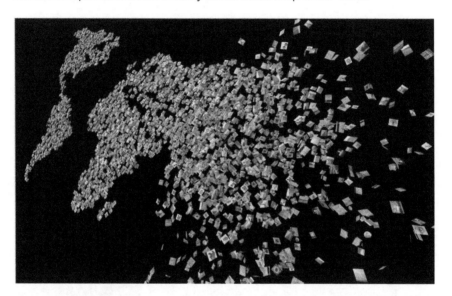

How it works...

Multi Shader is the key to making multiple textures to apply across all our clones. By adding the color shaders that we specify in the **Multi Shader** setting, we can set a **Random** effector to randomly distribute our colors across a lot of clones. It also works for image textures. By importing a folder full of images in the **Multi Shader** setting, we can apply different textures to all our images. This is an extremely easy way to get a lot of different images quickly applied across our clones randomly, without having to load separate images into lots of materials on an individual basis. The animation we added with the **Random** effector and **Falloff** provided an interesting bit of motion to the project.

There's more...

The example with our random colors was very simple with only three colors, so you can avoid the **Multi Shader** setting altogether. Just create three different materials with your red, green, and blue colors, and apply them to three different instances of your identical **Plane** clones under the **Grid** cloner. Under the **Object** tab for the **Grid** cloner, set the **Clones** mode from **Iterate** to **Random**, and your three identical clones with different materials will be distributed randomly across your grid. Use the **Multi Shader** setting if you have different types of clones or more than, let's say, five colors or textures to randomly distribute, it will be easier.

Creating a mosaic

We can also create a large mosaic image from lots of smaller images. This is quite a common technique and Cinema 4D release 14 makes it easy to do:

We can see an example of this technique in the previous image. Picture A is the original image and picture B is the image recreated with clones. This is the power of the technique. As it's now a cloner object, we can use the whole raft of Mograph features to manipulate it.

How to do it...

1. Create a **Cloner Object** and set it to **Grid Array**. Enter values, as shown in the following screenshot:

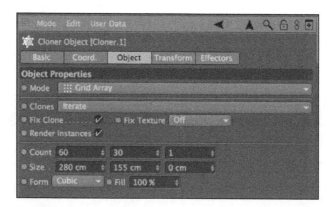

2. Now, drop a **Plane** object as the child of the **Cloner** object. Set the **Plane** object to be in orientation with -Z and make it 4.5 wide and high.

3. Create a new material and add the `Flags.jpg` image to the **Color** channel.

4. Select **Cloner** and create a **Shader Effector** node. Assign the new material to **Shader Effector** node and set it to **Flat** projection.

5. Set the Shader Effector's Channel to **Color** (in the **Shading** tab) and drop in the **Texture** tag into the **Texture Tag** field.

6. In the **Texture** mode, scale and rotate the image until it sits squarely on the **Cloner** object. Remember, you have to work in the **Axis Modification** mode (press *L*) to directly manipulate the projected texture with your normal scale and rotate tools:

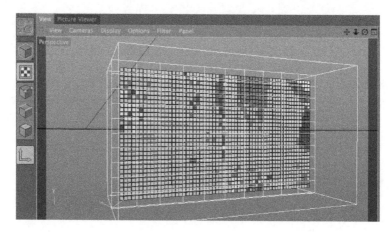

7. Now, create a new material and add a **Multi Shader** setting into the **Color** channel (**Texture/Mograph/Multi Shader**).

8. Go into the **Multi Shader** setting and in the **Texture 1** slot, add a **Color** shader. Go into the **Color** shader and pick a color which is somewhat similar to one within the image.

9. Go to **Add** and create another texture channel. Again, add in another **Color** channel and pick a new color.

10. Keep repeating this process until you have a good range of colors which are similar to the original image.

11. Now, switch the mode to **Average Color** (Euclidean Color Distance).

12. Now, drop this new material which contains the **Multi Shader** setting onto your **Cloner Object** and click on **Render**. You should see the image defined in your cloner.

13. The result may not be quite as exact as you were hoping for but fear not! We can tweak the setting to make it even more like the image. Go back into your **Multi Shader** setting, increase the **Blend Color** slider to **100%**, and set the **Mode** setting to **Color**. This should give you a much smoother result.

How it works...

The way this process works is rather clever. The **Multi Shader** setting can look at each of its channels and work out the average color of each one. It does this when you assign it the **Average Color** mode (both **Euclidean Color Distance** and **Hue Difference**). Then it looks at the image stored in the **Shader Effector** and decides which one of its channels to apply to each individual clone, to create the mosaic effect.

There's more...

We do not just have to use simple colors to color our clones. We can use images, in much the same way that we added a load of images within our Multi Shader with the Applying random textures to clones section on the world map we can do the same here.

Simply source a high number of images (the more the better) and add them to your **Multi Shader** setting instead of colors. Remember to use the **Add from Folder** button to save having to do it individually.

Combo #1 – building a 3D logo

The last three recipes in this chapter are going to focus on creating some specific results using various combinations of cloners and effectors. For this recipe, let's pretend your assignment is to create an animated logo for the company CubeCo, the largest manufacturer of cubes in the Western Hemisphere. We are going to build the logo animation within MoGraph using three effectors: the Step effector, the Delay effector, and the Random effector. Using these three tools will give us a nice flexible animation with minimal use of keyframes.

Getting ready...

Use the `CubeCo.c4d` file inside the C4D Content Pack as the starting point of this recipe.

How to do it...

1. Let's say this is the CubeCo logo, and we need to bring this to life. The font is Arial (in bold and italic), and they have a cube pivoted and colored with cyan, magenta, and yellow as the colors. Like a lot of clients, you may deal with the fact that the logo doesn't rock your socks off, but if we animate it nicely, it will be far more professional-looking than if we just faded it in over black or something more boring.

2. Start with a **MoText** object. Enter `CubeCo` in the **Text** field and change the **Align** value to **Middle**. Make sure the font is Arial (in bold and italic) to match the logo. Now, go under the **Caps** tab and change the **Start** and **End** value to **Fillet Cap** with a **Radius** value of **2**, just to give our edge a little bit of style. Our text now matches the letters in the logo, and has left enough space for our cube on the right.

3. Now, we could just make a normal colored cube to represent the logo like the client probably would imagine. But, let's aim higher and use **MoGraph** to make it a little more creative. Add a **Cube** primitive to the scene, and under the **Object** tab in the **Attribute Manager**, change its **Size** for the **X**, **Y**, and **Z** values to all be **10**, just so it's much smaller. Change your camera in the Viewer from the locked camera to **Default Camera**, so that we are free to move around, and zoom in on the cube so we can see it in a much better way. Press the **C** key to make it an editable polygon object.

4. Now, for the six faces of the cube. Click on the Use Polygon mode button on the left-hand side of the Command Palette and click on a face of the cube, then hold the **Shift** key and click on the opposite face of it to make a pair. Drag the corresponding colored materials from the **Material Manager** onto the highlighted faces, where they will be instantly applied and a **Set Selection** tag will appear for you in the **Object Manager**. Repeat so that each face and its opposing partner have the correct color applied like in the CubeCo logo.

5. The top and bottom faces should be cyan, the left and right faces should be magenta, and the front and back faces should be yellow. This tiny cube should look like the CubeCo cube, just smaller and not pivoted.

6. Switch back to the main camera, go up to the **MoGraph** menu, add a **Cloner** object, make your colored cube a child of the cloner, and then rename the cloner as Cube. Under the **Object** tab of the **Cloner** object, change the **Mode** value from **Linear** to **Grid Array**, change the **Count** to **11**, and the **Size** to **100** in all the three fields. Now, under the **Coordinates** tab, change the position in **X** to **480**, **Y** to **70**, and **Z** to **10**. Change the **Rotation** values in **R.H** to **-45** and **R.B** to **45**. Behold, we have created a big cube out of lots of little cubes. I guarantee this will come in handy:

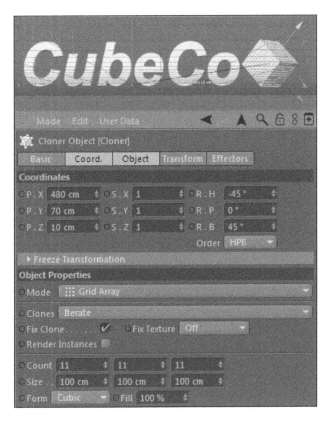

7. Highlight your **MoText** object in the **Object Manager** and then go up to the **MoGraph** menu. Under the **Effectors** submenu, select the **Step** effector. The **Step** effector applies sequential transformations to the position, scale, and rotation of clones based on the curve of the graph drawn under the **Effector** tab.

8. Right now it's applying a gradual scale transformation from left to right onto all of our letters. Go under the **Effector** tab and take note of the **Spline** field within the graph. The right side of the graph represents the clones in the beginning of the sequence and the left side corresponds to those at the end. Slide the far right point from the bottom of the graph to the top and you'll see all letters being scaled evenly, based on the shape of this curve. The curve can be animated and adjusted, but we want to leave it at the top of the graph so it affects all of our clones evenly.

9.   Uncheck the **Scale** box under our **Parameter** tab so that our logo is unaffected in every way. For our animation, let's make our letters fly in sequence from behind the camera. Check the box for **Position** and enter **-1500** in the **Z** value. You'll see our text is now very close to the camera.

10. Leave it here for now, switch over to the **Falloff** tab and select **Box** under the **Shape** menu. Now is a good time to switch to your **Editor Camera** and see your entire scene in a better way.

11. Adjust the **Size** value to be **1000** in the first field, and **500** in the second field, which correspond to **X** and **Y**. The yellow and red bounding box around your text represents the falloff; anything inside it is affected by the **Step** effector, and anything outside of it is not. If we keyframe the position of this box, we can have our logo zoom into the place where we had it before. Go to the first frame of your scene and set a keyframe at the **X** position for the **Step** effector in the **Coordinates** tab. Now, go to frame 45, change the **X** position to **1400**, set a keyframe, and then preview your animation. The letters slide into place once they are outside the bounding box of the falloff:

12. Switch back to the main camera and make sure your playhead is at frame 0. Notice how our text isn't completely behind the camera. The beauty of using the **Step** effector to do this kind of animation is that we can just change the **Position** values under the **Parameter** tab and the entire title moves accordingly without resetting keyframes. The keyframes merely affect the timing that the letters come in; the **Position** fields are where the starting position for our text is defined. Change the position **Y** value to **-100** so that the text is more towards the center of our camera. Then, increase the **Z** value from **-1500** to **-2000**, change the **X** value to **430**, and play your animation. The first C in CubeCo now passes right into the middle of our camera and frames the scene quite nicely, and the remaining letters follow suit.

13. But, we can add more to our logo animation. Check on the **Rotation** box and let's have the letters enter at an angle. Enter values of **-45** for **R.H** and **-90** for **R.P**, and now play your animation. The rotation definitely makes the entry a little nicer, but our C is blocking our camera to start now. As I pointed out before, the beauty of the **Step** effector is that all these adjustments we are making do not need to be entered as new keyframes. Simply change the **Y** value to **-135**, and now the C is out of the frame again, entering from the bottom.

> Stick to my numbers in these fields if you want, but feel free to make the animation your own and have it entered in a totally different way. Regardless of the changes you make in the **Parameter** tab, your animation will end up in the same spot every time.

14. Ready to make this animation even better without adding any keyframes? Good, me too. Select your **MoText** in the **Object Manager** and add another effector from the **MoGraph** menu called the **Delay** effector. The **Delay** effector takes any movement made by clones within **MoGraph** and applies a gradual temporal smoothing when they come to rest. Play your animation and you'll notice that your letters now ease into place a little more smoothly than before. That's because we added the **Delay** effector with the default **Blend** setting, under the **Mode** field in the **Effector** tab.

15. Change the **Mode** setting from **Blend** to **Spring** and you'll get an even more interesting animation. Play it from the top and you'll see your letters now bounce and gradually settle down once their move is complete. These effects are achieved without any keyframes. Imagine trying to draw **Bezier** curves to try to match this motion; it would be tedious to do once, much less for any and every clone you may have in your scene. I am an unabashed fan of the **Delay** effector. Pick whichever mode you like best; I'm going with **Blend**.

16. With our text in place, we can now figure out an interesting way for our logo to develop. Because we constructed our big cube out of our little cubes, we can do something interesting to build it up from the smaller pieces. These types of **Grid** cloners work well with **Random** effector, so let's highlight our **Cube** object and add a **Random** effector from the **MoGraph** menu.

17. Our logo is going to start with a bunch of displaced cubes, and as the animation plays, they will come together to form one. So, we need to offset the positions **X**, **Y**, and **Z** values to be much larger than what they are right now. Change each value to **3000** to get them scattered much farther away. They also need some random rotation so that they don't look rigid and uniform. Hence, check the **Rotation** box and increase each of the three fields to **360**.

18. Right now our cubes are scattered all over the map. This may be the effect you are looking for at times, but the screen should be blank and they should enter from the right from off-screen. You can control the range in which your values are randomized, in terms of positive and negative directions. Under the **Effector** tab, untwirl the Min/Max option and you'll see two sliders: set **100** for the **Maximum** option and **-100** for the **Minimum** option. Slide the slider over until the **Minimum** value reaches **0**; you'll see your clones end up on just the right side of the screen, because we are eliminating the range in which our values can be randomized in the negative direction.

19. Move to frame 10 and set a keyframe for the **Strength** setting to be **100**, under the **Effector** tab. Then, move ahead to frame 60 and reduce the **Strength** value all the way to **0**, to eliminate the randomness and set a new keyframe.

20. Preview your animation and you'll see our small cubes coming out of the frame to form our big cube. It might look nice if we add the effect of **Delay** effector to our cubes as well. Highlight the **Cube** cloner, switch over to the **Effectors** tab, and drag the **Delay** effector from the **Object Manager** into the **Effectors** field. Make sure it's below the **Random** effector because it won't apply its effect to any effector listed below it.

How it works...

This combination of effectors helps us create a simple, flexible, and effective logo animation rather quickly. The **Step** effector is the driving force behind our text entering the frame from behind the camera. We set keyframes that determine the speed of the animation. The keyframes control the falloff of our effector, which creates a zone in which the effector is applied and can be moved around to influence particular clones. The **Random** effector is the catalyst for bringing together our cube logo, which we developed out of small cubes aligned inside a **Grid** cloner. Both objects in the scene get a little something extra from the **Delay** effector. We set it to **Blend** and it gives a nice ease upon the completion of a move within **MoGraph**.

There's more...

There's a little glitch in Cinema 4D with the **Delay** effector that can cause your objects in the timeline to jump around and play improperly, if you scrub through the timeline. If you want to see an accurate preview when **Delay** effectors are enabled, you should play your animation from the very beginning of the timeline.

Combo #2 – dynamic stage lighting

Picture an assignment of having to create a concert or live performance in Cinema 4D. You can imagine lights spinning around at different angles creating a lively environment. Instead of positioning and animating these lights by hand, we are going to resort to MoGraph and some handy effectors to do the job for us. The **Spline** effector and the **Formula** effector are the main components of this recipe. With the right combination of effectors we will clone lights instead of objects and cause them to rotate and pivot around to create the feel of a concert's light setup.

Getting ready

Open the `Stage_Light.c4d` file from the C4D Content Pack and build your scene with this recipe.

How to do it...

1. Our star stands upon a star and needs to be lit, and a simple 3-point light setup isn't going to cut it. Use the traffic light to hide the **Star Stage**, **Floor**, and **Figure** objects for now, so that we can focus on our lights. We want to fit the lights around the stage and have them fit along the contours of the star. We also don't want the light just standing still; we need it rotating and moving like a concert light would do.

2. This requires us to plan ahead. The spot light in this scene will need to rotate from two positions: the pivot point, around where the light meets the mount, and the base of the light itself. For this, we will need to set up the main part of the light to be its own cloner, so that we have separate control over it. Untwirl the **Spot Light** group and add a **Cloner** object from within the **MoGraph** menu. Place the **Light** group as a child of the cloner, and rename the cloner as `Light Source`. Highlight this cloner in the **Object Manager** and select the **Object** tab in the **Attribute Manager**, reducing the default **Count** value from **3** to **1**. Our model looks the same, but now our light can be controlled with effectors as it is actually now a cloner.

3. Create another **Cloner** object and rename it as `Stage Lights`, and make your entire **Spot Light** group its child. The linear arrangement we have right now is no good. We need to get our lights around our **Star Stage** object. With the **Stage Lights** cloner selected, go to the **MoGraph** menu and find the **Spline** effector under the **Effector** menu.

4. The **Spline** effector will take our clones and align them around any spline we specify. Open the **Star Stage** group and untwirl the **Star3 Extrude NURBS** object, make a copy of this **Star** spline by pressing the *Ctrl* or *command* key and dragging it elsewhere in the **Object Manager**. This is the widest spline making up our stage, so it's the best fit for us.

5. Highlight the **Spline** effector in the **Object Manager** and go to the **Effector** tab. Take your newly-created **Star** spline and drag it into the **Spline** field from the **Object Manager**. You should notice that your lights have instantly snapped into place on the spline. If you reactivate the **Star Stage** object with the traffic light, you'll notice that they are overlapping the stage right now because the spline defining their path is not wide enough for them to fit. This is easily fixed by opening our **Star** spline and changing the **Scale** values for **X** and **Z** to **1.2** in the **Attribute Manager** under the **Coordinates** tab. Finally, go to the **Stage Lights** cloner and increase the **Count** value from 3 to 10:

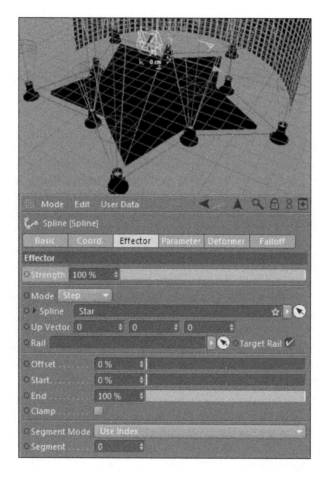

6. We now have 10 lights surrounding our stage, so let's get them moving. The next effector we will use is the **Time** effector, which applies a steady transformation over the course of time in your scene. Apply a **Time** effector from the **MoGraph** menu to your **Stage Lights** cloner. The default settings are too fast so reduce the **R.H** value to **45**. Play your animation and you'll see our lights start to rotate around their base.

7. Now, we need the actual light to pivot around. For this, we need to apply a **Formula** effector to our **Light Source** cloner that is inside our **Spot Light** group, so select it in the **Object Manager** and apply the effector from the **MoGraph** menu.

8. Load the **Formula** effector into the **Attribute Manager** and uncheck the **Position** and **Scale** boxes in the **Parameter** tab. Check on the **Rotation** box and enter a value of **90** in the **R.B** field, and then preview your animation. You'll see our lights spinning and rotating, but the rotation would probably make you nauseous or have a seizure if you were actually at the concert. Switch over to the **Effector** tab so we can tone down the movement. There are two ways to do it: by reducing the number **360** in the **Formula** field to a lower number, or by reducing the **Project Time** setting under the **Variables** options down from **1** to some fraction. Both these numbers are part of the formula, and decreasing them is the easiest way to slow down our lights. I prefer to not touch the **Formula** field and just lower the **Project Time** value from **1** to **0.1**, so now the lights will move at a fraction of the speed.

9. You may preview this animation and be satisfied, but we can change it up even more to make the movement of the light a little less uniform. The first thing we can do is apply a **Random** effector to the **Stage Lights** cloner. Apply this effector and deactivate the **Position** checkbox, then activate the **Rotation** box and put a value of **360** in the **R.H** field. Our lights are now rotated at a random angle, but they will still spin and flip at the same speed.

10. Our red light is good, but let's add in a blue light as well. When the lights cross, they will create a pink and purple light which will look pretty neat. Here's the key to this step: we need to have separate clones for our red light and blue light. So, inside your **Stage Lights** cloner, take your spot light, press the *Ctrl* or *command* key and drag another copy of the group right below it, making sure they both are children of the cloner.

11. Open the new **Spot Light** group and twirl down all the levels until you find the **Bulb** object with the red material on it. Drag the blue material from the **Material Manager** onto this tag so it will swap, then open the **Light** object below it and change it from a red-colored light to a blue light with the RGB sliders under the **General** tab. You'll see that our lights are now alternating in color from red to blue. Label your new spot lights as **Red Spot Light** and **Blue Spot Light**:

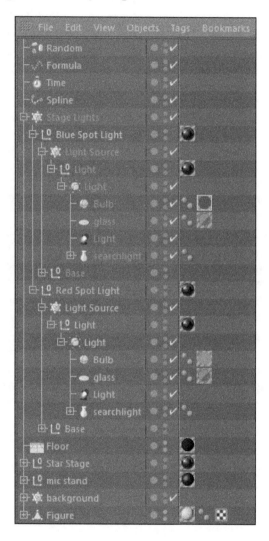

12. You can easily flip the direction in which your blue lights are rotating, by selecting the **Light Source** object of your **Blue Spot Light** group, and under the **Effectors** tab, you'll find the **Formula** effector listed with a percentage slider at the bottom. Change the value from **100** to **-100** and the effector will be inverted just for your blue lights.

13. Reactivate everything in the **Object Manager** with their traffic lights and play your animation. You'll see your rock star surrounded by colored spot lights, giving you a nice-looking light setup for your concert inside Cinema 4D:

How it works...

Our **Spline** effector can be used to align our clones along any spline. In this case, because our stage was created by the splines, it makes sense to use the same spline to align our lights around it. The **Time** effector provides a steady rotation for our lights, the **Random** effector changes the angle for all our lights so they aren't uniform, and the **Formula** effector creates the swinging pivot of our lights and sends them in different directions. These effectors combine to create a complicated light setup in just minutes, and we have complete control over the speed and pattern in which they move within MoGraph, allowing us to change everything about how our lights behave.

Did we just create all that movement and animation without setting a single keyframe? Why, yes. Yes, we did. Isn't MoGraph great?

Combo #3 – dancing music orb

One of the more fun effectors in MoGraph is the **Sound** effector, which measures the sound output from an audio file and processes that into transformations among your clones. This recipe combination will revolve around this effector, but use many of the concepts from the previous recipes to build a unique-looking design that dynamically moves to music. By now, you should realize that MoGraph gives us design and animation options that are just about impossible to achieve in any other way.

Getting ready

Find the `Music_Orb.c4d` file from the C4D Content Pack. It has an HDR Sky loaded and our render settings configured already, otherwise we'll be starting from scratch.

How to do it...

1. Start by creating a **Platonic** primitive from inside the Command Palette and switching its **Type** to **Bucky** and increasing the **Segments** value to **10** and **Radius** value to **200**. Go to the **MoGraph** menu, add a new **Cloner** object, and place the **Platonic** object as a child of the cloner. Select the cloner in the **Object Manager** to load its settings in the **Attribute Manager**, and switch the **Count** value down to **1** under the **Object** tab so that there is only one instance of our platonic shape. This will be the base shape for our dancing orb.

2. Next, we are going to load a couple of effectors into our scene, but we will use them to deform our **Platonic** object and not necessarily to affect it as a clone; it will prove to be a much more interesting result. Make sure the **Cloner** object is not selected in the **Object Manager** so that the effectors are not applied to the **Cloner** object. Go to the **MoGraph** menu to find the **Sound** effector and add it to your project as a child of the **Platonic** object.

3. Load the effector into the **Attribute Manager** and find the **Sound File** field under the **Effector** tab. Click on the ellipses button to navigate to the `Sound_Effector_Beat.wav` file found in the C4D Content Pack. Change the **Apply** mode to **Step**, which will apply the data seen in the **Frequency Graph** field as a transformation across all areas of your object. Switch to the **Parameter** tab and change all the **Position** fields to have a value of **100**. Lastly, we need to activate **Deformation** under the **Deformer** tab to be **Point**; you'll instantly notice the change in your orb's surface.

4. If you play your scene with the Animation toolbar, you'll see your shape twitching and deforming based on the sound in the audio file. We applied the deformation to the position of the points, which is the source for the erratic movement. You could apply the effector conventionally to the cloner itself, and this movement could be mapped across a series of orbs instead:

5. The next effector to add is the **Random** effector. Once again, make sure it's not applied to the cloner, but place it as a child of the platonic shape and move it below the **Sound** effector. Start by changing its **Deformation** type to **Point** and then loading the **Effector** tab to change its **Random** mode to **Turbulence**. These settings will cause our points to randomly shift around in a turbulent pattern and give a little noticeable motion to the surfaces of our orb, when they aren't affected by the **Sound** effector.

6. The next two effectors are just going to provide a little extra motion to the whole orb. Add a **Time** effector to the **Cloner** object, activate only its **Rotation** option under the **Parameter** tab, and change each of the three rotation values to **45**. This will spin our orb around a little bit so we can see more of it.

7. Now, add a **Formula** effector from the **MoGraph** menu. Change its **Y** position value to be **50** and **X** position value to be **0** under the **Parameter** tab, and then uncheck the box for **Scale**. This effector will make our orb bounce or wobble up and down a little bit.

8. If you preview your animation, you'll see our orb has quite a bit of interesting motion going on: it's bouncing, spinning, and shaking to the beat of our music. It looks good the way it is, but add a **HyperNURBS** object to the scene and place the whole cloner as a child inside it. Name the **HyperNURBS** object as Dancing Orb.

You'll notice that it is now very smooth and the sharp extrusions have been rounded off. More than likely, your computer won't be able to play this back in real time anymore, so deactivate the **HyperNURBS** object any time you want to play your animation:

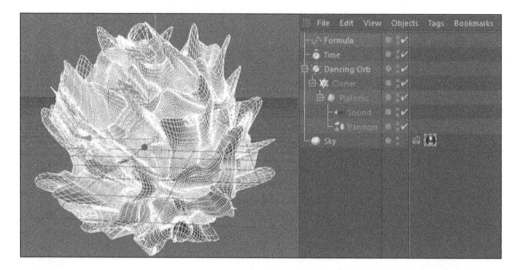

9. Apply the metal material from the **Material Manager** to your **Dancing Orb** object to give it a cool reflective look. Do a render preview with *Ctrl* or *command + R* and check out the result obtained.

10. Let's add some interesting lighting using some of the techniques we've learned in MoGraph. Add a **Light** object to your scene and make sure it's **Shadow** type is set to **Shadow Maps** under its **General** tab. Add a new cloner from the **MoGraph** menu and place the light inside the cloner. In the **Attribute Manager** under the **Object** tab, set the **Mode** type to **Radial**, and then bump up the **Count** value to **15** and **Radius** to **1000**. Then, switch to the **Coordinates** tab and move the whole cloner forward to **1000** in the **Z** position so that it's in front of our orb.

11. Right now, the lights are just plain white light. Let's add a splash of color to them by adding a **Random** effector to our new cloner and changing the **Color Mode** feature to **On** under the **Parameter** tab for the effector. Also, change the **Position** values for the **Transform** properties to be **500** in each field. Now, switch to the **Effector** tab and set the **Random Mode** feature to **Noise** and decrease the **Animation Speed** to **20**. This will cause our lights to change colors and move randomly in space over our orb, spilling different colors of light onto the faces of our dancing orb:

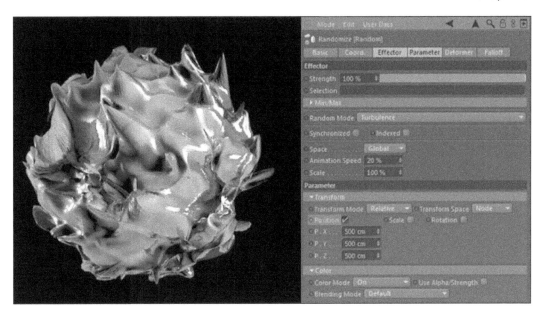

How it works...

This combination of MoGraph tools uses a little bit of everything to achieve the desired result. The **Sound** effector is the main component, driving the rhythmic motion of the faces of our **Platonic** object. The **Random** effector is also the key here; it deforms the points of our orb, giving it a more organic feel, like it won't sit still. The **Time** and **Formula** effectors are there to provide just a little bit of motion to the orb. It's interesting to see the orb floating in space while dancing to the music. Finally, we used the **Random** effector to not only colorize but also move our lights around the scene, so that we get a unique style of lighting that our reflective material picked up throughout the course of the animation. We didn't set a single keyframe, and still managed to arrive at this dynamic, shape-shifting, grooving little orb all thanks to some handy MoGraph skills.

9

XPresso Shots

In this chapter we will cover:

- ► Introduction to XPresso
- ► Creating and controlling user data
- ► Driving animations
- ► Adjusting outputs with Range Mapper
- ► Controlling lights with MoGraph and XPresso
- ► Creating a project control panel

Introduction

I once took karate classes for just two weeks as a child. I gave up on it because it was confusing my six-year-old brain and I wasn't becoming a fully certified ninja right away. One of my biggest issues was understanding the difference between left and right, and how if I'm facing the instructor his left hand is on the same side as my right, and vice versa. I probably wasn't the only kid who messed that part up, but I'm sure there were some kids that stuck with it and got a lot better at it. I gave up because I wasn't awesome at it right away.

XPresso is like my karate class, I'm surprised that some Cinema 4D users have never tried it, or gave up on it quickly because it was tricky at first. There aren't nearly as many tutorials and online resources for learning it compared to other parts of the program; it's much less heralded. But since I learned how to use parts of XPresso, I've been able to make projects that are much smarter than anything I could design before.

By smarter, I mean that I designed components that worked together and made sense. XPresso is a powerful tool that is used to link different properties and establish relationships between parameters. You can create visual relationships that make sense when you look at them, and the sky is the limit in terms of what it is capable of. Why change the values of 10 different objects when you can simplify it to just one automatic setting? Why keyframe the same position movements over and over again if you can find a way to get Cinema 4D to do it for you? You use output from one part of your project to control the input of another part, and before you know it you are saving time, simplifying your projects, and making it easier on yourself and anyone else who looks at your work.

Using XPresso can be a little intimidating at first but really you're just lifting up the bonnet, and beginning to work more directly with the underlying mechanisms. Sure the interface is a bit techy but once you begin to understand the engine more you'll get a lot more out of the whole system and it can be a much more powerful way to work. Plus it will give you a really strong foundation if you want to go on and work with other advanced features like Python or Thinking Particles.

This chapter is going to take you on an XPresso expedition and get you started towards being a smarter designer. Much like MoGraph, XPresso has enough content to fill its own book, so I'll do my best to introduce you to the basics and some of the most crucial pieces to get you going. So, let's figure out our right from our left, and hopefully lead you to one day being a black belt in XPresso.

Introduction to XPresso

This recipe will get us started and introduce you to how XPresso works. It's a simple example of how to link similar properties together to save some time on keyframing. Hopefully, you'll see some of the potential of XPresso here.

Getting ready

Use the `Spinning_Top.c4d` file from the C4D Content Pack for this recipe.

How to do it...

1. Click on **play** in the Animation toolbar and watch this top start spinning, and come to a complete stop by the end of the timeline. I already keyframed the animation for you, so you'll only need to focus on learning **XPresso**. **XPresso** is activated via a tag and it's opened in a separate window, cleverly named the XPresso Editor. You can apply the tag to any object and control all the objects in your scene from inside it; the changes made in the XPresso Editor influences any part of the project you specify.

2. A popular method for applying XPresso is to make a **Null** object, and rename it as XPresso or something like that, so that you know exactly where it is in your project. Go to the **Create** menu on top and, under **Object**, create a Null. Double-click on its name in the **Object Manager** and change it to **XPresso**. Now with it selected, click on the **Tags** | **Cinema 4D Tags** | **XPresso**. It adds a small tag with five blue squares on it, and a window will pop up: **this is the XPresso Editor**.

3. XPresso uses a node-based workflow, meaning you can add different nodes that represent either objects or modifiers to help establish relationships between parameters. Take the **Top** object from **Object Manager**, and click-and-drag it into the **XPresso Editor** to create a node for the object. It creates a small box with two tabs on both sides; a blue and a red one.

4. The blue tab represents the input properties for the node, and the red tab represents the output properties for the node. Click on the red tab to see a list of all the eligible properties we can use as output for our node. You may recognize most of the words because they are the same properties you can find inside the **Attribute Manager** when we are working normally in Cinema 4D. Look under **Coordinates**, then under the **Rotation** submenu, and click on the **Rotation** option. The word **Rotation** now appears inside the box with a red dot next to it, which is called a Port.

5. Output ports get connected to input ports to create links between different properties and drive movement in your projects. Let's say we wanted to have the **Spinning Top** text spin in sync with our Top that is keyframed. Instead of keyframing the object and trying to get it to look exactly the same as our Top, we can create a simple link in XPresso to do the work for us.

6. Drag the **Spinning Top** text from the **Object Manager** into the **XPresso Editor**, and click-and-drag the node so it's close to the node for the Top, but to the right of it. Click on the blue tab for the **Spinning Top** node, and find the same **Rotation** property as the **Top** node, which represents all the rotation properties instead of the individual settings below it.

7. Now, click on the red output port and drag over to the input port, which creates a line that is a link between the two properties. Now, close the **XPresso Editor** and check out your scene; click on **play** in the Animation toolbar, and watch how your text now has the same exact rotation properties as the top.

If we select the **Top** object from our **Object Manager** and click on the **Coord** tab you can see some little icons by the rotation values. These indicate that XPresso is being used in accordance with these values. If you select the **Spinning Top** object, you'll also see that it has similar icons next to the rotation values. If you look carefully, you'll see that the values driving the XPresso have a little triangle on the right of the icons, and the values being driven have the little triangle on the left. This is just to give the indication of what is controlling what. If you move your mouse over the icons, you'll see that it gives you information on the underlying XPresso:

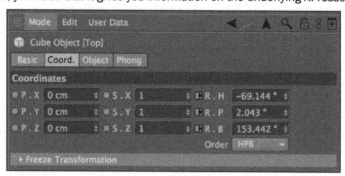

How it works...

Congratulations, you created your first bit of XPresso. This example was extremely simple, but hopefully you recognized the potential here. We took the rotation of one object and applied it to an entirely different object, thus linking their movement from now on. Any change we make to the keyframes of the **Spinning Top** will automatically be applied to the text as well. This can save tons of time when you are creating similar animations across different objects. You can have several objects to be dependent on one main object that can drive all of your animations.

There's more...

See the *Driving animations* recipe later in this chapter to see how we can create a more complex animation from just two keyframes.

Always optimize

Managing the screen space inside the **XPresso Editor** is a constant battle as you add more nodes and ports over time. One trick is to context-click or right-click on a node, and select **Optimize**. This resizes the node to accommodate all the ports and fit it properly so you can read everything within it.

You can also use the same navigation shortcuts that you use in the viewports. That is just press 1 or 2 pan or zoom around the XPresso window.

Result node

A good way to learn XPresso is trial and error. You'll never ruin your project by applying XPresso; once you delete the tag from the project you'll no longer have those nodes modifying your project. A good way to see what kinds of output you are getting is to add a Result node. To add a new node, context-click or right-click on an empty spot in the XPresso Editor, and you'll get all sorts of nodes to add. Cycle under **New Node** | **XPresso** | **General** and click on **Result**. Hook that blue port into any red port for output, and you'll be able to read what values are coming out of that particular output port.

Creating and controlling user data

In the last recipe, we linked two simple rotation properties together just to show how to establish a relationship between objects with XPresso. Every object has rotation properties, so it wasn't any sort of revolutionary use of XPresso. The unique uses of XPresso lie in your ability to create and manage **User Data**, which is custom information that you can feed into the properties of your objects to give yourself more control over your project. User Data can be created, labeled, and customized to fit within any sort of parameters you want to control. This recipe shows a short example about how to make an automatic counter with User Data, an effect that is a million times easier to pull off using some very simple XPresso than any other alternative in Cinema 4D.

How to do it...

1. Start a new project, and add a **Text** Spline from the Command Palette. Also, add an **Extrude NURBS** object and make the spline a child of it so we have an extrude text object. Change the name of the **Extrude NURBS** object to **Counter**.

2. So, instead of saying the word Text, we want to have numbers counting up or down from any point we choose. The problem is that you can't just enter the number 100 and have it cycle, in order, all the way down to zero. The **Text** field only accepts what you put in there; it doesn't have the ability to pull this off. But, every other numerical field in Cinema 4D is capable of doing this; you can start at the origin and move an object one unit at a time so that it goes sequentially to wherever you choose. With User Data, we can create a custom field just like that and use it to output counting numbers to our **Text** field.

3. Go up to the **Create** menu at the top, and create a new Null from inside the **Object** submenu. Name it as **XPresso**. Highlight it in the **Object Manager** and add an XPresso tag to it by clicking on **Tags | Cinema 4D Tags | XPresso**. You may have noticed it any time you have loaded something in the **Attribute Manager**, but there is always a menu at the top of the manager labeled **User Data**, which can be added to any object you want. Click on this menu, and then select **Add User Data**.

4. This opens a new window where you can manage as many User Data entries as you need to create. Under the **Properties** tab, we have all the information needed to customize the data to fit our needs. Under **Name**, change it to **Counter Value** so we know exactly what it is. Next, click on the menu for **Data Type**, and marvel at all the different types of data you can choose. You can create a piece of data that can represent everything from numbers, to fonts, to colors, and every other possible unit that you've ever come across in Cinema 4D.

5. Our **Data Type** should be set to **Integer**, because integers are whole numbers, and we want our counter using those kind of numbers instead of anything with decimal points or fractions. The **Interface** setting varies depending on the **Data Type**, and you can choose and sort the method for controlling the data; let's select **Integer Slider**.

6. Notice how there is an example of what your data will look like, both at the bottom of the **Properties** tab, and the separate **Example** tab. The **Step** value is important; its default of **1** means that our numbers will increase by one in each direction if we cycle through these values, but you may need this to represent larger or smaller numbers from time to time. **Limit Min** and **Limit Max** do exactly what they indicate: they set the upper and lower thresholds for your data. The defaults are **0** and **100**, meaning that you won't have numbers higher than 100 or any negative numbers to use. This works for us in this instance, but it's important to note that there are times where these need to be changed depending on the circumstance.

7. Lastly, the **Step** field indicates the increment in which you want your data to increase. We want ours to be set to the default value of **1**. Click on **OK** to make this User Data.

8. Now, there is a new tab in the **Attribute Manager** for our **XPresso Null**, and it's for our User Data. We can now control this data from this spot under the specifications we named in the last step. You can cycle through the numbers from 0 to 100 with the slider under our **Counter Value** field. But, it doesn't actually do anything until we connect it properly with XPresso.

9. Double-click on the **XPresso** tag to open the **XPresso Editor**. We need to drag in two items to the editor: the **Text** spline (not the **Extrude NURBS**, the actual spline) and our **XPresso Null**. Place them both in the editor, and now click on the red tab for your **XPresso Null** node, and head towards the bottom of the menu where you should see **User Data**. If you move your mouse over it, you'll see that our **Counter Value** is now eligible for use in XPresso, so select it as our output source. Now, click on the blue tab on the Text node and under **Object** Properties and select **Text**. Now, connect the Counter Value port to the **Text** port, and then switch out of **XPresso Editor**. You should now see that instead of the word **Text** we now have whatever number your **Counter Value** field is currently set at.

10. Go to frame 1 and change **Counter Value** to **1** and set a keyframe, then go to frame 50 and change the **Counter Value** to **50** and set a new keyframe. Play your animation from the Animation toolbar, and you'll see that our text is cycling through all of our numbers from 1 to 50. We have created a successful counter.

How it works...

User Data is the key towards using XPresso effectively, because it allows us to create parameters with our own specifications and easily link them to other properties to drive them how we wish. If we didn't set up this simple bit of XPresso, we couldn't have pulled this off without keyframing each individual number into the **Text** field for our spline; that is a nightmare. It makes me sad just thinking about it. Cinema 4D takes the **Counter Value** field and feeds it directly into our **Text** spline, so any changes we make with keyframes will be reflected inside among our text automatically.

There's more...

Check out the next example about *Driving animations* to see how the right User Data can be used to drive multiple objects and properties.

Go with linear

Use linear keyframes instead of Bezier keyframes when making a counter like this. It looks better when the numbers tick off evenly, but when you have a Bezier curve between values, the numbers ease into the keyframe values, and the numbers closest to the keyframe values will take longer to switch.

Compatible data types

Not every type of data can work together; you have to use compatible data types in XPresso. If you move your mouse over any port in **XPresso Editor**, at the bottom of the window you'll see text that tells you what kind of data type the port is outputting or accepting as input. For example, you can't connect the Y position value of an object to a User Data you made that is a Boolean checkbox, which is basically an on/off switch; it won't make sense.

Driving animations

By linking the right properties in XPresso, you can create seemingly complex animations from just one simple pair of keyframes. The same information can be used to power different pieces of your project in different ways, thus minimizing the amount of work you have to do outside of XPresso to control motion. This recipe will show you how we can make a complex shape spin and move in many different ways, all from setting two keyframes and using some simple XPresso.

Getting ready

This recipe requires the `XPresso_Rings.c4d` file from the C4D Content Pack.

How to do it...

1. Start by creating a new **Null** object from under **Create | Object** menu, and rename it **XPresso Null**. With the Null object selected, head over to the **Attribute Manager**, and click on the **User Data** menu, and select **Add New Data**. Inside the window, set the **Name** field as **Rotation Value**, and change **Unit** from **Percent** to **Degree**. Uncheck the **Limit Min** and **Limit Max** boxes so we are free to have any value we choose, and then click on **OK** at the bottom. Add an XPresso tag to it from inside **Object Manager** under **Tags | Cinema 4D Tags**. Double-click on the tag to open **XPresso Editor**.

2. Let's add all of our pieces that we want to control **XPresso Editor**. Click-and-drag the **XPresso Null** object into the editor, and place it towards the left-hand side of the window. Now, grab each of these five objects inside the **Spinning Rings** group, and place them on the right-side of the editor: **Inner Ring**, **Inner Thirds Ring**, **Middle Ring**, **Thin Outer Ring**, and **Thick Outer Ring**.

3. Click on the red tab of the **XPresso Null** node, and select the **User Data** option at the bottom, and create an output port for the **Rotation Value** field we created. This is the value we will use to drive the movement of each of the other five nodes we created. Exit **XPresso Editor**, and move to the first frame in the Animation toolbar. Highlight **XPresso Null** in the **Object Manager**, and then select its **User Data** tab in the **Attribute Manager**. Set a keyframe for **0** in the **Rotation Value** field, and then move to frame 150 and set a keyframe value for **359**. This will create a seamless-looking loop when we play our final animation back.

4. It's time to link the other nodes to **Rotation Value**. Back in the **XPresso Editor**, select the **Middle Ring** node and create a blue input port for Rotation B, by selecting **Coordinates | Rotation Value**. Play your animation in the Viewer, and you'll see the middle ring spinning around in accordance with our User Data. For the **Inner Ring** node, create an input port for **Position H** instead and link it back to the **Rotation Value**; now you'll see our innermost ring is spinning on a different axis, yet at the same rate as our **Middle Ring**.

5. We can also use the same keyframes to move an object, just at a different rate. Create **Rotation H** input ports for both the **Thin Outer Ring** node and the **Thick Outer Ring** node. If we simply link them back to the **Rotation Value** port, they will move at the same speed, but if we use a **Math** node, we can increase the rate in which they rotate.

6. There are two ways to find nodes in XPresso: by context-clicking or right-clicking inside the editor, and navigating under the **New Node** submenu, and searching for it, or by clicking on the **X-Pool** tab on the left-hand side, and clicking on the magnifying glass where you can type in the name of the node you want, and then drag the search result into the window. Try both methods and figure out which you'd prefer to use. Context-click or right-click and go under **New Node | XPresso | Calculate**, and then select the **Math** node.

7. The Math node creates simple mathematical expressions from the input we specify. Connect the **Rotation Value** port to the topmost blue input port on the Math node. Select the node to load it in the **Attribute Manager** and change the **Function** type to **Multiply** and the **Input [2]** value to **2**. Connect the Math node's output port to the Rotation H input port for the Thick Outer Ring node. This ring will now rotate twice as fast as the other rings.

8. Select the **Math** node and hold the *Ctrl* or *command* key, and drag it elsewhere in the **XPresso Editor** to create another copy. Change this **Input [2]** value to be **-2**, and connect the output to the **Rotation H** port of **Thin Outer Ring**, and the remaining input port back to **Rotation Value**. Now, the thin ring is spinning in the opposite direction as the thick ring, but just as fast.

9. Copy and create one more **Math** node and connect its top **Input** port to the **Rotation Value Output** port. Enter an **Input [2]** value of **-1**; this is a good way to invert any value inside XPresso. Connect its output to a **Rotation B** port on the **Inner Thirds Ring** node, and it will now rotate in the opposite direction as the middle ring. We now have five different pieces moving differently from just two keyframes.

How it works...

We only needed two keyframes to power this whole animation. By connecting the rotation ports for each of our objects to the User Data we created, we could get them all to spin in different directions depending on which input port we chose. We learned how to use a **Math** node to modify the output of a node, where we attached our User Data as input then created a simple math function to alter the same keyframed value the other nodes were using. Creating simple multiplication expressions inside the **Math** node is an easy way to increase the rate of any values or invert them by multiplying by **-1**. Remember I said earlier in the book the Cinema 4D is better at math than you are? Well, use this to your advantage and create some animations where Cinema 4D crunches the numbers for you.

Hook the ports up to different Rotation settings from the ones I gave you. You'll get a different-looking object, and you still won't have to change any keyframes.

Loops should be linear

When creating a loop, it's important to have the keyframes set to a linear interpolation so that they move at a constant rate. It doesn't look right to have your rings spinning slowly to start, then speed up quickly, and then slow down at the end of your animation. Click on **XPresso** and **Null** in the **Object Manager**, then click on the first keyframe in the Animation toolbar to load it into the **Attribute Manager**, and then change the **Interpolation** from **Spline** to **Linear**. This will provide a much better looping animation.

Keyframes control the length

The beauty of this setup is that you only have to slide the keyframes closer together to speed the animation up, or spread them farther apart to slow it down. The whole animation can be controlled this way, rather than having to adjust the timing of individual pairs of keyframes for each object.

Adjusting outputs with Range Mapper

There are times where you want to establish a link between two objects, but their input and output don't exactly match up perfectly. The values you want to use as input may be very small, but if they were magnified and reapplied somehow, they would be perfect. We can use a **Range Mapper** node to take a value input, and adjust it to fit within a different range of output. In this example, we take the Y position value of one object and translate its movement to affect the rotation of a different object, creating a gauge that pivots and displays our Y position value.

Getting ready

This recipe requires the Sine_Wave_Meter.c4d file from the C4D Content Pack.

How to do it...

1. Our project contains two main objects to start: a gauge and a cube. The cube will be programmed to move up and down in a sine wave pattern, and the gauge will swing back and forth measuring its Y position with the needle, all with the help of XPresso.

2. Start by creating a new Null object and renaming it to **XPresso**. Apply an **XPresso** tag to it in the **Object Manager**, and then click on the **User Data** menu in the **Attribute Manager** for the Null, and select **Add User Data**. **Name** for your data should be **Sine Scale**, and just change the **Unit** value to **Real**, and uncheck the **Limit Min** and **Limit Max** boxes. This will be the highest and lowest points for your sine wave movement that will power this cube.

3. Double-click on the **XPresso** tag to open the **XPresso Editor**, and then drag the following items inside: the **XPresso Null** object, the **Cube** object, the **Needle** group, and both the **Left Number** and **Right Number** splines (not the **Extrude NURBS** spline, the actual splines). Start by context-clicking or right-clicking in an empty spot inside the editor and find the **Trigonometric** node, under **New Node | XPresso | Calculate**. This node will create trigonometric functions for us when supplied with the proper input.

4. Now, under **New Node | XPresso | General**, select a **Time** node, which samples time values throughout our animation, and will give us a moving sine wave formula. Connect the **Time** output port to the **Value** input port on the **Trigonometric** node. Add an input node to the **Cube** for **Y Position** under **Position** inside **Coordinates**, and connect this port to the **Output** port for the **Trigonometric** node.

5. If you play your animation in the Viewer, you'll see your cube jumping ever so slightly; that's because the sine wave values being produced are less than 1 unit, which produces minimal displacement. Make a new **Result** node (found under **New Node | XPresso | General**), and connect it to the **Output** port of the **Trigonometric** node, and you'll see that the values represented are very small when you scrub through the timeline. We'll need to increase the ranges that our data corresponds to while keeping the motion our sine wave is generating, which is precisely what the **Range Mapper** does.

6. Add a new node for our **Range Mapper**, which is found under **XPresso | Calculate** inside the **context** menu. Place it between your **Trigonometric** node and your **Cube** node, connect the **Output** of the **Trigonometric** node to the **Input** port of the Range Mapper, then connect the **Output** port of the **Range Mapper** node to the **Position Y** input port.

7. Click on the **Range Mapper** node and load it into the **Attribute Manager**. You'll see that it has fields for **Input Lower**, **Input Upper**, **Output Lower**, and **Output Upper**. Basically, this node takes the range of your input and maps it to your specified range for your output. Right now, the **Input Lower** and **Input Upper** values are set to 0 and 1 respectively, so they are operating in a suitable range for our data. We need to adjust the **Output Upper** value to be a larger number so our sine wave covers a larger area to move our cube.

8. Load the **Sine Scale** port under the red tab of your **XPresso Null** node, and then click on the blue tab of the **Range Mapper** node and select the **Output Upper** option to create a port, and then connect these two. Now, click on **XPresso Null** in the **Object Manager**, and change **Sine Scale** under the **User Data** tab to **100** in the **Attribute Manager**. Play the animation; you'll see the cube moving up and down in a much larger range, thanks to the **Range Mapper** node.

9. The cube moves a bit too slow, so we need to increase the frequency in order to get more movement in our scene. Let's do this by adding a **Math** node, by clicking on **New Node | XPresso | Calculate | Math**. Place it between your **Time** node and your **Trigonometric** node, and connect the **Time** output port to the top input port on its blue side. Connect the red **Output** port of the **Math** node to the blue **Value** port of the **Trigonometric** node; now select the Math node and change the **Function** setting from **Add** to **Multiply** and the **Input [2]** value to **5**. This will multiply our time by five and result in a sine wave with a higher frequency.

10. Now that we have our cube moving the way we want it, we need to get the meter connected and moving properly. The cube's Y position is what we are going to get our values from, so click on the red tab of the **Cube** node, and create a **Position Y** port as to use as the output. The dilemma is that position values and rotation values are two different things; we need our needle to rotate with degrees, and our Y position doesn't provide that. But, we can use the **Range Mapper** once again to convert the units and map the output properly so that the rotation of the needle will be controlled by the movement of the cube.

11. Add a new **Range Mapper** node from the **context** menu or **X-Pool**. Search and add the **Input Lower** and **Input Upper** ports under the blue tab so that we can feed information into the node. We want our meter to read the same value as our **Sine Scale** User Data that we connected to our cube's movement, so let's actually feed this value into the input so there is never any discrepancy between the two and it will update automatically. Take the **Position Y** output port on the **Cube** node, and connect it to the **Input** port on the **Range Mapper** node. Grab the **Sine Scale** output port on the **XPresso Null** node, and connect it to the **Input Upper** port we just added.

12. The **Input Lower** port needs to be the **Sine Scale** value, but represents the values on the bottom of the wave, so add a new **Math** node to the editor, and change its **Function** to **Multiply** and the **Input [2]** value to **-1**. Then, connect the **Sine Scale** port to the first **Input** port, and you'll get a simple math expression multiplying our **Sine Scale** value by **-1** to invert it. Connect this to the **Input Lower** port on the **Range Mapper** node, and you've automatically linked **Sine Scale** to the inputs of the meter.

13. We can use this information to take this project one step further. For the remaining **Left Number** and **Right Number** nodes, add a **Text** port from their blue input tab under **Object Properties**, and connect **Sine Scale** to the **Right Number** port, and the **Output** port of the **Math** node inverting the value to the **Left Number**. Now, the text on our meter will read whatever number we enter in the Sine Scale automatically.

14. Select the **Needle** node, and click on the blue tab, and find the Rotation B value in the **context** menu under **Coordinates | Rotation**. Connect the **Output** port from the **Range Mapper** node to this blue input port for our needle rotation.

15. Play your animation and watch the needle move in sync with the cube, and give a reading of the Y position value throughout the length of your animation as shown in the following figure:

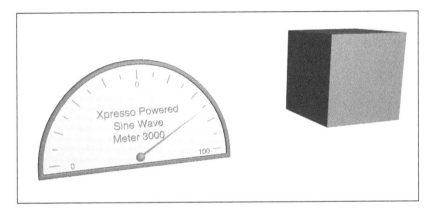

How it works...

The **Range Mapper** node is used to transfer input values that occur between one range of numbers, and apply them to a different range we specify. Our sine wave started very small and our cube was barely moving, but we amplified the wave with a **Range Mapper** node to have the same movements occur between much larger values. Then, we applied a second **Range Mapper** node to take these values and transfer them correctly to a different property altogether, where they could help create the accurate movement we were looking for. This node is pivotal to the success of the **XPresso Powered Sine Wave Meter 3000**, perhaps the greatest invention of all time.

There's more...

Check out the last recipe on creating a project control panel for another example using the **Range Mapper** node.

Controlling lights with MoGraph and XPresso

In this recipe, we will be learning how to control lights with MoGraph and XPresso. Controlling lights with MoGgraph and XPresso has the ability to create relationships between properties that we normally thought weren't really possible. In our last chapter, we used MoGraph's sound effector to deform a platonic object, basically creating a surface that moves and reacts to the beat by changing its position. The normal ways we have to use just about any effector is pertaining to the position, scale, and rotation of a clone or object; these were the transform properties we could select to manipulate. But with XPresso, we have the ability to take the output from any effector, and apply it in a totally different way beyond the standard transform properties.

Getting ready

Use the XPresso_Lights.c4d file that is available in the C4D Content Pack.

How to do it...

1. Our project is very similar to our Stage_Light.c4d project we did for *Chapter 8, The Awesome Power of MoGraph*, but we have a MoGraph cloner of Spot Lights above our stage instead of our randomly-moving colored lights. Instead, we are going to use XPresso to influence them in a totally different way with MoGraph's sound effector.

2. Go to the **MoGraph** menu, and add a sound effector under the **Effector** submenu. Highlight it to load it into the **Attribute Manager** under the **Effector** tab, click on the **ellipses** button under the **Sound File** field, and navigate inside the C4D Content Pack and find the Sound_Effector_Beat.wav we used for the *Dancing orb* recipe in *Chapter 8, The Awesome Power of MoGraph*. Change the **Falloff** from **0** to **50**; it will help smooth our movement out later on. With that audio loaded into the effector, we can use it to influence our lights with the help of the proper **XPresso** setup.

3. Add an **XPresso** tag, from the **Tags** menu under **Cinema 4D Tags**, to your **Sound effector** object. Double-click on the **XPresso** tag to open it in the **XPresso Editor** to get started. Drag **Sound effector** from the **Object Manager** to the middle of the empty **XPresso Editor** for your starting node. We are going to discover a couple of new nodes in this recipe, starting with the **Sample effector** node, which takes the output of an effector and applies it to any object using a variety of outputs.

4. Find it by context-clicking or right-clicking on an empty spot in the **XPresso Editor**, and looking under **New Node | Motion Graphics | Motion Objects | Sample** option. The default output in **Sample effector** is **Global Matrix**, which is simply the position, rotation, and scale information of an object. Click on the red tab of **Sound effector** node, and select the **Object** option, and connect that to the **Effector** input port on the **Sample** effector node.

5. Instead of using **Global Matrix**, we can click on the red tab and apply a **Strength** output port to use. Now, drag the **Light** object from inside **Lights Cloner**, and click on the blue tab, and find **Intensity** under the **General** submenu for our input port. Connect the **Strength** port to the **Intensity** port, and click on **play** on your Animation toolbar and watch the Viewer. Your lights are now reacting to the beat: the harder the music hits, the brighter your lights are as shown in the following figure:

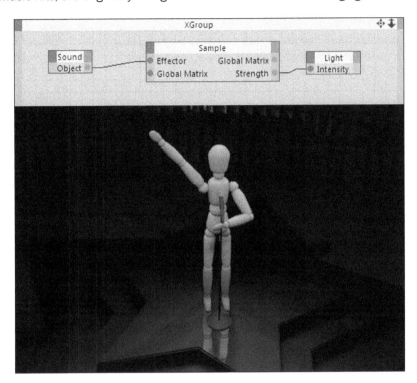

How it works...

The **Sample effector** node lets us take various outputs from an effector and apply it to different properties. In this instance, we were able to control the intensity of the lights in our scene with the measured strength of **Sound effector**, and have our lights brighten or darken based on the audio. Instead of using the default abilities of an effector to influence a clone's position, scale, or rotation, we created a unique relationship in XPresso. This setup right here is a good way to use audio to drive any sort of property from an object inside Cinema 4D.

There's more...

Still have that complete project with the rotating stage lights? Combine the two projects. Make the lights spin around the stage, but have them flicker on and off based on our audio file.

Creating a project control panel

One of the benefits of knowing XPresso is that you can create more organized and sophisticated projects. When you are designing, the objective shouldn't just be to make it look good cosmetically; you should make it functional and show that you planned things out properly. Some projects will be deep and complex, and you want to make it as easy as possible to understand how the different components of your work interact together. With XPresso, you can use User Data to create a separate control panel for your project that will control and move all the different pieces you need, and their properties will be neatly labeled so it will be easier to adjust and animate your work.

Getting ready

Open the `Elevator.c4d` file from the C4D Content Pack and buckle up: this XPresso is a bit more extensive than before. If you get lost, feel free to open the `Elevator_Complete.c4d` file, and peek at my completed XPresso if you get stuck.

How to do it...

1. The first step is to take a look at this project and think about what we want to achieve. It's a very plain office building with 10 identical floors and an elevator. Inside the elevator is a **Figure** object who wants to move between each floor. The elevator should be moving up and down, and when it reaches a floor, the elevator doors should open on that particular floor. We don't want the elevator doors to open on any floor except the one that we are on, since normal elevators don't do that, otherwise we'd be in danger of falling down the shaft.

2. We can use XPresso to achieve this, and we'll link the properties together so that we don't have to go keyframing each set of doors to open at a time, it will all be handled smartly from our control panel. Each floor has a group, so if you unfold the **Floor 1** group, you'll find all of the elements for that particular floor, notably the **Left Door 1st** and **Right Door 1st** objects, which are what we need to open to reveal the insides of our elevator only when it's on that floor.

3. As always, we need to start by creating our User Data and XPresso controller. Go to **Create** in the top menu, and create a new **Null** from the **Object** submenu. Rename it **Control Panel**. Highlight it to load it in the **Attribute Manager**, and click on the **User Data** menu and select **Add New Data**. We want to make only two properties to control everything we need. For your new data, change the **Name** to **Doors Open**, and that's all we need to do for that data. This will control the elevator doors opening, where 0 percent means the doors are completely closed and 100 percent means they are completely opened. Click on the **Add Data** button in the top-left corner, and change the **Name** field for this new data to **Floor**. Switch the **Unit** type to **Real** and change the **Min** value to **1** and the **Max** value to **10**. These will represent which floors our elevator can visit, so it has to be a number between 1 and 10.

We wanted real numbers here, capable of having decimal points, instead of just integers. Yes, the floor numbers will all be nice whole numbers, but our elevator needs to be able to move between the numbers and exist in a state between floors. If we had used integers, there would be no fractional numbers; our elevator would snap between floors and behave rather unnaturally. It's a small, yet important, distinction that is crucial to figure out before you start going crazy with a lot of XPresso.

1. Let's get the elevator movement down first. I suggest making the **Building** and **Shaft** object invisible in the editor for now, just so you can see inside the building and where the elevator is. Click on the top dot in the traffic light so it's red, and you'll see the scene more clearly, especially if you tilt the camera around to a good angle.

2. Add an **XPresso** tag to your Null object and get inside the **XPresso Editor**. Drag the **Control Panel** object into the editor as well as the entire **Elevator** group. Click on the blue tab for the **Elevator** group, and go under **Coordinates** and then **Position**, and select **Position Y** for the input port. This is the vertical position of our elevator, so we want it tied to the floor we are on. Click on the red tab of the **Control Panel** node and go to the bottom towards User Data, and select each option separately so we have a port for both our **Doors Open** and **Floor** User Data.

3. Each floor measures 100 units in height, so we want to have our elevator jump 100 units up to the next floor, and then 100 units higher for the one after that. No problem. Create a simple **Math** node by context-clicking, or right-clicking on an empty spot in the **XPresso Editor** and go to **New Node | XPresso | Calculate**, and then select **Math**. We want to take the floor number, and multiply that number by 100 to get the elevator to move the right amount, so select the node and change the **Function** field in the **Attribute Manager** to **Multiply**, and the **Input [2]** to **100**. Then, connect the red **Floor** port from our **Control Panel** node to the top **Input** port on the **Math** node, then feed the output into our **Position Y**.

4. If you change the **Floor** value inside the **User Data** tab in the **Attribute Manager**, you'll see our elevator move up and down, but the numbers are off and our elevator is on one floor too high. That's because the **Elevator** group actually belongs at 0 in the **Position Y** to be on floor 1, not 100 like our **Math** node is producing. No problem, we just need some more maths. Create a new **Math** node and change its **Function** to **Subtract** and the **Input [2]** value to **100**. Connect this node's output to the **Position Y** of the **Elevator** node instead, and the output of your other **Math** node doing the multiplication to **Input [1]**. Now, you'll see that our elevator corresponds to the right floor thanks to this extra part of the math equation.

5. We also have a **Target Camera** object that is set up to focus on the **Figure** inside the elevator. We need the camera to move upward with our elevator, so its Y position needs to be linked to the elevator. Drag the **Target Camera** object from the **Object Manager**, and create a **Position Y** port for its input on the blue side. Now, add an identical Y position output port for the **Elevator** node, and link these two together. Now, the camera will occupy the same Y position as our elevator, so it will follow it as it moves from floor to floor.

6. Now for the good stuff. We are going to set this up so we never have to select which doors to open; they will open automatically based on which floor the elevator is on. We'll introduce a few new nodes to help us accomplish this effect and minimize the amount of work we'll have to do when keyframing the elevator movement later on.

7. The best way to go about getting all the doors to work is to focus on one pair first, then apply the same technique to all 10 of them. Let's focus on the first floor, so change the **Floor** setting in the **Control Panel** object to **1** so that our **Target Camera** is on the first floor. We need to hook up the **Door Open** parameter we created to be able to open both doors.

8. For this, we'll need the **Range Mapper** node to take our percentage values in our **Door Open** value and translate that into how far apart our door will move in order to be open. Add a **Range Mapper** node to the **XPresso Editor** found inside the **context** menu under **New Node | XPresso | Calculate**, and then select **Range Mapper**. Take the red output port for our **Door Open** User Data and connect it to the **Input** port of the **Range Mapper**.

9. Cycle back into the **Object Manager** and unfold the Floor 1 group, and then locate the **Right Door 1st** and **Left Door 1st** objects. Click on one of them to load them in the **Attribute Manager**, and take note of their X position value under the **Coordinates** tab. In their current closed state, the X position value for the left door is **-7.417** and the right door is **28.417**. These are what I like to call ugly numbers: they have messy values with multiple decimal places, and they aren't as easy to work with as nice even numbers. In a scene like this with tons of objects of different sizes, it's almost impossible to not encounter an ugly number from time to time. But, the beauty of XPresso and using the **Range Mapper** node is that we can hide these numbers from our view, and set up this project to work with nice even numbers that make sense to us.

10. Add the **Right Door 1st** and **Left Door 1st** objects to the **XPresso Editor** by dragging them in from the **Object Manager**. Create a **Position X** port for both the input and output sides of the **Right Door 1st** node. Click on the **Range Mapper** node to load it into the **Attribute Manager** and leave the **Input Upper** and **Input Lower** fields as is; they represent our percentage of the **Door Open** field as a scale where 100 percent is equal to **1** as a real number.

11. We want to change the **Output Upper** and **Output Lower** to fit where our elevator door needs to move. Our door currently resides at **28.417** in its closed state, so we want this to be the lowest output value we can have. Enter this number as the **Output Lower** value. These door objects are 36 units wide, so to make it move enough distance it needs to move 36 units to the right. So, enter the following into the **Output Upper** field: **28.417 + 36**, and Cinema 4D will automatically come up with the right value of **64.417**.

12. This means that if the door is completely open, it will slide over 36 units. Connect the **Position X** input port of your **Right Door 1st** node to the output port of the **Range Mapper**, and then play with the slider for the **Door Open** parameter in the **Control Panel** object. You'll see our right door moving in accordance with our slider.

13. There's no need to re-map our values and hook them up separately to the left door; we can drive this movement with the motion of the right door we already configured. Create a blue input port on the **Left Door 1st** node for the **Position X** value and then create two different **Math** nodes from the contextual menu. Place them between the **Right Door 1st** node and the **Left Door 1st** node. Take the first **Math** node, and connect the top input port to the available **Position X** output port on the **Right 1st Door** node. Then, click on the **Math** node and change its **Function** to **Subtract**, then enter a value of **21** for the **Input [2]** field. **21** is the absolute value of the distance between the positions of the left and right doors, so it will offset our movement between them correctly. Connect the output of the first **Math** node to the top **Input** port for the second **Math** node. Select that **Math** node, and change its **Function** to **Multiply** and put **-1** in the **Input [2]** field. Connecting the second **Math** node's output to the **Position X** input node on the blue side of the **Left Door 1st** node will invert the movement of the other door, and drive it in the opposite direction of the right door.

14. So, our first floor doors now open, but the problem is that they will open regardless of what floor the elevator is on. We want the doors to only open when the **Floor** setting in **Control Panel** is set to one, otherwise your doors will be open and expose an empty elevator shaft. I don't want you to get in trouble for a hazard like that because of faulty XPresso. A solution to this lies in the logic nodes, which are nodes that can compare values and trigger results for us based on the statements we set up for our XPresso to follow. We need to create a conditional scenario that tells our first floor doors that it is only fine to open when the elevator is on the first floor.

15. Context-click or right-click on an empty spot and create a new node, by selecting **XPresso | Logic | Equal**. The **Equal** node takes two blue inputs and compares them. If the values are the same, it spits out a 1 and it spits out a 0 if the values are different. 1 is seen as the on state, and 0 is seen as the off state, a common concept in binary code. So, take the top **Input** port and connect it to the **Floor** port on our **Control Panel** node. Select the **Equal** node and change the **Input [2]** value in the **Attribute Manager** to **1**. So, when the **Floor** field in our **Control Panel** is set to **1**, our **Equal** node will output a **1** to say that the value is **ON**; when the **Floor** value is set to any other number it will output a 0 and say that it's off. This way the node will tell when the elevator is set to the first floor, and also tell us whenever the elevator is not set to the first floor.

16. We'll need one more logic node; create a **Condition** node from the same place in the **context** menu. The **Condition** node has a **Switch** port that reads an integer value fed into it and outputs the **Input** field that corresponds to that number. You can have more than the two default inputs, but this is all we will need in this case. We want our **Equal** node's output to be our switch, so connect its **Output** port to the **Switch** port on the **Condition** node. When the **Equal** node outputs a 0 it will cause the **Condition** node to output the value in the **Input [2]** field; when it outputs a 1 the **Condition** node will send out the **Input [3]** value as the output. This way, we can trigger two different values, based on whether the elevator is on the first floor or not.

17. Take your **Range Mapper Output** port, and disconnect it from the **Position X** input port on the **Right Door 1st** node. Connect it instead to the bottom **Input** port on our **Condition** node. Select the **Condition** node, and enter 28.417 for **Input [2]** in the **Attribute Manager** (which is the top input port; **Input [3]** is the bottom one). Now, take the **Output** for our **Condition** node, and connect it to the **Position X** input for our **Right Door 1st** node.

18. To recap, our **Equal** node compares the **Floor** number to the **Input** value of **1**, so if the elevator is on the first floor, it sends a number 1 to our switch in our **Condition** node. The number 1 triggers the **Input [3]**, which is now connected to our **Range Mapper**, which will send the right values to open our door coming all the way back from our **Door Open** setting. If the **Floor** value is set to any other number (try it, pick another number), the Equal node will compare the numbers and see that the **Floor** value does not match with the number 1 in the other input field, and it will send out a 0 that tells our **Condition** node to send out the **Input [2]** value instead, which is 28.417, a number that keeps our door closed.

19. We did it! The first floor works. Now, we need to apply this XPresso to all our other doors. The easiest way to do this is to select all the nodes that branch out from our **Control Panel** ports (except for the ones at the top that just control the Y position of our elevator). These nodes can be duplicated and swapped out to fit with our other doors. Click-and-drag a rectangle around these nodes until they are outlined in red. Make sure to exclude the **Control Panel** node and the four nodes leading to the **Target Camera** node (**Math: Multiply**, **Math: Subtract**, **Elevator**, and **Target Camera**). Then, context-click or right-click on one of the selected nodes in the editor, and select **Convert to XGroup**, which is basically an **XPresso Editor** inside the main **XPresso Editor**.

20. This creates a small, collapsible group where we can keep track of the important nodes easily. Highlight the new **XGroup** and change its **Name** under the **Basic** tab in the **Attribute Manager** to **1st**, so we can keep track of which floor it corresponds to.

21. Here's the key: highlight the first **XGroup** and hit *Ctrl* or *command* + *C* to copy it, then click inside the main **XPresso Editor** to paste a copy of the group (if you don't click out of the highlighted group, it will paste it inside there; you don't want that).

22. You need to make the following changes to this group, and repeat these steps eight more times so they correspond to the remaining floors. First, change the XGroup's Name to 2nd. Next, you need to reconnect the two output ports from the Control Panel node to the two input ports on the right of the XGroup. Connect the Doors Open port to the top port on the XGroup, and connect the Floors output value to the bottom input port.

23. Next, highlight the **Equal** node in this **XGroup** and change the **Input [2]** value to **2** so that this group triggers based on being matched up with the **Floor** value being **2** for our second floor. The final step is to import the **Left Door 2nd** and **Right Door 2nd** objects from inside the **Floor 2** group in the **Object Manager** into this **XGroup**, and connect them exactly how the current doors for the first floor are connected. Swap the **Right Door 1st** with **Right Door 2nd**, and connect a **Position X** input and output port to the same nodes, and place your **Left Door 2nd** in the place of the **Left Door 1st** at the end of the chain. Make sure you get all these steps right for all 10 of the floors to get your elevator XPresso to work properly. It's a repetitive process, but it's the only way to get it right.

24. Now, let's animate. Go to frame 1 and change the **Door Open** value to **100**, and set a keyframe in the **User Data** tab in **Control Panel Null**. Also, make sure you are set to **Floor 1**. Move to frame 15 and change **Door Open** to 0 and set a keyframe. Move five frames ahead to frame 20, and set a keyframe for the **Floor** value to be 1. Move ahead to frame 60, and change the **Floor** value to 2 and set a keyframe. Move 5 frames ahead to frame 65 and keyframe the **Door Open** value to be **0** again, but move 10 frames ahead to 80 and set **Door Open** all the way to **100**. Play your animation and watch your elevator work exactly how we planned it out as shown in the following figure:

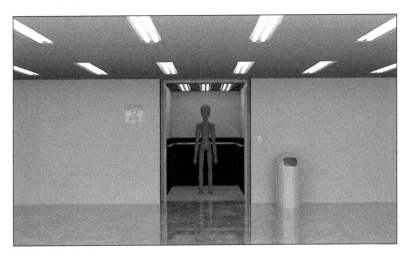

How it works...

Take a look back at all that XPresso did: it certainly came a long way. But if you retrace your steps, it doesn't seem as hard and the code makes sense. We started by controlling the elevator and camera to move up and down, based on our User Data to correspond to a particular floor. Then, we made it so our doors would open based on a percentage slider rather than keyframing their **Position X** values. We created a **Range Mapper** to hide those ugly numbers; it's much easier to understand the idea of the doors opening on a percentage scale than looking at a bunch of fractional position coordinates. Then, we introduced some logic nodes into our XPresso, which we crafted so that our doors only opened if the elevator was on that floor. This code makes it so that we don't need a door opening setting for each floor; Cinema 4D automatically knows to only open the correct door because that's what we told it to do. We eliminated a ton of keyframes and connected a bunch of buried parameters together to User Data that actually makes sense when we see it. You could give this project to someone who barely knows anything about Cinema 4D but has been in an elevator, tell them to open **Control Panel**, and they could understand how to change the floor and open the doors. Congratulations, you just made a smarter project.

There's more...

If you do a render preview, you'll see that Global Illumination is turned on, and that there's an HDR sky from our Dosch Design files. It adds a bit of a studio reflection to our surfaces to make it feel more like a real office. Our scene is lit by that and the fluorescent light bulbs arranged in the ceiling of each floor.

10
Configuring Dynamics

In this chapter we will cover:

- ▶ Introduction to dynamics – bowling
- ▶ Colliding clones – cereal bowl
- ▶ Aerodynamics – making a helicopter
- ▶ Dynamic trap #1 – trap door with connectors
- ▶ Dynamics trap #2 – soft body net
- ▶ Dynamics trap #3 – spring launcher and hair
- ▶ Cloth and Spline Dynamics – clothesline
- ▶ The final recipe – Rube Goldberg machine

Introduction

A producer I worked for always used the word "dynamic" to describe what he wanted to change about whatever project me or my fellow animators worked on. Whatever we made, it always needed something more. Instead of being specific and giving us a clue what to change, he would just use his catchphrase: "It needs to be more...dynamic."

So the word "dynamic" became a buzz word among us. We determined that we needed a button or a plugin that simply added more "dynamic" to our designs. More flares, more glows, more particles, more...dynamic!

By definition, I guess he used the word correctly, but when you put the word dynamics in the context of Cinema 4D, you can have relatively simple designs without throwing every effect in the book on them and they can still be dynamic. Dynamics are used in Cinema 4D to simulate interaction between objects, eliminating the need for keyframes and leaving their movement up to predetermined properties and physics within the project. Instead of keyframing exact movements of your objects, you set them up to collide, bounce, roll, and move like the objects you aim to create.

With dynamics in Cinema 4D, you have complete control over how your objects behave. You can start with a simple sphere and have it bounce really high like it's a superball, or hit the floor and stay in place like a bowling ball would; it's totally in your control. These dynamic properties can help us create a more realistic look and feel to your objects than any amount of keyframes would, because you are controlling the way in which it bounces, rather than how high and quickly it bounces at specific moments in time.

This chapter will get you on your way to creating dynamic objects. We'll work through an assortment of recipes to create everything from cereal to hair. We'll use other tools such as MoGraph and XPresso to help as well, creating complex movements without setting any keyframes whatsoever. Learning how to use dynamics in Cinema 4D will teach you a different style of designing animation, where you set up rules and properties for your objects to follow, and then sit back and watch the whole process come together.

Introduction to dynamics – bowling

The basic component behind dynamics in Cinema 4D is the collision. A **collision** occurs when two dynamic objects touch each other and interact. The objective is to try to set up your 3D objects to behave like the objects they represent when they collide, by tweaking their parameters to get the correct dynamic motion. This brings us to the bowling alley for our recipe. The most obvious collision you think of is the bowling ball smacking into the pins, but there's also a collision between the ball and the lane when it rolls, or perhaps with the gutter if you aren't very good. Collisions occur when the pins hit each other or land on the ground as well, and we need to set up the dynamics right so every object behaves as we expect it in our bowling alley.

Getting ready

Open and use the `Bowling.c4d` file from the **C4D Content Pack** with this recipe.

How to do it...

1. Our sample dynamics scene is a bowling lane, and we want to roll our bowling ball down the lane and hit our pins. Doing this with keyframes would simply be a nightmare. You wouldn't want to keyframe the movement of each pin once they are struck by the ball; it would be time consuming and ultimately wouldn't look very natural, and I can't even imagine how terrible it would be to tweak everything. With dynamics, we can aim our ball at the pins, let it fly, and watch them kick around like you would expect them to move in an actual bowling alley.

2. Select the **Bowling Ball** object in the **Object Manager**, and then navigate into the **Tags** menu and look under the **Simulation Tags** submenu. Here's where all of our dynamics tags can be found. We'll go over these as the chapter progresses, but let's start by selecting the **Rigid Body** tag to add it to our bowling ball. Think of a rigid body as any hard-surface object that you want to collide or interact with other objects or surfaces in the scene.

3. This adds a small purple **Dynamics Body** tag to your **Bowling Ball** object in the **Object Manager**. Here's where the magic starts. Head to the first frame of your timeline and press play in the Animation toolbar. Watch as the bowling ball drops straight down out of the frame. How exciting!

Whenever you are creating dynamic scenes, always preview them in the viewer by heading to the beginning of the timeline and playing from the first frame. For example, if your playhead is at frame 15 and you start adjusting the position of objects or the settings for the dynamics, you no longer have an accurate scene—the dynamics will be totally different. It's a good habit to go to the very beginning of your timeline and play it from there. Use the **Go to Start of Animation** button in the Animation toolbar; the keyboard shortcut is *Shift + G*.

4. You've successfully created a dynamic object, which is now affected by gravity, hence why the ball falls straight down. The controls for the gravity and various other dynamic settings are found in the **Edit** menu under **Project Settings**. There's a separate **Dynamics** tab where it loads in the **Attribute Manager**, where you have four tabs for **General**, **Cache**, **Expert**, and **Visualization**. More often than not, you don't need to mess with these settings, but if we need to change anything during our recipes I will call upon this box. The key here is the **Gravity** value of **1000**. The higher the number, the faster the objects fall. If it's set to zero or negative numbers, you'll get an outer space look to your scene.

5. So, we made our bowling ball dynamic and responsive to gravity. The problem is that we need it to hit the lane and stop, not pass right through it. If we want to have our dynamic ball interact with the lane, the lane has to be dynamic as well. Select the **Lane** object (the actual object, not the whole group) in the **Object Manager** and head back up to the **Simulation Tags** submenu. If we select **Rigid Body** for our **Lane** object, this will cause it to react just like our **Bowling Ball** object, causing it to fall with gravity. If you want an object to behave like a rigid body but remain in place and be unaffected by gravity, you need to select the **Collider Body** option. This adds the **Dynamics Body** tag to your **Lane** object just like the bowling ball, but it has a switch in the **Dynamics** tab in the **Attribute Manager** that says **Dynamic** and is switched to **Off**, instead of **On**. This means that it won't be affected by gravity but will still behave like a rigid body and react to collisions with other rigid bodies. Play your animation from the beginning, and you'll see the ball now hitting the floor instead of passing through it. Take the **Dynamics Body** tag from the **Lane** object and hold the **Ctrl** or **command** key to copy it to both your **Gutter** objects so they are rigid bodies as well.

6. We're not going to knock over many pins with our ball just landing in place on the lane. The ball is immediately affected by the gravity as soon as the scene starts, but there is no other force propelling it to the pins. Select the **Dynamics Body** tag for the **Bowling Ball** object to load it into the **Attribute Manager** and hit the checkbox for **Custom Initial Velocity**. This will allow us to give our ball some speed, rotation, and direction as soon as the scene begins. The three fields are for the **X**, **Y**, and **Z** direction for the **Linear Velocity** option and for **Heading**, **Pitch**, and **Bank** for the **Angular Velocity** option.

7. Change the third field in the **Initial Linear Velocity** option to **2000**, which controls the movement it has along the **Z** axis and will propel our ball to the pins. Then, change the second field under the **Custom Angular Velocity** option to **-360** so that the ball has a little roll to it from the start.

8. Play your animation now from the start. The ball rockets and almost flies off the lane and lands too far down. Go to the **Coordinates** tab in the **Attribute Manager** of the **Bowling Ball** object and adjust the **Z** position of the ball to be **-3000** so it starts farther back and rolls down the lane much better.

9. You may have also noticed that our pins do absolutely nothing when the ball supposedly hits them. That's because we need to apply a **Dynamics Body** tag to them as well. You could apply a tag to each pin, or you can just select the whole group, apply a **Rigid Body** tag from inside the **Simulation Tags** submenu, and then in the **Attribute Manager** under the **Collision** tab change the **Inherit Tag** value to **Apply Tag to Children**. This is a smarter workflow because it will apply the dynamics settings to all the children in the group, and any change we make to the single tag will affect all the pins at once.

10. One setting to change for our pins is under the **Mass** tab. Change the **Rotational Mass** value to just **50**. This value represents how much force it takes to rotate the dynamic object; a lower value here will make our pins spin and flip a little easier. Play your animation now and you'll see our ball hitting our pins. Every piece of the dynamic scene is now active.

11. Under the **Collision** tab is where you have some control over how your dynamic objects behave when they interact with other dynamic objects. Let's say you want your pins to scatter a little more than they do right now. Select the **Dynamics Body** tag for the **Pins** group and check out the **Bounce** setting under the **Collision** tab. Bounce is the reaction you get when objects collide; the higher the number, the more they will bounce away from the collision. Increase this value to 80 and play your animation from the beginning, and you'll see that the pins scatter much more now than before, making a better dispersion of the pins like real bowling. The setting two spots below **Bounce** is **Collision Noise**. This value gives a little randomness to objects involved in a collision so they don't all behave quite the same during the collision, so tweak that value to be **5** instead of **0.5**, just for a little more chaos during the strike.

12. **Friction** is the other editable value, and the one that acts against the collision to reduce the movement and inertia during and after the collision. Switch to the **Dynamics Body** tag for the **Lane** object and increase the **Friction** value to **150** under the **Collision** tab. Now if you play your animation from the start, you'll see that the ball travels a bit slower once it has hit the lane. It was hitting the pins at about frame 75 with the **Friction** value at **30**, and now it's hitting the pins at frame 90 with the **Friction** value at **150**. I think the animation looks better when **Friction** was lower, so change the value back to **30**.

13. The last setting we should change is the **Density** of the **Bowling Ball** object. You may have noted that there was a **Density** setting in the **Dynamics** options under the **Project Settings** window, which is universally applied to all dynamic objects in your scene. But in our case, the bowling ball should appear denser than the lighter pins. Switch to the top view in the Viewer and position the camera above the pins. Play the animation from the beginning of the timeline and watch how the bowling ball gets slightly redirected to the left upon collision. I think the ball should plough through the pins and its momentum should not really be affected by a light wooden pin standing completely still. Select the **Dynamics Body** tag on the **Bowling Ball** object and switch to the **Mass** tab. The setting for **Use** is set to **World Density**, meaning the value from **Project Settings** is applied flatly to this dynamic object. Change this to **Custom Density** and change the value to **5** instead of **1**. Now, watch as your ball doesn't get affected by the pins and goes straight through them, giving us a more satisfying dynamic action:

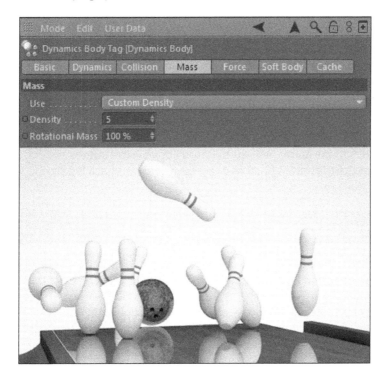

How it works...

We were able to create a dynamic bowling alley lane without keyframes inside Cinema 4D. By utilizing the **Dynamics Body** tag, we created rigid bodies and colliders to make our objects interact properly with each other. We set the **Custom Initial Velocity** value for our ball to roll it down our lane, which served as a collider, and crash into our pins. We tweaked a few settings for **Bounce**, **Custom Density**, and **Rotation Mass** to make our objects behave a little more realistically, and ultimately create a nice bowling scene.

There's more...

This was just a base for dynamics. We will get into some more specific uses of dynamics in the next recipes. Keep going!

Trial and error

If your dynamics settings don't work the way you want, keep tweaking and run the simulation again. The defaults can be pretty safe, but making fine adjustments to all the values in the **Dynamics Body** tag could pay off. If you're not thrilled with how something is bouncing or behaving, change the numbers and try them again. Try to think of how objects behave and interact with each other in the real world, and then get your dynamics to give you the correct look and feel of what you are thinking.

Adjusting the Custom Initial Velocity field some more

If you change the first value in the **Custom Initial Velocity** field, you'll be able to aim the ball left and right for a shot away from the center of the pins. If you adjust all those values, you can get some rolls with different levels of speed, accuracy, and rotation, thereby making each roll a bit different.

Don't roll a gutter ball

Don't roll the ball into the gutter just yet; they won't behave like gutters should. For dealing with dynamic objects that have contours or concave shapes, check out how to fix the mesh for these objects in the next recipe.

Colliding clones – cereal bowl

We learned earlier in the book that you can take MoGraph and clone an object so you suddenly have dozens, hundreds, or really as many instances of an object that your computer can possibly handle. We can combine this ability with dynamics, so we can have all of our clones colliding and bouncing around together as dynamic objects. Here's an example of how you can utilize dynamics to create a cereal box that pours you a bowlful of cereal.

Getting ready

Open and use the `Cereal_Bowl.c4d` file from the C4D Content Pack with this recipe.

How to do it...

1. So we have a scene here with a cereal box hovering over a bowl and three little particles to represent our cereal pieces. The brown one is the token boring grain piece, and the pink and blue ones are delicious, sugary **berries**. Go to the MoGraph menu up top and create a new cloner. Place the **Grain** and **Berry** objects as children of the **Cloner** object. Select the **Grain** object that's now a child, and hold the *Ctrl* or *command* key and drag another two instances of it so there are three **Grain** objects and two **Berry** objects as children; this will be the ratio of cereal pieces in your assortment, because they would never give you way more berries or marshmallow pieces, even though they always tasted way better. Change the name of the cloner to `Cereal`.

2. Instead of **Linear**, change the **Mode** value to **Grid Array**. Next, change the **Clones** setting from **Iterate** to **Random**, so our pieces are more naturally distributed in our box. Now, for perhaps the most important setting when working with heavy amounts of clones like this: check the box that says **Render Instances**. This can save your computer from certain death if you try to make hundreds of clones as it will hog all your RAM and CPU resources. It will help optimize the clones and save system resources. Whenever you are working with a large number of clones in a grid array like this, activate that checkbox. Now, change the **Size** settings to **200**, **300**, and **75** respectively, and the **Count** value to **12**, **15**, and **8**. Switch to the **Coordinates** tab in the **Attribute Manager** and change the **Y** position value to **530** so that our clones are contained inside our **Cereal Box** object. The box and floor already have their dynamic tags set up for you.

3. Now, with the **Cereal** cloner highlighted in the **Object Manager**, add a **Dynamics** tag inside the **Tags** menu, then go into the **Simulation Tags** submenu and click on the **Rigid Body** option. If you press play in the Animation toolbar from the start of your project and adjust the camera to see inside the box, you'll see the block of colored cereal pieces just kind of move together, with no individuality to the pieces. To fix this, go to the **Collision** tab of the **Dynamics Body** tag in the **Attribute Manager** and change the **Individual Elements** setting from **Off** to **All**. Now, play the animation from the beginning and you'll see the pieces fall as single units towards the bottom of the box; a much better start for our dynamic cereal.

4. Once your animation chugs to about frame 25, your cereal should have fallen into place at the bottom of the box, so pause the scene in the Animation toolbar and switch to the **Dynamics** tab in the **Attribute Manager** and click on the **Set Initial State** button. This sets our cereal to be in this position from the start, since we don't want it arranged unnaturally in rows and columns like our grid array does for us.

5. Move the **Cereal** cloner inside the **Cereal Box** group in the **Object Manager** to keep our **Object Manager** organized. Now, move to the start of the timeline and press play. You'll see nothing happens as our dynamic clones are ready to strike. Select the **Cereal Box** group and go to the **Coordinates** tab in the **Attribute Manager**. At frame 0, set a keyframe for the **R.B** value to be **0**, and then move to frame 45 and change the value to be **100** and set a keyframe for that value. This will animate our box tilting and pouring the cereal out.

6. Select the **Bowl** object and then go into the **Tags** menu and select the **Collider Body** tag in the **Simulation Tags** menu to add it to our bowl. If you play the animation now, you'll see our dynamics in action and our cereal pouring into our bowl.

7. Don't worry if your timeline doesn't play smoothly; it's part of the process of previewing dynamic clones. You'll notice that the cereal seems to have trouble landing in the bowl, like there is a **Force** field over the top of your bowl. This can be fixed in the **Dynamics Body** tag for the **Bowl** object, by changing the **Shape** value under the **Collision** tab from **Automatic** to an option such as **Static Mesh**, which is much more suitable for objects that are concave or contain crevices or contours. Now, test your animation out again and you should see the cereal landing in the bowl, so enjoy your breakfast.

Also, be sure to check the settings for **Steps per Frame**, buried inside the **Dynamics** options under the **Edit** menu, and then under **Project Settings**, switch to the **Dynamics** tab; do the same for the **Expert** tab. The default value is **5**; bump it up to **8** if you are experiencing clones that are poking through the edges of your other dynamic objects such as the cereal box or if the pieces are crashing through your floor like there was nothing there. This setting goes hand in hand with accurate dynamics calculations. It helps to get more precise values for dynamic objects traveling at higher velocities.

How it works...

We can apply dynamics to MoGraph cloners, allowing us to create lots of little pieces behaving dynamically together. We started with a simple grid array cloner with our cereal pieces and positioned it inside the box. We let the cereal fall into place and set it to have a new initial state, so that the cereal rests on top of each other and now line up perfectly in the original grid. Then we tilted the box over, added a **Dynamics** tag and adjusted its setting to fit our bowl, and watched the cereal fall into place.

There's more...

If some of your pieces fall out of the bowl, make some adjustments. Move the box and the bowl, and change the angle of the tilt. Reduce the **Bounce** setting of the cereal pieces. You've got a lot of options.

Aerodynamics – making a helicopter

Aerodynamics allow dynamic objects within Cinema 4D to act as if they have air flowing around them. For example, we could create a paper aeroplane with aerodynamics applied and expect it to act in a similar way to a real paper aeroplane.

For this recipe we're going to make a very simple helicopter which uses aerodynamics to fly (or crash!).

Getting ready

Open up `helicopter.c4d` from the C4D Content Pack.

How to do it...

1. As you see we already have a very simple setup. A simple helicopter and a ground plane. The **Floor** object has a **Collider Dynamic** tag already applied to it and the helicopter has a **Rigid Body Dynamics** tag applied.

2. Click on play button and watch what happens. Well not much! The model simply falls to the floor in much the way you'd expect. We're going to apply some aerodynamics to the helicopter to make it behave a little more realistically. Go to the **Rigid Body Dynamics** option and go to the **Force** tab. Under **Aerodynamics** increase the **Lift** attribute to **100**%. Also, go to the **Collision** tab and set the **Shape** value to **Moving Mesh**. Now, click on play button again. You should notice that the object behaves as if the air were acting upon it and making it spin as it falls. This is much more realistic.

3. Now, let's add in a motor to power our craft. Select the **Helicopter** object and with **Shift** held down go to **Simulate | Dynamics | Motor**.

4. Now, zero out the position coordinates of the **Motor** object and set the **P Rotation** value to **-90**.

5. Go to the **Object** tab and drop the **Helicopter** into Object A. Set the **Angular Target Speed** value to **-5000** and the **Torque** value to **200** and hit play.

6. You should see your helicopter spinning away and actually using aerodynamics to keep itself in the air.

7. Go to **Simulate | Particles | Turbulence** and set the **Mode** value to **Aerodynamics Wind** and set the **Strength** option to **30** cm. This should add a bit of random movement to the animation.

8. You can keep adding particles forces to affect how the helicopter moves. You can also try playing with the **Falloff** feature to decide where the **Particle** forces act. For example set a **Spherical Falloff** value to your **Turbulence** to create a patch of turbulent air!

How it works...

The aerodynamics system works in a very similar way to how objects behave aerodynamically in the real world. That is, the air around us has density and if objects move fast through the air they're slowed down by drag. That same drag force can become lift if the resistance pushes it upwards.

It is of course massively simplified within Cinema 4D but you can model things that look like aeroplane wings, arrows, propellers, or windmills and apply aerodynamics to them and they will behave very much like the real thing.

There's more...

Like any dynamic system there is an element of trial and error involved. It can be tricky to get what you want straight away so just stick at it!

The best way to understand the possibilities and limitations is to experiment and, of course, read the built-in help within Cinema 4D. Just go to **Help | Show Help** and search for Aerodynamics.

Dynamic trap #1 – trap door with connectors

In the next few recipes, we are going to create a few traps to help learn a few functions inside the dynamics in Cinema 4D. Connectors were added in Cinema 4D release 12, the dynamics package. They offer the ability to limit the movement of the rigid bodies and create an attached relationship between objects with dynamic properties. There are many different kinds of connectors you can create, and the default setting is **Hinge**, a useful property that can help simulate actual hinges. You'd find one on a door and its frame that restricts the movement to a certain range. In this recipe, we are creating a trap door inside Cinema 4D with a connector, and it will only trigger the trap when a dynamic object touches it.

Getting ready

Find and open the `Trap_Door.c4d` file inside the C4D Content Pack for this recipe.

How to do it...

1. Check out the infinite floor setup with the words **Trap Door** hanging above the floor. We are going to make this text drop down and land on a trap door that is flushed with the regular floor, which will swing open on a hinge and drop our text down below. Let's start by creating the actual trap door.

2. Go to your **Primitives** menu and create a new **Cube** object and change its **Size X** to be **80**, **Size Y** to be **6**, and **Size Z** to be **80** inside the **Attribute Manager**. Change the **Y** position in the **Coordinates** tab to be **-3** so that the cube is perfectly even with the floor in the scene.

3. Now, select the **Floor** object and press the **C** key to make it editable. The subdivision should line up nicely with the **Cube** object, so select the **Use Polygon** mode from the Command Palette and select the 16 cubes that are occupying the same parts on the floor as our trap door will be. Once you have them all selected, press the **Delete** key to remove them, and now our trap door should fill in the gap. Rename the cube as `Trap Door` and make it a child of the **Floor** object.

4. A render preview should show your scene looks exactly the same, but we know that we have this small cube cut out of the floor to trick unsuspecting victims. Now, let's add a **Connector** object, which is found under the **Simulate | Dynamics** submenu. The **Connector** object can be anywhere in the **Object Manager**, but we need to position it where we want in our scene to get it to interact properly.

5. Select and load the **Connector** object into the **Attribute Manager** and change the **Draw** Size under the **Display** tab to **5**, so that the object in the Viewer will be much smaller. The **Connector** object doesn't actually appear in the render; this is merely just a means of visualizing it while editing the project. Now, switch to the **Coordinates** tab and change the **X** position to **-40**, so it's at the edge of the **Trap Door** object.

6. Next, switch to the **Object** tab and check out the available settings for our **Connector**. The default **Type** value is **Hinge**, which is exactly what we want, but there are plenty of other special options in here that will help you tie together different objects in your dynamics simulation. The *Reference* documentation inside Cinema 4D has good illustrations and descriptions of what each type does.

7. The settings we are most concerned over are the **Object A** and **Object B** fields. Grab your **Trap Door** object in the **Object Manager** and place it as **Object A**, and then grab the **Floor** object and drag it in as **Object B**. This selects the two objects that will share a hinge connection. Uncheck the box below that says **Ignore Collisions**. With this activated by default, your **Object A** and **Object B** will not be allowed to crash into each other and collide, but this is precisely what we want, so make sure it's unchecked.

8. Nothing will happen to your door without the **Dynamics Body** tags. First, add one to our **Trap Door** object, so head under the **Tags | Simulation Tags** submenu and select **Rigid Body**. Without touching any settings, play your animation from the first frame and watch as your door swings open the instant your animation begins. There are two things we need to fix. We want the trap door to only activate when something hits it, and the trap door need not swing so far, especially over our **Floor** object.

9. The first fix can be made by selecting the **Dynamics Body** tag and loading it into the **Attribute Manager** and clicking on the drop-down menu for **Trigger** inside the **Dynamics** tab. The default is set to **Immediately**, but if we change it to **On Collision**, our door will only swing open when something hits it, which is exactly what we want.

10. The next fix needs to be remedied by making our **Floor** object a **Collider**. Select it in the **Object Manager** and go back up to the **Simulation Tags** submenu and find the **Collider Body** option. This means it won't move with gravity, but it will still act as an object capable of interacting with other dynamically moving objects. Change the **Shape** setting to **Static Mesh** under the **Collision** tab; automating it will ignore the hole that we cut out of it. Now, if you play the animation, nothing happens because we need to trigger our dynamics with a collision.

11. Add one more **Dynamics Body** tag to the **Trap Door** Text and watch what happens. The text block drops instantly because of gravity, and once it hits the floor the trap door springs into action and it falls through:

How it works...

The **Connector** object allowed us to link our trap door and the floor to having a relationship that links their movement to that of the hinge. The trap door was activated by our falling text, since we set its **Trigger** to be **On Collision** instead of **Immediately**. All three of the objects in our scene needed **Dynamics** tags so that they could all work together to create this short little animation.

There's more...

You could leave the **Ignore Collisions** box checked on and activate the **Angular Limit** box below it to limit the movement of your door, so it doesn't swing above the floor. With this box active, enter -90 in the **From** setting and leave the **To** setting to be 0 and you should have a similar result.

Dynamics trap #2 – soft body net

So far, we have only dealt with rigid body dynamics, which take our 3D objects and make them stiff and stable when they interact with other dynamic objects. However, there is another setting available for soft body dynamics, which makes objects appear more flexible in their collisions and interactions. Soft body dynamics are perfect for creating objects that can stretch, squish, wobble, and so on. In this recipe, we are going to use a net that traps and wraps around another dynamic object.

Getting ready

Open and use the `Soft_Body_Nets.c4d` project with this recipe.

How to do it...

1. Our scene consists of a sphere combined with the word `net` inside it, above our white environment. We are going to make a net that lands on top of this object and covers it up. Let's start by adding two **Dynamics Body** tags to our scene to both our **Floor** and **Nets Sphere** objects. Select the **Floor** object in the **Object Manager** inside the **Environment** group, and go under the **Tags** menu. Go under **Simulation Tags** and select **Collider Body** so this behaves like a floor.

2. Next, select the grouped **Nets Sphere** object and add a **Rigid Body** tag from the same menu, and then switch to the **Collision** tab in the **Attribute Manager** and change the **Inherit Tags** setting to **Compound Collision Shape** so that both our objects are included in the dynamics calculation as one object.

3. Now, let's create our net. Go to the **Primitives** menu in the Command Palette and select a **Plane** object. Change the **Width** and **Height** settings in the **Object** tab to **500**, and also move it up to **500** in the **Y** position inside the **Coordinates** tab.

4. Now, go back into the **Simulation Tags** menu and select the **Soft Body** option. The difference between a soft body and a rigid body is indicated in the **Soft Body** tab, where the **Soft Body** option is set to **Made of Polygons/Lines**, instead of **Off** like with a rigid body. If you play your scene from the first frame, you'll see our plane sort of acts like a blanket and drops over our spherical object.

5. Instead of a blanket, let's turn this into a net. Move your scene to the first frame in the Animation toolbar so your dynamics simulation is reset. Now, go up to the Array icon in the Command Palette and look inside for our **Atom Array** and add it to the scene. Place the **Plane** object as a child of **Atom Array**, which you should rename to Net. Inside the **Object** tab settings for the **Atom Array**, change the **Cylinder Radius** and **Sphere Radius** value to **1**, and reduce the **Subdivison** value to **3**. Apply the net material from the **Material Manager** to the **Net** object in the **Object Manager**. Now, if you play your animation from the start, you'll see the **Atom Array** has turned your plane into a net, but it's still behaving the same way with dynamics.

6. We need to fine tune a few settings to get this net to behave better. Open the **Soft Body** tab of your **Dynamics Body** tag on your **Plane** object. Let's focus on the properties under the **Springs** settings. Start with the **Structural** value set to **100** and decrease it to **50**. Tweak down the **Damping** value below it to just make the **Structural** setting preserve the outer edge of the shape. So decreasing it will cause our net to look less like the original square shape once the dynamics kick in. Below the **Damping** setting, change the **Shear** value to **1** and its **Damping** to 5. The **Shear** value set to this low will allow folding and make our surface a bit looser. Drop the **Flexion** value down to **1** and the **Damping** value paired with it to **5**. This will affect the angular behavior of all the springs that are inside the **Soft Body** calculations; a low value allows the squares in our net to bend at different angles and be more flexible. Finally, under **Shape Conservation**, change the **Damping** value down to **5** as well. These settings control how much of our original shape is retained during the soft deformation, so a lower value here will make our net capable of contouring to our object a little better.

7. Now, play your animation from the first frame and watch as our object becomes trapped under our net with the help of soft body dynamics:

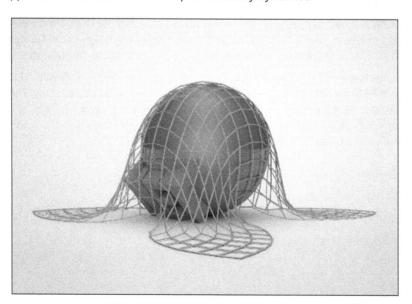

How it works...

Instead of using rigid body dynamics, we applied soft body dynamics to create a simple net. We adjusted our **Soft Body** tag to behave much differently, giving us a folding piece of geometry that wraps and contours to other dynamic objects. By placing a **Plane** object inside an **Atom Array**, we created the general shape of our net and fine tuned the dynamics settings to get it to behave properly.

There's more...

You could also use cloth to pull off a similar effect as well. Check out the *Cloth and Spline Dynamics – clothesline* recipe later in this chapter.

Dynamics trap #3 – spring launcher and hair

Let's create another fun trap for a 3D object using springs, which are dynamic objects inside Cinema 4D that contain and release bouncy energy just like in real life. If you remember our jack in the box from *Chapter 3, The Deformers*, we had to create the motion of the spring with keyframes, a **Bend** deformer, and there was even some hidden XPresso. In this recipe, we are going to create a spring-loaded launch pad that interacts with other dynamic objects in our scene. We'll also be introduced to **Hair**; we'll watch this dynamic feature interact with the launcher in our scene as well.

Getting ready

Open the `Spring_Loaded.c4d` file in the C4D Content Pack. It contains a nearly identical setup as the last recipe with the trap door, so it should seem familiar to you.

How to do it...

1. Start by taking the **Environment** group and making it invisible in the viewer. Hit the dot on top of the traffic light in the **Object Manager** and make it red. Now, you should only see two **Cube** objects: the **Launch Pad** object on top and the **Launch Base** object on the bottom. Just like our **Connectors** object, our **Spring** object needs any involved objects to have **Dynamics Body** tags on them, so select the **Launch Pad** object and add a **Rigid Body** tag, and then select the **Launch Base** object and pick the **Collider Body** tag, both found under the **Simulation Tags** submenu.

2. Next, go back to the **Simulate** menu up top and find the **Spring** object inside the **Dynamics** submenu. Click on it to add it to the **Object Manager**, and then with its properties loaded in the **Attribute Manager**, drag the **Launch Pad** object to the **Object A** field from the **Object Manager**, and drag the **Launch Base** object to the **Object B** field.

3. Click the play button in the Animation toolbar starting from the beginning of your timeline and watch what happens. Your spring bounces around and then the **Launch Pad** object flops downward. This is not a good look for our spring. Springs tend to need connectors to behave properly, so let's take what we applied in earlier recipes and use it here.

4. Add a **Connector** object from the **Simulate | Dynamics** submenu and place the **Launch Pad** object as **Object A** and the **Launch Base** object as **Object B**. Instead of using a **Hinge** object though, we want our spring to be able to rise as high as it needs to, but do not move it from side-to-side. This is perfect for the slider, so under **Type** change it from **Hinge** to **Slider**. Select the Rotate Tool from the Command Palette and grab the red handle, hold the Shift key, and rotate it 90 degrees so it's now standing vertically. Now play your animation from the start and you'll see the spring behave much better; it stays in place because we restricted the momentum with the Connector.

5. Hit the *Ctrl* or *command* key while holding down the *R* key to do a render preview and you'll see the big issue. In Cinema 4D R12 they introduced springs, but only as a way to create dynamic motion, not as an actual renderable object. The drawing in the viewer is just for reference, it doesn't get rendered. But, with some handy XPresso, we can create a bouncing spring that isn't dynamic, but will behave like it is.

6. Start by adding a **Helix** spline from inside the Command Palette to be the basis for our spring. In the **Attribute Manager**, change the **Orientation** value to **XZ**, the **Start Radius** and **End Radius** values to **20** and **End Angle** to **1800**. Switch to the **Coordinates** tab and change its **Y** position to be **-40** so its base starts at the top of the **Launch Base** object.

7. Now, add a new **Null** object from the **Object** submenu under the **Create** menu up top and rename it as XPresso in the **Object Manager**. Click on the **Tags** menu and add an **XPresso** tag to it from inside the **Cinema 4D Tags** submenu.

8. Double-click on the **XPresso** tag and drag the following objects into the **XPresso Editor**: the **Helix** spline, the **Launch Pad** object, and the **Launch Base** object. Right-click or context-click in the editor and go to **New Node | XPresso | Calculate**, and then select **Math**. Select this node to load it into the **Attribute Manager** and change its **Function** to **Subtract**.

9. Next, under both the **Launch Pad** and **Launch Base** objects, click on their red tabs and add a port for **Global Position Y**, under the **Coordinates** submenu. Take the red output port for the **Launch Pad** node and connect it to the top **Input** port on the **Math** node, and connect the red output port on the **Launch Base** node to the other blue **Input** port.

10. Under your **Helix** node, click on the blue tab and head under **Object Properties** and select the **Height** setting. Connect the red output for the **Math** node and connect it to the **Height** port of the **Helix** spline. This is taking the difference in position between the **Y** positions of the two components of our launcher and subtracting them to give us the correct height of our **Helix** spline.

The difference between global position and regular position is that global position is the exact location of the object in the world inside your project, and the position applies to just the values inside the **Coordinates** tab of the object. When objects are dynamic, they constantly have changing global position values, even though their regular position values aren't being changed. In this case, our **Launch Pad** object keeps changing its vertical position, but the change is not reflected in the **Y** position field under the **Coordinates** tab. Global position is something to use in XPresso when you have objects in MoGraph cloners or in nested groups, because the values in their **Coordinates** tab may differ from exactly where they appear in the scene.

11. Leave the **XPresso Editor** and add a **Sweep NURBS** object from inside the **NURBS** icon in the Command Palette. Place the **Helix** spline as a child of it and rename the **Sweep NURBS** object as `Spring`. Now add a **Circle** spline to the mix, place it as a child above the **Helix** spline in your **Spring**, and reduce its **Radius** all the way down to just **1**. If you play your animation, you'll see your spring now bounces correctly between the two objects, updating automatically based on the dynamic movement of the spring.

12. There's one tweak to be made here, however, as the **Global Position** value is being drawn from the middle of our pad and base. We want the spring to only exist from the bottom of the pad and the top of the base. Right now it's overlapping in the middle too much. We could fix it with more XPresso, but the easiest solution is to select the **Launch Pad** and the **Launch Base** objects in the **Object Manager** and hit the **C** key to convert them to polygon objects.

13. Now, make sure you return to the first frame of the animation before our dynamics are active, and select the **Enable Axis Modification** tool on the left-hand side of the Command Palette. Next, select the **Launch Pad** object and go down to the **Coordinate Manager** to enter a value of **-6** in the **Y** position field and you'll see the axis snap at the bottom of the pad instead of in the middle. Now, grab the **Launch Base** object and perform the same thing, but change the **Y** position value to **-40** instead of **-43**. The **Height** value of your spring should change automatically based on these new coordinates.

14. Right now, our spring activates at the very first frame of our scene. We want it to spring to action when something touches it, which makes for a better trap and a more interesting design. Click on the **Dynamics Body** tag on the **Launch Pad** node and change the **Trigger** value from **Immediately** to **On Collision**.

15. Now, we just need something to land on it to make it active. In the scene, there is a **Ball** object that is deactivated; click on the red **X** in the **Object Manager** to make it active and on the red dot for your **Environment** group so we can see our floor again. Also, take the **Launch Pad** object and place it as a child of the **Floor** object, so it absorbs its **Texture** tag and blends it in seamlessly. Apply a **Rigid Body** tag to our ball so it will be dynamic.

16. If you play the scene the ball drops to the floor but doesn't land on the pad because it's positioned too far away. We can give this ball a bit of movement that comes into play and sends it in a different direction, rather than just heading straight down with gravitational force. Click on the **Dynamics Body** tag for the ball and check the box for **Custom Initial Velocity**. Change the first number in the **Initial Linear Velocity** field to **300**, which controls the movement it has along the x axis. The higher the number, the more movement there is. Change each field under the **Custom Angular Velocity** option to **90** so that the ball has a little spin to it.

17. Let's add another aspect of dynamics to our scene with the Hair module. The Hair module is a great feature that allows you to add strands of hair to your objects, which behave dynamically when the object moves. It works great for character animators who want to add realistic hair and fur to their creations, but it can also be used to create great-looking grass, wavy wheat fields, or even feathers with the right settings.

18. Select the ball in the **Object Manager** and go under the **Simulate** menu, and select the **Add Hair** option under the **Hair Objects** menu. Head to the start of your timeline and check out your sphere; it has long blue lines poking out of it. If you press play, you'll see the guides flow and bounce with the ball as it crashes and bounces on the ground. Those are guides, and they represent how your hair behaves and where it's applied to the object.

19. There's a new **Hair Object** option inside the **Object Manager**; click on it and change the **Length of the Roots** from **100** to **20** under the **Guides** tab so that they are much shorter. Then, move to the next tab to the right, **Hairs**, and increase the **Count** value to **10000** so there are no bald spots.

20. If you do a render preview of the first frame with your hairy sphere in sight, you'll see it's brown and pretty bad-looking; the hair is straight as an arrow and doesn't act very naturally. The settings in the **Attribute Manager** for the **Hair** object tend to focus on how the hair is distributed and behaves, but we have to open the **Hair Material** created in the **Material Manager** to control how our hair actually looks.

21. Double-click on the **Hair Material** in the **Material Manager** to open the **Material Editor** and you'll see the same interface for editing regular materials, just with different options. Start with the first and most basic option, **Color**. Change the knots on the gradients to be something more colorful than plain brown. I picked a green and a blue color—this is entirely up to you. Next, move down to the **Specular** settings and reduce the **Strength** and **Sharpness** values down to **20**, just so the highlights aren't so bright.

22. All the settings such as **Length, Scale, Frizz,** and **Kink** are where you really get the detailed control over how your hair looks. The **Guides** represent where your hair is placed on the object, but these settings on the **Hair Material** control how it looks when applied to those guides. This is where you can create long silky strands or coarse, short, and scruffy fur. Activate the checkbox for **Length** and increase the **Variation** value to **80%** so the strands of hair have more difference in their individual lengths. Now, check on the **Frizz** checkbox and leave the defaults. This will send your hair in different directions so it won't appear so uniform.

23. For hair collisions to work properly, you'll need to add a **Hair Collider** tag from inside the **Hair Tags** menu in the **Object Manager**. Select the **Floor** object and add a **Hair Collider** tag to it, and then copy the tag from the **Floor** object to the **Launch Pad** object as well. Without these tags, your hair may poke through the objects it collides with, so add these tags to eliminate that problem.

24. Finally, do a render preview and you'll see much more interesting-looking hair on your ball, and with the dynamics the hair will automatically wave and bounce as your ball heads toward the launch pad. Once it hits the launch pad, you'll see it triggering our spring and it hitting it, but it is barely affected by the dynamic object. That's because our spring is pretty weak by default. Click on the **Connector** object in the **Object Manager** and change the **Stiffness** setting to **10**, and then play your animation back. The ball shoots way up into the air now and it's much better. Do a full render to see the output of your hair in action. You'll see we've created a much more interesting dynamic object with the addition of hair:

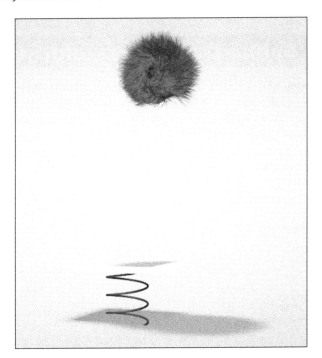

 Add a colored material to the sphere that matches your hair so it fills in the gaps with a better color than the basic gray.

How it works...

The **Spring** object is a way to link two objects together via a dynamic spring. Our **Launch Pad** objects came together by first creating the spring between the pad and the base, and then applying a **Slider Connector** to limit the movement of the object to be only vertical. Because the spring doesn't actually render a visible object, we had to create one through a **Helix** spline, **Sweep NURBS**, and **XPresso**. The **XPresso** code basically took the difference between the pad and the base and allocated that value as the height of our visible spring. Then, we set the **Launch Pad** object to be triggered with a collision, and we learned how to adjust the custom initial velocity so our ball bounced with some rotation and direction instead of just dropping straight down. It got launched high into the air when we raised our stiffness of the spring, which increases the amount of potential energy available in our dynamic spring. Finally, we added hair into the mix, which made a little more interesting-looking object. **Hair** is another dynamic tool to utilize inside Cinema 4D. We got some cool and quick results with its dynamics interacting with the other objects in our scene.

Cloth and Spline Dynamics – clothesline

Cloth and **Spline Dynamics** are two other dynamic options we have inside Cinema 4D. **Cloth** does exactly what you would expect: it simulates the unique way the clothing and fabrics behave. It can be used to create garments, flags, tablecloths, blankets, basically just about anything you'd find in the laundry hamper. **Spline Dynamics** comes with the **Hair** module and can create things such as swinging ropes and chains, by setting up realistic behaviors for how simple splines would hang, dangle, or tighten when interacting with other objects and forces. This recipe will combine the two dynamic objects, and you'll create a clothesline that has a nice, flowing sheet hanging from it.

Getting ready

Open and use the `Clothesline.c4d` file from the C4D Content Pack with this recipe.

How to do it...

1. The setup here is pretty simple. We have two small clothespins and two posts that resemble a combination of a T and a Y fused together. A clothesline can hang from anything—windows, fences, trees, balconies, and there are a couple more example photos I found where there were poles like this in the yard. It's a simple model to make, and it isn't the main focus of our recipe, so let's get to the good stuff.

2. Start by switching the viewer to the top view and then selecting your **Linear Spline** tool from the Command Palette. The objective here is to draw a spline to represent our clothesline. It shows stretch from the little ring on the left-hand side pole to the little ring on the right pole. Click on the small ring on the left-hand side and then click on the small ring on the right-hand side so that you draw a straight line. Now, hit *Ctrl* or *command + A* key to select both points, and now context-click or right-click and find the **Subdivide** setting option at the bottom. Click on the small black window tab to the right side of the option to open the **Subdivide** box and enter a value of 8:

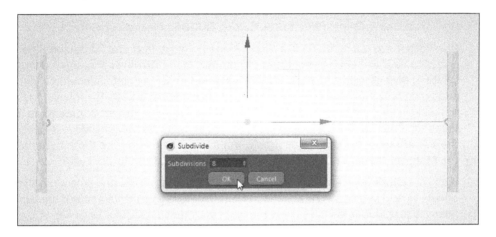

3. Switch to the **Front** view and move your entire spline up in the Y position so it's even with your two rings (make sure to hit the **Use Model** mode to move the whole spline and not just one of the points) using the **Move** tool. Spline dynamics is activated by selecting your Spline and going under **Tags** in the **Object Manager**, then under **Hair Tags**, and then picking **Spline Dynamics**. As soon as you activate this, you can play your animation from the start and watch as your **Spline** object falls down with gravity, signifying its dynamic state. Splines like these need what we call constraints, which are tags that lock the point of a spline to the position of another object. With the Spline still highlighted, go up to **Tags** again, and then in **Hair Tags** select **Constraint**. Do it again so you have two **Constraint** tags on the **Spline** object in the **Object Manager**.

4. Each **Constraint** tag will correspond to one ring on our poles. Open the **Pole Left** and **Pole Right** groups so the ring objects are visible in the **Object Manager**. Zoom in on the **Left Pole** group and then switch to the **Use Point** mode and select the end point of the spline, the last point on the left-hand side (make the ring temporarily invisible if you can't see it). Now, select the first **Constraint** tag in the **Object Manager** and drag the **Ring Left** object into the **Object** field in the **Attribute Manager**, and then hit the **Set** button. This attaches the point you selected on the spline to the **Ring Left** object you specified.

5. Now, move to the other side and repeat the same steps for the **Ring Right** object. Make sure you are using the second **Constraint** tag. With both constraints set, play your scene from the first frame. You'll see our spline dips in the middle and bounces between our two poles, like it's tied to the rings.

6. As of now our clothesline is just an invisible spline. Add a **Sweep NURBS** object to the project as well as a **Circle** spline from the Command Palette. Select the **Circle** object and change the **Radius** value to **2** in the **Attribute Manager**. Place both the **Circle** and **Spline** objects as children of **Sweep NURBS**, and make sure your **Circle** spline is on top. Apply the **Rope** material to the **Sweep NURBS** object. Now, we have a defined line for your clothesline. Rename the **Sweep NURBS** object as `Clothesline`.

7. Now, let's make our cloth. Create a new **Plane** primitive from the Command Palette and rename it to `Cloth` in the **Object Manager**. In the **Attribute Manager**, change its **Width** to **800**, **Height** to **530**, and its **Orientation** to **-Z**. The cloth simulations depend heavily on how much subdivision there is on your original object. Too many polygons will make your cloth wrinkly. Reduce **Width Segments** and **Height Segments** to **10**. Press the **C** key to make this **Plane** object into an editable polygon. Move it down in the **Y Position** to **-100** so it's just below your clothesline. Apply the **Cloth** material in the **Material Manager** so you have a nice tablecloth pattern to work with.

8. With your **Cloth** object selected, go to **Tags | Simulation** Tags, and select the **Cloth** option. Now, if you play your animation from the start, you'll have another uninspiring falling object, but at least we know the cloth is dynamic now. In a lot of cases, you'll create a cloth that has what are called fix points, which are set points on the geometry of the cloth where it's attached. Think of it like using thumb tacks to pin the cloth to a wall.

9. The problem with fix points, in this instance, is we want our points to move and flow with the movement of our dynamic spline and not stick in one place. So for this, we'll use the **Belt** tag and add it to your **Cloth** by going back under the **Cloth Tags** menu and selecting the **Cloth Belt** option. We then add another copy of it as well so you have two **Cloth Belt** tags.

10. The **Cloth Belt** tag is a way to attach cloth to other objects such as polygons. Think of it as an actual belt that secures your pants (cloth) to your waist (object). We are going to belt the cloth to the clothespins, which have been waiting patiently in our project so far. Take the **Clothespin 1** group and add an **Align to Spline** tag from the **Cinema 4D Tags** menu in the **Object Manager**. Drag the spline corresponding to your clothesline into the **Spline Path** field in the **Attribute Manager**. Adjust the **Position** value so that the value moves the clothespin along your spline into a position that is right on top of a point along the geometry of your cloth. This will be where it will hold up the right-hand side of the cloth. For my spline, a value of 39.9 works and yours should be somewhat close to it. Now, hold the **Ctrl** or **command** key and drag a copy of the **Align to Spline** tag to the **Clothespin 2** group. Adjust the **Position** value of this tag to be 61.2 so that it will hold up the left-hand side of the cloth and lands right on top of another point on our cloth geometry:

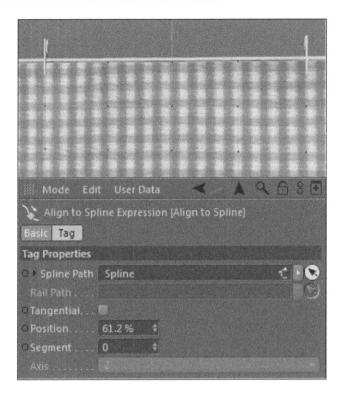

11. Now, we are going to belt our cloth to the clothespins. Switch on the **Use Point** mode and select your **Cloth** object, and grab the point closest to the left-hand side clothespin and the point directly below it as well. Next, select the first **Cloth Belt** tag and drag the **Wood Right** object from inside the **Clothespin 1** group into the **Belt on** field, then press the **Set** button. Cinema 4D draws yellow dots and lines to attach the belt, and now our **Cloth** object will stick to our clothespin, which sticks to the spline. Repeat the process for the other two points closest to the clothespin on the right, making sure to set it on the other **Cloth Belt** tag and apply it to the **Wood Left** object.

12. Click on the **Cloth** tag and head under the **Expert** tab, and click the checkbox for **Self Collision**, which will give our cloth a better-looking simulation and not have it pass through itself. Switch to the **Tag** tab and reduce the **Stiffness** value down to **5%** so the cloth will flow a little more loosely. Now, go to the **Cache** tab and click on **Calculate Cache** and your **Cloth** simulation will be stored.

13. Go into the **Simulate** menu up top and select the **Cloth NURBS** option under the **Cloth** submenu. This works similarly to **HyperNURBS**. Place your **Cloth** object as a child of it. Increase the **Subdivision** value to **3** under the **Object** tab in the **Attribute Manager**. Now, head to frame 0 in your timeline and watch your dynamic clothesline and cloth dance in the viewer:

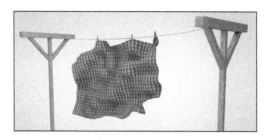

 If you change any of the dynamics settings under the **Cloth** tag, you need to empty the cache and start over. The animation is stored here and won't update without clearing the cache and starting over, so your animation won't appear any different until you recalculate it.

How it works...

Our clothesline works thanks to both the **Spline Dynamics** and **Cloth** tags in Cinema 4D. We made the actual clothesline with a simple spline between two constraints, and with the **Spline Dynamics** tag, our spline immediately sinks with gravity and bounces like it's tied to the poles. Then, our **Cloth** tag is used to turn a simple **Plane** object into a flowing piece of fabric, and we are able to use the **Cloth Belt** tag to pin the cloth to our clothespins. The final result is the sheet flowing in a breeze while being fixed to the dynamic clothesline; a good combination of two different dynamic objects.

Add some more pieces of laundry to the clothesline if you'd like.

Tying the knot

If you want a knot on the rings where the clothesline would be tied, just use the **Freehand Spline** tool to draw a twisted knot, and then apply the same kind of **Sweep NURBS** to it. It's a small detail, but it counts.

The final recipe – Rube Goldberg machine

Let's end with something fun. A **Rube Goldberg** machine is a mixture of items that all work together to create a chain reaction to usually perform a simple task. Individually the items are usually simple and they have a specific function, but when you place them in the right sequence and position, their movements trigger another component and you can reach your end result. This recipe is going to use dynamics to create a complex machine with simple household items. The way they are set up in our dynamics will result in a very epic finish—we are going to ring a bell.

Getting ready

Open and use the `Rube_Goldberg_Machine.c4d` file from the C4D Content Pack with this recipe. I also provided a `Rube_Goldberg_Machine_Final.c4d` file for you to see how it works in case you get stuck anywhere.

How to do it...

Take some time to examine this project carefully. I had to construct something similar to this in my Physics class in high school. It's a machine that performs a simple task made up of components you'd find around the house, garage, and maybe in the hardware store. The objective of our machine is to ring the service bell on the far right-hand side. I had to make all the components and position them properly; otherwise this recipe would give you tons of headaches and take over 100 pages to explain how to set up the whole thing. You'll be taking the objects and making them dynamic and creating all the motion.

The sequence in which we accomplish it will go like this: the balloon will rise up and hit the coffee can, which will roll on its side and then hit the wave of dominoes. The dominoes will fall and the last one will kick a golf ball off the edge and onto a slide that will send it into another slide. Once the golf ball flies off this slide, it will hit a bowling ball and give it just enough of a roll to push the ball off the edge of the table. The bowling ball lands on a seesaw that sends it downward to the floor, where it blasts through a house of cards, hits the boxes, which cause the bowling pin on top to fall, landing on our bell and making it ring. Sounds simple, right? Let's get started:

14. Let's start by adding **Collider Body** tags to objects that will need to be dynamic, but will simply stay stationary in one spot on our machine. Select the following items in the **Object Manager** by holding the *Ctrl* or *command* key to select multiple, non-consecutive items in your hierarchy, such as **Board, Slide 1, Slide 2**, all six items in the **Slide Supports** group, **Table Top, Tilt** (inside the **Seesaw** group), **Bell Base, Bell Middle** (inside the **Service Bell** group), and **Floor**. With these items selected, go to the **Simulation Tags** submenu and select **Collider Body**. These are the objects that are sitting still in our simulation. We'll make a couple of tweaks to their collision settings along the way:

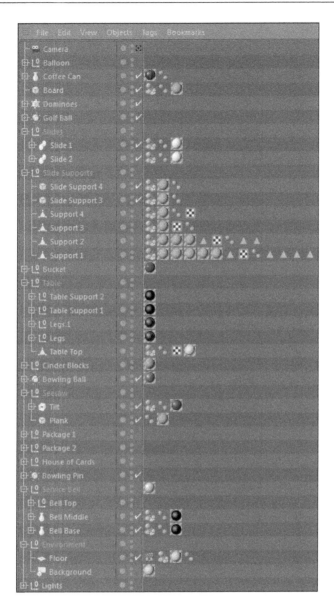

15. Now, let's create our rigid bodies, and let's just start at the beginning of our machine and work our way through. The items are arranged in a sequential order in the **Object Manager** from top to bottom, so let's start with our **Balloon** object. Open the group and select the **Balloon** object and apply a **Rigid Body** tag to it. Adjust the **Bounce** value to be **80** inside the **Collision** tab of the **Attribute Manager**. Switch to the **Mass** tab and change the **Use** setting to **Custom Density** and enter a value of **0.1** and reduce the **Rotational Mass** value to **15**, which will help make our balloon appear lighter.

16. The problem is, we want our balloon to rise like it's filled with helium, and since it's a rigid body, it's going to sink with our gravity. One method for fixing this is to apply **Forces**. Go under the **Simulate** menu and then inside the **Particles** submenu to locate the **Wind** object. Place this object inside the **Balloon** group and load it into the **Attribute Manager**.

17. The default **Wind Speed** value is too low, so bump it up from **5** to **50**. You can see that the **Wind** object appears as a yellow fan in the viewer, so we need to position it so it blows our balloon upwards against the gravity. Switch to the **Coordinates** tab in the **Attribute Manager** and move it up to **50** in the **Y** position and change the **R.P** value to **90**, so it changes its rotation to blow upwards. We aren't finished, because by default you have to add a force such as **Wind** to your **Rigid Body** tag so that you know to include it. Click on the **Rigid Body** tag for the **Balloon** object and go to the **Force** tab, and drag the **Wind** item from the **Object Manager** into the **Force List** field. Switch the **Force Mode** value to **Include** and watch as your balloon will now fly up to the sky.

18. However, because the wind is now active in the scene this will affect any new rigid bodies we add from here on in as, by default, the new tags are not excluding the forces when the tags are created. There's a solution for this. Once we create all our **Rigid Body** tags, we will select them all and change them just one time from the **Exclude** to **Include** mode, so that our wind is omitted from all the tags.

19. Select the **Coffee Can** object in the **Object Manager** and add a **Rigid Body** tag to it from the **Simulation Tags** submenu. Now, switch to its **Dynamics** tab and set the **Trigger** value to be **On Collision**, so it will only become active when the balloon hits it. Under the **Mass** tab, change the **Rotational Mass** value to **30** so that it will take less of a collision to get it rotating, and it will roll towards our dominoes.

20. The dominoes are set up via a linear **MoGraph** cloner, spacing them out evenly with the **Clones** object set to be **Random**, so the different game pieces get shuffled around. Apply a new **Rigid Body** tag to the **Dominoes** cloner. Under the **Collision** tab, change the **Individual Elements** option to **Top Level**, which will make all of our clones dynamic. Reduce the **Bounce** value to just **10** and the **Friction** value to **100**. Switch to the **Dynamics** tab and change the **Trigger** option to **On Collision**. Now, switch to the **Board** object, which is what our dominoes are placed upon, and click on its **Dynamics Body** tag and change its **Friction** value under the **Collision** tab to **100**. These higher friction values are aiming to keep the dominoes from tilting out of place and sliding around.

21. The dominoes will knock our **Golf Ball** object off the edge, so apply a **Rigid Body** tag to the **Golf Ball** object. There are only a couple of settings to change for this item. Change the **Bounce** value under the **Collision** tab to **80**, reduce the **Friction** value to **15**, and give it a **Custom Density** value under the **Mass** tab: a very high value of **10**. These changes aim for our golf ball to have enough power to get our big bowling ball rolling ever so slightly so it falls off the edge of the table. Set the **Trigger** option to **On Collision** under the **Dynamics** tab as well.

22. Our **Golf Ball** object will roll down our two slides, so open the **Slides** group and make the same changes to both of these **Collider Body** tags. Reduce the **Friction** value to **10%** under the **Collision** tab and then switch the Shape value from **Automatic** to **Static Mesh**. Since our slides are concave, they need to have a setting other than **Automatic**, which won't fully recognize their concave shape. Switching to **Static Mesh** is a must here, and unfortunately it will require the most calculations to be made and slow your computer down a bit.

23. Once the ball slides down, it will crash into our **Bowling Ball** object on the edge of the table, giving it just the slight little push to get it to spill over. Add a **Rigid Body** tag to the **Bowling Ball** object. Change its **Bounce** setting to be **80**, then switch to the **Dynamics** tab and set the **Trigger** value to be **On Collision**. Next, go to the **Mass** tab and switch it to have **Custom Density** with a value of 5.

24. Go into the **Dynamics** tab of the **Table Top** object it rests upon and reduce the **Friction** value to just **10%**. The objective of all these settings is to make the ball roll, slowly and slightly, with just enough movement to get it to fall off after anticipating.

25. The **Bowling Ball** object will fall onto the **Seesaw** object, which will redirect it properly towards the next pieces of the machine. We are going to use **Connector** to make our seesaw behave correctly, so add one from the **Simulate** menu up top under the **Dynamics** submenu, and place it inside the **Seesaw** group. The **Type** value is set to **Hinge**, and that's exactly what we want in our seesaw, so just place **Tilt** as **Object A** and **Plank** as **Object B** by dragging them from the **Object Manager** to the appropriate fields inside the **Attribute Manager** for the **Connector** object. Make sure to uncheck the box that is for **Ignore Collisions**, so that the seesaw will react when the bowling ball hits it. Switch to the **Coordinates** tab of the **Connector** object and move it to be **-33** in the **X** position and **18** in the **Y** Position, with a **-90** degrees rotation in the **R.H** value. This will position it in the right spot to serve as the hinge of our seesaw. The only thing left to do is apply a **Rigid Body** tag from the **Simulation Tags** menu to **Plank** and leave the defaults on and, you know, have a dynamic seesaw that will send the bowling ball in the right direction.

26. The next object is a fun one: a house of cards. It's also the trickiest effect to pull off in our Rube Goldberg machine, even though it's probably a million times easier to create in Cinema 4D than in real life. If you open the **House of Cards** group in the **Object Manager**, you'll see that there is a **MoGraph** cloner set to **Object**, and there's a triangular polygon labeled **House of Cards Shape** that it is applying the clones to. The clones are set to be applied to the edge and are rotated to fit together, such as they are stacked together.

27. You know the drill: apply a **Rigid Body** tag to the **House of Cards** cloner. The key here when you are dealing with lots of dynamic clones is to get them to stop colliding and settle down once your action happens. Cinema 4D will keep calculating some very small dynamic collisions when all your cards scatter to the floor, and it will cause your cards to shake and wiggle constantly. There are a few settings we can use to try to get our clones to stop moving.

28. First, under the **Dynamics** tab, change their **Trigger** to be **On Collision**. Under the **Deactivation** options below, change the **Linear Velocity Threshold** and **Angular Velocity Threshold** values to be **200**, which will remove any objects from the dynamics calculations once they stop moving at a rate below this value for a couple of seconds, after they finish colliding. The value can be set very high in order to make sure there's no way these cards will keep moving after they stop colliding with each other. Switch to the **Collision** tab and set the **Individual Elements** setting to be **All** so that the clones are affected individually. Set the **Size Increment** value to **1** so that our cards won't be so skinny and they have a larger area in the calculations This way they won't poke through the floor and each other so much. Reduce the **Bounce** value to **0** and increase **Friction** to **50**, which will perhaps do the most to get these cards to settle down. Lastly, switch to the **Force** tab and increase the **Linear Damping** and **Angular Damping** values to **50**, which is a sort of manual way to remove energy from your dynamics. It will cause your clones to settle down faster.

29. The **Bowling Ball** object is aimed to go through the house of cards and hit the two packages blocking the service bell. Highlight **Package 1** and apply a **Rigid Body** tag to the group. Change the **Inherit Tag** setting to be **Compound Collision Shape**, so the **Tape** object on the package will be included in the calculation too. Set the **Trigger** value to be **On Collision** and set a **Custom Density** value of **0.5** under the **Mass** tab. Then, hold down the *Ctrl* or *command* key and drag another copy of the **Dynamics Body** tag from **Package 1** to **Package 2** to keep the same exact settings.

30. **Bowling Pin** is the object that will fall from the top of the boxes and land on our bell, causing it to ring. Apply a **Rigid Body** tag to it and head to the **Mass** tab, where it needs to have a **Custom Density** value of **0.25** and **Rotational Mass** of **5**, just so it seems a little lighter.

31. The finish line is our **Service Bell** object. We need to add a spring to this object so it bounces and behaves like a bell when the **Bowling Pin** object hits it. Open the **Service Bell** group and look inside, and then add **Spring** and **Connector** from the **Dynamics** submenu inside the **Simulate** menu and place them inside the group. Take **Spring** and place the **Bell Base** object as **Object A** and the **Main Bell** object as **Object B** by dragging them in from the **Object Manager**. Set the **Rest Length** value to **20** and **Stiffness** to **5** so the bell won't have such a wobbly bounce, and also adjust its position coordinates so it appears at **0** in the **X** position and **5** in the **Y** position as a child of this group.

32. The **Bell Base** object already has a **Dynamics Body** tag on it from the beginning, so apply one to the **Main Bell** object so it becomes a rigid body. Set the **Trigger** value for this tag to be **On Collision**, so it only becomes active when the **Bowling Pin** object hits it. Then, change the **Inherit Tag** setting to **Compound Collision Shape** under the **Collision** tab. Now, we just need to configure the **Connector** object. Load it into the **Attribute Manager** and place the **Bell Base** object as **Object A** and **Main Bell** as **Object B**. Also uncheck the **Ignore Collisions** checkbox. Change the **Type** value to **Slider** and rotate it **-90** in the **R.P** value so it's pointing straight up, and place it at **0** in the X position and **5** in the Y position inside the **Service Bell** group.

33. Now, for the last step. We have to remove that pesky **Wind** object from interfering with anything else in our scene. So, use the *Ctrl* or *command* key to click and select all the **Rigid Body** tags we applied (not the **Collider Body** tags). The following objects should be included in your selection: **Coffee Can**, **Dominoes**, **Golf Ball**, **Bowling Ball**, **House of Cards**, **Package 1**, **Package 2**, **Bowling Pin**, and **Main Bell**. Change their setting under **Force Mode** in the **Force** tab from **Exclude** to **Include**.

34. Save your machine as a new project, and test it out by playing it from the first frame. Everything should work together because of the dynamics, and you now have a state-of-the-art, 100 percent certified bell-ringing machine:

How it works...

Just like a real Rube Goldberg machine, ours relies on the dynamic properties and correct positioning of all components to accomplish the final task. We added the proper **Dynamics Body** tags to each of the objects, as well as a couple of connectors and springs, to make all the components work together to ring our bell. I arrived at the settings with tons of trial and error, which is necessary in an open-ended exercise like this. There is no one correct method towards ringing the bell; the components can be moved and swapped to have an entirely different look, but still arrive at the same conclusion. The design is to try to build the momentum and anticipation by having slower objects develop like the golf ball rolling slowly, the bowling ball crawling towards the edge, and the bowling pin wobbling on top of the boxes before it falls on the bell. We accomplished this entire animation without any keyframes whatsoever, meaning that utilizing dynamics in Cinema 4D is hands down the best way to pull off a complex sequence of movements like this.

There's more...

Where to go from here? Go anywhere you please. Create your own objects, customize their dynamics settings, and make your own Rube Goldberg machine that's better than mine.

11
Thinking about Particles

In this chapter we will cover:

- ▶ Standard Particles
- ▶ Let the water flow (a simple particle simulation)
- ▶ Using Thinking Particles to create complex behavior
- ▶ Adding geometry to Thinking Particles
- ▶ Making it rain

Introduction

Particles will allow you to create all sorts of interesting effects such as rain, explosions, bubbles, smoke, or even cool abstract animations for motion graphics. There are two types of particle systems in Cinema 4D: The Standard Particles and Thinking Particles. **Standard Particles** are fun, easy to get your head around, and don't require too much previous experience with the program. I recommend you thoroughly understand Standard Particles before moving onto **Thinking Particles**. Thinking Particles are much more powerful and flexible although they're not as user-friendly to begin with. They work in a node-based system, much the same as XPresso, so I definitely recommend you become familiar with the XPresso workflow before embarking with Thinking Particles. Personally, I love working with Thinking Particles and get a real kick out of the power and flexibility of the system, but you do have to be patient whilst learning it, it can be frustrating at first but it's definitely worth sticking with if you want to create stunning visuals.

Particles work a little differently than directly keyframed objects within Cinema 4D as they are a simulation. Each time you play your particles simulation you should do so from the very start of the animation otherwise you may get strange results. This is because the program needs to calculate each frame in sequence rather than just jumping to any old point you fancy.

Secondly, make sure you set your playback to **All Frames**. If you have your playback on real time (for example, **All Frames** not ticked) then your simulation will be jumping, inconsistent, and may not work at all as shown in the following screenshot:

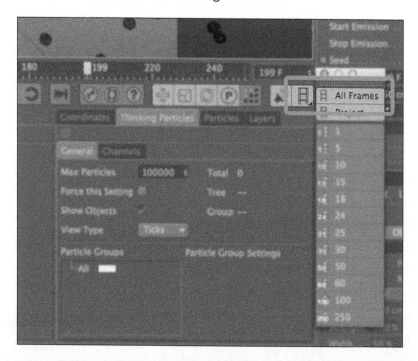

Standard Particles

Standard Particles (SP) are created by the **Emitter Object**. We use this to control how the particles are created and some of their basic attributes such as speed, life, and so on. We then use particle Modifiers to add different behaviors to the simulation which include things such as wind or gravity or even rotation. We can use various different objects as our particles such as geometry or lights or even tracer objects. So, let's get cooking!

Getting ready

Create a new project and make sure **All Frames** is activated.

How to do it...

1. Go to **Simulate | Particles | Emitter** and click on **play**. Congratulations! You've just created your first particle simulation! Have a play around with the settings of **Emitter**, increase the **Birthrate** to create more particles, make the particles faster with the **Speed** setting. Don't be afraid, just give it a whirl. Remember, any setting you're curious about, simply right-click and go to Show Help. You'll also notice there is a **Birthrate Editor** and **Birthrate Render** setting. The **Editor** setting allows you to set how many particles you see in the viewport whilst the **Render** settings will define how many particles are created for the final render.

2. Let's make our project a little longer, let's say 250 frames. This will help us see what's going better.

3. Now, let's make them do something a little more interesting, go to **Simulation | Particles | Rotation** and you'll see their behavior changes immediately.

4. Select the Emitter object again, and go to **Mograph | Tracer**. In the **Tracer** settings, go to **Limit** and set to From End and set the value to 20. This will allow us to see what the particles are doing and just generally look a bit nicer. As you may have guessed, **Tracer** traces the movement of whatever you drop into it; it draws a spline which follows the movement of anything you drop in the **Trace Link** field. In this case, as you had **Emitter** already selected, automatically add it to the **Trace Link** field.

5. Just try adding in some new particle forces and just see what they do—they add Deflectors, Attractors, Gravity, and so on. It's worth trying them just one at a time so you can see clearly what the effect is.

How it works...

You should have now grasped the basic idea that particles are created by the **Particle Emitter Object**. Once they are created the Emitter Object no longer affects them, the only way to control them after this point is to use the Particle Forces. It's a bit like a billiard ball, when you strike it you give the ball its direction and speed (or velocity). This is like the Emitter. The other balls and the cushions are like the particle forces. They can redirect or change the behavior of the ball once it has been set in motion.

There's more...

Maybe we don't want to use the **Tracer** object to visualize our particles, well, we can use almost any object we like as a particle. This is done by making our object a child of the Particle Emitter Object. Then make sure that in the **Particle settings** tab of the Particle Emitter Object, the **Show Objects** checkbox is ticked. You should now be able to see the object you've selected being applied to every single particle which is being generated by the Emitter Object.

Let the water flow (a simple water simulation)

Let's create a very simple simulation of some water running from a tap using Standard Particles and the **Metaballs** generator.

Getting ready

Open Tap.c4d from the C4D Content Pack.

How to do it...

1. First, create an **Emitter (Simulate | Particles | Emitter)** object, and move it to the nozzle of the tap. Make sure the z axis (the blue one) is facing downwards slightly. Scale the Emitter object until it's contained nicely within the nozzle. Press **play** just to make sure you've got it facing the right direction as shown in the following figure:

2. Now, add a **Sphere** object as the child of the Emitter. Set the sphere to a **Radius** of **16**. Now, tick the **Show Objects** box in the **Particle** tab of the **Emitter** settings.
3. Add in a **Gravity** particle force from the **Simulation | Particles menu**.

4. Make **Emitter** the child of a **Metaballs** object. (**Create | Modeling | Metaball**) Change the **Metaballs** settings in the **Object** tab to: **Hull Value: 625%, Editor Subdivision 5cm**.

5. Finally, search the **Content Browser (Window | Content Browser)** for **Water**, and add in a water material of your choice to the **Metaball** object. You can do this by simply dragging the material from the **Content Browser** onto your **Metaball** object or by double-clicking it, and then dragging it on.

How it works...

We already have an understanding of the principles of standard particles from the previous recipe, but we've introduced a new object here, or more technically, **Generator**, which is the **Metaball** object. The **Metaball** object behaves like an elastic skin which tries to envelope all the objects within it. The **Metaball** object is designed to work with particles and it creates a generated polygonal skin around them but it also works with primitives, splines or polygons.

There's more...

As you can see, our simulation won't behave like real water; you'd need a third-party plugin for that such as Real Flow, Navie, or even X-Particles. But this will give us something fun and stylized, and should give you an idea of how you can apply particle behavior to your scenes. As you get better at understanding how particles and forces work, you'll be able to create more believable or impressive simulations. It's surprising what can be achieved with Standard Particles. But if you want to go further, you'll have to take a look at Thinking Particles which we'll look at next.

Thinking Particles

Thinking Particles are the more complex and powerful older brother of Standard Particles. They can be quite frustrating to start with, but offer much more power and flexibility than their little brother. I also think they're a lot of fun! Make sure you are familiar with XPresso before you dive into these recipes, even if it's just understanding how to link different nodes together because Thinking Particles are a node-based system as well.

If you're new to Thinking Particles, we'll call them TP from now on, and then don't expect it to all make sense instantly. Just stick with it, and things will become clearer as you learn more and get used to the flow.

A lot of the power comes from being able to pass particles from one group to another. This means you can emit a set of particles and when they hit the wall they move to another group and their behavior changes. You can create multiple groups with lots of complex behaviors. The particles can move in and out of groups and change dynamically. This may not make an awful lot of sense straight away so let's just dive right in and start cooking!

Using Thinking Particles to create complex behavior

In this recipe, we will be learning about how to use thinking particles to create complex behavior.

How to do it...

1. Firstly, create a new document and make sure it has at least 500 frames. Then create a new null object and name it **Emitter**. Now, add an **XPresso** tag (**Tags | Cinema 4D Tags | XPresso**).

2. Select the **X-Pool** tab from inside your **XPresso Editor** window as shown in the following screenshot:

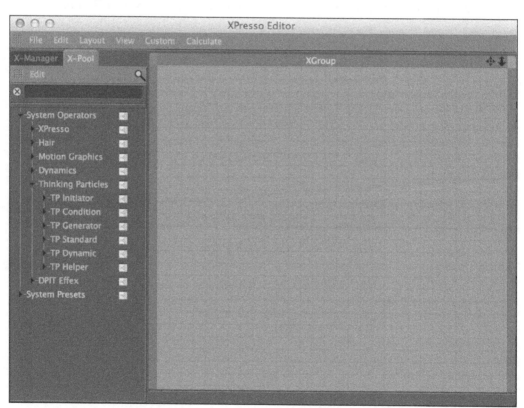

3. Flip down the **System Operators** delta (the little triangle), then the **Thinking Particles** delta, and we can now see our main groups of nodes: **TP Initiator/TP Condition** and so on. These are the nodes for controlling Thinking Particles (or 'TP' for short). It may seem confusing now but will begin to make sense. Flip down **TP Generator**, and drag **PStorm** into the main window of **XPresso Editor**. You can also access all the nodes by right-clicking in the main window of **XPresso Editor**, and navigating to **New Node/ Thinking Particles | TP Generator | PStorm**.

4. Click on the **PStorm** node and you'll see lots of attributes. These are somewhat similar to the standard particle **Emitter**. Let's just press **play**, and you'll see particles being emitted!

5. You'll notice that if you try and move the **Emitter Null** object around it doesn't affect where the particles are emitted from. To fix this, drag the **Emitter Null** object directly into the **XPresso Editor**. Now, click on the red box on the **Emitter Null** node, and navigate to **Coordinates | Global Position | Global Position**. Now, drag with the left mouse button pressed, from the newly created output node to the **PStorm** position input port as shown in the following screenshot:

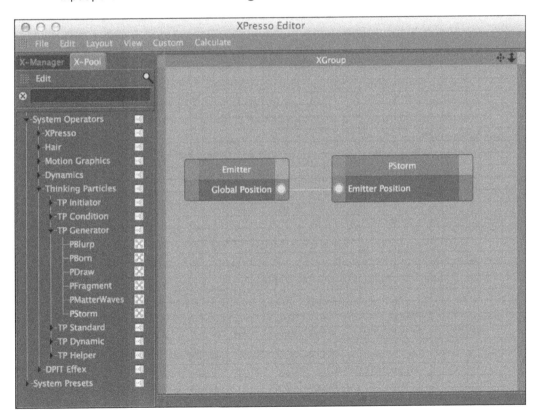

6. Now, click on the red box on the **Emitter Null** node again, and select **Global Matrix** to create another output port. Connect that to **Emitter Alignment** on the **PStorm** input port. This may seem long-winded and it sort of is but you're best off getting used to it because you'll have to do it many times! Eventually, you'll be able to do it really fast and it'll even make sense. Now, when you move **Emitter Null** around, it moves where the particles emit from.

7. You can press **play** and select the **PStorm** node in the **XPresso Editor** you'll see it emitting. The settings are somewhat similar to **Emitter** in Standard Particles or **Particular** in **After Effects** if you've used that. Let's increase the **Life** to **500** and **Count** to **250**.

8. We need to create a group for the particles created by our **PStorm** node. Remember the power of TP is in the ability to create complex behaviors by moving particles from group to group. So, go to X-Pool again, and select a **PGroup** node and drag it into the **XPresso Editor**. This can be found in **System Operators | Thinking Particles | TP Standard | PGroup**. You could also search for it using the little magnifying glass at the top right of **X-Pool**.

9. Now, we need to connect the **PStorm** node to our **PGroup** node. Select **Particle Birth** from the right hand output port of the **PStorm** node, and drag the wire to the input port of the **PGroup** node. This now puts all the particles from the **PStorm** emitter into our selected group. We haven't created any groups yet so let's do that.

10. Navigate to **Simulate | Thinking Particle Settings**. This will bring up a new dialog box where we can view our **Thinking Particle** groups. Now, right click on the **All** type, and select **Add**. Now, click in the **Color** dialog box, and change it to pink.

11. Right-click again on the **All** type, and click on **Add** again, and then change the group color to light blue. We have now created two particle groups.

12. Drag **Group.1** onto the **PGroup** node in our **XPresso Editor**. You should see the name change from **All** to **Group.1**. Sometimes you have to do this more than once as sometimes the program fails to update properly, and keeps the previous particle group in the field. Always check that you have the right particle groups on the **P Pass** and **PGroup** fields as this is quite a common problem.

13. Press **play** and you should see that your **PStorm** emitter is now shooting out red particles! It's emitting particles into **Group.1**.

14. Now, let's create a dynamic effect. Flip down the **TP Dynamic** switch in **X-Pool**, and then drag **PWind** into **XPresso Editor**. Now, create a new null object, and name it **Wind**, then drag it onto your **PWind** node. Don't worry if it's not doing anything yet.

15. Go to **System Operators | Thinking Particles | TP Initiator | P Pass**. Drag this **P Pass** node into your **XPresso** window. Then, open your **Thinking Particles Settings** again (as per step 9), and drag **Group.1** onto the **P Pass** node. Make sure you can see the type in the **P Pass** node change to **Group.1**. If this doesn't work, do it again!

16. Now, connect the output of the **P Pass** node to the input port of the **PWind** node.

17. Change the **PWind** node settings to **Type Spherical** and **Strength** to **-500**. We are basically creating an attractor that will suck all the particles towards our **Wind Null**.

18. Move **Wind null 300cm** along the z axis so that it's clear of the emitter and press **play**. You should see your particles orbiting **Wind null**. If not, go back through the steps carefully, and check the pictures to make sure you're doing everything correctly.

19. So, this is all well and good but you can do something very similar with Standard Particles. Let's add some more complex behavior! Let's tell our particles that when they're 200 frames old to go and do something else. In this case, follow another null.

20. We need something to test how old the particles are, and when they get to 200 frames old to move into a new group. We can then tell this new group to follow our new null. So let's get going! First create a new **PGroup** node (as per step 7) but this time, drag **Group.2** into it from **Thinking Particle Settings**. Now, create a **PAge** node from **System Operators | Thinking Particles | TP Condition | PAge**. Now wire it up as follows:

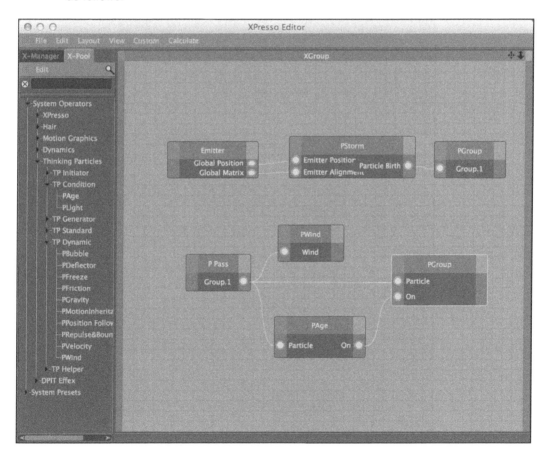

21. You can create the new **On** input port on the **PGroup** node by simply clicking on the blue square and selecting **On**. If you want to see the port names right-click on any node, and navigate to **Ports | Show Names**. Now, change the settings of the **PAge** node. Set it to **Type Absolute** and change **Absolute T1** to **100**, and **Absolute T2** to **200**.

22. What we've done here is say to each particle if you're between 100 and 200 frames old then I'm moving you to **Group.2**.

23. As you'll see when you play back (from the start!) that when the particles get to 100 frames old, they'll go blue! Congratulations, you're well on your way!

24. Let's make our new blue particles from **Group.2** do something different rather than just drift off. Create a new **Null** and rename it **Follow**.

25. Add a **Vibrate** tag to (**Tags | Cinema 4D | Vibrate**) it with the following settings:

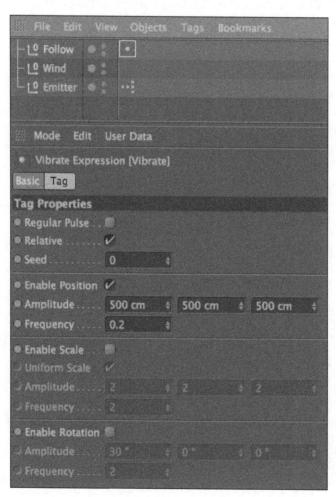

26. Drag the new Follow Null into **XPresso Editor**.

27. Create a new **P Pass** node (as we did in Step 15) and this time, drop **Group.2** into it from the Thinking Particle settings.

28. Add a **PPosition Follow** node from **System Operators | Thinking Particles | TP Dynamic | PPosition Follow**. Set the **Type** to **Spring**.

29. Then wire it up as follows. When you press **play**, the particles should orbit **Wind Null** for 100 frames then begin to follow **Follow Null** as shown in the following screenshot:

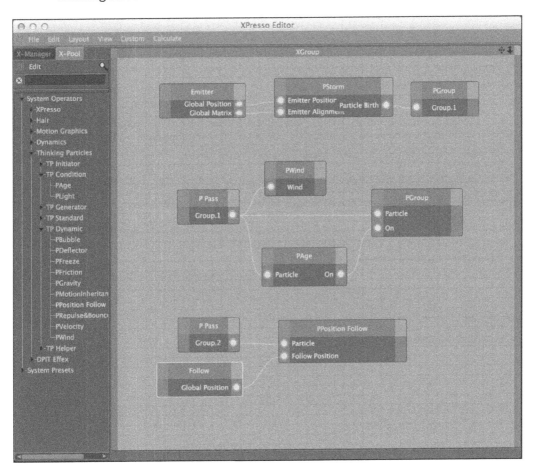

How it works...

We're controlling our entire particle setup from inside the **XPresso** tag. We do, of course, reference other objects within our scene (for example, our **Emitter Null**), but the power of Thinking Particles lies in this tag. You should think of the **PStorm** node as our Emitter Object in Standard Particles. Then, the other nodes are simply different ways to apply forces to the particles it has generated.

There's more...

Hopefully, you'll be beginning to see that you can keep on adding groups and making the behaviors more and more sophisticated. Once you master the general principles you'll begin to see the power of Thinking Particles. It allows for a wide range of creative expression and problem solving. But, it can be frustrating and does require a different mentality to normal animation within Cinema 4D. But, if you have enjoyed dipping your toe into Thinking Particles, then keep on playing because there's a lot to explore. And make sure you familiarize yourself with all the different nodes. At first, it's a bit intimidating but really there's not that much to learn and you can pick it up fairly quickly.

Adding geometry to Thinking Particles

If you press render you will see nothing! So let's add some geometry. Often tutorials show you how to use the **PShape** node with the particle geometry object but I've found using a **Cloner** object to add geometry is more effective, flexible, and faster. There are plenty of tutorials online showing you how to use the **PShape** node so feel free to look it up but I recommend you start with the following approach.

Getting ready

Make sure that you've followed the previous recipe because this will follow directly on from that!

How to do it...

1. Add a **Cloner** object to the scene, and set it to **Object** mode. Now, add a **Pyramid Primitive** object as a child of the **Cloner** object. Make the Pyramid a bit smaller, say 20cm on each axis.

2. In the **Object** slot of **Cloner**, drop in particle **Group.1** from the **Thinking Particles Settings** dialog box. Boom! You have created some geometry for your particles which you can now render. And as it's a **Mograph** object you can add Effectors to it too! But let's not get ahead of ourselves.

3. Let's make our particle geometry align with the direction the particles are travelling. Add a new **P Pass** node to our **XPresso Editor**. Check back to part 1 of this recipe if you're not sure how to do it. You needn't drag a particle group into the **P Pass** node as it is automatically set to **All**. This default setting means that all the particle groups will be affected which is exactly what we want.

4. Also add a **PAlignment** node from **X-Pool: System Operators | Thinking Particles | TP Standard | PAlignment**. Wire that up to new **P Pass** node, and make sure the **Type** field is set to **Direction Of Travel**. Also, change the **Source** to **Y**. Now, press **play** again, and you should see the particle geometry align itself to the way the particle is moving, creating a much more interesting effect.

5. Now, we will create some geometry for our second group. Let's repeat the process, create a new **Cloner** object, and set it to **Object Mode** again. This time, add **Group.2** to the **Object** slot and then make a Torus Primitive the child of the **Cloner** object. Scale the Torus down so it doesn't look ridiculous! Now, when you play (from the beginning!) you should see the particle geometry change from a pyramid to a torus when the particles change group.

How it works...

We're taking the power of Thinking Particles and moving it into the Mograph module which is a powerful and flexible combination. Essentially the program is adding a clone onto every Thinking Particle. Simple!

There's more...

Hopefully, that's given you a taste of the power of Thinking Particles. You should now begin to be able to see that you can create lots of different groups and behaviors to create interesting effects. Don't be disheartened if it all seems a little abstract and strange, it does take a little while to get your head around. Keep playing and it will begin to make sense.

But, there are certainly more things to play with. Try some of the following once you have played around and feel comfortable:

▸ Add Mograph Effectors to your particle geometry Cloners. Adding **Random** and **Formula** Effectors should give you an interesting effect straight away.

▸ Try adding some values to the **Velocity Stretch** in the **Object** field of your **Cloner** object.

▸ You can add a **Rigid Body Dynamics** tag to the objects you are cloning. In the tag, make sure you go to **Force/Follow Position**, and put the value above 1. Maybe even to **10**. This will make sure that it follows the particle rather than just falling away!

- ▸ Use the **Matrix** object to emit particles. Set it to **Generete Thinking Particles** rather than **Matrices**. Make sure you drop in your **TP Group** to the correct slot in the **Object** mode.

- ▸ Read the Thinking Particles built-in help section, it may seem dry at first but it will really help you understand what each node does.

Making it Rain

Let's use what we've learnt so far and create a rain simulation. This isn't any more complex than the previous tutorial, but it is a more practical application, and it uses a couple of new techniques such as using the Hair module to render. You should definitely do the previous recipe before embarking on this one so you are familiar with the techniques involved.

Getting ready

Create a new scene with at least 500 frames.

How to do it...

1. Create a null object and rename it as **Rain Emitter**. Move the null up so the Y position value is **500cm**.

2. Create three new null objects, and name them **Gravity**, **Wind**, and **Up**. Rotate the **Gravity** null by -90° on the p axis, and rotate the **Up** null by 90° on the p axis. We'll use these a little later to help control our simulation.

3. Create a **Plane Object** and make it nice and big, **3000cm** on both **Width** and **Height**.

4. Create two particle groups by opening the **Particle Settings** dialog (**Simulate | Thinking Particles | Thinking Particle Settings**), and right-clicking on the **All** group, and selecting **Add**. Name the groups **Rain** and **Splash**. Change the colors of the groups so that they are different from each other. This helps us to see what's going on. Make the **Rain** group green, and the **Splash** group blue.

5. Change the **View Type** to **Drops** in **Thinking Particle Settings**. Firstly, this will look more like rain, and secondly it should make it easier for us to see what we're doing.

6. Add an **XPresso** tag to your **Rain Emitter Null**, and open the **XPresso Editor** by double-clicking on the tag.

7. Drag our **Rain Emitter** null into the **XPresso Editor**, and add a **PStorm** node and a **PGroup** node. You can do this by either finding them in **X-Pool** which is a tab on the right-hand side of the **XPresso Editor**, or by right-clicking and selecting **New Node**. You will be able to find **PStorm** under **TP Generator**, and the **PGroup** node under **TP Standard**. If you're not sure about this go back to the previous tutorial.

8. Adjust the **PStorm** settings so that they match the following screenshot:

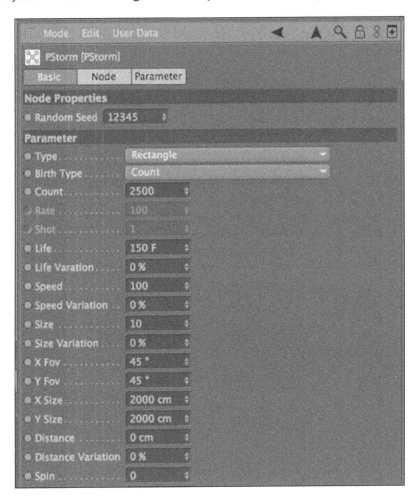

9. Now, wire them up as shown in the following figure, taking care to create **Global Matrix** and **Global position** in the **Rain Emitter** node as shown in the following screenshot:

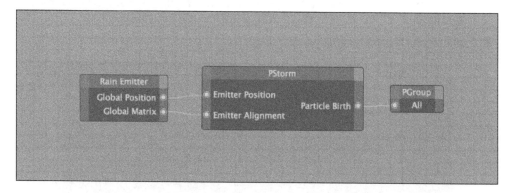

10. Drag your **Rain** particle group from your **Thinking Particle Settings** dialog box into **PGroup** in the **XPresso Editor**. This makes sure all particles created by the **PStorm** node are in the **Rain** group.

11. Create a **P Pass**, a **PWind**, and a **PGravity** node. Again, drop the **Rain** particle group into the **P Pass** node from **Thinking Particle Settings**. Drag the **Wind** null onto your **PWind** node, and your **Gravity** null onto your **Gravity** node. Wire them up as per the following screenshot:

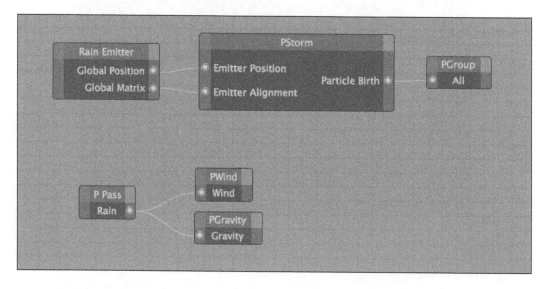

12. Change the **PWind** strength to **50** and increase the **Turbulence** to **100**. Press **play** and we should have the first part of our simulation. Feel free to adjust the settings to get a feel you're happy with.

Now, we're ready to create a little splash each time a raindrop hits the floor. To do that we must test each particle and see if its position is 0 or less on the y axis. This is the level of the floor and where we want our splashes. If it is 0 or less then we want to do two things. We want to emit some more particles which splash upwards, and we also want our initial raindrop to die. So let's begin!

1. Create a **PGetData** node. You can find this in **Thinking Particles/TP Helper**. This node will get information that we can use about the position of our particles. As you get more into Thinking Particles, you'll use this a lot. Create a Position output port by selecting it from the red box at the right-hand side of the node. This gives us the position of each particle, but we're only interested in the Y position (or height) of each particle. We need another node for this.

2. Create a **Vectors2Real** node which you can find in the **X-Pool** tab, or by right-clicking, and selecting **New Node**. You'll find it under **XPresso/Adapter**.

3. Now, take the output from your **PGetData** node, and enter it into your **Vectors2Real** node. This is taking the position data of each particle, and splitting it into **X,Y**, and **Z**.

4. We just want to see if the Y value of each particle is equal to or less than 0 (where the ground plane is). For this we use a compare node. Add a compare object from **XPresso/Logic/Compare**. Set the **Compare** nodes function to **<=** and **Input 2** to **0**.

5. Finally, we want a **PDie** node which can be found in **Thinking Particles/TP Standard/ PDie**. Wire everything together as per the following screenshot:

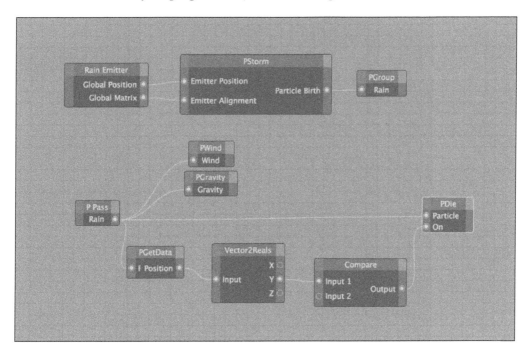

6. This whole system is now checking every particle, if the particle is lower than 0 on the y axis then it is being killed with the **PDie** node. We're nearly there! But, we also want to create a splash so let's look at that.

7. Add another **PStorm** node and add an **Emitter Alignment** input port and an On input port. Again, just do this by clicking on the blue square on the left of the node.

8. Add a new **PGroup** node and connect it to the **PStorm** node. Drop the **Splash** particle group into this node.

9. Drag in the **Up** null from the **Object Manager**, and connect its **Global Matrix** to the **Emitter Alignment** of the **PStorm** node. This just makes sure our new **PStorm** node fires upwards. Remember we rotated the **Up** null at the start of the tutorial.

10. Now, let's connect it to the rest of our system! We want to create the new **Splash** emitter at the exact point where the rain hits the floor. So, let's wire the port from the **PGetData** node to our new **PStorms** Emitter Position input port. We also only want it to fire if the raindrop is at Y Position 0 or less. Connect the output from our **Compare** node to the new **PStorms On** input. This should give us exactly what we want!

11. Input the following values to new **Splash PStorm** node as shown in the following screenshot:

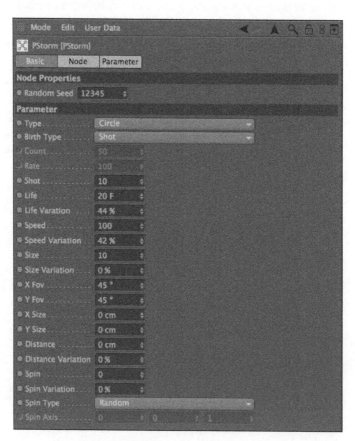

12. For the final part of our simulation, we want to add a little more gravity to our Splash particles. So, create a new **P Pass** node and a new **PGravity** node and connect them. Drop the **Gravity** null into the **PGravity** node, and make sure the **Splash** particle group is in the **P Pass** node. Crank up the settings so **Strength** of **Gravity** is **200**.

13. Now, rewind and press **play**! You should have a lovely dynamic rain animation! Your final TP setup should look like the following screenshot:

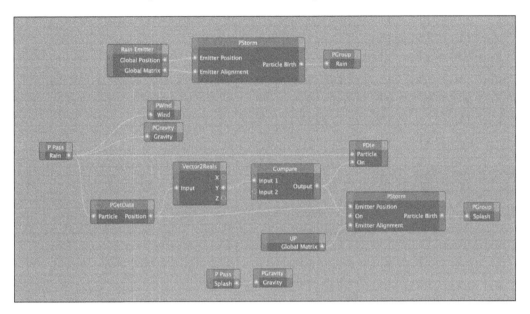

14. You can also open `Rain.c4d` file from the C4D Content Pack if you're having any problems.

15. The only drawback now is that it won't render, so let's use **Hair** to render it with. This may sound strange but it's a very good way to render particle systems, it's very fast and looks nice! It's a **Post** effect so doesn't use geometry which makes it very quick.

16. Add in a **Tracer** object. (**Mograph/Tracer**). Drag the **Rain** particle group into the **Trace Link** field from the **Thinking Particle Settings** dialog box. Then, also add the **Splash** particle group.

17. Set its **Limit** to **From End** and set the value to **3**. If you want longer raindrops, increase the value.

18. Right-click on **Tracer** and select **Hair Tags/Render**. Now, when you press render you can see the raindrops. But they're not looking quite right yet. Now, we need to create a **Hair** Material.

19. In the **Material Manager**, click **Create/New Shader/Hair Material**. Double-click on the new **Hair** material, and change the **Color** gradient from a light blue to a white (or whatever you choose). Also, go to the **Thickness** parameter, and change the **Root** field to **0.1cm** and the **Tip** field to **1cm**.

20. Now, drop the new **Hair** Material onto your **Tracer** and press **render**. You should have something that looks a bit nicer and more like rain! Have a play with your **Hair** material and **Tracer** options to create a look you're happy with.

How it works...

We have emitted particles and added dynamic behaviors to them. We've also tested the particles and based on the results of that test we've created new groups with new behaviors. This is all quite complex stuff, and if you fully understand it, you're well on your way to creating much more complex simulations. But don't worry if it is all a little vague still, just play around, and you'll slowly begin to understand it.

There's more...

There's plenty more to try in the world of Thinking Particles, hopefully this has got you started and if you've enjoyed it I'm sure you'll keep on experimenting. There are lots of different types of Emitters and Dynamic effects which you can link together in all sorts of interesting ways.

Index

D

deformation
  applying, with effectors 289-291
Deformation tab 291
deformers
  about 89
  Bend 94
  Collision 111
  Displacer 100
  FFD 100
  in 3D cinema 90
  Shear 96
  Squash & Stretch 98
  Taper 90
  unconventional animations 103-105
  used, for breaking objects 105-108
Delete key 217
Diffusion channel 213
Digital sculpting. *See* **sculpting**
Disc primitive 194
displacement channels
  about 220
  adding, to 3D model 220-226
Displacer
  used, for asteroid creating 100-103
dollying 12
Dutch Angle 13
dynamics
  about 341, 342
  bowling 342
dynamic stage lighting
  about 309
  steps 309-313

E

edges 42
effectors
  about 278-281
  deformation, applying 289-291
  Random effector 282
  working 282

Effects button 272
Emitter Object 376
Enable Axis Modification tool 359
Explosion FX deformer 108
External Compositing tag 265-268
Extrude NURBS
  about 49-53, 194, 196
  MoText, using 53

F

Falloff tab 300
F-Curves 26
FFD
  used, for asteroid creating 100-103
focal lengths
  about 125
  adjusting 125, 126
  working 126, 127
Formula effector 309
Frame Range option 236
Free Form Deformation. *See* **FFD**
Freehand Spline tool 217, 367
Fresnel button 218
Fresnel gradient 213
Fresnel shader
  reflective materials 211
  reflective materials with 212-215

G

Gaussian Blur filter 275
geometry
  adding, to Thinking Particles 386, 387
gizmo 14
glass material
  creating 216-219
Global Illumination
  about 174
  Ambient Occlusion 178
  applying 174-177
  working 177, 178
Grab brush 82

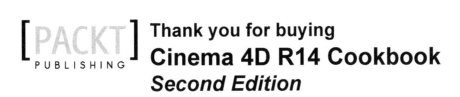

Thank you for buying
Cinema 4D R14 Cookbook
Second Edition

About Packt Publishing

Packt, pronounced 'packed', published its first book "*Mastering phpMyAdmin for Effective MySQL Management*" in April 2004 and subsequently continued to specialize in publishing highly focused books on specific technologies and solutions.

Our books and publications share the experiences of your fellow IT professionals in adapting and customizing today's systems, applications, and frameworks. Our solution based books give you the knowledge and power to customize the software and technologies you're using to get the job done. Packt books are more specific and less general than the IT books you have seen in the past. Our unique business model allows us to bring you more focused information, giving you more of what you need to know, and less of what you don't.

Packt is a modern, yet unique publishing company, which focuses on producing quality, cutting-edge books for communities of developers, administrators, and newbies alike. For more information, please visit our website: www.packtpub.com.

Writing for Packt

We welcome all inquiries from people who are interested in authoring. Book proposals should be sent to author@packtpub.com. If your book idea is still at an early stage and you would like to discuss it first before writing a formal book proposal, contact us; one of our commissioning editors will get in touch with you.

We're not just looking for published authors; if you have strong technical skills but no writing experience, our experienced editors can help you develop a writing career, or simply get some additional reward for your expertise.

Cinema 4D R13 Cookbook

ISBN: 978-1-849691-86-4   Paperback: 514 pages

Elevate your art to the fourth dimension with Cinema 4D

1. Master all the important aspects of Cinema 4D

2. Learn how real-world knowledge of cameras and lighting translates onto a 3D canvas

3. Learn advanced features like Mograph, Xpresso, and Dynamics

4. Become an advanced Cinema 4D user with concise and effective recipes

Cinema 4D Beginner's Guide

ISBN: 978-1-849692-14-4   Paperback: 274 pages

Model, animate, and render like a Pro!

1. Step-by-step instructions on modeling, texturing, lighting, and rendering a photorealistic 3D interior scene

2. Dynamic animations using MoGraph

3. Node-based programming to link parameters using XPresso

4. Stylized rendering with Sketch and Toon

Please check **www.PacktPub.com** for information on our titles

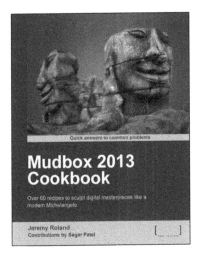

Mudbox 2013 Cookbook

ISBN: 978-1-849691-56-7   Paperback: 260 pages

Over 60 recipes to sculpt digital masterpieces like
a modern Michelangelo

1. Create amazing, high detail sculpts for games,
    movies, and more

2. Extract high-resolution texture maps to use
    on your low poly 3D models

3. Create terrain that you can walk on in
    a virtual world

4. Learn professional tricks that will improve
    your workflow

Away3D 3.6 Cookbook

ISBN: 978-1-849512-80-0   Paperback: 480 pages

Over 80 practical recipes for creating stunning graphics
and effects with the fascinating Away3D engine

1. Invaluable tips and techniques to take your
    Away 3D applications to the top

2. Reveals the secrets of cleaning your scene
    from z-sorting artifacts without killing your CPU

3. Get 2D objects into the 3D world by learning to
    work with TextField3D and extracting graphics
    from vector graphics

Please check **www.PacktPub.com** for information on our titles

Cinema 4D R14 Cookbook *Second Edition*

Cinema 4D is a 3D modeling, animation, and rendering application developed by MAXON.

Cinema 4D R14 Cookbook provides all the Cinema 4D knowledge you need to become well-versed with the software in the form of short recipes. Along the way you'll learn how to set up lights, cameras, and materials to turn your work into something that feels more like art and design. Towards the end of the book you will be introduced to powerful tools like XPresso, MoGraph, Particles, Sculpting, and Dynamics to take your work to the next level. You'll be impressed by how easy it is to design top quality work once you lay the foundation for the entire program through this book.

What this book will do for you...

- **Learn useful tools and methods for creating your own 3D objects**

- **Use deformers to manipulate and adjust your designs**

- **Create camera setups that capture your design in every dimension and mimic real world camera movements**

- **Texture your objects to give them unique properties and qualities**

- **Develop complex animations using Mograph**

- **Create sophisticated and smarter projects using XPresso**

- **Take your work to the next level using the Cinema 4D Dynamic system**

- **Learn how to create sophisticated particle systems**

Inside the Cookbook...

- Straightforward and easy-to-follow format

- A selection of the most important tasks and problems

- Carefully organized instructions for solving the problem efficiently

- Clear explanations for what you did

- Apply the solution to other situations

$ 49.99 US
£ 30.99 UK

Prices do not include
local sales tax or VAT
where applicable

ISBN 978-1-84969-668-5

54999

9 781849 696685

Visit **www.PacktPub.com** for books, eBooks, code, downloads, and PacktLib.